ACTION AND VALUE
IN CRIMINAL LAW

Action and Value in Criminal Law

Edited by
STEPHEN SHUTE
JOHN GARDNER
and
JEREMY HORDER

CLARENDON PRESS · OXFORD
1993

Oxford University Press, Walton Street, Oxford OX2 6DP
Oxford New York Toronto
Delhi Bombay Calcutta Madras Karachi
Kuala Lumpur Singapore Hong Kong Tokyo
Nairobi Dar es Salaam Cape Town
Melbourne Auckland Madrid
and associated companies in
Berlin Ibadan

Oxford is a trade mark of Oxford University Press

Published in the United States
by Oxford University Press Inc., New York

British Library Cataloguing in Publication Data
Data available

Library of Congress Cataloging in Publication Data
Action and value in criminal law / edited by Stephen Shute, John
Gardner, and Jeremy Horder.
Includes indexes.
1. Criminal law—Philosophy.   I. Shute, Stephen, 1955-   .
II. Gardner, John, tutor in law.   III. Horder, Jeremy.
K5018.Z9A27   1993 345'.001—dc20 [342.501]   93–28961
ISBN 0–19–825806–2

1 3 5 7 9 10 8 6 4 2

Typeset by Graphicraft Typesetters Ltd, Hong Kong
Printed in Great Britain
on acid-free paper by
Biddles Ltd., Guildford and King's Lynn

For Tony Honoré

In memory of H. L. A. Hart (1907–1992)

Preface

The seeds of this book were planted in 1989, when the three of us first convened, at All Souls College, Oxford, a series of seminars on the philosophical foundations of criminal law. It was to be an annual forum, not just for the presentation of our own tentative efforts at understanding the subject, but also for the exchange of ideas with friends and colleagues who shared our interests. A number of the essays which follow are based on, or related to, papers delivered at these seminars. To these we have added essays by other scholars whose participation we would have valued, but who were separated from the seminars by the expanse of the Atlantic Ocean and the limits of our budget. Mindful of the differences between conveners and editors, however, we have resisted the temptation to include essays of our own. Our compensation for that forbearance has been the joint preparation, with the generous co-operation of our contributors, of a critical introduction. Although such an introduction may be thought unorthodox in a collection of original essays, we hope that it helps this book to retain some of the spirit of the seminars.

We are very grateful to all those who have helped to give the seminars a spirit worth retaining. Our good friend Heike Jung attended the whole series in 1990, forcing us, with genial manner but enduring influence, to confront our common-law parochialism. Many other colleagues from Oxford and elsewhere have paid memorable visits. Nor should the critical mass be left out of account: conveners and visiting speakers alike have regularly benefited from the daunting interrogations and stern rebukes of successive groups of talented graduate students, some of whom have also presented valuable papers of their own. In the transition from seminar to book, meanwhile, we have been assisted not only by the friendliness and assiduousness of our contributors, but also by the enthusiastic guidance of the editorially experienced. Jules Coleman gave us early encouragement, while Richard Hart at Oxford University Press was our editorial mentor once the project got under way.

Mentors of a different kind are revealed in our dedication. Our common interest in the philosophical foundations of legal doctrine owes much to Tony Honoré, whose seminars on causation have inspired and captivated so many generations of graduate students in Oxford. In his formidable array of published work, Tony has perhaps done more than anyone else to dispel the comforting lawyers' myth that philosophical thinking about the law must be grandiose and remote from the particulars of doctrine and practice. The essays in this book are, we believe, more in Tony's tradition

than in the tradition of the grandiose. They are also, we hope, faithful
to the memory of Herbert Hart, whose death just before Christmas 1992
introduced a note of sadness into the otherwise festive final stages of our
editorial activity. No work on the philosophical foundations of criminal
law can escape Herbert's pervasive influence. The subject was his to begin
with, and the essays in this book reaffirm, to us at least, that it will remain
his for ever.

Oxford   S. C. S.
January 1993   J. B. G.
                                                                J. C. N. H.

Contents

LIST OF CONTRIBUTORS   X

Introduction: The Logic of Criminal Law   1
   Stephen Shute, John Gardner, and Jeremy Horder

Agency and Welfare in the Penal Law   21
   Alan Brudner

On What's Intentionally Done   55
   Jennifer Hornsby

Acting, Trying, and Criminal Liability   75
   R. A. Duff

Taking the Consequences   107
   Andrew Ashworth

Foreseeing Harm Opaquely   125
   Michael S. Moore

Culpability and Mistake of Law   157
   Douglas Husak and Andrew von Hirsch

The Nature of Justification   175
   George P. Fletcher

Should the Criminal Law Abandon the
   Actus Reus–Mens Rea Distinction?   187
   Paul H. Robinson

Subjectivism and Objectivism: Towards Synthesis   213
   Richard H. S. Tur

Diminished Capacity   239
   Stephen J. Morse

Value, Action, Mental Illness, and the Law   279
   K. W. M. Fulford

INDEX OF SUBJECTS   311
INDEX OF NAMES   313

Contributors

Andrew Ashworth is Edmund-Davies Professor of Criminal Law and Criminal Justice at King's College, London.

Alan Brudner is Professor of Law and Political Science at the University of Toronto.

R. A. Duff is Professor of Philosophy at the University of Stirling.

George P. Fletcher is Beekman Professor of Law at Columbia University.

K. W. M. Fulford is Research Psychiatrist at the Department of Psychiatry, University of Oxford.

John Gardner is Fellow and Tutor in Law at Brasenose College, Oxford.

Jeremy Horder is Fellow and Tutor in Law at Worcester College, Oxford.

Jennifer Hornsby is Fellow and Tutor in Philosophy at Corpus Christi College, Oxford.

Douglas Husak is Professor of Philosophy at Rutgers University.

Michael S. Moore is Leon Meltzer Professor of Law and Philosophy at the University of Pennsylvania.

Stephen J. Morse is Ferdinand Wakeman Hubbell Professor of Law at the University of Pennsylvania.

Paul H. Robinson is Professor of Law at Northwestern University.

Stephen Shute is Fellow and Tutor in Law at Corpus Christi College, Oxford.

Richard H. S. Tur is Fellow and Tutor in Law at Oriel College, Oxford.

Andrew von Hirsch is Professor of Criminal Justice at Rutgers University.

Introduction:
The Logic of Criminal Law

STEPHEN SHUTE, JOHN GARDNER, AND JEREMY HORDER

1. Critique without Philosophy?

Criminal law has been described as a 'species of political and moral philosophy'.[1] We would not go so far as to say that criminal law itself is a form of philosophy, nor that its philosophical dimension is exhausted by concerns with morality and politics. But we would say that it can and should be the subject of philosophical study. The aim of this book is to explore some of the philosophical foundations of the criminal law. Modern textbook writers often claim to be laying bare these foundations in their accounts of criminal law, but their attempts tend to be thin and insubstantial. If this book gives some depth and substance to such claims in the future, then it will have served its purpose.

But some may find that purpose too narrow. There are many urgent questions to which academic criminal lawyers now commonly feel that they must address themselves, such as the question of the correlation between 'law in the books' and 'law in action', and the question of whether the criminal law plays a key role in sustaining institutionalized forms of injustice and oppression. These are indeed important issues, and academic lawyers ignore them at their peril. Devoting a book to the philosophical foundations of criminal law may seem insignificant by comparison, like fiddling while Rome burns. None the less, the philosophical foundations are of crucial significance. The concepts of 'law', 'criminal', 'injustice', and 'oppression' are not self-explanatory, and different accounts of them compete for our allegiance. Revealing the nature and source of such differences and their impact upon our thinking cannot be done without philosophy. A central task of philosophy is to break down conventional false associations and establish true ones in their place. It is to challenge our preconceptions and reconstruct with greater candour our patterns of thinking about the world, if not the world itself.

Yet some people may think that the essays in this book fail to go deep

We would like to thank Christopher Shields and Andrew Simester for their comments on earlier drafts of this introduction. We have also benefited from the comments of many of the contributors to this volume. Jennifer Hornsby gave particularly helpful advice.
[1] George Fletcher, *Rethinking Criminal Law* (Boston 1978), p. xix.

enough into our preconceptions and patterns of thinking. Impatient to get on to the grand issues of injustice and oppression, such critics will regard the concentration on seemingly mundane concepts like action, intention, foreseeability, and responsibility as little more than an ideological smoke-screen, giving far too much credence to the complacent self-image of the criminal law. This is a mistake. It ignores the fact that a social practice has its own internal logic. One cannot properly understand its strengths and weaknesses until one understands its workings from within. Consider, for example, the ferocious contemporary debate over the denial to battered women of a defence to murder on the ground of provocation when they kill their violent abusers after what the law regards as a 'cooling-off' period. In order to bring out the injustice of this denial, one might point out that it reflects a failure to appreciate the predicament of women trapped in violent relationships. That casts the denial as a denial of an excuse. But it is easy to drift into a different argument, in which the denial is portrayed as a failure to see that the death of an abuser is a reasonable price to pay for the ending of abuse. This is a justificatory drift: it is an attempt to justify the conduct rather than excuse it. If what one is interested in exploiting is the gendered aspect of the denial, the second argument is evidently a weaker one. One can use the stronger first argument, however, only if the provocation defence, when it is granted, takes the form of an excuse. For there is no injustice in refusing to extend the excuse to abused women, if there is no excuse to extend. Thus one must begin by exploring the nature of the provocation defence, establishing that it is indeed an excuse and not a justification.[2] That is exactly the sort of distinction which some would be inclined to dismiss at first sight as remote from the grand issues which ought to concern criminal lawyers today.

2. Beyond Punishment

One of the reasons why some have come to resist the philosophical study of the criminal law relates to an underestimation of the range of philosophical problems to which the criminal law gives rise. In recent years, self-consciously philosophical discussion of the proper scope and structure of the criminal law has been treated by many writers as a mere adjunct to discussion of the justification of punishment.[3] It is widely thought that the

[2] A case where the facts raise this issue is R v. *Pearson (William)* [1992] *Criminal LR* 193, considering the position of close relatives who kill an abuser.
[3] e.g. Nicola Lacey, *State Punishment: Political Principles and Community Values* (London 1988); Alan Norrie, *Law, Ideology, and Punishment: Retrieval and Critique of the Liberal Idea of Justice* (Dordrecht 1990); C. L. Ten, *Crime, Guilt, and Punishment* (Oxford 1987).

conditions for legitimate criminalization are largely dictated by the conditions for legitimate punishment. This is in many ways unfortunate. In the first place, the theory of punishment has become a battleground in which the most fanatical moral outlooks are routinely pitted against one another: uncompromising Benthamites against unyielding Kantians. Such crude extremism readily spills over to create rival caricatures of the criminal law as a whole. Second, the annexation of criminal-law theory to the theory of punishment has led some to take a highly selective view of what they need to justify when justifying the workings of the criminal law. There are many forms of sentencing which are not punitive. There is also much of moral consequence which takes place in criminal proceedings before the question of sentence is reached. These matters have been almost studiously neglected in the literature. Finally, there is a dangerous feedback, whereby the study of punishment is itself corrupted by using this highly selective view of the criminal law as the exemplar of all punitive practice. In reality, much punishment takes place outside the criminal justice system—among friends, in families, at school—and such punishment calls for justification no less than criminal punishment.

Take, for example, the problem of infancy. The punishment of children is an everyday practice; yet the criminal liability of children begins only at age 10. Those who append the theory of criminal liability to the theory of punishment must see this as a difficulty. If they want to defend the asymmetry, they must either portray the legal practice or the extra-legal practice as anomalous. Either the legal practice is an institutional concession, or the extra-legal practice is marginal, not strictly speaking punishment, but something that looks like it. If, on the other hand, the asymmetry is to be condemned, then the source and the object of the condemnation will be predictable. Some will present the extra-legal practice as a utilitarian device, while others will see the legal practice as a retributivist hang-up. In these responses to the asymmetry, the baneful influence of the annexation of criminal-law theory to the theory of punishment is all too evident.

It will come as no surprise, therefore, that the contributors to this volume have been asked to consider the philosophical foundations of criminal law from perspectives other than that of argument about punishment. They have made commendable efforts to comply with this (as some would have it, unreasonable) demand. The result has been a group of essays which, while in many respects diverse, are joined together in more than one union. There are small-scale unions that have frequently allowed us to group essays together around a particular topic. Those brave enough to attempt a beginning-to-end reading of the volume will be struck (if we have succeeded) by the common concerns of neighbouring essays. But there are also larger unities of theme, broadly concerned with the inner logic of the criminal law, which cut across the localized commonalities of topic. These include the relationship between 'real crimes' and 'mere regulatory offences', the size and shape of the 'general part' of the criminal law, the relationship between substantive criminal law and the law of criminal evidence and procedure, the nature of criminal 'wrongs', criminal 'harms', and criminal 'responsibility', and the existence and importance of the criminal lawyer's distinction between *actus reus* and *mens rea*.

3. Value in Action

The contours of several of these themes are charted in Alan Brudner's essay. Although he avoids dwelling on the theory of punishment, his starting-point is with the Kantian and Benthamite extremes so beloved of many who write about punishment. At the heart of his essay lies the idea that there need be no irreconcilable conflict between instrumental and intrinsic concerns in the criminal law, between values which the criminal law must promote and values which it must honour.[4] For Brudner, it is welfare which must be promoted and agency which must be honoured. The removal of any impression of irreconcilable conflict is achieved, not by attempting to subsume one under the other, as some have tried to do, but by showing that each depends upon the other. Whereas welfare would be meaningless without agency, agency would be unconsummated without welfare (p. 50).[5] This is said to have significant pay-offs for the structure of the criminal law. The most important pay-off is that it shows how and why 'true crimes' are to be distinguished from merely regulatory offences: for the reconciliation of the conflict between agency and welfare generates more than one set of principles for the criminal law (pp. 50–1). Here, Brudner gives us a welcome reminder that the interesting moral issues raised by the criminal law are not exhausted by a study of killing, rape, and pillage; pollution, milk-adulteration, and speeding are no less rich in morally intriguing detail. Too often it has been suggested or implied that philosophical method gives rise to a myopic concentration on a narrow band of crimes which are not representative of the criminal law as experienced by most of those who fall foul of it. Brudner shows what an ill-considered criticism this is.

What is striking about Brudner's argument, however, is that he seeks to rectify this myopia by relying on an unexpectedly parsimonious set of abstract premises. Brudner's starting-point seems to be that it is agency that falls to be honoured, and welfare that falls to be promoted; but why limit our moral concerns to these? Morality is a good deal more plural

---

[4] Philip Pettit, 'Consequentialism and Respect for Persons', (1989) 100 *Ethics* 116.
[5] Throughout this introduction, page references to the essays in this volume are shown in brackets in the text.

than this. In protecting endangered species, for example, one might be promoting natural diversity for its own sake, irrespective of agency or welfare. In decrying the desecration of graves, meanwhile, one is perhaps concerned with honouring the dignity of the dead rather than honouring the agency or promoting the welfare of the living. Brudner does not say how these values (and values they undoubtedly are) might fit into his moral outlook. Of course, there may be reasons to doubt whether the criminal law should be concerned with these values. One might argue that the killing of endangered species or the desecration of graves should be prohibited, if at all, only on grounds other than the values of natural diversity and the dignity of the dead. This is the job that the traditional liberal 'harm principle' is supposed to do. Brudner has some trenchant criticisms to make of this principle, which he sees as excessively welfarist, in his sense (p. 25). But the harm principle is an exclusory principle, whereas what Brudner offers us appears to be an inclusory principle. The harm principle explains why some activities should not be criminalized, whereas Brudner's 'dialogic community' explains why certain activities should be criminalized. It may be that 'dialogic community' is meant to be exclusory as well, but Brudner gives no arguments for thinking that this is so.

4. From Action to Responsibility

Even if morally selective, Brudner's focus on agency does draw attention to a recurrent theme in some of the essays which follow. This is the concern with action, the unit of agency. While several other contributors draw connections between problems about the concept of action and problems about the criminal law, Brudner is the most explicit in offering a reason for making such connections. It is that agency is at the heart of value, and the value of the criminal law therefore depends upon the honouring of agency as well as the promotion of its consummation. This has ramifications for the structure of criminal law, for its enforcement, and not least, as Brudner stresses, for its proper scope.

When the concept of agency is introduced into discussions of criminal law, the emphasis is often not on these issues, but on issues of responsibility. It is often supposed that the key to understanding responsibility will be found in a study of action. This supposition is apt to mislead. Normal breathing does not involve action. It has a semi-automatic aspect which means that it cannot be put on all fours with writing a letter or eating lunch. Nevertheless, we can be straightforwardly responsible for our normal breathing. Suppose someone with healthy respiratory powers is told by the doctor to hold his breath for a few seconds while she conducts a tricky test. If the test fails because he forgetfully breathes again too soon, he is responsible for the test's failure. That is because he is responsible for the breathing, although it is no action. Nor is this merely the derivative sense of responsibility sometimes used as a substitute for 'cause' (as where one says that a storm was responsible for damage to a house); rather, this is normatively significant responsibility, of the sort that can be labelled legal or moral. He is responsible in this latter sense because he has, for a limited period, control over his breathing. What this case suggests is that control, while at the heart of responsibility, has no special role to play in action that it does not play elsewhere in our lives. This reveals that there is nothing special about action that provides the key to understanding responsibility. Indeed, as we will discover later, a focus on what makes action special will seriously distort one's account of responsibility. Yet Jennifer Hornsby and Antony Duff focus on precisely this. Neither of them suggests that action is a necessary condition of responsibility. For Duff it is the 'paradigm' (pp. 77–8); for Hornsby there is merely a 'connection' (p. 70). Even these relatively modest proposals, however, seem to us to herald the same difficulties. Both authors also mention the importance of control for responsibility, but neither takes the natural further step, when thinking about responsibility, of shifting attention away from what is special about action to cases of control more generally.

Hornsby stresses the logical link between action and intention: 'an action is a person's doing something intentionally' (p. 55). Her main point is that while intention may be central to action, and understanding action may be the key to understanding responsibility, it does not follow that one is responsible only or even paradigmatically for that which one intends to do or intentionally does. That is because when one acts, one does many things: every action, as other philosophers have put it, bears many descriptions. While at least one of these things that is done is in each case of action done intentionally, it does not follow that all are. Therefore, it may be possible to define actions by reference to the fact that in each action one thing at least is done intentionally, and it may be possible to use the concept of action thus defined to help with one's account of responsibility, without committing oneself to the position that one is responsible only or paradigmatically for what one intends doing or intentionally does. One's account of responsibility may extend, even paradigmatically, to the many things one unintentionally does in action.

Although Hornsby here works with an account of action in which intention is central, she is eager to show that different accounts of action need not be rivals. Thus, actions for her are not only things done intentionally, but also attemptings or tryings, as well as (in some sense) bodily movements (p. 60). Elsewhere she has concentrated on the element of attempting or trying;[6] and her views on that subject are briefly reiterated in her essay. It is to accounts of action in which trying plays a pivotal role that Duff addresses his contribution to this volume; but he interprets these accounts, as Hornsby herself clearly does not, as ventures to identify a single, exclusive essence of action. The focus may be on 'trying' accounts of action, but the real target is what Duff sees as a reductive tendency throughout the philosophy of action. One of the practical dangers in such reductiveness, according to Duff, is the effect that it can have upon our understanding of the criminal law. If, for example, one insists that actions are essentially tryings, and nothing else, then one will end up exaggerating the extent to which the criminal law should focus attention on our tryings. So, it is said, a trying-based account of action will tend to lend false support to an extreme form of subjectivism in the criminal law (p. 89). Here Duff tries to set the trap which, according to Hornsby, he has himself fallen into on other occasions. In his earlier ground-breaking work, Duff notices the link between action and intention, but then goes on as a result to exaggerate the pervasive importance of intention in the criminal law.[7] Now he accuses those who emphasize trying, rather than intention, of getting into the very same kind of trouble.

This is not to say that Duff overlooks the distinction between an action and its descriptions, or, as Hornsby reconstructs it, the distinction between an action and things done in that action. On the contrary, he points out that this distinction is a matter of some significance for the criminal law. The general requirement that there be a 'voluntary act' does not require, for example, that the defendant acted voluntarily under the particular description which has legal salience, but only that the defendant acted voluntarily *tout court* (p. 77). Thus, Duff's opposition to essentialism about action is seemingly not an opposition to distinguishing actions from their descriptions. On the other hand, Duff appears to remain attracted by a holistic view of action, according to which the description applicable to an action makes a difference to what action it is (p. 105). In the last analysis, Duff stands by his instinct to deny the possibility of distinguishing actions, in anything other than name, from their circumstances and consequences (i.e. from the facts and events in terms of which they are described). This may be Duff the moralist speaking, rather than Duff the analyst. He may be reacting to the tendency of some criminal lawyers, faced with the possibility of distinguishing an action from its circumstances and consequences, to exaggerate the normative significance of the distinction. He may be reacting, for example, to the tendency to play down the relevance of consequences to moral and legal responsibility.

[6] See Jennifer Hornsby, *Actions* (London 1980), ch. 3.
[7] R. A. Duff, *Intention, Agency and Criminal Liability* (Oxford 1990), esp. chs. 3 and 5.

5. Counting Consequences

Andrew Ashworth's essay not only exemplifies but defends that tendency. He believes that actions are essentially 'tryings'—the analytical point.[8] He also believes that, other things being equal, criminal responsibility should (because moral responsibility does) extend to and only to what the criminal tries to achieve—the normative point. But he does not mix up the two points. It is merely that the same thought underlies both of them: that trying is all that we have control over. We think this fails to secure the analytical point—not on Duff's grounds, but on the simpler ground that there are events in our lives over which we have control but which are not actions (remember the 'forgetful breathing' example). There is no reason to define actions in some artificially wide way to accommodate such cases. Meanwhile, the normative point is also affected by such cases, because the things which we have control over other than actions (such as the forgetful breathing), are also not tryings. They are cases in which, if one had tried, one would have made a difference: that is the element of control. But the fact is that one did not try. So it cannot be the case that the dependence of responsibility upon control also makes responsibility depend upon trying.

Ashworth might reply that even though there can be responsibility without trying, in cases in which trying is in play responsibility only goes as far as the trying does (i.e. when one tries, one is not responsible for what one does not try to do). Ashworth appears to equate the view that responsibility only goes as far as trying with the view that once one gets to descriptions of one's actions which refer to unforeseen (or at any rate unforeseeable) consequences, one's responsibility runs out. What is not made clear is how one leaps from questions about trying, to questions about foresight and foreseeability. What about the foreseen and foreseeable things which we do without trying to do, which are merely side-effects of the things that we try to do? Even if we set this problem aside,[9] however, Ashworth faces deeper difficulties. He wishes to combine his 'trying' principle, which is supposed to make criminal law insensitive to certain important kinds of luck, with another principle of which he was the original articulator, namely the principle of 'representative labelling' (or 'fair labelling', as he now calls it).[10] The principle of representative

[8] Although he denies making the mistake which Duff warns against, of viewing a 'trying' as some kind of mysterious mental act detached from the actual things that one does (p. 109).

[9] Elsewhere Ashworth has attempted to fill this gap by using what he dubs the 'belief' principle; see A. Ashworth, 'Belief, Intent and Criminal Liability', in J. Eekelaar and J. Bell (eds.), *Oxford Essays in Jurisprudence, Third Series* (Oxford 1989).

[10] The principle is introduced in Ashworth, 'The Elasticity of Mens Rea', in Colin Tapper (ed.), *Crime, Proof, and Punishment* (London 1981), 45 at 53. The name change was proposed for no obvious reason by Glanville Williams in 'Convictions and Fair Labelling', (1983) 42 *Cambridge LJ* 85.

labelling requires that the names given to criminal offences, and the labels accordingly attached to convicted offenders, should give an accurate picture of the offence of which they have been convicted, including its gravity. One might assume, then, that it would be important to include in the label a clear indication of the harm, if any, which the offender is supposed to have brought about. In deploying the trying principle, however, Ashworth resists precisely this. Take his example of the batterer whose battery causes death (p. 118). English law would label her a manslaughterer, and at first sight it is hard to think of a more representative label; but Ashworth's trying principle would make her, under certain conditions, a batterer and no more.

Perhaps there is simply a conflict here between Ashworth's two principles, the trying principle and the representative labelling principle. In his contribution, however, Ashworth seems to envisage that they are in harmony. Harmony is presumably achieved only at the expense of a modification to the representative labelling principle itself. Not only must the label give an accurate representation of what the defendant did, but it must also give a representation which makes no reference to features of what the defendant did which lie beyond what he tried to do. That may explain why Ashworth has now accepted the name 'fair' labelling for his principle, instead of representative labelling. The extra work is now done by the idea of 'fairness', an idea which is not explicitly elaborated in Ashworth's contribution.

Ashworth assumes throughout that the law can in principle (if not in practice) be shaped so as to eliminate the important kinds of luck, sensitivity to which would fall foul of his 'trying' principle. Michael Moore's essay seeks to cast doubt on the coherence of some of the law's attempts to narrow down the field of luck by the use of foreseeability criteria. His argument echoes several of the points made by Hornsby. Once we have realized that there are many things done in every action, we can see that any other eventuality, be it a death or a solar eclipse or a gas explosion, may also be both one thing and many things. Each is one thing in the sense that it is a particular incident occurring at a particular place and time, but also many things in the sense that it can be variously described. Think of a death. In a sense, a death is something that happens, with its own spatio-temporal location: it is what Moore and Hornsby, following philosophical convention, term a 'particular' (pp. 56, 127). Particulars may be variously described. Depending on the circumstances, a death may be described as a bereavement, a murder, a poisoning, a tragedy, a blessed release, or the supreme self-sacrifice. Or it may simply be described as a death. The result is that when we say 'that death was intended (or foreseen or foreseeable)', the question arises: was it the death *qua* particular that was intended, foreseen, or foreseeable, or was it the death, understood as just one of many descriptions which that particular may bear? The answer is that mentalistic terms like 'intended', 'foreseen', and 'foreseeable' cannot by their nature be predicated of particulars. They introduce traces of what are often called 'propositional attitudes' (i.e. mental states the content of which takes the form of a proposition). Moore claims that this gives rise to problems in certain areas of the law. Sometimes, if we are to be legally liable, what the law requires us to intend or foresee, or what the law stipulates must be foreseeable, is merely 'harm' or 'damage'. It seems to Moore that the law cannot mean 'harm' or 'damage' to count as a description of something: these terms are too open-ended to give any useful guidance as to the limits of legal liability, and yet the law claims to find useful guidance in the intention–foresight–foreseeability tests which take this form. Moore runs through the other things that 'harm' could be if it is not a description, but shows that the law gives too little specification for it to be a useful test, however it is meant.

Moore takes this situation to yield a fundamental 'incoherence' in certain mentalistic tests of legal liability, notably those used in determining legal causation (pp. 154–5). This way of putting the point is reminiscent, perhaps, of those sceptics that Moore describes (citing Morris Cohen) as the 'stray dogs of the intellectual world' (p. 130). His talk of incoherence seems in fact to be a dramatic way of expressing the point that the law could sometimes be sharpened up. We are all familiar with situations in which legal tests are ripe for more detailed specification. There may be doubts, for example, about the level of generality of the law's description of the damage which must be foreseen or foreseeable for an arson conviction. Is it merely the destruction of the building which must have been foreseen or foreseeable, or is it the destruction of the building *by fire*?[11] The law is open to interpretation here, but (unless you are a stray dog) it is hardly a case of incoherence.

6. Knowing Right from Wrong

Perhaps this is, however, to overlook a further subtlety, with which Moore does not concern himself. The subtlety concerns what it means for one to foresee something under its legally salient description. It could mean that one foresees it under the description which happens, unbeknown to one, to have legal salience. One knows the facts but not the law. Or it could mean that one actually appreciates the legal salience as well. One knows the facts and the law. Should it matter, for the purposes of criminal liability,

[11] Compare J. C. Smith and B. Hogan, *Criminal Law* (7th edn., London 1992), 708: 'D must intend or be reckless as to destruction or damage *by fire*', with Marise Cremona, *Criminal Law* (London 1989), 193: 'The serious offence of arson requires no additional *mens rea*', presumably beyond that required for ordinary criminal damage.

into which category one falls? English law generally says no: *ignorantia juris neminem excusat*. Some critics have linked the emergence of this doctrine to a time (surely imaginary) when English criminal law was broadly coterminous with morality.[12] This would suggest that *ignorantia juris neminem excusat* is a doctrine which is easier to defend concerning crimes *mala in se* (crimes which would be wrongs even if there were no applicable legal prohibition) than it is concerning crimes *mala prohibita* (crimes which are wrongs only because of the applicable legal prohibition). This might be thought of as the traditional view. Douglas Husak and Andrew von Hirsch take a different view, envisaging a dividing line between those who can avail themselves of a mistake-of-law defence and those who cannot, that would cut across the *mala in se/mala prohibita* distinction. The central plank of their argument is that certain mistakes of law affect culpability. They recognize that criminal liability does not always turn on culpability, although they are, we think, too inclined to play down the incidence of strict liability and the importance of regulatory offences (p. 157). This may be wishful thinking: by contrast with Brudner, Husak and von Hirsch appear to think that a unified doctrine of culpability should prevail across the whole criminal law.

According to the doctrine of culpability which Husak and von Hirsch prefer, the effect of mistakes of law depends on a number of considerations. In the first place such mistakes should only furnish a defence if they are, in a stipulated sense, reasonable. But even that will not suffice by itself. The defendant must also have made a mistake, with some rational basis, as to the 'injuriousness' of her allegedly criminal conduct (p. 168). The relevant sense of 'injuriousness' is evidently heavily moralized: even the seemingly implausible view that euthanasia is not 'injurious' is among those that might count as 'plausible' on the Husak and von Hirsch account (p. 165). 'Injuriousness' appears to mean something like 'all things considered wrongness'. The requirement that one make a 'plausible' mistake as to 'injuriousness' in this sense rules out the use of Husak and von Hirsch's mistake-of-law defence in many, but not all, *mala in se* crimes. One can use the defence even where what one did was wrong apart from the law, so long as one had the requisite 'plausible' belief that it was not. The position with crimes *mala prohibita* is a little more complicated. The whole point about these crimes is that they would not be wrongs apart from the law. That means, if we read Husak and von Hirsch right, that the 'injuriousness' element in such crimes would be lacking, apart from the law. If one has no reason to know the law, then one has no reason to know of the 'injuriousness'. Leaving aside those who find 'injuriousness' on spurious grounds, then, those who reasonably mistake the law concerning a

---

[12] See Glanville Williams, *Textbook of Criminal Law* (2nd edn., London 1983), 451.

malum prohibitum crime appear automatically to meet the conditions for the Husak and von Hirsch defence. This all assumes, however, that the offence in question carries a culpability requirement: for if it does not, the Husak and von Hirsch argument does not apply anyway. Given the profusion of *mala prohibita* crimes which are strict liability crimes, this should not be dismissed as a minor caveat. Its effect is to generate many counter-examples to the traditional view that a mistake-of-law defence is easier to justify for *mala prohibita* crimes than for *mala in se* crimes.

Husak and von Hirsch's essay illuminates the case of the defendant who did not know that he was breaking the law, but admits the moral wrong. They expressly decline to take a view on the converse case: the defendant who knows she is breaking the law, but denies the moral wrong (p. 165). That case, they say, can only be dealt with once one considers the arguments for a general moral obligation to obey the law. George Fletcher, on the other hand, feels able to discuss this case without going into that wider problem. His strategy is to distinguish the function of the legislature in criminal law from that of the judiciary. The legislature must strive for certainty in virtue of the *nullum crimen sine lege* principle. Judges, he thinks, are also bound by this principle to the extent that they may not alter the definition of offences as such. They may, however, respond to the facts of particular cases by altering the scope of defences. This they must do in accordance with what Fletcher calls 'the Right', a moralized account of legality (p. 177). One's nominal legal wrongdoing may be eclipsed in court by some justification derived from that moralized account.

This suggests that justifications need not come to light until the deed is done. It might be thought, however, that justifications must, by their nature, be accessible *ex ante* to potential offenders as well as *ex post* to judges. Fletcher himself claims that whether one will benefit from a justification depends on whether one knows of the justificatory facts (p. 179). Sometimes he seems to be going even further. There are hints that what really matters is whether one acted by reason of the justificatory facts, and not merely with knowledge of them: Fletcher speaks of justificatory 'intent' (p. 179). If the argument can be pushed that far, it is hard to see how justifications can be held to arise independently of defendants' reliance upon them, as Fletcher later suggests that they do (p. 186). One way out of this apparent dilemma would be to distinguish the justificatory facts from the fact of the justification. In other words, any defendant who is to benefit from a justification must act for the reason that the justificatory facts obtain, but need not act for the reason that they count as justificatory, which is an *ex post* matter for the judge. It is hard to see, however, why anyone would act for the reason that justificatory facts obtain if she did not also act by reason of the justificatory force of those facts. It is true that she might not act for the reason that they constitute a *legal* justification, and thus the law would not be relied upon. Instead, she might be acting on the moral justificatory force of the facts. Thus Fletcher's talk of *Recht* could be recast in more positivist terms, as the judges' giving *ex post* legal recognition to *ex ante* moral arguments, or at any rate *ex ante* moral arguments which can be fitted into established legal categories.

7. Distinguishing Prohibition from Responsibility

Paul Robinson also lays much stress on the distinction between *ex ante* and *ex post* aspects of the criminal law, between the prohibitions addressed to potential perpetrators and the rules of responsibility addressed to judges. Robinson is concerned with the merits and demerits of the traditional lawyer's distinction between the *actus reus* of a crime and its *mens rea*. One of the merits of this distinction, in Robinson's eyes, is that it attempts to mark the important line between the definition of the prohibited conduct and the rules of responsibility. One of the demerits of the distinction is that it fails to mark this line properly (p. 206). Robinson is right to find a failure here, and right to think that many criminal lawyers too readily identify *mens rea* with responsibility.[13] The *actus reus–mens rea* distinction cuts across the distinction between prohibition elements and elements of responsibility. In the English law of theft, for example, the requirement of an 'intention permanently to deprive' is plainly part of the *mens rea* of theft, if anything is. Nevertheless, and equally plainly, it goes to define the nature of the wrong itself rather than what makes the wrongdoer responsible for the wrong. The test for determining which of these it goes to (a test which Robinson does not spell out) relates to the nature of the justification for including in the definition of the crime the element of intention permanently to deprive. We all have certain special reasons, symbolic and instrumental, not to take others' property permanently, which are supplementary to our reasons not to take it temporarily. These give rise to further reasons, again symbolic and instrumental, for us not to intend to deprive permanently. So the reasons which drive this part of the definition of theft are reasons for us, in so far as we are potential perpetrators, rather than for judges. They are *ex ante* rather than *ex post*.

In recognition of all this, and unable to find any other use for the *actus reus–mens rea* distinction, Robinson argues that the criminal lawyer would be well advised to dispense with the distinction altogether. It would be better, he thinks, to divide criminal-law definitions up directly into the elements of prohibited conduct, on the one hand, and the rules of

---

[13] See e.g. C. M. V. Clarkson and H. M. Keating, *Criminal Law: Text and Materials* (2nd edn., London 1990), 149–50.

responsibility on the other. The former he calls 'rule articulation' elements, while the latter are described, depending on how exactly they operate, as rules of 'liability' and of 'grading'. The problem for Robinson is that he would like to preserve the kind of organizational tidiness which the *actus reus–mens rea* distinction has always been used to supply. He wants to be able to say something general (i.e. crossing the boundaries between different crimes) about what kinds of things will be found in each of the three classifications. 'Future-conduct intention' can bear on 'rule articulation', whereas 'present-conduct intention' will be found in the 'liability' category and 'future-result culpability' will matter for 'grading'. The truth is that things are less tidy (even) than this. Consider the example of homicide. Robinson uses the distinction between murder and manslaughter to illustrate 'grading', a matter of *ex post* responsibility (p. 208). On his analysis, the distinction relates to grading because it is a distinction of 'future-result culpability', i.e. a distinction between intention and recklessness as to the death. But it is really a distinction between two different wrongs, between two different prohibitions. The distinction between murder and manslaughter is analogous, in all relevant respects, to the distinction between theft and a crime of temporary deprivation (e.g. 'joy-riding'); yet Robinson would happily classify the latter as a difference of rule articulation because it involves what he calls future-conduct intention (p. 209). Once again, the point is that we all have special reasons, symbolic and instrumental, not to intend to kill, which are supplementary to the reasons we have for not taking the risk of death, knowingly or otherwise. In the end, Robinson's classificatory system faces the same difficulty which makes the *actus reus– mens rea* distinction a distinction of limited use. It is that little can be said, at least of a kind that will help criminal lawyers, about the logical structure of crimes in general. Those things that one can say about the logical structure of crimes in general are doubtless of great philosophical interest, but they will not, as Robinson hopes, help to make the textbooks better.

8. Defeasibility

Richard Tur's arguments bear this out. He characterizes the law in general, and the criminal law in particular, as a set of 'defeasible normative conditional propositions' (p. 214), but illustrates how this is compatible with there being criminal offences of many different configurations. Thus, what is part of the definition of one crime (i.e. bears on conditionality) may be merely the absence of a defence in another (i.e. bears on defeasibility).[14] As it stands, this is merely a formal philosophical distinction. In order to

---

[14] On defeasibility, see H. L. A. Hart's 'The Ascription of Responsibility and Rights', in (1948) 48 *Proceedings of the Aristotelian Society* 121, which he overhastily disowned in the preface to *Punishment and Responsibility* (Oxford 1968).

make it a matter of concern to criminal lawyers one must add certain normative premisses. To some extent, in Tur's essay, these normative premisses are moral propositions independent of law (p. 222). In large measure, however, the normative premisses are themselves propositions of law. Tur's view is evidently that some aspects of the criminal law must be taken as 'givens' when others are being contested. It is only because and to the extent that the law already happens to make something turn on the distinction between the elements of an offence and the conditions of a defence that it is a matter of moral consequence whether one is a 'definitional maximalist' or a 'definitional minimalist': whether, in other words, one is predisposed to count any particular legal doctrine bearing on criminal liability as going to conditionality or to defeasibility. So, for example, if there are general principles of law which make the whole *actus reus* subject to *mens rea*, and dictate what kind of *mens rea* that will be, then the only way to get away from the general requirement of *mens rea* may be to shift a certain part of the *actus reus* into a defensive role where the general principles of law dictating *mens rea* do not apply.

Tur himself is willing, however, to subvert the 'givens' on which he relies. Having built his definitional minimalism on the back of the assumption that putting elements on the 'offence side' constrains one to take a strict view of the *mens rea* required, he goes on to present a view of the criminal law in which things are apparently much less strict. There can be crimes of 'partial' *mens rea*, or no *mens rea* at all: there are many permutations. That being so, it is not so clear why one need have a general view about how much or how little is to be included in the definition of a crime. It is not clear, in other words, why one needs to choose some general position on the scale from definitional minimalism to definitional maximalism. One motivation for so choosing might be that, like Fletcher, one considers the definition of crimes to be a matter for the legislature (by virtue of the principle of *nullum crimen sine lege*), and one also considers that judges are better placed to deal with certain problems of responsibility.[15] In that case, one might need to say that those problems of responsibility belong to the realm of defences rather than to the definition of offences. There are certainly hints of this argument to be found in Tur's essay. He indicates that the list of defeating circumstances is always open to change, presumably in contradistinction to the element of conditionality in criminal offences, and he indicates a preference that the openness to change of the former be exploited: judicial justice over legislative certainty (p. 215).

[15] See J. C. Smith, *Justification and Excuse in the Criminal Law* (London 1989), 5–6. Smith supports the view taken by the Law Commission in its 1985 proposals for codification of the English criminal law, that no attempt should be made to codify all defences to crime, even though all offences should be codified.

The contrast between conditionality and defeasibility also plays a major role in Stephen Morse's essay. He points out that the symptoms of mental illness can be significant on both sides of the equation. They can be used both to deny *mens rea* and to provide a positive defence. In the former role they have an instrumental (evidentiary) significance; that is to say, they can help one to establish lack of *mens rea*, but do not constitute lack of *mens rea*. In the latter role, however, they are of intrinsic significance. The fact that one suffers from certain symptoms of mental illness actually constitutes the defence. The puzzle about Morse's proposal, at least from the point of view of an English lawyer, is that he finds no constitutive significance for mental illness on the conditionality side of criminal liability. It is a commonplace among English criminal lawyers that voluntary conduct is a (general) positive requirement of criminal liability, quite separate from any element of *mens rea* which may be required by the definition of particular crimes.[16] It is also a commonplace that the so-called 'defence' of automatism is in reality no more than a denial of voluntary conduct. And there can be no doubt that, whatever automatism may be, it is sometimes a symptom of mental illness; hence 'insane automatism'. If all this is correct, then (*pace* Morse) the mere fact that a symptom of mental illness is pleaded constitutively rather than instrumentally should not lead one to think that it necessarily belongs to the realm of defeasibility. It is not necessarily, in other words, being treated as a positive defence.

It may be thought that this matter is important only because of the twists and turns of criminal procedure and evidence: all that turns on whether something is a matter of conditionality rather than a matter of defeasibility are things like the evidentiary burden and who is allowed to raise the issue. But there is also a moral distinction at work. Morality deals with responsibility in two stages. There is prima-facie responsibility, and then there is all-things-considered responsibility. The questions which arise at the stage of prima-facie responsibility are about one's susceptibility to moral judgments in the light of what one did, irrespective of what exactly it was one did. They concern, in other words, whether one falls (for the time being) under the judgmental jurisdiction of morality. All-things-considered responsibility, on the other hand, is sensitive to what one actually did. It is here that questions of excuse come in.[17] That excuse belongs here and not at the stage of establishing prima-facie responsibility is demonstrated by the familiar fact that some wrongs are inexcusable.

Morse holds that when the symptoms of mental illness are not used instrumentally (to help deny *mens rea*), they can only be used as excuses. They are in that respect (although apparently not in other respects)

---

[16] See e.g. Smith and Hogan, *Criminal Law*, above n. 11, 37–42.

[17] Just as justification comes in when we move from the question of prima-facie wrong-doing to that of all-things-considered wrongdoing.

analogous to coercion (p. 265). The result of this is that the symptoms of mental illness can never be enough to take one outside the province of criminal liability altogether, whatever the crime may be. They cannot be used to eliminate liability for inexcusable crimes. Are there any such crimes in force today? In recent times, English law has given a firm 'yes'. There is the now familiar rule that murder cannot be excused by duress, a rule which the judges purport to justify by presenting murder as always inexcusable.[18] Morse's argument would suggest that if the judges are right here, then mental-illness arguments should not be available in murder cases either. The diminished-responsibility defence, which operates in England in relation only to murder, is therefore turned on its head. Oddly enough, on Morse's argument, murder is the very last place in which the defence should operate.

9. Science and Reason

Bill Fulford shares Morse's preference for describing mental illness as an excuse. He also shares with Morse a view according to which the exculpatory significance of mental illness lies in its impact upon practical reasoning. But whereas Morse defends this view against a naïve moralist's insistence upon assimilating mental illness to coercion, Fulford defends it against a naïve psychiatrist's insistence upon reducing mental illness to disease. Fulford is anxious to distinguish illness from disease. Illness is the sufferer's experience of disease, and disease the medical expert's account of illness. If we accept this reclassification, then we have been guilty of pleonasm in speaking (up to now) of 'the symptoms of mental illness': the mental illness actually *is* the symptoms, as experienced by the sufferer; it is not something which *has* symptoms. What does not follow, but what psychiatrists are said to take too often for granted, is that our interest in mental illness must reflect its role in evidencing the presence of mental disease. On the contrary, argues Fulford, it is the illness itself which matters, and the search for an underlying disease should be viewed as a matter of derivative concern. If a disease can be found, so much the better, since that will open up new channels for treatment and cure, as well as proof of the illness. But if, as in the case of many a psychosis, the illness is unsupported by any (known) disease, we should not be led to doubt for a moment that

---

[18] See *DPP* v. *Lynch* [1975] AC 653, *Abbott* v. *R* [1977] AC 755, *R* v. *Howe* [1987] AC 417, *R* v. *Gotts* [1991] 1 QB 660. It might be thought that the view that murder is always inexcusable is inconsistent with the doctrine of provocation. In the view of Lord Diplock, provocation is 'an anomaly in English law' (see *DPP* v. *Camplin* [1978] AC 705, 713). Another explanation of the provocation doctrine would point to the fact that it is only a partial excuse, and would reinterpret the view that murder is always inexcusable as a view that there is no *complete* excuse for murder.

it can truly qualify as an illness. Nor, therefore, should we be led to doubt that it is capable of affecting responsibility. As Fulford notices, the criminal law typically errs here in treating the disease as pivotal.[19]

In shifting our attention from the disease to the illness, Fulford also brings our thoughts back to questions with which we began, questions about the role of action and value in criminal law. According to Fulford, the disease paradigm restricts our attention, with scientistic zeal, to matters of 'fact' and 'functioning', sidelining the discourse of action and value in terms of which the moral and legal significance of mental illness must be cast. Here Fulford works with a sharp distinction between fact and value, which has been at the heart of his earlier work on conceptual problems in medicine.[20] To this he adds another distinction, perhaps less sharp, between matters of mental and physical functioning on the one hand and matters of reasoning and action on the other. The shift of attention from disease to illness brings with it a shift of attention from the discourse of functioning to the discourse of action. Here Fulford associates himself with a view that we criticized in our discussion of Hornsby and Duff. He appears to identify the boundaries of action with the boundaries of responsibility, and also appears to identify the boundaries of intention with the boundaries of action (pp. 300, 305). These false identifications have led some to subscribe to distorted accounts of responsibility in which questions of cause and effect are paramount. That is because the causes of actions (some say, the intentions which cause them) are what distinguish actions, first and foremost, from other kinds of conduct (such as the conduct of the forgetful breather), and so viewing the presence of action as the key to questions of responsibility makes questions of responsibility seem to turn, in part, on the presence of certain causal factors. Fulford, however, does not let his false identifications lead him down such a dangerous path. One of the main achievements of his essay is to distance questions of responsibility from questions of cause and effect. He does this by observing that the causal role of mental disease in disrupting practical reason is a contingency; that is to say, to ask whether one is rational or not is different from asking how it came about that one is rational or not. And what matters for responsibility, Fulford argues, is one's rationality or irrationality. The causal origins are neither here nor there. On the same grounds, the causal origins of one's *conduct* are neither here nor there: the forgetful breather is responsible for his breathing, even though that breathing is caused entirely by spontaneous reflex movements in his chest cavity. And so would he be, as Fulford's argument reminds us, even if those reflex movements were in turn caused by some disease. So long as he is in control

---

[19] Fulford correctly cites, in this regard, *Bratty* v. *Attorney-General for Northern Ireland* [1961] 3 All ER 523, and *R* v. *Quick* [1973] 3 All ER 347.
[20] K. W. M. Fulford, *Moral Theory and Medical Practice* (Cambridge 1989).

of the breathing, his responsibility is intact. As in the body, so in the mind.

It is not hard to see where the confusion creeps in. The control relation is in a loose sense causal. It belongs to a family of relations, of which the relation of cause and effect in a stricter sense is simply another member. There are some family resemblances. Both relations have counterfactual elements and both have what may be called a 'direction of operation'.[21] So the two are easily mistaken for one another. Nevertheless, there are important differences. To be in control of something is not necessarily to be its cause, nor vice versa. Take the example of a guided missile. The missile's guidance system may be in control of the missile—the missile may be under control—even though its movements are so far entirely caused by the launch momentum. The control is lost if no adjustment in the guidance system would make a difference to the missile's movements.[22] But so long as no adjustment is necessary, the control of the system may be maintained throughout the operation of numerous external causes. It does not even matter, for the guidance system to be in control, what caused the working of the guidance system. If we understand ourselves as complex guidance systems, which is how we must be understood if the guidance of morality and law is to apply to us and be applied by us, then it is not hard to see how the causal history of our reasoning and our conduct can be left on one side when our responsibility is being assessed.[23] Those who think that real responsibility is hostage to the facts about determinism are often accused of misunderstanding determinism or its role in the world. Our suggestion is much more mundane. They have merely misunderstood the conditions of responsibility.

10. Liberal Values

The misunderstanding is compounded by the introduction of a third concept, that of choice. Those who reject the modern criminal law and its philosophical foundations often do so because they think it is permeated with assumptions about human freedom which liberalism makes but determinism unseats. The rejection is ill-considered on two fronts. The preoccupation with responsibility, and with the grounds of responsibility which we find in the modern criminal law, are not peculiarly liberal. And neither the preoccupations of liberalism nor the foundations of the modern

[21] For an illuminating discussion of counterfactuals and 'directions' in causal relationships, see John Mackie, *The Cement of the Universe* (Oxford 1974), chs. 2 and 7.

[22] See Harry Frankfurt, 'The Problem of Action', in his *The Importance of What We Care About* (Cambridge 1988).

[23] Of course, the causal history of many other things is of vital importance for responsibility. Hence our earlier reservations about the tendency to play down the relevance of consequences to responsibility.

criminal law are especially challenged by determinism. The Liberal ideology is dominated by a concern with choices, ranging from small choices about what to do here and now to big choices about how to lead one's life. Certainly the criminal law is not immune to such concerns. They serve to justify the harm principle, for example, if anything does. They play a large part in the shaping of criminal prohibitions. But they do not play such a large role as critics are wont to claim in our doctrines of criminal *responsibility*. One's conduct may be voluntary even though one had no options; and without options, of course, one has no choices. Choices entail alternatives, but basic criminal responsibility is largely unaffected by the presence or absence of alternatives. Nor is moral responsibility much different. It depends primarily on control of conduct and self-control, not on choice. An account of it compatible with that gestured towards here has been defended at least since Aristotle, and throughout the works of many (Aristotle included) who could scarcely be described as liberals. It may be fashionable to lay all the problems of our criminal justice system at the door of our ideological tradition, but one of the aims of this book—and certainly of this introduction—is to show that the philosophical foundations of criminal-law doctrine are far from being that simple. Liberalism claims to be open to many values, to many moral concerns which are not dictated by liberalism itself. Nowhere is that openness more vividly illustrated than in the diverse preoccupations of criminal-law doctrine.

Agency and Welfare in the Penal Law

ALAN BRUDNER

1. Introduction: The Problem of Harm

In his monumental work on the moral limits of the criminal law, Joel Feinberg makes the concept of harm—understood as a set-back to interests—central to the definition of crime. The 'common element,' he writes, in wilful homicide, rape, aggravated assault, battery, burglary, and grand larceny, 'is the direct production of serious harm to individual persons and groups'.[1] Other acts somewhat further removed from the core of uncontroversial crimes sound variations on the theme of harm. Thus counterfeiting, smuggling, income-tax evasion, contempt of court, and the violation of zoning and anti-pollution ordinances are offences because, while seldom harming specific persons or groups, they nevertheless cause harm to 'the public', 'society', 'the general ambience of neighbourhoods, the economy, the climate, or the environment'.[2] Generalizing from these clear cases of permissible criminalization, Feinberg concludes that penal restrictions on individual liberty are morally justified when they prevent harm or the unreasonable risk of harm to parties other than the person whose liberty is curtailed.[3]

No sooner, however, does Feinberg begin to define the harm principle than the principle slips away. Clearly, not all cases of harming are crimes, for individuals have interests—commercial or amorous—that often conflict with those of others, and the satisfaction of one person will often mean the thwarting of a competitor. We thus need a criterion of seriousness to distinguish harming that is wrong from harming that is permissible. For Feinberg, serious harms are those that invade 'welfare interests'—that is, interests in the possession of goods which everyone needs in order to attain his or her personal goals.[4] Obvious examples are the interest in life, physical health, financial security, and liberty. Yet this formulation soon

I would like to thank the editors of this volume for their helpful comments on an earlier draft of this essay.

[1] Joel Feinberg, *The Moral Limits of the Criminal Law*, i. *Harm to Others* (New York 1984), 11. [2] Ibid.
[3] Feinberg would also allow offence to others as a criterion of permissible criminalization; see Joel Feinberg, *The Moral Limits of the Criminal Law*, ii. *Offence to Others* (New York 1985).
[4] Feinberg, *Harm to Others*, above n. 1, 37.

runs up against the depressive who has no interest in life (because no goal seems worthwhile to him), the vagabond who has no interest in property, the ascetic who has no interest in bodily health, or the multi-millionaire for whom the theft of a dollar threatens no basic interest in security. These problematic examples drive Feinberg to the postulate of a 'standard person', who has normal interests and whom legislators must have in view when they formulate general laws.[5] Yet this device places Feinberg on the horns of a dilemma. The standard person is standard either in a statistical or in an ideal sense. If the standard person has interests that *most* people have, then killing the depressive who has no interest in living is not wrong, though the law may punish it in order to forestall a defence (harmless killing) that may tempt the unscrupulous and give too worrisome a discretion to authorities. If the standard person has interests that the rational agent has, then killing the depressive is wrong although no interest *of his* is set back, in which case the harm principle as Feinberg conceives it does no work in defining crime. Since it is doubtful that Feinberg would deny that killing the depressive is wrong, he will likely be impaled on the second horn rather than on the first.

The disjunction of wronging and harming illustrated by the examples of the depressive and the millionaire is well known to the law of torts and crimes.[6] A *damnum absque injuria* is not actionable, whereas an *injuria* is often actionable without proof of damage. A trespass to land may incidentally benefit the landowner's interest and yet none the less be a proscribable wrong.[7] Feinberg explains such 'hard examples' by arguing that the trespass is a harm to a proprietary interest, although one that is possibly outweighed by other benefits. But why, if the prevention of harm is the theme of the least controversial criminal laws, do we punish if the invasion of the proprietary interest works a net increase of benefits for the property-owner? The fact that the trespass is 'to some extent' a harm ceases to have explanatory power if we can punish even though the harm is more trivial than some we do not proscribe (for example, the harms from economic competition), and even if the trespass produces an overall benefit.

The idea to which Feinberg continually returns in order to rationalize these cases of apparently harmless wrongdoing is that of freedom of choice.[8] Stealing a dollar from a millionaire, killing a suicidal depressive, or trespassing on another's property deprive someone of the freedom to decide what to do with his or her life or wealth; and since everyone (we can assume) has a strong interest in such a liberty, these actions too are harmful. This idea also explains what is otherwise mysterious from the standpoint of the harm principle: it explains why the consent of the victim

[5] Ibid., 112.   [6] *Restatement (Second) of the Law of Torts* (1965), ch. 1, § 7.
[7] Ibid.   [8] Feinberg, *Harm to Others*, above n. 1, 113 and 206–14.

negates the wrongfulness even of serious set-backs to welfare interests. However, the idea that is hurried in to rescue the harm principle in these problematic cases actually demolishes it. This becomes evident when we juxtapose the following two examples.

Suppose V is suffering great pain from a disease that is curable by drugs. The disease is so debilitating that V is unable to perform any but the simplest of life-preserving functions. Nevertheless, V obstinately refuses treatment. He refuses not from any religious or moral convictions but from an ungrounded fear that the treatment will produce side-effects worse than his illness. One day D forcibly injects V with the appropriate medication, and V recovers to lead a normal and productive life. D is here unquestionably guilty of an assault, and the fact that his act was of untold benefit to V is irrelevant to his culpability. Contrast this situation with one in which V is rendered a lifelong quadriplegic by D in a sporting match in which V is a willing participant. Here D is innocent of wrongdoing if his act imposed a risk within the range to which V consented.

Some may be inclined to explain these cases by attributing to the interest in freedom of choice a preponderant weight, one that tips the welfare scales in its favour when measured against other interests. But this explanation is unconvincing. Few would doubt that the person who refuses treatment because of a gross misperception of its likely effects on his welfare is on balance better rather than worse off for the assault; and no one will say that absolving D in the second case enhances V's welfare by giving effect to his choices, as if choice were the one thing needful for a life valuable to the agent. What these examples show, on the contrary, is that the criminal law does not weigh violations of freedom in the same scales with set-backs to welfare interests. Instead, it assigns freedom a privilege or absolute value such that disrespect thereof is a crime *regardless* of the benefits it confers on the victim (and regardless of whether the victim subjectively values freedom) and such that respect for a person's freedom of choice absolves a defendant regardless of the magnitude of harm inflicted on him.[9] This means, however, that disrespect for another's freedom performs the thematic role that Feinberg wished to assign to the harm principle. It and not the infliction of harm is the gravamen of crime.

If we pursue this suggestion, other features of the criminal law that are unintelligible from the standpoint of the harm principle begin to cohere. For example, it is no excuse to an intentional homicide that society has been rid of someone who is a source of far greater suffering in the world than good. It is as wrong to kill an unreconstructed Scrooge as it is to

---

[9] The fact that the consent of the victim is no defence to murder does not refute this proposition. On the contrary, it is because liberty is the foundational principle for the criminal law that one cannot effectively alienate it.

kill a Tiny Tim. Nor is it an excuse to theft that the accused redistributed wealth from those for whom the loss was barely felt to those for whom the gain meant the difference between misery and contentment. Disrespect for freedom is a wrong no matter how great the consequential benefits to society.[10] Conversely, the excuses recognized by the criminal law appear perverse from the standpoint of preventing harm to others. An involuntary agent is excused even though someone is seriously harmed by his physical movements and even though he is thereby freed perhaps to inflict harm again. Taking someone's property in the belief that the object is one's own is not a crime, nor is an assault in the mistaken belief that the victim consented to contact. In all these cases someone is harmed—perhaps seriously—but the accused has shown no disrespect for the victim's freedom of choice.

Regarded as a whole, these phenomena support a thesis that is the antithesis of Feinberg's: that the criminal law—or at least that part of it with a common-law origin—systematically excludes considerations of harm and benefit from the concept of criminal wrongdoing. This exclusion is masked by the fact that most cases of wronging are also cases of harming, but the independence of wrongdoing from harm is revealed by thought experiments in which one alternately isolates set-backs to interests and violations of freedom. Moreover, the repulsion of harm from the notion of wrongdoing is the obverse of a rigorously exclusive focus on personality, agency, or free will as the concept that gives thematic unity to the criminal law.[11] The *actus reus* of crime is the subjugation to oneself of the body or external property that embodies the free will of another; the *mens rea* of crime is the intentional or reckless disdain for the autonomy of another self; penal justice consists in the connection between punishment and the free choice of the criminal; and the paradigmatic form of punishment is imprisonment, which may or may not disadvantage the prisoner (he may be a vagrant who prefers the security of prison), but which certainly deprives him of liberty and of the dignity based thereon.

Having drawn this stark picture, however, we must now point out its one-sidedness. The thoroughgoing exclusion of considerations of harm from the concept of crime applies only to wrongs that one person may commit against another in a context abstracted from any human association for a common end. That is to say, it applies only to wrongs that one may commit in a prepolitical state of nature and that are of common-law

---

[10] The defence of necessity has sometimes been interpreted as a counter-example to this principle, but I have elsewhere suggested an interpretation of necessity that coheres with it; see Alan Brudner, 'A Theory of Necessity', (1987) 7 *Oxford Journal of Legal Studies* 339. Moreover, the lesser-harm theory of necessity has been rejected by the Supreme Court of Canada; see *Perka* v. *R* (1985) 13 DLR (4th) 1.

[11] We will see, however, that this exclusiveness cannot coherently be maintained.

origin, to wrongs against the life, bodily integrity, and property of the person. This means that the exclusion applies to a very narrow segment of the penal law of the modern, regulatory State. Beyond this segment, the welfare of individuals is undeniably the aim of the penal law. For example, the promotion of welfare is the point of laws controlling the use and sale of narcotics and liquors, of laws regulating the production and marketing of food, of laws protecting the environment, and of laws promoting road, air, and industrial safety. Under these laws, one may incur penalties for acts that do not dominate the free will of others, either because (as in the case of a breach of a safety regulation) they involve no transaction with another person, or because (as in the case of trafficking in narcotics) the transaction is consensual. Judges often refer to acts that violate these laws as 'public welfare offences' to distinguish them from 'true crimes', and typically require standards of fault for a conviction that fall short of the wilfulness required for criminal liability.[12]

Ultimately, then, the problem with Feinberg's harm principle is not that it fails to capture intuitions about wrongdoing embedded in the penal law, but that it obliterates a distinction within the penal law between two paradigms of wrongdoing. I shall call these paradigms the agency paradigm and the welfarist paradigm, and I shall use the term 'criminal law' to designate that part of the penal law governed by principles unique to the framework of agency. The questions I want to discuss emerge from the coexistence of these two normative frameworks within the penal law. First, what assumptions about the nature of personality and freedom underlie the agency paradigm, and is this view of freedom internally coherent? Second, is the conception of freedom underlying the welfarist paradigm a superior understanding of freedom, and if so, why has it not succeeded in establishing its hegemony over the whole domain of the penal law? Is its failure to do so a matter of historical inertia, or is there a conceptual basis for a differentiation of paradigms within the penal law, each with its characteristic aim, standard of fault, and criterion of penal justice? Can these paradigms be grasped as interconnected parts of a totality that requires both?

My thesis is that the agency paradigm of the penal law rests on an untenable conception of freedom, but that it is nevertheless essential to a whole that embodies an adequate conception. The agency paradigm errs in so far as it claims to contain the whole content of penal justice; but it is preserved as a subordinate sector of a totality that also includes the welfarist framework. This thesis (the Hegelian origins of which will be plain) bears implications across a broad front of jurisprudential controversy. As long as it appears that the two frameworks exist independently

---

[12] See *Sherras* v. *De Rutzen* [1985] 1 QB 918; *Proudman* v. *Dayman* (1941) 67 CLR 536.

of each other, legal argument will appear rooted in a prior, ungrounded choice between them. Hence legal discourse will be vulnerable to a critique exposing its structured modes of reasoning from underlying principles as a façade for political advocacy.[13] Moreover, if the paradigms are unconnected, there will be a theoretical imperative to absolutize the normative principle of one or the other. The frameworks will thus be antagonistic, and any *modus vivendi* achieved between them will appear as an intellectually disreputable compromise. Principled adherents of each paradigm will seek to extend its dominion over the entire penal law, while moderate pluralists will seem bereft of principle as well as unclear about the boundaries of the frameworks. So, for example, an advocate of the subjective standard of fault in the criminal law will insist on its application to welfare offences as well;[14] while the welfarist who favours a negligence standard will urge its extension to all crimes, which he will reinterpret as harms.[15] Similarly, those for whom criminal justice consists in meting out punishment to the deserving will want to make desert the criterion of just punishment throughout the penal law;[16] while those who see the irrelevance of desert in a paradigm ordered to the prevention of harm will want to eliminate it entirely (as part of an outmoded retributivism) in favour of a welfare-justified constraint of respect for autonomy.[17] In the absence of a principle for demarcating the paradigms, those dissatisfied with the consequences of either extreme position will tend to mix agency and welfarist doctrines throughout, leaving the penal law in the muddle in which we currently find it.

Suppose, however, that the two paradigms were internally connected as subordinate and complementary aspects of a whole. In that case, their differentiated and mutually tolerant existence would have a solid conceptual foundation. We would coherently have a system of criminal law, ordered around respect for agency (that is, agency abstracted from embodiment in determinate values), and a system of welfare law aimed at the promotion of good. The choice between frameworks would not be open-ended, for each would apply to a distinctive category of offences whose (otherwise elusive) boundary would be stabilized by the primacy of the whole over its parts. Moreover, each paradigm would have the features necessitated by its thematic principle. In the agency paradigm, the standard

---

[13] Mark Kelman, 'Interpretive Construction in the Substantive Criminal Law', (1981) 33 *Stanford LR* 591.

[14] Jerome Hall, 'Negligent Behaviour Should be Excluded from Penal Liability', (1963) 63 *Columbia LR* 632.

[15] Oliver Wendell Holmes, *The Common Law* (ed. M. De W. Howe, Boston 1963), 42–62.

[16] See *Reference Re Section 94(2) of the Motor Vehicle Act* [1985] 2 SCR 486, at 514, per Lamer CJ.

[17] See H. L. A. Hart, *Punishment and Responsibility* (Oxford 1968), 22–4, 44–53 and 180–5.

of fault would be the wilful disrespect of freedom, and the point of punishment would be the vindication of mutual respect as the sole coherent foundation of the person's worth. In the welfarist paradigm, the point of sanctions would be the prevention of harm, and the standard of fault would be negligence. Each paradigm would thus be liberated from the tyranny of the other; and the quarrel between subjectivists and objectivists, retributivists and consequentialists would be pacified, for each would hold sway within its respective sphere.

The aim of this essay, then, is to disclose the conceptual ground for the reconciliation of the agency and welfarist paradigms in the penal law. I begin by describing the internal coherence of the agency model, relating its basic features to the abstract conception of freedom that informs it. I then try to show how the limitations of this conception are revealed within the agency paradigm itself, notably in the concessions the law must make to considerations of welfare in differentiating wrongs according to seriousness and in dealing with conflicts between property and the right to self-preservation. I then set out the welfarist paradigm and show how the absolutization of this model negates the autonomy of the self that it means to actualize. The self-contradictoriness of each principle, when absolutized to the exclusion of the other, reveals the genuine ground of law as the totality that includes both as subordinate moments. This totality I call dialogic community, whose structure of mutual recognition is the latent theme of both paradigms.

A final introductory word about the method of argument employed in this essay: because I shall be partly concerned with describing the internal coherence of paradigms, my theoretical attitude will be one of immersion in the standpoint of each of the paradigms in turn. As a result, it may sometimes be unclear whether I am stating positions I mean to endorse. To avoid this problem, I shall state at the outset my theoretical stance toward the legal principles and doctrines generated by the models. Since my thesis is that penal justice consists in the unity of the paradigms, I mean to endorse all the principles and doctrines derived from the foundational norm of a paradigm in so far as that norm keeps within bounds consistent with a recognition that the paradigm is merely part of a whole. On the other hand, I mean to criticize those implications of the model that flow from treating its norm as the whole itself. What these implications are will become clear in due course.

2. The Paradigm of Formal Agency

2.1. *Mutual Recognition as the Basis of Rights*

A legal paradigm is ordered by a particular conception of the end that grounds valid duties. Because a legal order seeks to differentiate itself categorically from a condition of violence, its conception of a foundational end must be a philosophically plausible (though not necessarily adequate) conception of an absolute end, of one that is necessarily valid for all agents. The connection between law and an absolute end was taught to the modern world by Kant.[18] No value that is relative to the desire of a particular agent can ground a duty in another to respect or promote it, for the particular good of one individual (or group) provides no sufficient reason for another's renouncing his own. Subjective values can hold sway over others only by compulsion—that is, only by an appeal to fear and self-interest incompatible with the idea of an unconditionally valid obligation. Binding duties are possible only if there is an end that transcends the objects of particularistic appetite and that necessarily commands the respect of all agents.

There are, of course, various ways in which one might conceive such an end. One might, for example, conceive of it as thinkers of antiquity did, as a good common to all agents by virtue of their rational natures, a good consisting in the full development of the civic and intellectual potentialities inherent in that nature. On this understanding of the foundational end, penal law appears primarily as an instrument of moral education, one whose function is to inculcate, through the creation of appropriate incentives, the habits and attitudes necessary to the full development of one's humanity.[19] Yet, whatever one might think of the classical conception of law's foundation as a philosophical idea, it is quite clearly not the conception of the absolute end that informs the common law. Here, thought repudiates the assumption of an immutable human nature given independently of the will and to whose ethical prescriptions the will must conform; and because it identifies the idea of a common good with a good rooted in such a nature, legal thought repudiates the common good as such, treating all value as relative to individual desire.[20] Given this identification of value with preference, thought can reach an absolute end only by rigorously abstracting from all determinate values to the bare capacity of the agent spontaneously to form, pursue, and revise values, that is to say, to the capacity for action or freedom. This capacity legal thought calls personality. The person is an absolute end not in the sense of an excellence

---

[18] See Immanuel Kant, *Foundations of the Metaphysics of Morals* (trans. Lewis White Beck, Indianapolis 1959), 43–7.

[19] See e.g. Plato, *Laws* 642b–645c; *Gorgias* 472d–479d.

[20] The common-law view of the status of values finds its classic expression in Thomas Hobbes, *Leviathan* (Oxford 1957), 32: 'But whatsoever is the object of any man's appetite or desire, that is it which he for his part calls *good*; and the object of his hate and aversion, *evil*; and of his contempt, *vile* and *inconsiderable*. For these words of good, evil, and contemptible are ever used with relation to the person that uses them, there being nothing simply and absolutely so, nor any common rule of good and evil to be taken from the nature of the objects themselves . . .' (emphasis in original).

of human nature to be attained through cultivation, but in the sense of a self-conscious purposiveness necessarily given with all goal-orientated action, the background end to which all purposive activity is ultimately directed. Moreover, as the end that is universally and necessarily posited in the pursuit of all relative ends, the abstract person or self is the unconditioned end that supports valid obligation, or so the agency paradigm assumes.

We can perhaps now see why considerations of harm and benefit are assiduously repressed within this framework. If harm and benefit are considered to be relative to individual preference, then they must be excluded from any public conception of normativity. There can be no coercive duty to confer benefits on others or even to abstain from harming them, for (unless part of a bargain) such a duty would be a servile one to cater to the pleasure of others, an ideological mask for interpersonal domination. The only duty generated by this framework is one to respect personality, both in oneself and in another, as an absolute end.[21] To respect personality in oneself is to refuse to acknowledge any duty to subordinate oneself unilaterally to the particular interests of another; to respect personality in another is to abstain from one-sidedly subordinating the other to one's will. The exclusively negative character of the duty toward others is determined by the formal conception of freedom regnant within the agency paradigm. Where freedom is understood reflexively (from causal determination) as a capacity for choice without regard to whether the ends chosen are authentically one's own or externally imposed, the duty to respect personality is simply a duty not to interfere with choices that are compatible with a like liberty for oneself.

At the foundation of the agency paradigm, then, is a claim about the absolute worth of individual personality, considered as a formal capacity for choice. By virtue of this capacity, persons are fundamentally distinguished from 'things', which are seen as naturally instrumental to persons. To begin with, however, the claim of personality to be an absolute end is a subjective one, challenged by the apparent independence of things in the external world. An end that is absolute only for itself is self-contradictory, and so personality is subject to a conceptual imperative to act in order to objectify itself as an end or to verify its claim of absolute worth.[22] Here, of course, we advance no empirical hypothesis about the psychological dispositions or behaviour of actual individuals; rather, we are describing the ideal conception or theory of the person that organizes a legal paradigm, as well as the model of action to which this person is understood to be necessarily impelled. The action of the person consists in the subjugation of things to its will. Thus, the person confirms itself as an absolute

[21] See Hegel's *Philosophy of Right* (trans. T. M. Knox, Oxford 1967), para. 36, hereafter *PhR*.   [22] *PhR*, para. 39.

end by reducing its body to an obedient instrument of its purposes; and its end-status is validated in the legally enforced respect each shows for the other's exclusive authority over his or her body. The person also takes possession of, shapes, and uses external things, and its dignity gains objective reality in the recognition it receives for its ownership of the things it originally possesses or receives through exchange.[23] The agency paradigm of law can thus best be understood as the objective realization of the self's claim of primacy over the world of things.

The conceptual demand that the end-status of personality acquire objective reality draws the person into relationships with others. Within the agency paradigm, the social bond takes the form not of a co-operative association of individuals for a common good but of an external connection between putatively self-sufficient selves, each of whom claims to be an absolute end in isolation from others and yet paradoxically requires others to validate its worth. The need for the other arises because one's property in a thing is decisively established as an objective reality (as distinct from a subjective claim) only when it is freely recognized by a being radically independent of oneself—which is to say, by a being who, by virtue of a like capacity for freedom, also claims to be an absolute end. However, a person may recognize the absolute end-status of another without compromising his own (and so without disqualifying himself as one competent to deliver objective reality to another) only if the other reciprocally recognizes the first. The end-status of personality is thus real only within a relationship of mutual recognition of ownership between free and equal persons.[24]

That the mutual recognition of persons as ends is the ground of individual rights to liberty and property is instantiated throughout private law. For example, one's property in uses of land is never determined simply by one's desires. This would imply a duty in neighbouring owners to defer to one's pleasure without any reciprocal deference to them. Reciprocity is ensured by defining one's property in terms of a social standard of 'ordinary use' to which all are equally entitled, and by requiring anyone who wishes protection for an exceptional use to bargain for it.[25] Similarly, the

---

[23] While the duty to respect personality in an external thing is conditional on the person's having reduced it to his possession, the same is not true of the duty to respect personality in its body. One may not forcibly use another's body (make him a slave) even if the person has always neglected it. This is so because the end-status of personality is unintelligible apart from its being the end *of* action. It is only the union of self and bodily motion that makes the former an end and the latter action. Accordingly, to use for one's own purposes the necessary instrumentalities of another's action leaves personality with nothing of which to be an end. Obversely, his physical movements are no longer actions but the mechanical operations of a thing. On the other hand, it makes no sense to say that the person is the end of any external thing until he has actually reduced it to his purposes.

[24] *PhR*, para. 71; cf. Hegel's *Phenomenology of Spirit* (trans. A. V. Miller, Oxford 1977), 109–11.

[25] *Bamford* v. *Turnley* (1862) 122 ER 27, at 33, per Bramwell B: '[T]hose acts necessary for the common and ordinary use and occupation of land and houses may be done, if

right to impose risks on others is limited to those risks ordinarily concomitant with action in society, which the self-respecting agent would thus consent to suffer as being consistent with an equal liberty for himself.[26] Accordingly, the end-status of the person exists objectively only within an intersubjective exchange of respect that I shall call dialogic community.

2.2. The Nature of Criminal Wrong

Having established the intersubjective matrix within which alone the right of the person exists, we are now in a position to understand the nature of wrong as conceived within the agency paradigm. A wrong is an exercise of freedom wherein the self claims a right of action *vis-à-vis* another that the other cannot, consistently with his equal end-status, recognize as valid; or wherein the will makes claims for its worth in excess of those objectively validated through the framework of mutual recognition. An agent may make such a claim in two fundamentally different ways.

First of all he may do so in the mistaken belief that he is acting within limits consistent with the equal end-status of the other. He may, for example, take something out of the possession of another, believing it to be his own; or he may injure someone as a consequence of imposing a risk greater than that ordinarily incidental to the equal freedom of both, believing the risk to be within these limits. In these cases, one agent wrongs another because he asserts a freedom of action in relation to the other that the other cannot recognize without subordinating himself to the pre-eminence of the first, hence without disqualifying himself as an absolute end capable of objectively confirming the end-status of a self. The fact that the defendant acts in good faith cannot nullify the wrong, for otherwise the subjective beliefs of the defendant would unilaterally determine the rights of the plaintiff contrary to the norm of reciprocity. The rights of persons are determined intersubjectively; hence the ubiquitous standard of the reasonable person in private law. Nevertheless, the unintentional character of the wrong is not insignificant. In so far as the wrongdoer oversteps the bounds of rightful liberty unwittingly, he does not deny the intersubjective foundation of his rights. On the contrary, he acknowledges this foundation but errs as to what the standard permits.[27] Consequently, the actualization of the standard takes the form not of a subjugation of a contrary principle but of an adjustment of the relation between plaintiff

conveniently done, without subjecting those who do them to an action . . . There is an obvious necessity for such a principle . . . It is as much for the advantage of one owner as of another; for the very nuisance the one complains of, as the result of the ordinary use of his neighbour's land, he himself will create in the ordinary use of his own, and the reciprocal nuisances are of a trifling character. The convenience of such a rule may be indicated by calling it a rule of give and take, live and let live.'

[26] *Bolton* v. *Stone* [1951] AC 850.   [27] *PhR*, para. 85.

and defendant in accordance with its requirements. Thus the tortfeasor unilaterally defers to his victim's agency to the degree necessary to redress the asymmetry produced by his earlier action. By compensating the plaintiff for the damage caused by his excess, the tortfeasor relinquishes the preeminence over the other that his action implied; by receiving compensation, the victim gains recognition for the dignity previously offended. Both are thus returned to the normative position of equality and mutual respect.

Suppose, however, that the wrongdoer knowingly exercises a degree of freedom inconsistent with the equal freedom of the other, say, by knowingly taking another's property, or by having his way with another's body in defiance of the other's refusal of consent, or by knowingly imposing an excessive degree of risk and injuring someone as a consequence. In these cases, the wrongdoer not only transgresses the moral boundary reconciling his freedom with another's; he challenges the intersubjective foundation of valid claims to respect, claiming an absolute worth for his singular self and denying worth to the other. When I unintentionally wrong a person, I do not deny his capacity for rights, but merely err as to the scope of those rights or as to the things to which they extend. However, when I intentionally wrong him, I deny his right as a person to respect and therewith deny personality itself as an absolute end. I thus not only infringe *this* person's right; I challenge the conceptual basis of rights as such.[28] However, in denying personality as an end, I also deny my own right to respect and so contradict my original claim to an absolute worth in isolation. This is the internal nemesis of the criminal principle, one that is brought home to the wrongdoer either in the form of his victim's revenge (which he impliedly authorizes) or in the form of punishment meted out by a dispassionate (and therefore more fitting) executive of the intersubjective will. The significance of punishment within the agency paradigm, then, is twofold: it is the self-destructive implication of the claimed end-status of the isolated will and therewith the invalidation of that claim; concomitantly, it is the objective confirmation of intersubjectivity as the sole coherent foundation of the person's right to respect.

From this account of the nature of criminal wrong and the annulment thereof we can derive the criteria of penal justice generated by the agency paradigm. First, punishment within this framework has the significance of retribution, of the recoiling against the criminal of his own disdain for personality. Its justification therefore lies in a past intentional wrong rather than in a desired goal to which punishment is a means. Stated otherwise, penal justice here consists in the inner connection between the principle of the criminal's act and his liability to coercion rather than in the maximization or promotion of good. This idea yields two possible formulations of the

[28] *PhR*, para. 95.

criterion of just punishment. One can say that penal justice consists in the deservedness of punishment, where desert is understood stringently as the entailment of the criminal's moral vulnerability by the disrespect for personhood implied in his deed;[29] or one can say that penal justice consists in the congruence of punishment with the autonomy of the agent or in the immanence of punishment in the criminal's own will. Punishment is immanent in the criminal will—that is, assented to—in a dual sense. First, it is immanent in his *criminal* will, for it is the application to him of the principle contained in his intentional act; secondly, punishment is immanent in his *rational* will, for it aggrandizes not another particular will (not even that of a majority) external to the criminal's but the intersubjective will in which his own end-status is confirmed.[30]

From the foregoing account of criminal wrong and punishment we can also derive the basic elements of criminal culpability recognized by the common law. These are the elements that make coercion of the agent just (deserved) punishment immanent in his will rather than the external violence of another particular will. Thus, the *mens rea* requirement is the requirement that there be the denial of the end-status of personality that entails the nullity of one's own right to liberty as its necessary implication. This requirement is satisfied, as we have seen, when the wrong to another is intended. However, the *mens rea* requirement is met not only by the central case of intention—that is, by desiring the (believed to be possible) product of one's act and acting from that desire;[31] it is also met by any state of mind that signifies disrespect for the equal freedom of another self. Thus, mental states one might want to distinguish for the purpose of assessing moral character or for the purposes of a philosophical psychology are treated as equivalents from the standpoint of criminal wrong and the annulment thereof. One manifests disrespect for the free will of another when one destroys, uses, or alters the embodiments of his will without his consent whether one desires that very outcome or, knowing that it will certainly or probably result from one's act, is indifferent to whether it does; when one knowingly imposes an asymmetrical degree of risk on another and accidentally injures him; or when one is wilfully blind to the circumstances that render one's act a wrong. On the other hand, states of mind that fall short of denying the end-status of personality imply no negation of right that could rebound against the wrongdoer; hence they

---

[29] *PhR*, para. 100.

[30] This sense of penal desert is stringent because the criminal's forfeiture of his right to respect is entailed by his intentional act, quite apart from positive law. Later, I contrast a weaker sense of desert according to which someone deserves punishment if the unlawful act is morally attributable to him and regardless of whether doing the act (e.g. possessing a narcotic) would imply one's liability to coercion apart from positive law.

[31] See R. A. Duff, *Intention, Agency and Criminal Liability: Philosophy of Action and the Criminal Law* (Oxford 1990), 58–63.

cannot justify the degradation of criminal treatment, however compatible with the responsibility of the agent or morally censurable they may be. Thus, an unwitting imposition of excessive risk is not a legitimate ground of criminal liability, no matter how far below the standard of care the agent fell, and regardless of his capacity to conform to the standard. Though proscribable (as we shall see) by a regulatory statute, such an act is not deserving of criminal punishment in the rigorous sense of desert understood within the agency paradigm, for it implies no denial of an obligation to respect liberty and hence no licence for the disrespect of one's own. Moreover, if disrespect for his freedom is not licensed by the agent, then it amounts to a forcible use of the individual for the benefit of others, indistinguishable in principle from crime.

The *actus reus* requirement of criminal liability is likewise intelligible from the standpoint of the agency account of criminal wrong. In order that there be a *criminal* wrong, there must first be a wrong in the sense we have explained, an exercise of liberty inconsistent with the equal liberty of another. A wrong against a specific person will obviously satisfy this requirement, so that a tort, if committed intentionally or recklessly (that is, with advertence to the excessiveness of the risk), becomes an *actus reus* as well as a tort. However, because a criminal act presupposes the intentionality of wrongdoing, it has a significance different from that of a tort. When coupled with intention, the wrongful act signifies the objective realization—the transition into outward and public reality—of the claimed end-status of the isolated will. Without this external movement, the claim of right to an absolute liberty (and the corollary denial of the right of persons) remains a subjective conceit or fancy; it does not rise to the status of a trans-individual principle implicitly claiming universal validity. One may harbour private fantasies of one's domination of others and even communicate one's intention to realize them, but until there is action for the sake of the goal, the intention is a private wish and not a principle *of* action. If, however, the intention does not attain the dignity of a principle, there is no logical impetus to universalize it, hence no inner determination of punishment. Accordingly, just as (within the agency paradigm) a wrongful act becomes an *actus reus* only when united with intention, so does an intention become a *mens rea* only when united with an act that embodies it. Each element of criminal culpability presupposes the other; hence only their union produces a criminal wrong justifying punishment. However, if the significance of the *actus reus* is that it objectifies the claimed end-status of the isolated will, there is no reason to limit criminal wrongs to torts. An act (for example, of driving) manifesting a reckless indifference toward the life or physical integrity of persons is a crime whether or not it results in injury to a victim. Similarly, an act intended to work one's will with the life, body, or property of another but which fails to realize the agent's purpose may none the less amount to an *actus reus* if it, no less than the completed act, outwardly embodies the criminal intent.[32] Thus attempts are crimes if there is an act that, viewed in all the circumstances, cannot reasonably be interpreted as having other than a criminal purpose; and if this test is met, the fact that it was (factually or legally) impossible to commit the crime or that the accused desisted is irrelevant.[33]

The account of criminal wrong generated by the agency paradigm also explains the common-law excuses based on absence of *mens rea* and indicates solutions to venerable controversies. The *mens rea of* criminal culpability is not whatever state of mind or level of fault a lawmaker has stipulated for an offence; nor is it the level of moral blameworthiness needed to justify the severest sanctions a legal system administers;[34] nor is it any one of several states of mind that a philosophical psychology tells us is consistent with the idea of a responsible agent.[35] The morally obvious fact that a competent but thoughtless agent is responsible for the reasonably foreseeable consequences of his act does not logically take us to liability to punishment as a criminal (as distinct from tort liability, liability to regulatory penalties, or moral blameworthiness). What alone takes us to criminal punishment is the intentional or (advertently) reckless disdain for the autonomy of another self that, when absolutized as a principle, involves the insecurity of one's own liberty as its necessary consequence. Accordingly, since liability to criminal punishment requires a subjective *mens rea*, a mistake concerning some fact essential to the *actus reus* excuses from liability for that crime (though the mistake may indicate the *mens rea* for an included or attempted offence), and it is sufficient if the mistake is honest. The requirement of a reasonable mistake belongs, as we shall see, to the paradigm of welfare. Moreover, if intoxication rendered the accused incapable of forming the requisite intent, then he is excused whether the intent is 'basic' or 'specific', though he is guilty of criminal negligence causing the unlawful consequence if he adverted to the hazards of getting drunk and took no precautions. Insanity excuses if it rendered the accused incapable of foreseeing the consequences of his act or of

---

[32] The *mens rea* for attempts is properly determined not by semantic considerations but by the role of *mens rea* in the justification of punishment. Since the requirement of an explicit denial of the intersubjective basis of rights is satisfied by a reckless disdain for the end-status of another no less than by an intentional one, there is no reason to limit the *mens rea* for attempts to intention.

[33] The 'unequivocality test' for the *actus reus* of attempt is out of favour with courts and commentators; however, it is, I think, the test demanded by the agency paradigm. The other tests proposed fail to do justice to the independent act requirement, for they treat the act as evidence of a dangerous resolve and so effectively punish for intent alone; see below, n. 58.

[34] This is currently the view of a majority of the Supreme Court of Canada; see *R* v. *Martineau* (1990) 58 CCC (3d) 353.

[35] Hart, *Punishment and Responsibility*, above n. 17, 149–57; Brenda Baker, 'Mens Rea, Negligence, and Criminal Law Reform', (1987) 6 *Law and Philosophy* 53, at 79–86.

knowing it was wrong (not only legally but according to the standard of reasonable persons), for in either case there is lacking the devaluation of personality that alone implies the nugatoriness of one's own rights.[36] The fact that ignorance of the law is no excuse is no counter-example to the subjectivist theory (as Holmes thought),[37] for it merely reflects the assumption, justified by the self-contradictoriness of a right to absolute liberty, that rational agents know the wrongfulness of crimes. A plea of ignorance is thus admissible as an excuse for true crimes (as distinct from welfare offences) only within the context of a plea of insanity.[38]

All of these conclusions flow from the basic norm of the agency paradigm. As part of a non-instrumentalist understanding of punishment, they follow logically from a normative standpoint that takes the choosing self as the sole absolute end, and that therefore recognizes no common goal or value for the sake of which the self could, consistently with its autonomy, be coerced. As we have thus far derived them, the doctrines of the agency paradigm of the penal law merely form a coherent system ordered by a certain conception of an unconditioned end. They do not yet have an absolute justification, for the theory of the unconditioned from which they flow is itself a particular and contestable one. Our endorsement of these doctrines has so far merely anticipated what has yet to appear: the legal foundation that justifies within limits a doctrinal paradigm serving no value.

For anyone immersed in this paradigm, of course, there is no such higher justification. The conception of the unconditioned on which the model rests is, from this standpoint, not simply *a* conception of the unconditioned. It is the unconditioned itself and, as such, forms the horizon of legal thought. For this pre-sceptical attitude, the mere demonstration of the coherence of a doctrine with the foundational principle will be enough to establish its absolute validity, for it is in the nature of a foundational principle that it cannot itself be further justified; it is self-justifying and everything else is justified (or not) through it. As we shall now see, however, there are phenomena within the agency paradigm itself that testify to the incoherence of its principle as a conception of the unconditioned and that drive us to a welfarist principle formative of a new paradigm of penal justice. Once this new framework comes into view, the agency paradigm

---

[36] Incapacity to know the act's wrongfulness is crucial here, for every criminal impliedly asserts a right to do the wrong and in that sense is ignorant of the wrongfulness of his act. What distinguishes the legally insane or infant agent from the criminal is that the latter knowingly asserts his claim of right against the intersubjective will (or the standard of reasonable persons), while the legally incompetent agent (much like the tortfeasor) believes that his act conforms to that standard.

[37] Holmes, *The Common Law*, above n. 15, 41.

[38] As we shall see, there is no reason to carry this blanket exclusion forward to the context of welfare offences.

can no longer be self-justifying; one can no longer persuasively argue for the doctrines native to it simply by appealing to its foundational norm, for this norm has now been revealed in its particularity and historical relativity. As a result, the elements of criminal justice that formerly seemed fixed and certain—elements such as the centrality of desert, the subjective standard of fault, and the independent-act requirement—are now called radically into question. They may yet turn out to be absolutely justified. However, whether they are will now depend on whether we can vindicate the agency paradigm and the defective principle that informs it from the standpoint of a normative foundation beyond and inclusive of that framework.

2.3. *The Limits of the Formal Agency Paradigm*

We have seen that the agency paradigm is organized by a conception of the absolute end as the abstract and vacuous self. Because all value is treated as subjective, it is excluded from the unconditioned end that supports valid duties. And because welfare denotes the satisfaction of value, it too must be regarded as without public significance and hence as irrelevant to the notion of wrongdoing. Yet the instability of this abstract conception of the unconditioned is revealed within the agency paradigm itself. This formation recognizes that the self must embody itself in order to objectify or confirm its status as an end. It recognizes this necessity in treating interferences with the physical integrity and property of the person as violations *of* personality. Such interferences are not, after all, coercive of the pure will as such. Strictly speaking, the pure will cannot be coerced, for it is theoretically capable of renouncing its attachment to life, body, and property when the latter are threatened. Since it *can* renounce these values, its submission to someone who holds them in his power signifies a choice not to do so; hence, if freedom were identified with this purely formal capacity to choose, one would be compelled to say that the person who submits to another's will under threat of death or bodily harm has not been coerced. Of course, the agency paradigm does not say this. On the contrary, it is the criminal who, by repudiating the freedom embodied in the mutual recognition of property, privileges abstract over objective freedom and who therefore takes the formalist premise of the agency paradigm to its logical and self-destructive conclusion. The self-contradictoriness of crime is thus also the self-contradictoriness of the abstract conception of the unconditioned on which the agency paradigm is overtly based and which it is always covertly denying. In treating interferences with life, physical well-being, and property as wrongfully coercive, the agency paradigm acknowledges these objects as aspects of personality indispensable to its freedom, *as values the self is not free to renounce*. But then it is embodied and not abstract freedom that is the unconditioned end supportive of valid duties. And once we acknowledge the necessity to freedom of embodiment, we grant the existence of objects universally valuable for agency, and hence too the possibility of being harmed in ways that are juridically cognizable.

The inescapability of value for a coherent conception of agency is also revealed in the way that the agency paradigm apportions punishments to crimes. The popular notion that the punishment must fit the crime is an intuitive perception of the inner connection between crime and retribution within the agency paradigm. Because, however, this connection is conceptual and abstract rather than empirical or quantitative, it cannot determine how much punishment any particular crime deserves; hence the concrete application of the fitness criterion requires a gradation of crimes according to their 'seriousness', to which order a parallel scale of punishments is then roughly fitted. This ranking of crimes cannot occur, however, without comparing the embodiments of freedom in terms of their value for agency.[39] Thus theft is punished less severely than assault, because personality is more integrally connected with the body than with any particular external object; and assault is punished less severely than culpable homicide because the former impairs agency while the latter extinguishes it altogether. Accordingly, in concretely applying its principle of equality between crime and punishment, the agency paradigm cannot avoid grading wrongs according to the harm they inflict on valuable objects.

The same tacit acknowledgement of the normative relevance of harm can be seen in the significance the criminal law attaches to consequences. An attempt is criminal because it implies the same denial of equal liberty as does the accomplished purpose; yet the completed offence is punished more severely than the attempted one. An assault causing death attracts more punishment than one of equal ferocity from which the victim recovers. Reckless conduct that materializes in death is punished more severely than that which produces 'bodily harm', which in turn draws more punishment than reckless conduct by itself, even though the significance for equality of all three acts is the same. Thus, while liability to punishment *per se* flows from a theory of criminal wrong that excludes all mention of harm—from the wilful disdain for the free will of another—the *measure* of punishment depends on relative harm to fundamental interests. The puzzle here is not, as some believe, that fortuities are credited to an agent whose moral blameworthiness or dangerousness is no different from that of someone whose intentional or reckless act happened to produce unlawful consequences. This will not surprise us once we see that the basis of criminal liability has nothing to do with one's moral worth or dangerousness and

---

[39] *PhR*, para. 96.

everything to do with one's denial of equal liberty as the basis of rights (thus a saint who performs a mercy killing is a murderer).[40] What is interesting about the relevance of consequences is that acts having the same juridical significance as denials of equal rights of agency are differentiated normatively on the basis of a factor that plays no role in the account of liability. This occurs, of course, because the embodiments of freedom matter to freedom, because agents thus have objective in addition to subjective interests, and because they can therefore be harmed in ways that affect the relative gravity of wrongs.

There are, finally, defences in the criminal law that further reflect the equivocation of the formalist paradigm with respect to the subjectivity of all values. The overt indifference of this paradigm (for we must now contrast this to a covert attention) to considerations of welfare is exemplified in the normal irrelevance of motive to criminal culpability.[41] It is no defence to a wilful interference with the embodiments of another's freedom that one acted not from malice toward the victim but in order to promote the well-being of a friend, of one's family, of an oppressed group, or of the victim himself. However, the limits of this exclusion of motive are revealed in situations where the essential embodiments of agency—life, bodily integrity, and property—come into conflict. If someone jettisons cargo in the reasonable belief that death from drowning is otherwise imminent, or if someone steals under threat of death or serious bodily harm from another person, he will be exonerated under the laws of necessity and duress respectively.[42] Whether one conceives these defences as excuses or justifications, one cannot treat them as exculpatory without acknowledging an objective scale of value based on the importance of an object for the expression of freedom. If one sees necessity and duress as excuses negating voluntariness, one will have to admit that the act is involuntary only because the accused is entitled to treat his life or health as inalienable when they conflict with another's property in some particular thing; he would not be entitled to do so if they conflicted with another's life.[43] Hence the judgment that the act is involuntary presupposes a ranking of goods according to their value for agency. If, on the other hand, one treats these defences as justifications, one explicitly postulates a hierarchy of goods according to which property must yield to values more important to the foundational end—personality—through which property is itself justified.

---

[40] For a contrary view, see Michael Moore, 'The Moral and Metaphysical Sources of the Criminal Law', in J. Roland Pennock and John W. Chapman (eds.), *Criminal Justice: Nomos XXII* (New York 1985), 11 at 14.   [41] See *Lewis* v. *R* (1979) 98 DLR (3d) 111.
[42] *Mouse's Case* (1608) 12 Co. Rep. 63; *R* v. *Gill* [1963] 1 WLR 841.
[43] See *R* v. *Dudley and Stephens* (1884) 14 QBD 273; *R* v. *Howe* [1987] 1 All ER 771.

3. The Paradigm of Welfare

I have argued that the agency paradigm, while explicitly based on a conception of the unconditioned as abstract selfhood, acknowledges *sub silentio* the impossibility of such a conception; and that it implicitly identifies the unconditioned end with freedom embodied in life, physical integrity, and property, and recognized by other selves. That is to say, it implicitly recognizes realized rather than formal freedom as a right of the person and so as the basis of valid duty. The self-conscious elevation of this principle to the status of a foundational norm generates the paradigm of welfare.

What are the characteristic features of the welfarist model of the penal law? To begin with, we must distinguish between two senses of welfare. Welfare may denote the satisfaction of values relative to individual desire, or it may denote the satisfaction of values derived from the concept of a free agent. Both conceptions have a place within the welfarist paradigm, and each constitutes a subsystem of its own. I shall use the term 'general happiness' to designate the system of law based on subjective values and the term 'common good' to refer to the system based on values essential to agency. Before deriving the principles of right respectively native to these systems, let us see how the subjective values excluded from relevance under the agency paradigm acquire standing under the welfarist model.

The recognition that agency is real only as outwardly embodied entails a rehabilitation of the subjective goals of the individual as something whose realization is a matter of public importance. Because the choice and pursuit of individual values are the medium through which generic agency expresses itself, the authoritative actualization of the common freedom involves (in addition to the enforcement of negative rights against torts and crimes) the promotion of the general happiness understood as some universalizing operation performed on the satisfactions of discrete individuals. Whether this operation will be a maximization of an impersonal sum or average, an equalization, or a maximization of the welfare of the least well-off, will depend on the justification for treating preference-satisfaction as a public good, as something a public authority ought to facilitate. The justification that informs the welfarist legal paradigm is action-based. That is to say, it begins not from the brute fact of desire (as does utilitarianism) but from freedom and the requirements of its self-expression. The public authority does not promote happiness because the gratification of preference is in itself a good. As subjectively contingent ends, preferences by themselves have no standing in normative discourse; they generate no duties in others to respect or serve them. Thus, a penal restriction of liberty justified in terms of the majority's pleasure would be arbitrary force. Rather, the public authority promotes happiness because the realization of agency is a universal end, and because this process necessarily involves the formation and pursuit of subjective values.

This justification for the promotion through penal laws of the general happiness is egalitarian. If my subjective welfare is worth promoting because I am a free agent whose freedom requires concrete expression, then the felicity of all other agents is equally worthy of public concern. Accordingly, the agency-based argument for the moral salience of the general happiness rules out any interpretation of this norm that countenances the sacrifice of the satisfactions of some for a greater happiness overall; or that treats certain substantive choices regarding how best to live as inherently less worthy of public support than others.[44] We see here another manifestation of dialogic community as the foundation of valid claims against others. Within the pure agency paradigm, the normative force of mutual recognition appeared solely as a demand that valid laws reflect mutual restraints on liberty, or mutual respect for spheres of private sovereignty. Within the welfarist paradigm it manifests itself further as the idea that authentic laws must reflect an equal concern of each citizen for the welfare of all; hence that penal laws must be neutral with respect to preferences respectful of equal liberty, and inequalities of welfare must work to the long-run advantage of everyone whom the laws oblige.

Once we justify the welfarist goal by reference to the realization of agency, we see that the promotion of the general happiness cannot exhaust the agenda of a public authority founded on the normativity of the intersubjective will. Viewed from the standpoint of realized freedom, welfare means not only the satisfaction of contingent preferences, but also the satisfaction of values indispensable to the coherent self-expression of agency, values whose goodness is thus based on reason rather than on subjective desire. In order that the goals one chooses be authentically one's own or self-determined, one must have a minimum degree of security of life, physical health, education, and economic wherewithal. One must also be nurtured in an environment of habits and attitudes that fosters a rational sense of one's worth and of one's capacity to be author of what one becomes. And one must be protected from those who would enslave others by procuring their addiction to substances the need for which exerts a tyranny over one's life-choices. These are not primary goods in Rawls's sense, because they are not things every rational agent would want more of in order to achieve the ends that he has. Rather, they are goods every rational agent

[44] These elements of the welfarist paradigm have, of course, been thoroughly worked out by John Rawls and Ronald Dworkin; see especially Rawls, *A Theory of Justice* (Cambridge, Mass. 1971), 150–92; Dworkin, *Taking Rights Seriously* (Cambridge, Mass. 1977), 184–205, 266–78. We shall presently see that there are rational limits to the requirement of State neutrality toward preferences.

would want to a sufficient degree in order that the ends he pursues can be freely chosen rather than chosen under prejudice or constraint. They are thus necessary conditions of authentic freedom rather than of success or happiness; and when pursued within bounds drawn by the requisites of freedom, they are normatively prior to (and so properly constrain the pursuit of) subjective ends, for the latter become morally salient only as expressions of freedom.

The conditions of freedom can be produced in part by penal laws protecting the health, safety, and self-respect of citizens. To distinguish these values from those relative to individual desire, let us call them aspects of the common good of autonomy; and let us correspondingly distinguish between penal laws aiming to increase the general happiness, taking individual values as given, and those aiming to promote the effective autonomy of all. Laws promoting competition in the market or regulating the harvesting of a depletable resource are examples of the former, while laws regulating the sale of food, liquor, and drugs, prohibiting environmental pollution, demanding a certain standard of safety in factories and on highways, and prohibiting the dissemination of hatred toward a racial group, are examples of the latter.

We can now delineate the basic features of the welfarist paradigm through a contrast with the pure agency model. First, the point of penal sanctions is not retribution for a past denial of the end-status of personality, but the deterrence of activity inimical to a fair distribution of satisfactions or harmful to essential goods. Since the rationale for sanctions is goal-orientated or instrumentalist, the concept of desert no longer plays the pivotal role in justifying punishment that it did within the agency paradigm. There desert was the *model* of justification; punishment could not be justified otherwise than by a crime. Here the moral force of the goal justifies the sanction; and the requirement of desert is retained only as reinterpreted from the welfarist standpoint, as a constraint on policy that is itself teleologically justified by the goal of individual autonomy. So interpreted, desert is no longer meant stringently as the entailment of the agent's coercibility by his deed, for this sense will not always be available where punishment is a prospective means to an end; rather, it is understood in the weaker sense of the moral responsibility of the agent for the *actus reus* of the offence. In a society ordered to the goal of individual autonomy, instrumentalist punishment is justified only if one's liability to use for the deterrence of others is a fate over which one may exercise control.

Secondly, the doctrine of *mens rea* as understood within the agency paradigm has no theoretical support within the welfarist model. Recall that in the agency paradigm, subjective *mens rea* was an essential element of criminal desert because it triggered the conceptual circuit between wrongdoing and punishment. The wilful infringement of a right to respect implied a denial of personality's worth whose universalization recoiled upon the criminal in the nullification of his own right to liberty. In the welfarist paradigm, however, there is no necessary connection between the intentional deed and punishment.[45] Apart from positive law, my catching of undersized lobsters does not entail the nullity of my rights as a necessary implication; nor even does my possession or sale of a narcotic. Here the punishment is justified not by the deed but by a goal; and because it is justified by a goal (which might conceivably be attained in other ways) it is contingently justified. Accordingly, the doctrine of *mens rea* has no role to play in the theoretical account of punishment within the welfarist paradigm; it is not part of an account of the inner necessity and deservedness of punishment, because there is here no inner necessity or deservedness to comprehend.[46] The requirement of subjective *mens rea* is thus firmly embedded within the agency paradigm and hence within the sphere of crimes against the formal liberty of persons. When transplanted to the welfarist paradigm, *mens rea* becomes a flexible concept referring to any of the morally blameworthy or responsible states of mind from which a legislature may choose in seeking the least costly (to autonomy) achievement of its goal. Moreover, since a requirement of subjective *mens rea* (with its defence of unreasonable mistake) would frustrate the purpose of a welfare statute, liability within the welfarist paradigm is standardly based on negligence.[47]

If penal justice within the welfarist framework does not consist in punishing in accordance with desert, in what does it consist? What are the principles of justice applicable to statutes creating welfare offences? The utilitarian one—that the welfare goal be attained at the least cost in human suffering—is an obvious possibility, but we have already seen that it is ruled out by the agency-based justification for the public promotion of welfare. That justification supports principles of penal justice in the form of priority rules—that is, of rules that resolve conflicts between competing principles not by reducing them to some common measure but by establishing a rank order between them.[48] Since the State's promotion of the general happiness was justified with reference to the self-expression of agency, that enterprise must be constrained by respect for rights of equal freedom. One cannot commit wrongs for the sake of the general happiness, for one cannot coherently pursue happiness at the expense of the

---

[45] I am speaking here of the situation anterior to the enactment of a statute. Once a welfare statute is in place, punishment can be deserved, since an intentional breach of positive law also implies an elevation of self above the legal order that, when universalized, negates rights. However, because the rationale for the penal sanction is in the first place a goal, desert (in the strong sense) will not here be a necessary condition of penalization.

[46] This is the underlying rationale for the doctrine in *Sherras* v. *De Rutzen*, above n. 12, that *mens rea* is not required for convictions for public-welfare offences.

[47] See *Proudman* v. *Dayman*, above n. 12; *R* v. *City of Sault Ste Marie* [1978] 2 SCR 1299.

[48] See Rawls, *A Theory of Justice*, above n. 44, 40–5.

principle through which preference-satisfaction first rises to moral and public significance.[49] Accordingly, the principle of penal justice applicable to laws promoting the general happiness is the priority of autonomy over welfare or of the right over the good. This principle forbids (*inter alia*) the pursuit of happiness by means of sanctions that impinge upon the agent as an incalculable and unavoidable fate, and that, by failing to respect the person as a self-determining agent, one-sidedly reduce him to a means for the deterrence of others. Thus, the State cannot enforce the policy behind a welfare statute by penalizing someone innocent of the *actus reus*; nor can it do so by imposing absolute liability; nor can it penalize under the authority of a retroactive, unpublished, or vague law; nor if the accused reasonably relied on an erroneous official statement of the law;[50] nor without a hearing by an impartial tribunal wherein responsibility for the unlawful act is established by proofs tested by independent counsel and open to rational scrutiny. Here is yet another manifestation of dialogic community as the foundation of valid obligations. The individual can be legitimately coerced for the sake of the general happiness only in so far as the enforcement of the general happiness reciprocally respects the individual agent as an end.

The principle of penal justice applicable to laws promoting the common good is different. Here we cannot speak about the priority of autonomy over welfare, because welfare in this context denotes the satisfaction of the conditions of *effective* autonomy, by which rights of formal liberty must be circumscribed if they are to be consistent with the equal end-status of persons (and so coherent as rights). Here, in other words, dialogic community manifests itself as the priority of the common good over formal liberty, since the unlimited exercise of negative rights leaves to chance the satisfaction of the conditions for the equal effective autonomy of all. This does not mean that the strictures against punishing the innocent apply with less force here than in the system ordered to the general happiness. All the substantive and procedural rights against arbitrary coercion secured by the priority of the right over happiness are equally guaranteed by the priority of the good where the good is itself understood as the effective autonomy of the agent. More particularly, they are guaranteed by what may be called the non-contradiction proviso. The latter states that the common freedom cannot be enforced by legislative means that gain autonomy for some by denying it to others. This principle too excludes absolute liability, for the common good of autonomy cannot coherently be enforced against the individual through a liability over which he has no control.

[49] *PhR*, para. 126.   [50] *R* v. *MacDougall* (1981) 60 CCC (2d) 137.

There is another principle of justice applicable to laws ordered to the common good that is not applicable to laws directed to the general happiness. In the latter context, rights of formal liberty are normatively prior to the exigencies of preference-satisfaction, so that rights of free speech or freedom of religion (for example) are absolute constraints on the pursuit of happiness. The public authority may not restrict speech or worship merely because the subjective welfare of the least happy in society would be enhanced by the suppression of certain opinions and faiths. In the present context, by contrast, rights of formal liberty are subordinate to the common good, for the same mutual respect of persons that defines the scope of rights to formal liberty demands that these negative rights be exercised in a manner consistent with the equal effective autonomy of everyone. Subordination, however, does not mean immersion. The rights of formal liberty generated within the agency paradigm retain an independent normative weight, one resistant to thoroughgoing definition by the common good. This is so, because the inward determination of rights by the common good submerges the discrete end-status of the individual agent and so contradicts the essence of the common good, which is the autonomy *of* the individual. Accordingly, the primacy of the good must manifest itself through an override of pre-established rights that retain their force rather than through an internal limitation of rights. The second principle of justice applicable to penal laws ordered to the common good is that rights of formal liberty may be abridged by such laws only to the extent necessary to achieve the social purpose. Thus, an abridgement is unjust if there is available an alternative means of achieving the goal that is less restrictive to liberty.[51] This principle is, however, subject to the non-contradiction proviso: the public authority may not adopt means that negate the autonomy of some persons, even if no other instrument would effectively achieve its goal, for such means are inherently incompatible with the common good.

[51] The three principles of justice indigenous to the welfare paradigm (the priority of autonomy over happiness, the non-contradiction proviso, and the requirement of the least restrictive means) are embodied (albeit confusedly) in the test devised by the Supreme Court of Canada to determine whether statutory infringements of constitutionally entrenched rights are 'reasonable limits' in a 'free and democratic society'; see *R v. Oakes* [1986] 1 SCR 103. Limitations of rights are justified, first of all, only if the goal served by the impugned statute is 'pressing and substantial'. This test intuitively grasps the distinction between goals relative to desire, which cannot override fundamental rights, and goals relevant to the common good of autonomy, which can. However, the common good can limit rights only to the extent necessary to achieve the goal; hence the proportionality test in *Oakes* demands that the means be rationally related to the end and that they limit rights as little as possible. The third aspect of the *Oakes* proportionality test—that the deleterious effects of the statute not outweigh the expected benefits—appears to be part of a utilitarian model, but can also be understood as screening out self-contradictory attempts to promote the effective autonomy of all by denying it to some.

4. The Imperialism of Welfare

We have thus far distinguished an agency and a welfarist model (itself internally differentiated) of the penal law, each based on a certain conception of an absolute end and each displaying features derived from that conception. Since the principle underlying each paradigm purports to be the ground of law, it will exhibit an intellectual drive to subdue the whole of the penal law to its exclusive hegemony.[52] If formal liberty is the sole end that grounds valid duty, then coercion of the agent is justified only if that consequence is willed by him. Coercion of oneself is willed, however, only if the boundary of another's rightful liberty has been knowingly or recklessly transgressed, for only conscious wrongdoing affirms a principle subversive of all rights to liberty. But then, it seems, any coercive sanction applied against the individual requires a subjective *mens rea*, and it makes no difference whether the offence committed is a violation of rights to life, liberty, or property, or a breach of a regulatory statute. And if a requirement of subjective *mens rea* defeats the prophylactic point of a welfare statute, then let the regulatory aim be pursued by non-penal means.[53]

If, on the other hand, the absolute end is effective or realized freedom, then the ground of law is a goal rather than a background condition of action. Hence the structure of legal justification is consequentialist rather than retrospective. Penal laws are justified if they serve this goal in ways that are consistent with individual autonomy. Moreover, because the end of law is human welfare in the two senses distinguished above, the aim of penal laws is the prevention of harm, and the point of punishment is the correction and incapacitation of the dangerous, as well as the deterrence of others. From this standpoint, the wrongs visible to the formalist paradigm—those against life, liberty, and property—are reinterpreted as harms to basic welfare interests, so that no essential difference is recognized between criminal and regulatory law. The aim of all penal law is the prevention of harm, and it can make no difference whether the harm averted threatens a specific individual or everyone collectively.

We have already seen how the absolutization of the principle of the pure agency paradigm leads to its self-contradiction in crime and punishment, and how this paradigm is thus led into a pattern of dissimulation whereby it covertly acknowledges the normative relevance of factors excluded by its overt principle. The revealed inadequacy of this principle as the ground of law is the argument for the validity of the welfarist norm and of the

---

[52] The figures who best personify these opposing tendencies are Jerome Hall and H. L. A. Hart.

[53] See Jerome Hall, *General Principles of Criminal Law* (2nd edn., Indianapolis 1947), 351–9.

doctrinal innovations (basically, the due-diligence defence to 'public welfare' offences) it generates. However, if it is also true that the absolutization of the welfarist norm at the expense of the formalist one leads to its self-contradiction, then the ground of law will have been revealed as a totality that embraces both principles as subordinate elements. If the principle of each paradigm contradicts itself when pursued to the exclusion of the other, then each requires the other for its own coherence; and this notional continuity of the principles discloses a totality in which both agency and welfarist paradigms are preserved as mutually complementary normative frameworks.

Let us then consider what follows if we make the effective autonomy of agents the absolute end of the penal law. Since the end of law is now a goal, *all* punishment is justified instrumentally. Hence the strong sense of desert as the entailment of coercibility by crime has no justificatory role to play anywhere in the penal law. Indeed, since the connection to which desert refers has been buried in the instrumentalist relation, talk of desert now seems 'mystical' or 'mysterious'.[54] Concomitantly, the rationale for subjective *mens rea* disappears. The forward-looking aims of punishment are now constrained only by the requirement that the agent have a fair opportunity to avoid liability to sanctions. This requirement is equally met by intentional, reckless, or negligent wrongdoing, so that *mens rea* is now an empty vessel into which one can pour whatever content accords with the social purpose. Intention and advertent recklessness are disqualified, however, for the availability of excuses of unreasonable mistake, voluntary intoxication, and inadvertence to risk subverts the preventative aims of the law. Hence the 'subjectivist orthodoxy' native to the obsolete framework is overthrown in favour of a modified negligence regime that, consistently with autonomy, considers the accused's capacity to conform to the law.[55] Yet one may question the depth of this regime's commitment to individual autonomy. Since the basis of criminal liability is now negligence, the right to liberty is no longer lost by implication of one's deed. If not implicitly forfeited, then the right has been infringed for the sake of collective security.

[54] See Holmes, *The Common Law*, above n. 15, 37; Ted Honderich, 'Culpability and Mystery', in Antony Duff and Nigel Simmonds (eds.), *Philosophy and the Criminal Law* (Wiesbaden 1984), 71.

[55] Hart, *Punishment and Responsibility*, above n. 17, 136–57; Don Stuart, *Canadian Criminal Law: A Treatise* (2nd edn., Toronto 1987), 194–5; *R v. Tutton and Tutton* (1989) 48 CCC (3d) 129, per Lamer CJ. Under a negligence regime one is punishable for 'murder' if one causes death by an act whose fatal consequences one ought to have foreseen; see *DPP v. Smith* [1961] AC 290. One is liable for manslaughter if one negligently breaches a legal duty of care and death results; see *R v. Lawrence* [1982] AC 510. One is guilty of sexual assault if one has non-consensual intercourse with a person in the unreasonable belief that she consented; Criminal Code of Canada 1985 s. 273.2. One is punishable for any offence committed as a result of negligently becoming intoxicated; see *DPP v. Majewski* [1977] AC 443.

This is an override of a right to liberty by the common good that must satisfy the relevant principles of justice. Yet it violates the non-contradiction proviso, for it promotes the autonomy of some by denying it to others.

The requirement of subjective fault is not the only casualty of welfare's empire. If the point of punishment is the prevention of harm, the retributivist rationale for the act requirement also disappears. The point of this requirement is now to provide evidence of a dangerous character, of someone who lacks internal controls on impulses and fantasies. Accordingly, if someone inflicts harm while unconscious, the absence of an act will not preclude State coercion if the unconscious episode itself indicates someone dangerous to others. It will not matter whether the episode manifested clinical insanity or a physiological disorder such as epilepsy, arteriosclerosis, or a brain tumour. If the accused's condition is dangerous, we will call him insane and forcibly confine him.[56] We will also reinterpret the act requirement of attempts. One will now be guilty of an attempt if one has the intent to commit an offence and takes steps indicative of a dangerous resolve, whether or not the act can be said to embody or objectify a criminal intent.[57] Thus, the act ceases to play an independent role in establishing criminal liability; its sole function is to *evidence* a firm intent (which, if sufficiently proved by other evidence, will relieve the burden on the act) and hence a suitable candidate for restraining and corrective measures. One will be punished for intent alone.

The lesson of these doctrinal consequences seems to be this: the absolutization of individual autonomy as the ground of law negates the autonomy of the agent. In a sphere of wrongdoing where it is conceptually possible to deserve punishment in the strictest sense, the individual is subjected to coercion he does not deserve in that sense. Where (as in the context of regulatory offences) no intelligible meaning can be ascribed to the notion of desert, punishment for negligence is not undeserved, for punishment can be undeserved only if it is possible to deserve it. Where, however, desert refers to an intelligible connection between deed and retribution, a punisher who ignores this connection imposes undeserved and hence arbitrary 'punishment'. Similarly, where crime is intelligible as a specific category of wrong essentially distinguished from tort, the individual who is named a criminal, though lacking any of the mental states definitive of that category, bears a stigma he does not deserve. Relative to the possibility for the conceptual self-imposition of punishment in the sphere of crimes, the accused who is punished as a criminal for a negligent infringement of rights is subjected to external violence. And the same may be said of someone punished for a criminal intent that does not attain

[56] *Bratty* v. *A-G Northern Ireland* [1963] AC 386; *Rabey* v. *R* (1980) 54 CCC (2d) 1.
[57] *R* v. *Sorrell and Bondett* (1978) 41 CCC (2d) 9; *Deutsch* v. *R* (1986) 30 DLR (4th) 435.

objective embodiment as determined by the test of Salmond J in *The King* v. *Barker*.[58] To the extent, however, that punishment is not self-determined, the agent is used for the aggrandizement of a common good that fails reciprocally to recognize him as an end, and that thus reveals itself as neither common nor a good.

5. Toward a Differentiated Standard of Penal Justice

The self-contradictoriness as grounds of law of both formal liberty and positive freedom produces the phenomenon of mixture to which interpretative sceptics are fond of pointing as indicative of law's essential incoherence. Thus, an accessory may be liable for the consequential offences of the principal on a foreseeability standard, even though the principal is liable only on a subjective standard. Automatism or an honest mistake of fact excuses from a crime of basic intent unless the mistake or automatism was attributable to the accused's drunkenness. Mental disorder negating intent excuses from murder if the accused is insane, but results in a conviction for manslaughter if he is not. To the same point are legal fictions designed to feign a commitment to the subjective standard even as that standard is eroded; thus the rule that intoxication is no defence to a crime of basic intent is supported on the theory that the intention to get drunk supplies the *mens rea* for the offence charged.[59]

The sceptic's claim that such inconsistencies are innate in the penal law can be justified only on the premiss that the antagonism of the paradigms is a necessary and constant reality. This would be the case if there were indeed a logical imperative to absolutize one or the other principle as the ground of law. Yet the process whereby each fell into contradiction when absolutized in isolation shows us that there is no such imperative. If the elevation as an end of both formal agency and positive freedom leads to their self-contradiction, then neither can alone be the ground of law. That

---

[58] [1924] NZLR 865, at 875, per Salmond J: 'That a man's unfulfilled criminal purposes should be punishable they must be manifested not by his words merely, or by acts which are in themselves of innocent or ambiguous significance, but by overt acts which are sufficient in themselves to declare and proclaim the guilty purpose with which they are done.' The objection usually raised against the unequivocality test for attempts is that acts falling short of the completed purpose will rarely manifest a *specific* criminal intent unambiguously, and it seems irrational to exclude evidence of intent in deciding what the accused was up to; see Glanville Williams, *Criminal Law: The General Part* (2nd edn., London 1961), 630. This objection mistakes the nature of the end that the act must signify. The account of the unequivocality test we have given shows that the act must, to be punishable, manifest criminality unequivocally, not any specific criminal purpose. The identification of the particular purpose is needed only to determine the appropriate *measure* of punishment. Accordingly, once the issue of punishability is settled by the unequivocality test, there can be no objection to using evidence of the accused's intent to determine the precise offence attempted.

[59] *DPP* v. *Majewski*, above n. 55.

each suffers inversion when pursued at the other's expense shows that each needs the other for its own self-consistency. This should not be surprising. Formal agency was objectively an end only in so far as it manifested itself as such in property and bodily autonomy, so that it already implicitly contained the welfare dimension it purported to exclude. Similarly, both the general happiness and the common good were interpreted in terms of individual autonomy, so that they too implicated the end-status of the individual that their absolutization negated. Because each principle implicitly contains the other within itself, its domination of the other nullifies an element of its own nature and so results in its self-destruction.

The contradiction into which each principle falls when pursued at the other's expense discloses a conceptual whole wherein each is preserved as a constituent principle informing a distinctive but bounded subsystem of law. The genuine ground of law is neither formal agency nor the common good but the whole, of which both are mutually complementary parts. This whole evinces the structure of mutual recognition we have called dialogic community and is indeed the archetype of which the relationships seen earlier are exemplars. The common good is both authentically common and authentically a good only in so far as it respects the discrete end-status of the individual agent and hence the distinctive legal paradigm ordered by that principle. Conversely, the individual agent is an end only in so far as he recognizes the authority of the common good whose self-inadequacy alone first establishes his end-status as an authentic reality. That this structure of reciprocal deference is the authentic ground of law was revealed in the self-realization of the pretenders to that title; for it was, as we saw, the sub-textual theme of both paradigms. And it was decisively revealed in the process whereby each of these pretenders collapsed when absolutized to the exclusion of the other. Accordingly, the validation of dialogic community as the ground of law is just the process of its manifestation in (and emergence from) paradigms ordered to rival principles; and since the justification of a foundational end must be internal to its notion, these paradigms (for all their defects) are constituent elements of the foundation.[60]

If the ground of law is dialogic community, then the principle of each paradigm is normatively resistant to the expansionist claims of the other. Though each principle is deficient in so far as it pretends to be the absolute ground of law, each is none the less preserved as an essential component of an adequate conception. The implication is that the penal law is a differentiated totality composed of two principal subsystems of law, each characterized by indigenous principles of justice and standards of fault. There is thus no 'general part' (in the sense of a single set of principles

[60] *PhR*, paras. 129–30.

applicable throughout) of the penal law; and yet the penal law is a unity, for each special system embodies in a distinctive way the ground of law that connects the systems to each other.[61]

That the penal law is a differentiated totality implies that the principle of each paradigm is valid only within limits consistent with the distinctive existence of the other. Once the whole comes forward as the ground of law, the hegemonic claims of the constituent principles cease to appear logically natural and become indicative instead of conceptual pathology. Conversely, their mutual respect is no longer a compromise of principle but a demand thereof. Neither is there any longer a 'choice' between paradigms to undermine *ab initio* the rationality of legal discourse; for the principle of each model applies only within definite boundaries. The border between the systems is marked by the difference between the formal liberty of the abstract person and the positive freedom of the individuated self. What judges call true crimes are denials of the end-status of abstract personality as embodied in the authority it exercises over its body as well as over its external possessions. Welfare offences are breaches of statutes aiming at the general happiness, taking individual values as given, or protecting the social conditions of effective autonomy.

Because each system is part of a whole, each must be actualized by judges and legislators with a moderation that reflects this constituent status. It is a mistake to extend the principle of either the pure agency or the welfarist paradigm over the whole penal law, for this absolutizes a principle whose validity is inherently relative to a specific context. Hence it is a mistake to make negligence the basis of liability for crimes against personality or to weaken the strict retributivist understanding of desert for such offences. Subjectivist orthodoxy is appropriate for true crimes. However, it is also a mistake to make subjective fault the standard of blameworthiness for welfare offences or to assess the justice of penalties for such offences from the standpoint of desert. Because welfare laws are justified instrumentally, the concept of desert strictly understood has (with one exception I will mention presently) no intelligible application within this sphere.

Even within the sphere of welfare offences, the principle of penal justice is not monolithic. It varies, as we have seen, according to the meaning of

---

[61] George Fletcher has also argued that the criminal law is a unity of different paradigms; see *Rethinking Criminal Law* (Boston 1978), 388–90. However, for Fletcher the three patterns of criminality (manifest criminality, subjective criminality, and harmful consequences) have no immanent connection; they are alternative and equally plausible theories of criminality that could singly order the whole of the criminal law. Hence the unifying general part does not embrace the patterns as parts of a whole; it merely states general propositions or defines concepts that happen to cut across all three. Despite the general part, the criminal law remains 'polycentric'. In the view presented here, by contrast, the penal law is a differentiated whole; one pulse beats in all divisions.

welfare. Where welfare means the satisfaction of preferences undetermined by the idea of effective autonomy, the appropriate principle of justice is the priority of autonomy over happiness, for the latter becomes normatively significant only through the end-status of personality. Applied at the level of adjudication, this principle rules out offences of absolute liability (for persons but perhaps not for corporations) and favours defences of reasonable mistake of fact and of due diligence in seeking to comply with or ascertain the law. At the legislative level, it screens out utilitarian (or other aggregative) justifications for penal laws, as well as what Feinberg calls legal moralism: the penalization of activity (for example, the consumption of alcohol) to advance a relative view of the good life; for these justifications signify the coercion of persons for the benefit of others. In so far, however, as welfare means the satisfaction of values essential to effective autonomy, the appropriate principles of justice are that rights of formal liberty are validly limited by the common good to the extent necessary to achieve the aims of the law, and to the extent that the legislative means do not contradict the end they purport to further. The latter proviso excludes absolute-liability offences in this context as well.

The principles of right applicable to welfare statutes yield a position regarding the legitimacy of imprisonment within this sphere. The priority of autonomy over happiness rules out prison sentences for offences against non-fundamental values unless the statutory breach is intentional or advertently reckless. Imprisonment is justified for wilful breaches, for although the intentional act would not have deserved punishment apart from positive law, the intentional breach of statute posits a principle subversive of law and so also of the lawbreaker's liberty. Thus imprisonment is here justified by desert. Incarceration is also ruled out for inadvertent breaches of laws promoting fundamental values, for the common good of autonomy cannot coherently be furthered through a total deprivation of liberty unwilled by the agent; here the means would contradict the end. We may conclude that the penalty of imprisonment understood as a qualitative deprivation of freedom is justified by desert or not at all.

However, this result need not render welfare laws ineffectual. Where a statute protects interests essential to autonomy, the legitimacy of the means least restrictive to liberty implies that partial or quantitative restrictions of liberty are justified not only by a wilful breach but also where monetary penalties sufficiently heavy to deter would be beyond the financial capacity of most lawbreakers. Partial restrictions include probation orders and—at the extreme—confinement for intermittent periods. The latter penalty is justified, however, only if there exists a distinct class of penal institution for the non-criminal offender. Where restrictions on liberty are justified by a goal but not by desert (for example, in the case of inadvertently dangerous driving), special institutions and administrative leniencies are required in order to reflect the categorical difference between welfare offenders and criminals. In their absence, confinement even for intermittent periods is wrong as a penalty for regulatory offences. In general, there should be no implication of depersonalization for the welfare offender; his penalty is the intermittent confinement and nothing else. Further, the maximum overall term should be lower than that of the lowest maximum for crimes; and since the point of the sanction is deterrence rather than retribution for a wrong, the penalty should not vary with the consequences of the conduct.

6. Epilogue

The Canadian counterpart to *Proudman* v. *Dayman*[62] in Australia is a case called *R* v. *City of Sault Ste Marie*.[63] There the Supreme Court of Canada decided that statutes creating regulatory offences would henceforth be construed as incorporating defences of due diligence and reasonable mistake of fact. The judgment of the Court was given by Justice (later Chief Justice) Brian Dickson, now retired. Endorsing the common-law distinction between true crimes and public-welfare offences, Dickson J. argued that the principles of penal justice applicable to the former had no place in the latter. Welfare statutes served collective rather than individual interests; they thus belonged to the sphere of administrative law to which the requirement of subjective fault was inappropriate. However, absolute responsibility offended traditional principles of penal liability founded on respect for individual autonomy, and so the standard of fault in this setting must be negligence. In a number of other cases, Justice Dickson laboured with equal diligence in fighting the expansion of negligence into the sphere of crimes. Thus, in *Leary* v. *R*[64] and again in *Bernard* v. *R*,[65] he condemned the distinction in the law of intoxication between offences of specific and basic intent, urging that evidence of intoxication be put to the jury in all cases on the question of intent. In *R* v. *Tutton and Tutton*[66] he concurred in an opinion that gross inadvertent negligence was an insufficient level of fault for criminal negligence; and in *Pappajohn* v. *R*[67] he insisted that a mistake as to consent excused from the crime of sexual assault even if the mistake was unreasonable. If we can compare the imperialists of the penal law to inebriates who know no inhibitions, then Justice Dickson stands out as a model of sobriety, moderation, and good sense. This essay is dedicated to him.

---

[62] Above n. 12.   [63] Above n. 47.   [64] [1978] 1 SCR 29.
[65] (1988) 45 CCC (3d) 5.   [66] Above n. 55.   [67] (1980) 52 CCC (2d) 481.

On What's Intentionally Done

JENNIFER HORNSBY

I want to raise the question of how far some recent philosophy of action assists in explicating the moral psychological notions that are of concern in jurisprudence. The focus of my overall argument will be a distinction used by Antony Duff in his *Intention, Agency and Criminal Liability*[1]—a distinction, Duff says, between 'a broader and a narrower conception of intention'. I doubt whether the distinction can do the work that Duff wants it to. And I believe that Duff rests as much upon it as he does only because of a certain optimism: he hopes that conceptual analysis of *intention* may reveal what many of the interesting questions about *mens rea* really turn on, and so deliver the goods for the criminal lawyer. But—I suggest— this hope is vain.

I shall begin with some basic philosophy of action. A presentation of an account of actions which highlights some essential conceptual connections, and which introduces the concept of *attempt* into the framework, can provide a setting for a clear view of Duff's distinction. Exposition of this material takes up the first part of what follows. I bring it into relation with issues in criminal liability in the second part, where I show its connection with the notions of *actus reus* and *mens rea*. In the third part, I explain and argue for the view I take of Duff's distinction, which differs from his. In the final parts, I consider how far an understanding of the concept of *intention* can take the criminal lawyer.

I

Philosophers have wanted to know how to demarcate the class of events in which human beings' capacity for agency is exhibited. So they have asked what distinguishes actions from other events. A definition of 'an action' which provides an answer is this:

(A) An *action* is a person's doing something *intentionally*.

(A) has seldom been explicitly formulated; but it has probably found as much favour as any rival defintion.[2]

---

[1] R. A. Duff, *Intention, Agency and Criminal Liability: Philosophy of Action and the Criminal Law* (Oxford 1990). Page references to Duff are to this book.

[2] (A) is not usually so simply put: it is the idea behind (A) that has found favour. The simplification I go in for results from eschewing the terminology of 'intentional under a

To appreciate the force of (A), we evidently need to understand the difference between 'an action' (which is being defined) and 'a something' that a person does (in terms of which the definition is given). *Actions* are particulars—unrepeatable things, named by phrases like 'Hyam's setting light to the petrol at two o'clock on the fateful day', and 'my reading this paper now'. *Something done*, on the other hand, is not a particular: things done are named by phrases like 'inflict damage', or 'eat an egg', or 'throw a brick'. In order to see how the definition works out, one has to realize that a person's doing one thing may be the same as her doing another thing, and that when a person does two things, she may do one intentionally and the other not intentionally. For example: someone who inflicts damage by throwing a brick, might throw the brick intentionally, but not inflict damage intentionally. (A), then, relies on the fact that a single action can be variously described as the agent's doing one thing, and another (and, perhaps, a third and fourth thing . . .). For an event actually to have been an action of some person's, according to (A), it has to be true only that she has done intentionally at least one of the things she did.[3]

---

description'. I think that it has led to more confusion than it was intended to eradicate, and that (in any case) if we want to keep track of what we are committed to, we do best to cast our claims in ordinary English as far as possible. In order to theorize about action, one has to speak at a level of generalization which exceeds what is ordinary: hence my recourse, in (A) and elsewhere, to the schematic (or pro-verb) 'do something'; but this seems to me fully intelligible, where 'do something under a description' is not.

The philosophers who go in for 'under-a-description' talk correctly see that in order to be in a position to make the right distinctions between what an agent intended and what she didn't, one must have on the scene a mode of individuation which cuts as finely as (interpreted) action *descriptions*. (Actions themselves, of course, being particulars, have many descriptions: see next paragraph of text.) But these philosophers incorrectly suppose that an agent's intentions are directed on to actions (albeit, now, 'actions under descriptions'). This is incorrect, because the objects of agent's intentions are *not* actions (whether or not these be 'under descriptions'). The things that agents intend to do are things of the same sort as those that they do; and these things—that agents do—, unlike actions, are themselves as finely discriminated as (interpreted) descriptions of actions.

[3] The argument of this paragraph takes it for granted that there are true statements of identity using two action descriptions. It may well be that this is something that Duff wishes to deny. He himself puts phrases like 'her action' in scare quotes, saying, for instance, that which of the 'possible descriptions we offer depends not on some objective truth about what "the action" really is (since there is no such truth), but on our own interests . . .' (Duff, 41). This makes it sound as though someone who believes that there are actions is committed to privileging some one description of any action—as if we could be told about any action what it 'really' is. But this is the opposite of the truth: someone (like me) who thinks that actions are variously describable particulars is someone who thinks that there is no single truth about what the action is: rather (she will say) any description which has application to it, will, equally, be a description of an action. She thinks (roughly) that where an agent does one thing in or by doing another, her doing the one thing is (identical with) her doing the other, so that 'doing the one thing' and 'doing the other' both apply to her action.

Despite being suspicious of actions, Duff often uses the terminology of 'acting under a description' (which is usually prompted by the recognition that there *are* actions, and that they can be variously described). The terminology is eliminable (compare n. 1). For example, when Duff says (at 43) 'we must ask what it is to act intentionally or with intent under a

The most striking thing about (A) as a definition of *action* is the paucity of the resources that it uses—the only word of any apparent interest in it is the adverb 'intentionally'. If (A) is to cast any light, the concept that 'intentionally' introduces will need to be connected with others. (1) and (2) are theses which start to spell out some connections.

(1) If someone did something *intentionally*, then there is an *explanation* of why she did it, which mentions that she thinks something and that she wants something—that is, which mentions a *belief* and a *desire* (or *pro-attitude*[4]) of hers).

(2) Someone who has a *belief* and a *desire* that are relevantly related, has a *reason* for doing a particular thing. (If, for example, she believes that she can bring it about that q by ϕ-ing, and she desires that it be the case that q, then she has a reason to ϕ.)

(1) and (2) serve to bring together notions of *agency* and of *practical rationality*, by seeing *wanting, thinking,* and *intentionally doing* as an interdependent triad of concepts. The underlying idea is that, in so far as they are agents and do things intentionally, people are beings with motivating reasons—they are apt to do those things that, so they believe, will get them what they want. A person who has a motivating reason to do something is in a state potentially explanatory of her doing it. If she actually does the thing for the reason, then she does it intentionally, and there is an explanation which shows it as a reasonable thing to do from her perspective.[5]

specified description', he means that we must always ask what it is to do some particular thing intentionally, the point being that there can be no one answer to the question whether 'that' was intentional, where 'that' alludes to an occasion when more than one thing was done.

[4] The only notion of 'want' or 'desire' that makes (2) true is an extremely thin one, corresponding to what Davidson introduced with 'pro-attitude' (compare Duff, 54). Given how thin it is, we may wonder whether it is dispensable. Duff for his part thinks that it is dispensable—that we can use 'believe' on its own to define 'intentionally' (67); but he also thinks that we should retain it for the sake of preserving conceptual connections (69). I suggest that Duff makes 'want', or 'pro-attitude', seem dispensable only because he introduces a kind of belief which in fact could not be present in the absence of any pro-attitude. For a defence of the view that we cannot understand *practical* reason and *agency* without introducing attitudes of people that have a world-to-word direction of fit (the pro-attitudes) as well as those that have a word-to-world direction (beliefs and the like), see Michael Smith, 'The Humean Theory of Motivation', (1987) 96 *Mind* 35.

[5] The qualification 'from the perspective of the agent' is essential. I acknowledge that a person may have a motivating reason even where we should find it odd to think of the person as having a reason. In Bernard Williams's example, where the agent wants gin and tonic, and believes of stuff that is in fact petrol that it is gin, the agent has (according to my usage) a (motivating) reason to mix the stuff with tonic and drink it. (The example is in Williams's 'Internal and External Reasons', reprinted in his *Moral Luck* (Cambridge 1981), 102–3.) Williams would reject my legislative policy: he wants to be free to say that the agent has no reason (in any sense) to make and drink the mixture. I believe that the policy *need* not lead us astray in the ways that Williams fears that it will.

(1) and (2) are fairly uncontroversial. Or at least they can be made uncontroversial by making it clear how thin is the notion of 'want' used in (1) (see n. 4 above), and how thin is the justificatory role of the notion of *reason* used in (2) (thin, because confined to the agent's own perspective: see n. 5 above). A third conceptual thesis is less likely to seem immediately acceptable. This is (3):

(3) A person who acts because she has a *reason* to do some particular thing, *attempts* to do that thing.

Combined with (1) and (2), (3) requires us to say that people attempt to do all of those things that they intentionally do. This may strike one as wrong when it is first brought to the surface and enunciated as a general, conceptual truth. But I should claim that it is actually implicit in our ordinary thinking.[6] One can appreciate this by seeing how easily we find ourselves committed to it. It may be argued for example, that Duff, while explicitly denying it,[7] implicitly endorses the claim that we attempt—or try—to do what we intentionally do.

Duff's own concern over attempts is with the question of why a failed attempt should be counted as a lesser offence than 'the relevant complete offence'.[8] The picture he uses is one in which there is an element common to two cases—the case of someone who attempts to do something but fails, and the case of someone who actually does the something. (His question arises because if it were the common element that constituted a person guilty, then it would seem that there ought to be no difference in respect of guiltiness between people who fail and people who succeed.) Now, what could the element common to a failure and a success be? Someone who does something intentionally differs from the person who attempts-it-but-fails, because she is someone who does not fail but succeeds. But is this not to allow that she, also, attempts? She succeeds precisely in that in which her counterpart fails: where what she does is to φ (say), what her counterpart failed in was an attempt at φ-ing. If so, then, we have deduced that she attempted something, by using (besides a piece of comparison) only the assumption that whatever led her to do the thing ensured that she did it intentionally. But then, generally, what agents do intentionally, they attempt to do.

For this general idea to strike us as even remotely plausible, we have to recognize that, in particular cases, it can be true that someone attempts

---

[6] I gave some arguments to this effect (less cursory than the one offered in the present paper) in ch. 3 of my *Actions* (London 1980).
[7] Duff's denial of the claim is made at n. 10 on 188. He is there considering the views of Ashworth, in e.g. 'Belief, Intent and Criminal Liability', J. Eekelaar and J. Bell (eds.), *Oxford Essays in Jurisprudence, Third Series* (Oxford 1987), 1.
[8] At 184 ff.

something, without the fact that she attempts it being at all a usual or useful thing to point out. Where someone is unsuccessful in some attempt, she has a reason to do something, which, in circumstances more propitious to her, might have led to her actually doing the thing; as it is, she fails in the thing, and we think of her as having attempted it. But where an agent is successful, her having a reason to do something leads to her actually doing the thing, and we have no need to think of her as having attempted to do it. Yet the explanation of why we do not think of her this way need not be that it is untrue that she has attempted it, but only that we can think of her instead, more interestingly, as having done the thing.

Just as we must not suppose that we would ordinarily think of someone as having attempted something when she succeeded, so, equally, we must not suppose that agents themselves think of themselves as attempting anything whenever, as a matter of fact, they are attempting something. (For most of the things that we do from day to day, we have no doubts about our success: we simply get on and do them.) Nor should we suppose that the reasons that agents have for doing the things they do provide them with reasons to attempt to do those things. For an agent to do something intentionally she must (according to (1) and (2)) have a reason to do it. And equally (by (3)) an agent who in fact attempts to do something, typically has a reason to do the thing, whatever it is. But it would be a mistake to infer that someone who attempts to do something because she has a reason to do it must also have a reason to attempt to do it.

Once all this is clear, perhaps (3) and its consequences may be easier to swallow.[9] Just as ascriptions of beliefs, desires, and things intentionally done form a trio, so there are interdependencies in the correct applications of the three concepts of *belief*, *desire*, and *attempt*. This is because explanations of what people do are based on seeing how their beliefs and desires combine to yield a practical conclusion; when we understand people, we know what they are up to, or what they are attempting. But since, of course, most of the time people are right about what they can do, and thus *do* do what they attempt to do, we do not ordinarily need to introduce the concept of attempting in order to make sense of them.

[9] Duff himself finds it hard to swallow because he links it with volitionalism, which aims to uncover 'the essence of action' in the will. The position of Ashworth ('Belief, Intent and Criminal Liability', above n. 7) makes it plain that acceptance of volitionalist thinking need be no part of the reason for accepting (3) and its consequences. In his paper in the present volume, Duff persists in linking claims about *trying* to 'philosophers' search for the essence of agency'; and I am found guilty by association. But it has never been my view that we can 'analyse actions down into tryings', or that trying is what action 'ultimately consists in'. And in ch. 4 of *Actions*, above n. 6, I attempted to dissociate (3) (and other related theses about the ubiquitousness of the applicability of 'try' or 'attempt') from the philosophical project with which Duff connects it.

In the present context, I move to and fro between 'try' and 'attempt'. There are certainly differences between the two that matter, but they don't matter here (I hope).

So an agent who attempts something, typically has a reason to do it but typically lacks a reason to attempt to do it. It is worth noticing that there are untypical cases: one can have a reason which is a reason precisely for attempting to do something; and if one does have such a reason, then one may attempt to do the thing without having any reason to do it. Suppose that someone is quite confident that she stands no chance whatever of success in saving a drowning child; but suppose that she thinks that no one else is likely to appreciate how adverse the conditions were, and that she is anxious not to be seen to have done nothing. Then she may have a desire to be seen to have attempted to save the child, and there may be nothing to do about this except dive in and attempt a rescue. In this case a person has a reason to attempt something (save the child) which is different from any reason she has to do it. This is a possibility relevant to some judicial reasoning,[10] and one which I return to in section III.

If the account here of *attempts* is correct, then criterion (A) of actionhood might be replaced with (B):

(B) An action is a person's doing something in *attempting* to do something.

Equipped with (B), we see that we could, if we wanted, say (in English) what an action is without using the word 'intention' or any of its cognates at all. This shows that *intention* does not have to be the concept around which everything else turns. And it makes it plain that an account which puts 'attempt' or 'trying' at centre-stage does not have to be a rival to one which does not. Sometimes we are given the impression that philosophers have to make up their minds whether 'action consists basically or essentially' in *bodily movement* or in *trying*. But on the account given here: any event which is an action consists only in what it is; and it is (*a*) a person's moving her body in some way, *and* (*b*) her doing something intentionally, *and* (*c*) her trying (attempting) to do something.[11]

[10] The possibility of such examples makes it plain that people can attempt to do what they believe to be impossible. English judges have doubted whether it is possible to attempt the impossible, even when the impossible is not believed to be so. Perhaps they have reasoned: 'You couldn't have a reason to do what [you believe] is impossible, and you will only attempt what you have a reason to do. So you won't attempt to do what [you believe] is impossible.' Such reasoning overlooks the fact that you might attempt to do something not because you have a reason to do it but because you have a reason to attempt to do it (see the example in n. 20 below). A thorough onslaught on the mistakes in this area is undertaken by Herbert Hart. (See 'The House of Lords on Attempting the Impossible', reprinted in H. L. A. Hart, *Essays in Jurisprudence and Philosophy* (Oxford 1983).) Here I add one small piece to Hart's diagnosis of the Lords' errors.
[11] Just as we may identify someone's doing one thing with her doing another (see above n. 3), so we may identify her doing something with her trying to do something. If a pickpocket takes a coin (say), then his attempt to steal the coin is the same as his action of stealing it; so if his stealing it is his moving his hand (in the pickpocketing way), then his attempt cannot be distinct from, because it is the same as, his making the bodily movements

II

(A) relies on a distinction between actions (particulars) on the one hand, and things that may be done (not particulars) on the other. The *actus rei* of criminal law are evidently a species of the latter: they are things that people may do which the criminal law proscribes (or in terms of which the law defines what it proscribes). Part of the endless list of things people do, including both *actus rei* and criminally less significant things done, goes like this: *inflict damage on someone else's property, eat an egg, murder someone, board a plane to Manchester, drive, cause serious injury....*

The discussion of *attempts* makes it plain that *attempt to do such and such* will itself be something that someone does (even if something she has no reason to do) when she is led to action by having a reason to do something. (*Attempt to get to Liverpool*, would be something that had been done by Smith, for example, if he had got on a plane to Manchester believing that it was destined for Liverpool.) This ensures that, for anything on our list of things done, we could prefix it with 'attempt to' and put the result on the list too. The list would then register the fact that attempting is a species of doing.[12] When *attempt* is introduced, it becomes particularly evident that questions about what people have done are tangled up with questions about what they were up to. This may be evident already, in the fact that a *mens rea* condition is a necessary condition for some of the things that may be done—for *murder*, for example.

Even if those things that may be done which require the satisfaction of some *mens rea* condition were excluded from *actus rei*, a distinction between actions and things done would still not fix the sense of '*actus reus*': a potential ambiguity remains here. On the one hand, we might say that the notion of *actus reus* starts to have application only where there is an action. On this understanding, it is a condition even of raising a question about whether there has been some *actus reus* that at least something has

that he does. This shows that Duff is wrong to connect the account of attempts given here with one that 'portrays the "trying" or "exertion" [or attempt] as a mental act distinct from the agent's external bodily movements' (Duff, 188, n. 10). (There are questions about how a person's making a movement is related to what Duff calls an 'external bodily movement'; but (B) itself makes no commitments to any particular view about this.)

I surmise that it is Duff's own conception of the 'mental', combined with the natural assumption that *trying* is 'mental', which leads him (e.g. in his paper in the present volume) to think that there is an incompatibility in holding that an agent is especially well placed to know what she has tried to do while denying that events of trying are conscious occurrences. The conception is not shared by Ashworth or me (see also n. 13 below).

[12] Slightly more accurately: *attempting to* φ (a thing of that sort) is a member of a species of which *things done/actus rei* are the genus. A different claim, about actions (as opposed to things done), is also true: actions are themselves attempts; when an attempt is a success, it is an action. (This is to say that the events whose occurrence is explained in the distinctive way which (2) outlines are describable both as attempts and as actions: compare the end of section I and nn. 3 and 11 above.)

been intentionally done, so that a positive answer to a general *mens rea* question is presupposed in the ascription of any *actus reus*. On the other hand, we might say that the question of whether we have a case of a certain *actus reus* is supposed to be a 'pure' or 'merely external' question, which we can answer simply by reference to someone's visible interactions with the world, without worrying at all about her states of mind.

This distinction between two different ways of using *actus reus* shows up in a distinction between two possible places for a legal defence of automatism. Intuitively, such a defence makes the claim that the defendant's part in the putative crime was not the part of an agent, so that there could have been no actual crime. If *actus reus* is used so as have application only when there is an action, then the defence would naturally come prior to any consideration of what specific things D might have done; for if the defence were successful, there could have been no *actus reus*. If, on the other hand, *actus reus* is used so that it is the 'pure', psychologically un-contaminated notion, then the automatism defence will be more or less on a par with other possible defences that appeal to particular aspects of *mens rea*. Questions about any *actus reus* could now be thought of as questions merely about whether an event in which D (or his body) participated led to some consequence—to someone's death, say; and the defence of auto-matism would amount to the claim that, although there was an *actus reus*, nevertheless D cannot be a criminal killer, because he did not satisfy certain psychological conditions at the time of the killing.

Different systems of criminal law, with their different rules of evidence, go different ways on this matter. But even if it is decided to use *actus reus* in the second, restrictive way—so that in the first instance, questions about *actus rei* come free from all questions about *mens rea*—that would do nothing to vindicate a dualist (Cartesian) attitude to the *mens/actus* dis-tinction. It can be true that, through philosophical analysis and a stipulation about *actus reus*, one may make a sharp division among requirements of culpability between those which are and those which are not psychological requirements. But it would be an error to suppose that this division could be founded in any distinction used in our ordinary practices of interpre-tation. In courts of law, there can be subtle questions about people's states of mind, and these questions may remain unanswered even when every question about *actus reus* in the restrictive sense seems to have been settled. But this legal situation must not encourage a picture by which our attitude to people is in the first instance as to automata, so that it is at a second stage that we turn to questions about their 'internal' or 'mental' states.[13]

---

[13] The picture of people as automata with superadded minds is, I think, the one that Duff is concerned to reject in some of his discussion of dualism (116 ff.). Duff suggests that the *mens/actus* distinction will be freed from dualist commitments if *actus reus* is so defined as to include mental elements (117). But it is hard to see how entering a stipulation that '*actus*

Artificial principles that may be useful for analytical purposes may reveal nothing about our actual (human, moral) predicament.

III

The account of *action* in section I, whether it is cast using 'intentionally' (as in (A)), or using 'attempt' (as in (B)), makes no use whatever of the verb 'intend'. Yet the verb 'intend' has sometimes been given most of the attention by jurisprudents.

In the 1970s, much philosophy of action trundled along on the assumption that uses of the adverb 'intentionally' and of the verb 'intend' were, for many purposes, interchangeable. It was allowed, of course, that a person might intend to do something and do nothing about it; but the assumption was that where a person had actually done some particular thing, speaking of her as having *intended* to do it and speaking of her as having *intentionally* done it were different ways of saying the same thing. More recent philosophical work challenges the assumption, and takes intentions seriously as distinctive states of mind.[14] It has been recognized that any full account of the phenomena must treat both the adverb 'intentionally' and the verb 'intend' (and its various nominalizations), and that there is plenty to be said under the latter head. The distinction of Duff's, out of which he wants to get much legal mileage, is in fact a distinction between what people intend to do and what they intentionally do.[15]

The distinction makes its first appearance in Duff's book as a distinction between 'two shades of meaning'. But this account of it could be mislead-

reus' has application only where there is an action could make a difference to whether one's outlook was a dualist one.

Duff's view sometimes seems to be that one is committed to dualism to the extent that one believes that psychological states cause physical things (e.g. 118). But, as his subsequent discussion makes clear, the ills of dualism that we need to avoid are those of the epistemological outlook that it provokes. I suggest that Duff shares with a dualist the assumption that the psychological/physical distinction marks the same line as the internal/external distinction; and that if he could free himself from that assumption (and the conception of the mental that goes with it: see n. 11), then he would less readily reject accounts like my own. (See my 'Bodily Movements, Actions and Mental Epistemology', (1986) 10 *Mid-West Studies in Philosophy* 275.)

[14] See esp. Michael E. Bratman, *Intention, Plans and Practical Reason* (Cambridge, Mass. 1987).

[15] Duff is clearest that this is *the* distinction he wants at 76. 'Intend' and 'intentionally' are not the only locutions in play in Duff, however: he also uses 'with an intention' and 'intentional agency'; the consequence is that the central distinction he is after can be unclear. Where Duff is most explicit about making his central distinction, he equates that which an agent acts 'with the intention' of bringing about with what is *intended* (see Duff, 76), but he equates this elsewhere with what is *intentionally* done (43)). Again: 'intentional agency' as used by Duff goes hand in hand sometimes with what is *intended* (e.g. 83), but sometimes with what is *intentionally* done (e.g. 95).

ing. Certainly there may be 'shadiness' where each of 'intentionally' and 'intend' is concerned (both may be vague); but the distinction of verb from adverb itself would not seem to be a distinction between shades.[16] Duff later describes his distinction as that between two 'conceptions' of intention—a 'broader' and a 'narrower'.[17] But again this may mislead. What Duff actually has in mind is that among the things that someone did when there was an action of hers, there may be more that she intentionally did than that she intended to do. Duff thinks, that is, that we have to deny that the following makes a valid inferential step:

(I) *A intentionally* did something → *A intended* to do the thing.

But we can agree with Duff's denial of (I) without being led to say that we have two different 'conceptions of intention', of which one ('intend') is more restricted. As soon as we think about the role of intentions generally, outside the context introduced by (I), it appears that the verb 'intend' in fact can have a greater breadth of application than the adverb 'intentionally'. And if *intending* has importance in its own right, then it has a breadth of its own, and it will be inaccurate to think of the verb as introducing a 'narrow conception', the adverb a 'broader' one.

These are quibbles about Duff's own formulations (in terms of 'shades' and 'breadth'). But they may not be pointless quibbles, and I shall return to them. For the time being, I want to question Duff's view of the extent to which (I) is false. Duff thinks that counter-examples to (I) are much more prevalent than I do: he believes that there is a great deal that is done intentionally without being intended.

Duff asserts that someone who 'intends to travel on this plane despite the fact that the pilot is a woman' is someone who intentionally travels on a plane piloted by a woman but who does not intend to be piloted by a woman.[18] This will strike some people as wrong. The fact that a man prefers not to be piloted by a woman tends to rule it out that any statement of his reason for action should mention a woman pilot. And it is hard to see why, when the plane's having a woman pilot has nothing to

---

[16] Duff takes over 'shades' from the judgment of Lord Cross in *Hyam* v. *DPP* [1975] AC 55, at 96 (Duff, 33, and see also 76). In that judgment, vagueness was surely the point. I suspect that Duff is apt to see shades of meaning where I see different locutions partly because he fails to keep track of his own terminology (see n. 15 above). His association of 'intend' and 'intentionally' with 'different aspects of the ordinary concept of intention' presumably springs from the idea (dubious in my opinion) that there is a single concept that all words cognate with 'intend' latch on to (or latch on to some aspect of).

Duff is also motivated by the thought that 'a concept whose legal applications determine something as significant as a defendant's liability to punishment, must . . . have a clear, unambiguous and consistent legal meaning.' But it is not obvious how, even if we were to legislate that 'intend' and 'intentionally' each correspond to a different range of meaning, we could prevent either of them from being vague. (Where 'F' is vague, 'definitely F' and 'strictly F' are usually also vague.)

[17] Duff, 37.   [18] Duff, 81.

do with the traveller's reasons, we should have any inclination to think that he intentionally travels on a plane piloted by a woman. Certainly this man intentionally travels on a plane, and he wittingly travels on a plane piloted by a woman, and the plane he intentionally travels on is piloted by a woman. But with all this acknowledged, do we want to say that something he does which is contrary to what he would want to do is something that he *intentionally* does?

Different people have different intuitions about cases like this, and I should try to clarify the theoretical basis of my own view of it. I need to say something about when I might allow that there is something intentionally done but not intended. So here are two kinds of case where I think that it is arguable that we have to acknowledge counter-examples to (I).

The first kind we might call emergency behaviour. It is arguable that someone who has to react extremely quickly and instinctively does what she does intentionally, but doesn't intend to do it. If I suddenly see a ball coming towards me, but hadn't realized that it was going to be thrown my way, it may be right to think that I never intended to catch it. Yet in so far as I had a perfectly good reason to catch it, grounded in my standing cognitive and affective states, I caught it intentionally.

The second sort of case has more complexity, and relies on the possibility (noted above) that a person may have a reason to attempt what she doesn't have a reason to do. Suppose that there are two things you might do, each one of which is such that if it were to come off, you would realize some end of yours. But suppose that neither of these things seems to you very likely to be something you will actually succeed in; and suppose that success in both is not part of your end—that succeeding in both would be going beyond anything you wanted and have some result that you did not want. You might decide that your best chance of realizing your end was to attempt both of the things: if everything were to go the way of the probabilities, you would succeed in one, but only one, of the things, which is exactly what you want. Now it seems that if everything does in fact go according to plan, then the one thing you then do, you do intentionally. But it is very much less obvious that you would have *intended* to do this thing. You had reason to do at most one of the two things; in respect of the one which (as it so happened) you actually did, your plan involved you only in attempting to do it.[19]

---

[19] The example is structurally similar to Bratman's video-games example: *Intention, Plans and Practical Reason*, above n. 14, ch. 8. And it is like Bratman's example in purporting to be one of something intentionally done but not intended. But it is unlike Bratman's example in an important respect: in the present example, it is not impossible, but only undesirable for the agent, that both of the two things should be done. So the description I offer does not rest on Bratman's premises, and is free from what I take to be the most controversial premise. (In fact, however, Bratman himself would reject the view about *attempting* on which my description does rest.)

What leads us to think that the person in these two cases may not have intended to do that which she intentionally did? (What matters is not so much whether we have genuine counter-examples to (I) in these two kinds of case, as what the grounds are of someone who thinks that they are counter-examples.) Well, in the first kind of case, we exploit the fact that my reason was in place before the ball came my way: I already believed that I could avoid being hit by a ball by catching it, and already desired not to be hit, so that—arguably—no specific intention to catch this particular ball (which is the one I intentionally caught) needs to enter into the picture. In the second kind of case, we exploit the fact that your doing something intentionally can derive from a reason you have to attempt to do it;[20] in that way we can make it plausible that any intention actually to do the thing was missing. In both kinds of case, then, we latch on to an idea of something which suffices for intentionally doing, which, however, does not suffice for intending; but we maintain a connection between what someone has reason to do and what is intentionally done by her.

Neither of these kinds of case seems to have much legal relevance. And Duff is not concerned with them. The putative counter-examples which he adduces are ones which would have us sever the link between what is *intentionally* done and what is done because of a *reason* the agent has. We may argue next against severing this link.

The argument requires an assumption—that whether someone did something intentionally is, in a certain sense, a question about her. More precisely, the assumption is that if a person did a number of things, and we raise the question in the case of a particular one of whether it was intentionally done, then it is to her states of mind that we need to advert in order to settle the question. With this assumption in place, three suggestions would seem to exhaust the possibilities for extending the things an agent intentionally did beyond those which she had a reason to do. One suggestion would be that agents may have *beliefs* or *knowledge* about what they are doing which suffice for their doing those things intentionally even in the absence of any reason to do them. A second would be that agents' *desires* might increase the scope of what they intentionally do. A third would be that an agent's having a *reason* to do or not to do something, even when it is not the reason which explains why she did what she did, might render something (else) that she did intentionally done.

First: *belief* or *knowledge*. The fact that a person knew for sure, or was

---

[20] This is not to say that the presence of a reason to attempt something is sufficient for the thing's being done (if it is done) intentionally. If, for instance, I believe that a stone is impossibly heavy to lift and I try to pick it up in order (as I suppose) to demonstrate the impossibility to you, then, if I am wrong and I succeed in lifting it, I do not lift it intentionally. Roughly: a pro-attitude towards ϕ-ing, as well as a successful attempt to ϕ, is required for someone to ϕ intentionally; and we have this in the example in the text.

aware, that she was, or might be, doing something seems not to have much to do with whether she was doing it intentionally. I know that I contract the muscles of my body whenever I move, but I do not contract the muscles of my body intentionally. You may be aware that you cause your electricity meter to tick over more rapidly when you switch on the fire, but even while you focus on this fact (perhaps finding it undesirable because you will have to pay the electricity bill), you can intentionally switch on the fire without affecting the meter intentionally. A purely cognitive condition seems unlikely to provide what Duff needs. In one particular case—of the terror bomber—Duff seems to rely on such a condition. He says that the terror bomber who does not intend to kill with her bomb, but who omits to give a timely warning, kills intentionally.[21] Here he cites, apparently with approval, the principle that 'I bring about intentionally both such relevant side-effects as I am sure *will* ensue, and such as I am sure will ensue *if* I achieve what I intend.'[22] But this principle obviously does not stand up to the examples just noted. And if we find Duff's description of the bomber persuasive, this may be because, outraged by her act, we want to say something about her which makes her look bad; but there is surely plenty to be said against her without saying the particular thing that Duff does.[23]

Second: *desire*. The idea that we can get something intentionally done out of, merely, a desire to do it seems to have no promise at all; and Duff never so much as seems to rely on the idea. If it was no part of someone's reason for doing something that she wanted to φ, then, even if it turns out that she has φ-d in doing the thing, the fact (if it is one) that she wanted to φ has no tendency to show that she intentionally φ-d.[24]

---

[21] Duff, 81.

[22] Duff in fact does not accept the principle, despite the fact that he seems to use it in his argument here. (Perhaps he would want to give an independent explanation of 'relevant' as it figures within it.) In his official view, the extended application of 'intentionally' results not from principles like this, but from principles which require him to reject the assumption that we are working with here: see below.

[23] Another factor also may weigh with us here: in thinking of the bomber as feeling certain of causing death, we may find that we can't really avoid viewing her as acting from a reason she has for a possible fatal upshot. But then we shall have a case in which the bomber *intends* consequences which may include deaths, and not a case of the kind that Duff wants.

Notice that if there are two means of achieving some end, and the only difference between them is that the first but not the second causes deaths, then, if the agent knows all this and chooses the first, the presumption must be that she prefers to cause deaths than not to. And of course we hold it against someone that she prefers to cause deaths. On the conception of 'intentionally' I am defending it will be an error to suppose that 'I did not do it intentionally' is any sort of excuse all by itself: manifestly it is not an excuse in the case of the terror bomber if she killed knowing that she might kill and that she could avoid doing so.

[24] It is a question for me why it should be so much more tempting to suppose that 'intentionally' is (to use Bratman's terminology) 'belief-extendable' than to suppose that it is 'desire-extendable'. A relevant difference is this: whereas typically an agent acts out of just a single pro-attitude (unless she can kill two birds with one stone), she acts out of more than

Third: *reasons.* A person may have reasons for, or against, doing what she does, or, also at the level of reasons, she may be neutral. Duff's air-traveller who wanted a male pilot was someone who had a reason against doing something that Duff holds that he intentionally did. The strangeness of Duff's description is accentuated when we compare the misogynist with someone quite indifferent about the sex of his pilot. Presumably we have no inclination to say that someone with no preference either way but who happens to have discovered that the pilot is a woman is someone who intentionally boards a plane piloted by a woman. And it seems incredible, where Smith is someone to whom it makes no odds but Jones really wants to be piloted by a man, that it should be Jones of the pair who intentionally boards a plane piloted by a woman. It is a curious feature of Duff's position that he hopes to persuade us sometimes to extend 'intentionally' to cases where the agent has a reason against something, but not to extend it to comparable cases where the agent is indifferent to the thing.[25]

None of the three possible ways of extending the application of 'intentionally' seems to work. But then, in the presence of our assumption, we are left without any case for thinking that the account I gave in section I, which connects doing something intentionally with possession of a *reason* to do it, falls short on its attributions of things intentionally done.

Duff's own case for thinking that 'intentionally' has a more extensive application seems bound to fail if the further connection that I made, between what is attempted and what is intentionally done, is accepted. For if that connection is right, then taking Duff's view about 'intentionally', we should have to think of the air-traveller who wants not to be piloted by a woman as attempting to be piloted by a woman—which is evidently wrong. Once 'attempt' is introduced, it becomes very hard indeed to resist the assumption about the application of 'intentionally' which I introduced

one belief (i.e. more than one belief can be adduced in explanation of her doing what she does: have it in mind here that when there is an action, there will typically be more than one thing that the agent intentionally does). Thus there is much more scope for doubt in the case of any particular belief than there is in the case of any particular desire, about whether it is one which was part of the agent's reason for doing what she does (whether, in Benthamite terminology, it concerns one of 'the links in the chain of causes by which the person was determined').

[25] Duff's stated position is that 'intentionally' applies in cases where there is a reason against, and whether there *is* a reason against doing the thing does not turn on whether the agent *has* this reason against doing it. But Duff's account of the misogynist—like that of the terror bomber—relies on a point about the states of minds of the relevant agent, i.e. on reasons she *had*: Duff wants us to take account of what the bomber believed and of what the misogynist wanted in relation to what he knew. (Unless this is so, we have to attribute to Duff the view that there *is* a reason for the misogynist to travel on male-piloted planes, so that he could be blamed if, e.g. he failed to take steps to avoid women pilots. I hope that that is not Duff's view.) It now looks as if Duff himself is tempted by the assumption which is the basis of the present argument, although this is an assumption that he officially rejects. (I leave Duff's stated position to the next section.)

above. By seeing the different, but related, ways in which beliefs and desires may lead (*a*) to the possession of intentions, and (*b*) to the initiation of attempts, perhaps we can remove any inclination to suppose that 'intentionally' could have the ready application that Duff thinks it does.

IV

Someone might set out with a grand hope. She might think that the concept of *intention* is the one that really matters to criminality, so that conceptual work on the topic of *intention* will expose the essence of what concerns the criminal lawyer. If that were so, then all the conceptual work of philosophers and jurisprudents which uses 'intend' and 'intentionally' could be put to good use, in seeing what the crux is in judging difficult cases. The hope might be supported with the thought that the real villain is someone who goes in for some awful *actus reus* and moreover intends to do exactly that.

If the hope were to explicate all *mens rea* concepts in term of *intention*, it would evidently be misplaced. This is clear as soon as we think of recklessness or of negligence or of crimes of strict liability. It is quite plainly not generally sufficient to be rendered blameless in law to demonstrate that one had no intention of causing the harm that one did. But someone might hold on to a more moderate hope, and think that at least in many categories of case, we could uncover, or we could posit, some notion of *intention* to play a leading role in an account of responsibility. (We may have in mind the defendant who acted in spite of realizing, or in spite of being in a position to realize, the possibility of disastrous consequences.) Such a hope may have inspired the introduction of the contrived idea of *oblique intention* (by which, roughly, foreseen consequences of actions, although not directly intended, are obliquely so).[26] Duff wants 'intentionally' to do the same sort of work that 'oblique intention' was supposed to—to provide a class of potentially culpable things that is wider than the class of intended things. And if we speak, as Duff did, of different shades of meaning (compare my first quibble in section III), then it may seem as though we have only to rely on an aspect of the central notion of intention (rather than any specially invented notion, such as oblique intention) to latch on to what the moderate hope requires.

My argument in section III, which, relative to Duff's view, cuts back on what is intentionally done, would frustrate this moderate hope. But the

---

[26] Duff quotes Bentham, *Introduction to the Principles of Morals and Legislation* (eds. J. Burns and H. L. A. Hart, London 1970), s. 8.6 on oblique intention.

argument as it stands would carry little weight with Duff, because he is committed to denying the assumption on which I rested it. The assumption was that, once it is given that an agent has done some particular thing for a particular reason, we can confine ourselves to her states of mind in thinking about what else she then intentionally did. Duff, though, wants to persuade us that the things intentionally done by a person encompass those 'which are properly ascribed to her as their responsible agent', those which 'she must justify or excuse if she is to avoid blame'; he believes that we have to look beyond the agent and consider how we feel about what she did and what we should attribute blame to her for in order to settle questions about what she intentionally did.[27] The disagreement between Duff and me comes down to this, then: whether, with Duff, we should allow that our general conception of responsibility properly affects our view of what people intentionally do; or whether we should accept that questions about what people are responsible for, and to be blamed for, are questions which by and large are unresolved when we have answered the questions about what they intentionally did.

Duff gives some indication of why he thinks that questions about what is intentionally done are caught up with questions of responsibility.[28] He points out, correctly enough, that the adverb 'intentionally' has seemed to philosophers to be absolutely crucial in an account of action. And he points out, again correctly, that philosophers have been interested in the category of action precisely because it is connected with *responsibility* which is an evidently important concept.[29] But these two points do not establish that we have more materials for dealing with responsibility when we bring in 'intentionally'. For first, the fact that 'intentionally', but not 'intend', may be used (as it is in (A)) to single out the class of events that are actions, does not automatically give 'intentionally' any breadth that 'intend' lacks.[30] (Talking of 'intentionally' as a broader concept than 'intending' is likely to set us on the wrong track here; compare my second quibble in section III.) Second, even if it be true that 'intentionally' has application whenever there is an action and true that attributions of responsibility can only be made when there is an action, no particular link

[27] Duff, 78, 79. At 82, Duff introduces his idea that 'blame and praise involve different criteria of intentional agency'. But I shall say nothing specifically about this, because I take it to be another symptom of what I see as his underlying mistake.

[28] I suggest that Duff manages to make it seem plausible that there is a connection by making it seem plausible that we can deny the assumption which was the basis of the argument against his view in the previous section. The seeming plausibility is achieved by inducing myopia—by encouraging us to suppose that our judgments of responsibility must somehow be expressible using the language of *intention*: reading Duff's book, we find *intention* at the forefront and are offered no other resources for expressing them.

[29] Duff, 99.

[30] Of course we are likely to need something adverbial, and not the name of a state of mind, to single out the class of actions: nothing ventured, nothing done.

between the things an agent intentionally does (on the one hand) and the things she is to be held responsible for doing (on the other) is forged.[31] I suggest that there is no real basis for the sorts of connection that Duff thinks he sees between '*e* was intentionally brought about by D' and 'D is to be held responsible for *e*'.

And there are difficulties about Duff's thought that we must accord 'intentionally' a prominent place in jurisprudence in consequence of its prominent place in philosophy of action. Philosophers have been concerned with actions as (A) defines them in part because they have wanted to mark out a particular class of events in order to be able to raise clear questions about the place of reasoning beings in a causal world; the discovery has been that one very significant class of events can be marked using the idea of doing something intentionally. But in marking out this class, one does not necessarily illuminatingly circumscribe the area in which questions of responsibility properly arise. For one thing, a person may be responsible for failing to do something, and there may be no event of her not doing the thing. It is true that the absence of an event in such a case need not destroy a link between 'intentionally' and a notion of action, since 'intentionally' can have application other than in virtue of an event — as it often does when someone intentionally doesn't do something. We should allow that there are more instances of the phenomenon of action than there are events which are actions: an area of responsible agency is overlooked when philosophers direct us towards the events that are actions.

Earlier, we considered the defence that D's part was not that of an agent at all (see the discussion of two uses of *actus reus* in section II). It seems right to think of this defence as claiming that the minimal psychological notions appropriate to an imputation of responsibility have no application. But it is not at all obvious that the particular way of understanding the defence to which the philosophy of action will lead us—that nothing was intentionally done—is any improvement on an older idea, where the claim was that there was no voluntary act. In considering whether a defence of automatism is appropriate, we seem to be involved in thinking not so much about whether the agent had a motivating reason to do something she did, as about whether the agent was in a position to control her movements in accord with any such reason. The idea that an action is a prerequisite of any ascription of legal responsibility may not be most happily understood in the context of a definition of 'an action' in which 'intentionally' has entered.

---

[31] Someone who conflated actions with things done would, when he linked 'intentionally' and 'responsible' via 'action', tend to conflate what is intentionally done with what the agent is responsible for doing. The 'under-a-description' language (compare n. 2 above) can lead to the conflation.

Jennifer Hornsby

Whether or not 'intentionally' can be used to define the general notion of action that matters most to lawyers, there are two respects in which it will fail to delimit the area in which concerns about responsibility are exercised. First, a person may be culpably absent-minded: she brings about some bad consequence by making some careless but avoidable motion, although she was not intentionally doing anything. Second, a person may be responsible for an event or state of affairs, not because she brought it about, but because she should have seen to it that it did not come about. Many acts of omission would provide cases in this category; here an agent could have done, but failed to do, what would have prevented some unwanted occurrence. In some omissions, the agent intentionally doesn't do something. But in some omissions 'intentionally' has no application. No doubt such cases will be covered using *mens rea* terminology other than 'intend' or 'intentionally', so that Duff will want to deal with them under a separate head.[32] But they demonstrate the inadequacy of any account of responsible agency which confines its range to motivated participation on the part of an agent. They thus expose the limitations of the work that 'intentionally' is cut out for.

Cases like these may also remind us of a more general, and important, point—of the extent to which expectations of people bear on our view of their culpability. If, with Duff, we suppose that our view of culpability reflects on what is done intentionally, then there will be a danger that what we take it to be reasonable to expect of people will infect our account of what a particular person was up to: judgments of what people must answer for will prejudice questions about what someone is answerable for.[33] Since this danger is surely to be avoided, Duff's view of the importance

---

[32] See e.g. the qualification 'at least for the kind of moral culpability which flows from moral wrong-*doing*' at 102. The italics are presumably supposed to signal the exclusion of acts of omission.

[33] Culpable absent-mindedness and culpable omissions show that 'intentionally' cannot figure in a condition which is necessary for answerability, but not that it does not figure in a condition that is sufficient. And I agree with Duff that anything someone intentionally does is something that she may be answerable for. I introduce 'answerable' and say 'may be answerable for' because there are many things that we intentionally do which lack all moral or legal significance, so that no question of being actually answerable arises, and our intuitions about responsibility are then not secure.

Duff's way of registering that no interesting moral conceptions need have been brought in when we have only got as far as introducing 'intentionally' is to say that 'we ascribe intentional agency when blame is not at issue' (78). But then he says something about the way 'intentionally' gets in which appears to run against his own view. He says that even though 'A marked the snow intentionally' need not imply 'that A is liable to be blamed for marking the snow', at least it implies 'that we can properly ask A why she marked the snow'. But if we think with Duff that people may intentionally do what they have no reason to do and may have a reason against doing (see section III above), then our 'proper' question may be a question without an answer. Duff seems to me to get things backwards here. If one is confident that A marked the snow intentionally (and this isn't something that one has taken on trust), then one is already on the way to knowing why A marked the snow. (*Belief, desire,*

of 'intentionally' must be criticized not only for being based in error, but for tending to lead us astray.

V

Over the last twenty years, much philosophy of action has been at the service of philosophy of mind, not of moral psychology. The explanation for this state of affairs is (I surmise) a shift of philosophical interest in agency—a shift away from questions in ethics, and towards questions in metaphysics about explanation and causation and about the status of subjects of beliefs and desires and the like. The thinness of the notions of 'reason' and of 'want' (or 'pro-attitude') that are employed in explicating 'intentionally' (see nn. 4 and 5 above) is a symptom of the fact that to bring in 'intentionally' is not yet to bring in much with moral (or, presumably, legal) content.[34] And placing 'attempt' on the conceptual scene (along with 'believe', 'desire', 'have a reason', 'intend', 'do intentionally') may suggest that there is a cluster of concepts of practical rationality which, though foundational in moral psychology, are not yet imbued with determinate evaluative import.

If the particular aspirations of this philosophy of action are understood, then perhaps it can be clear that even Duff's moderate hope was ill-founded. When that is clear, we may be prepared to deny the (to my mind) counterintuitive claims that he makes about where 'intentionally' has application, and we may be content to allow 'intentionally' to be defined in terms of the notions of a 'motivating reason' and willing to see a link

and *intentionally* apply hand in hand, so that one could not have adequate grounds for the application of one in the absence of taking any view about how the others apply.) Thus I should say: of course she had a reason if she did the thing intentionally. The next question (which will reveal whether she must actually answer for what it has been established she may be answerable for) can be whether her reason counts as a proper justification (or might reasonably have been expected to lead someone to do the thing). And then, of course, there are further questions (which will reveal whether she must answer for anything else): whether there was anything else she did which she could have avoided doing and which she either knew she was doing, or could have known she was doing, or might if she had been reasonable thought of herself as doing, or had wilful disregard for, or . . .

[34] If you found section I of this paper boring, then you now have an explanation of that: it isn't addressed to the interesting questions about responsibility. Much analytical work (and some of Duff's book) has been devoted to refining (1) and (2) and to attempting to develop them into an actual analysis. I am doubtful whether this work does much to advance the kind of conceptual understanding that is relevant to jurisprudence. Duff himself registers scepticism in the case of philosophical work with volitionalist or dualist leanings (compare nn. 9, 11, and 13 above). My scepticism about philosophy of action's relevance is prompted by different anxieties. But of course I do not deny that the work of philosophers can provide a firm basis and a good context for jurisprudential questions: section I might be correct and apposite even if it were not very interesting.

between this notion of 'reason' and that of 'attempt'. If we remain hopeful of demonstrating 'how fruitfully philosophy can interact with jurisprudence',[35] then we shall need to look further afield than the specific work on action out of which Duff hopes to build so much.

[35] This is the last phrase of Duff's book (at 206).

Acting, Trying, and Criminal Liability

R. A. DUFF

1. Action and Criminal Liability

Philosophers of action often think that one of their main tasks is to answer the question 'What is action?' This question cannot be answered merely by enumerating examples of action: such examples are rather the data on which the philosopher must work. Her task, it is thought, is to find that 'common character' shared by all actions, in virtue of which we 'call them actions';[1] that 'mark of action' which distinguishes (human) actions from other kinds of event.[2] So begins a search for the essence of action: for the defining features which constitute actions as actions rather than mere happenings.

To one concerned with the practicalities of the criminal law, this question and this search might seem peculiarly and esoterically philosophical. Like other 'What is X?' questions which philosophers ask ('What is knowledge?' 'What is mind?'), it has a metaphysical, abstract generality which seems distant from the concerns of those who try to work out, for instance, the proper structure and content of the criminal law. Legal theorists have, however, sometimes felt impelled to ask the nearly identical question 'What is an act?'

The legal theorist's interest in this question may be, in part, analytical. The *actus reus* of a crime, it is often said, typically consists in an 'act' (conduct), done in certain circumstances, and having certain consequences:[3] a clear understanding of the structure of criminal liability, and of the substance of particular offences, might therefore be thought to require a clear

---

[1] H. A. Prichard, 'Acting, Willing, Desiring', in A. R. White (ed.), *The Philosophy of Action* (Oxford 1968), 59, at 59.

[2] C. Ginet, *On Action* (Cambridge 1990), 6. See also L. H. Davis, *Theory of Action*, (Englewood Cliffs, NJ 1979), 2; D. Davidson, 'Agency', in his *Essays on Actions and Events* (Oxford 1980), 43, at 43–4; C. McGinn, *The Character of Mind* (Oxford 1982), hereafter McGinn, 84; A. C. Danto, *Analytical Philosophy of Action* (Cambridge 1973), pp. x–xi. I leave aside here the question of whether we should define human action as a subclass of a larger category which includes the 'actions' of non-human agents: see McGinn, 84–5; F. Dretske, *Explaining Behavior: Reasons in a World of Causes* (Cambridge, Mass. 1988), ch. 1.

[3] See e.g. J. C. Smith and B. Hogan, *Criminal Law* (6th ed., London 1988), 34 and 39; C. M. V. Clarkson and H. M. Keating, *Criminal Law: Text and Materials* (2nd ed., London 1990), 105; W. R. LaFave and A. W. Scott, *Criminal Law* (2nd ed., St Paul 1986), 195; Model Penal Code, § 1. 13(9).

distinction between an 'act' and its circumstances and consequences, allowing us to analyse each *actus reus* into these three elements.[4]

Such an analysis can also have a normative significance. It is sometimes argued, for example, that criminal attempts should require intention as to the 'act' and consequences involved in the relevant complete offence, but only recklessness (or whatever *mens rea* that complete offence requires) as to its circumstances: attempted rape should require an intention to have sexual intercourse, but only recklessness as to the woman's lack of consent.[5] Much can then hang on whether an element of the complete offence is classified as part of the 'act', or a consequence, which must be intended by one who attempts to commit the offence; or as a circumstance, as to which recklessness suffices.[6] Any such classification, however, requires a general distinction between acts, circumstances, and consequences. In discussing 'impossible attempts', courts have sometimes argued that the defendant should be acquitted if, had his 'intended acts', 'the contemplated sequence of actions', been completed, he would not have committed the relevant substantive crime.[7] But to apply this slogan, we need to know how to identify a defendant's 'intended acts', the 'sequence of actions' that he contemplated. If someone handles goods which she mistakenly believes to be stolen, does her 'contemplated sequence of actions' include 'handling stolen goods' (so that she is guilty of attempting to handle stolen goods); or merely 'handling these goods' (so that she must be acquitted)?[8] If someone shoots at what is actually a tree, mistakenly thinking it is his enemy, is his 'intended act' 'killing a person' (which convicts him of attempted murder); or 'shooting that object' (which acquits him)?[9]

---

[4] See e.g. P. H. Robinson and J. A. Grall, 'Element Analysis in Defining Criminal Liability: The Model Penal Code and Beyond', (1983) 35 *Stanford LR* 681; R. L. Gainer, 'The Culpability Provisions of the Model Penal Code', (1988) 19 *Rutgers LJ* 575.

[5] See *R* v. *Khan* [1990] 1 WLR 813; Law Commission No. 177: Draft Criminal Code Bill, cl. 49 (2) (1977); G. Williams, 'The Problem of Reckless Attempts', [1983] *Criminal LR* 365; Model Penal Code, § 5.01, on which see Commentary 301–2; J. C. Smith, 'Two Problems in Criminal Attempts', (1957) 70 *Harvard LR* 422, at 422–35, 'Two Problems in Criminal Attempts Re-examined', [1962] *Criminal LR* 135; D. Stuart, 'Mens Rea, Negligence and Attempts', [1968] *Criminal LR* 647 (contrast his *Canadian Criminal Law* (Toronto 1982), 529). For criticisms, see R. Buxton, 'The Working Paper on Inchoate Offences: Incitement and Attempt', [1973] *Criminal LR* 656, at 662–4, and 'Circumstances, Consequences and Attempted Rape', [1984] *Criminal LR* 25.

[6] See Buxton and Williams on abduction under the Sexual Offences Act 1956, s. 20: Buxton, 'The Working Paper on Inchoate Offences', 662–4, 'Circumstances, Consequences and Attempted Rape'; Williams, 'The Problem of Reckless Attempts', 368. And see my 'The Circumstances of an Attempt', (1991) 50 *Cambridge LJ* 100.

[7] *US* v. *Berrigan* (1973) 482 F 2d 171, 188 (and see *People* v. *Jaffe* (1906) 78 NE 169); *Haughton* v. *Smith* [1975] AC 476, 495–6 per Lord Hailsham; and see *DPP* v. *Nock* [1978] 3 WLR 57; *Anderton* v. *Ryan* [1985] 1 AC 560. See also my 'Attempts and the Problem of the Missing Circumstance', (1991) 42 *Northern Ireland Law Quarterly* 87.

[8] See *Haughton* v. *Smith*, *Anderton* v. *Ryan*, above n. 7.

[9] See *Berrigan*, above n. 7, 188.

But the notion of an 'act' has a larger normative significance in the criminal law. Criminal liability, it is said (even 'strict' liability), always requires a 'voluntary act'.[10] Now it is not clear whether this principle, whose status is anyway disputed,[11] declares a univocal requirement for criminal liability: 'acts' are contrasted with mere thoughts, with omissions, or with involuntary movements or happenings; and we cannot assume that 'act' means the same in each contrast.[12] If we are to apply the principle, however, we must ask not just what makes an act 'voluntary', but what counts as an 'act'.

The definition of any offence, we could say, includes a more or less complex action-description: 'destroying or damaging property belonging to another';[13] 'inflicting grievous bodily harm upon any other person'.[14] A defendant is guilty of the offence only if we can properly ascribe to him an action matching that description: the criteria for such an ascription are provided partly by the general principles of the criminal law, and partly by the full definition of the offence. Now the principle that criminal liability requires a 'voluntary act' cannot require that the defendant acted voluntarily under a description matching that embodied in the definition of the offence. Such a requirement would, for instance, convict a person of murder only if he voluntarily 'caused death': but the 'voluntary-act' requirement does not preclude convictions for murder based on 'felony-murder' rules or 'constructive malice', when the defendant might not even realize that he might cause death, and so could not be said to 'cause death' voluntarily.[15] It would convict a person of dangerous driving only if she voluntarily 'drove dangerously': but one who did not realize that she was driving dangerously, who thus could not be said to have voluntarily 'driven dangerously', can be convicted of dangerous driving without flouting the 'voluntary-act' principle.[16] So what does the 'voluntary-act' principle amount to: just what is required if that principle is to be observed?

The concept of action is also related to normative issues about criminal liability in the following way. One reason for portraying the definitions of offences as action-descriptions, under which a person's conduct must fall if she is to be convicted, concerns the connection between action and responsibility. A criminal conviction holds a defendant culpably responsible,

[10] See e.g. Model Penal Code, § 2.01(1); and the oft-quoted dictum in *Woolmington* v. *DPP* [1935] AC 462, 482.
[11] See P. R. Glazebrook, 'Situational Liability', in Glazebrook (ed.), *Reshaping the Criminal Law* (London 1978), 108.
[12] But see M. S. Moore, *Act and Crime* (Oxford 1993), chs. 1–3.
[13] Criminal Damage Act 1971, s. 1(1).
[14] Offences against the Person Act 1861, s. 20.
[15] See e.g. *Ryan* v. *R* (1967) 40 ALJR 488. For useful discussions of how the requisite 'voluntary act' should be identified, see also *Vallance* v. *R* (1961) 108 CLR 56; *Timbu Kollian* v. *R* (1968) 119 CLR 47.
[16] See, famously, *Hill* v. *Baxter* [1958] 1 QB 277.

answerable, for something;[17] and if we ask what it holds her responsible for, the answer 'for an action' seems appropriate. Such an answer seems appropriate, first, as emphasizing that mere thoughts or bare intentions should not make a person criminally liable. I bring myself within the reach of the criminal law only when I act: only when thought and intention are given active embodiment in conduct which engages with the world, and which may thus impinge on the rights and interests that the criminal law aims to protect.[18] It also, and in this context more relevantly, seems appropriate because we can surely be held culpably responsible only for what is within our control; and, once we move beyond the realm of (mere) thought, it is our actions that we paradigmatically control. The concept of action marks the fundamental

contrast between what an agent does and what merely happens to him, or between the bodily movements that he makes and those that occur without his making them.[19]

We can be held responsible for what we do, since that is (normally) within our control.[20] We cannot be held responsible for what 'merely happens to' us, or for events that are determined by factors outside our control; nor can such events be counted as actions of ours.

(To say that the criminal law holds us responsible, and convicts and punishes us, for our actions, seems inconsistent with the view that the real focus of criminal conviction and punishment is not the particular action which brings the defendant to the attention of the court, or her choice to do that action, but the defective character-trait which that action manifested.[21] Though I cannot discuss this view here, I suspect that the dispute between 'choice' theorists and 'character' theorists rests on a mistaken dichotomy between 'choice' and 'character' as possible foundations for criminal liability; and that we can capture what is true in each of these competing views, whilst avoiding their errors, by insisting that criminal liability is, as it seems to be, for actions.)

But if it is for our actions that we are responsible, and can properly be

[17] See further my *Trials and Punishments* (Cambridge 1986), ch. 4.
[18] I cannot discuss the meaning or foundations of this principle here: but see especially H. Morris, 'Punishment for Thoughts', in his *Guilt and Innocence* (Los Angeles 1976), 1; B. Chapman, 'Agency and Contingency: The Case of Criminal Attempts', (1988) 38 *University of Toronto LJ* 355.
[19] H. Frankfurt, 'The Problem of Action', in his *The Importance of What We Care About* (Cambridge 1988), 69 at 69.
[20] Only normally, because the possibility of such excuses as insanity or various kinds of compulsion show that action is not a sufficient condition of responsibility.
[21] See M. D. Bayles, 'Character, Purpose, and Criminal Responsibility', (1982) 1 *Law and Philosophy* 5; N. Lacey, *State Punishment* (London 1988), ch. 3: for some criticisms see M. S. Moore, 'Choice, Character and Excuse', (1990) 7 *Social Philosophy and Policy* 29; S. H. Pillsbury, 'The Meaning of Deserved Punishment: An Essay on Choice, Character and Responsibility', (1992) 67 *Indiana LJ* 719; R. A. Duff, 'Choice, Character, and Criminal Liability', (1993) 12 *Law and Philosophy* 1.

held criminally liable, we need to know what action is. We need to know what can count as an action (as a 'voluntary act'), as distinct from a mere happening. We also need to know what falls within the scope of an action: what events or outcomes can properly be ascribed to an agent as something which she did, for which she can be held liable. For instance, the law distinguishes completed crimes from failed attempts: if I succeed in injuring the person I attack, I am guilty of wounding; if I try but fail to wound him, I am guilty only of attempted wounding, and will probably receive a lighter sentence. This implies that we can ascribe different actions to a successful and an unsuccessful assailant: one 'wounded another person', the other only 'tried to wound another person'. Likewise, in distinguishing between (and providing different maximum penalties for) reckless driving and causing death by reckless driving,[22] the law implies that we can ascribe relevantly different actions to the reckless driver who causes death and to one who does not: the fact of causing, or of not causing, death properly enters into the law's description of the defendant's action—into the description of that for which he is to be held responsible.

Our ordinary action-descriptions do reflect the actual effects of an agent's conduct: we say that one person 'killed V' or 'caused death'; another 'tried but failed to kill V', or 'drove recklessly but did not, fortunately, cause death'. But the practice of allowing actual outcomes to affect criminal liability is also controversial: surely, it is argued, it is neither rational nor just to allow what may be the chance fact of causing or not causing harm to make such a difference to the agent's criminal liability.[23] One way to support this argument is, we will see, by so defining the notion of 'action' that the agent's action (that which can properly be ascribed to her) does not include such outcomes: by arguing that, in the strict or appropriate sense of 'action', a successful and a failed would-be killer, or a reckless driver who causes death and one who does not, have both done the same action, and should thus suffer the same punishment.[24] Here again, then, substantive questions about the proper foundations and scope of criminal liability seem to connect with questions about the concept of action.

A legal theorist's interest in the question 'What is action?' or 'What is

---

[22] Road Traffic Act 1988, ss. 1–2. The offences mentioned have now been replaced with offences of dangerous driving under the Road Traffic Act 1991.

[23] See e.g. S. J. Schulhofer, 'Harm and Punishment: A Critique of Emphasis on the Results of Conduct in the Criminal Law', (1974) 122 *University of Pennsylvania LR* 1497; H. L. A Hart, 'Intention and Punishment', in his *Punishment and Responsibility* (Oxford 1968), 113, at 129–31; R. Parker, 'Blame, Punishment and the Role of Results', (1984) 21 *American Philosophical Quarterly* 269.

[24] See A. J. Ashworth, 'Sharpening the Subjective Element in Criminal Liability', in R. A. Duff and N. E. Simmonds (eds.), *Philosophy and the Criminal Law* (Wiesbaden 1984), 79, hereafter 'Sharpening'; 'Belief, Intent and Criminal Liability', in J. Eekelaar and J Bell (eds.), *Oxford Essays in Jurisprudence: Third Series* (Oxford 1987), 1, hereafter 'Belief'; D. Lewis, 'The Punishment That Leaves Something to Chance', (1989) 18 *Philosophy & Public Affairs* 53, at 56; and text at nn. 61–2 below.

an act?' is thus both analytical and normative. So too is a philosopher's interest in these questions. Her concern might be simply to understand action as a central dimension of human life and experience: but she might also hope that an adequate understanding of the 'contrast between what an agent does and what merely happens to him' will cast light on the question of whether, in what sense, and to what extent, we are free and responsible agents. To be a free and responsible agent is, at least, to be an agent who can act, rather than a being who is merely the passive victim of external forces:[25] to discover what it is to act will thus also be to discover at least part of what it is to be a free agent.

2. Action, Basic Action, and Volition

The question 'What is action?' invites a search for the essence of action— for the 'common character' shared by all human actions. But how can we begin this search, faced by the manifold diversity of human action? How can we hope to identify the common character which unites such disparate actions as driving a car, writing an article, stealing a wallet, killing some-one? Many actions involve intention: the intention to do the particular action, a further intention with which it is done. But even if every action is intentional under some description,[26] intention is not the essence of action. For to intend is not yet to act: but we want to know what it is to act.

2.1. The Philosopher's Basic Actions

Philosophers have sometimes thought that the 'common character' of action can be found by a reductive analysis which identifies the essential core of all our diverse and complex actions. We note first that many actions are 'non-basic', done by doing something else: I make a contract by signing a document; I kill someone by shooting or poisoning her. Now when I do X by doing Y, Y is basic relative to X: but an action which is basic relative to another action, as signing a document is basic relative to making a contract, is itself often non-basic relative to (is itself done by doing) some other action; I sign a document by moving my hand. If any action is to be possible, however, there must be some absolutely basic actions which we just do, not by doing something else.[27] So perhaps the essence of action consists in absolutely basic action: in those actions which

[25] Compare Hart's remarks on the 'fundamental defect' in human conduct, when 'the movements of the human body seem more like the movements of an inanimate thing than the actions of a person'; 'Acts of Will and Responsibility', in Hart, *Punishment and Responsibility* (Oxford 1968), 90, at 91–2.

[26] Davidson, 'Agency', above n. 2, 45–7.

[27] See A. C. Danto, 'Basic Actions', in A. R. White (ed.), *The Philosophy of Action* (Oxford 1968), 43, at 50–1.

we just do, and by doing which we can do all our more complex, non-basic actions. Furthermore, if we could show that absolutely basic actions are all of one kind, we would have identified the 'common character' of all actions.

Some have thought that we can show precisely this. All basic actions are bodily movements: action thus consists, essentially, in moving one's body.

We must conclude, perhaps with a shock of surprise, that our primitive actions, the ones we do not do by doing something else, mere movements of the body— these are all the actions there are. We never do more than move our bodies: the rest is up to nature.[28]

Non-basic actions are done (ultimately) by moving our bodies, but we do not normally move our bodies by doing anything else: we just move them.

The comment that 'the rest is up to nature' points to another aspect of basic actions. The success of non-basic action depends on factors independent of the agent: my killing V depends on the proper working of my gun, on V's not moving, etc. Non-basic action is thus fallible. One who aims to do X by doing Y might do Y, thus playing her part in doing X, but fail to do X: for the relation between Y and X, which makes doing Y a method of doing X, depends on factors outside her control. I aim and fire the gun, but it malfunctions, or V moves. My basic actions, however, are not vulnerable to this kind of failure: they are within my control; it is up to me whether they are done; they are authentically mine.

What is 'mine' is not, of course, only a bodily movement. I make the movement given certain beliefs (that this is a contract, that this is a poison), and with a certain intention (to make a contract, to kill V). What is 'mine' is making that movement in that belief, with that intention. But beliefs and intentions are not themselves actions: so we could say that my action, strictly speaking, consists in making that movement.

2.2. Basic Actions and the Law

Just as philosophers have found the essence of agency in bodily movements as basic actions, so legal theorists have defined an 'act' as a (voluntary) bodily movement.[29] The 'voluntary act' required for criminal liability is

[28] Davidson, 'Agency', above n. 2, 59: see Danto, 'Basic Actions', above n. 27; A. I. Goldman, *A Theory of Human Action* (Englewood Cliffs, NJ 1970), chs. 1–3; also J. Hornsby, *Actions*, (London 1980), hereafter Hornsby, ch. 1.

[29] See e.g. J. Austin, *Lectures on Jurisprudence* (5th edn., London 1885), i, 407–17; J. C. Smith, 'Two Problems in Criminal Attempts', above n. 5, 422–3; G. Williams, *Textbook of Criminal Law* (2nd ed., London 1983), 147–8, and 'The Problem of Reckless Attempts', above n. 5, 369; LaFave and Scott, *Criminal Law*, above n. 3, 195; Model Penal Code, § 1.13(2); Robinson and Grall, 'Element Analysis in Defining Criminal Liability', above n. 4, at 719; A. Enker, 'Impossibility in Criminal Attempts—Legality and the Legal Process', (1969) 53 *Minnesota LR* 665, at 665; *Berrigan*, above n. 7, 187.

thus to be understood as a (voluntary) bodily movement,[30] and an *actus reus* can be analysed into a (set of) bodily movement(s), and certain specified circumstances and consequences.[31]

Now, the application of this conception of 'basic action' to the criminal law might raise some doubts about its utility. We may note first that even its advocates do not always apply it consistently. Enker defines 'act' as 'the defendant's physical bodily movements', but describes the 'act' in possessing stolen goods as 'possession of stolen goods', and the 'act' in smuggling as 'bringing goods into the country without paying a duty'.[32] Robinson and Grall similarly define the 'conduct' element 'literally, and thus narrowly', as 'the actual physical movement of the actor', but describe the 'conduct element' in harassment as 'the simple act of speaking', and say that reckless driving 'requires only conduct (driving) under a particular circumstance'.[33] Such descriptions, however, describe much more than simple bodily movements. Nor have courts, in discussing (explicitly or implicitly) the minimal demand for a 'voluntary act', taken it to require only a voluntary bodily movement: they have, rather, talked of such acts as 'driving';[34] of 'striking a child';[35] or of 'firing a gun' or 'pointing a gun'.[36]

Second, an account of basic actions simply as bodily movements does not help to solve the particular problems in criminal law which seem to require a clear definition of an 'act'. The real problem in the case of 'reckless attempts', for instance,[37] concerns not the identity of the 'act', but the distinction between circumstances and consequences: a distinction which this account does not help us to draw. The slogan that one whose 'intended acts, even if completed, would not amount to a crime' does not commit a criminal attempt,[38] cannot plausibly mean that she commits no attempt if her intended bodily movements would not amount to a crime. This might be the only way to make sense of the claim that the would-be

[30] See text at n. 10 above; M. S. Moore, *Act and Crime*, above n. 12, chs. 2–5 (the 'act requirement' requires 'willed bodily movement').

[31] See esp. Robinson and Grall, 'Element Analysis in Defining Criminal Liability', above n. 4, 719–25.

[32] Enker, 'Impossibility in Criminal Attempts—Legality and the Legal Process', above n. 29, 665–6. See also *Berrigan*, above n. 7, 187–9: having adopted Enker's definition of 'act', and held that there is no criminal attempt if the agent performed his 'intended physical act' without committing a substantive offence, the court talked of such acts as having intercourse with a woman, taking an umbrella, shooting an object, and sending a letter.

[33] Robinson and Grall, 'Element Analysis in Defining Criminal Liability', above n. 4, 719, 720 and 750. See also *Haughton* v. *Smith* [1975] AC 476, 501 (Lord Morris: the defendant 'did all the physical acts that he planned to do' without handling stolen goods; but the 'act' that he ascribed to Mr Smith was 'handling goods'); *Vallance*, above n. 15, 64–5 (Kitto J.: the requisite 'voluntary act' is the 'physical ["bodily"] action'; but he goes on to talk of 'firing the gun' as not being involuntary).

[34] See *Hill* v. *Baxter* above n. 16.   [35] See *Timbu Kolian*, above n. 15.

[36] See *Ryan* v. *R*, above n. 15, 494 (Barwick CJ), 499 (Taylor and Owen JJ), and 502 (Windeyer J.).   [37] See text at nn. 5–6 above.

[38] *Berrigan*, above n. 7, 188; see also text at nn. 7–9 above.

picker of an empty pocket is not guilty of attempted theft:[39] but it would also acquit the would-be killer whose gun was not loaded, or whose shot missed, which would clearly be absurd. And, finally, what worries courts in applying the 'voluntary-act' requirement is more usually the problem of whether the defendant's bodily movements were 'voluntary', rather than the problem of whether those movements, if they were voluntary, constituted the requisite 'act': but a claim that basic actions are bodily movements does not tell us how to distinguish voluntary from involuntary movements.

2.3. *From Basic Actions to Volitions*

The philosophical doctrine of basic actions as bodily movements (on which the analogous legal doctrine relies) is anyway vulnerable to serious objections. I can only sketch these objections here: they show that once we start down the road leading to bodily movements as basic actions, we cannot avoid going further, to locate the essence of agency in something lying behind such movements.[40]

First, not every action involves bodily movement: a guardsman who keeps himself from moving acts, but acts precisely by not moving his body.

Second, even if we can decide what counts as 'bodily movement', there is no plausible criterion which counts only bodily movements as basic actions. An intentional criterion, by which an action is basic if it is the immediate object of the agent's intention, counts some more complex actions (such as changing gear, typing a word) as basic. A causal criterion, by which an action is basic if its result is not caused by another action of the agent's, counts some of the causes of our bodily movements (muscular contractions, for instance) as basic to those movements.

Third, a 'basic-action' theory does not help with the 'result-problem'.[41] A movement of my arm occurs when I move my arm, and when my arm moves in involuntary spasm. If we are to understand what it is to act we must ask what distinguishes these cases: but the 'basic-action' theorist can say only that moving my arm is intrinsically, but indefinably, different from my arm moving involuntarily.

Fourth, bodily movements are fallible. Whether I move my arm depends on conditions outside my control: if those conditions are not satisfied (if my arm is paralysed, or tied down), I might fail to move my arm although,

[39] See e.g. *Haughton* v. *Smith* above n. 7, 494–6.

[40] See especially A. C. Baier, 'The Search for Basic Actions', (1971) 8 *American Philosophical Quarterly* 161; J Annas, 'How Basic are Basic Actions?', (1977–8) 78 *Proceedings of the Aristotelian Society* 195; C. J. Moya, *The Philosophy of Action* (Cambridge 1990), 14–18.

[41] See H. McCann, 'Volition and Basic Action', (1974) 83 *Philosophical Review* 451; Moya, *The Philosophy of Action*, above n. 40, 12–17; also Hornsby, chs. 1–2.

as we would naturally say, I try to move it. I might even believe that I have moved my arm when it has not actually moved: this happens when someone's arm is anaesthetized, he is asked to shut his eyes and raise his arm, and the arm is held down.[42] This person has not been merely inactive (like someone who simply refuses to obey the request to raise his arm): but a 'basic-action' theorist seems able to say nothing about him except that he has not acted.

The last two objections seem to make it necessary to ask, and to try to answer, Wittgenstein's famous question (though he thought it could not be answered, and should not be asked):

[W]hen 'I raise my arm', my arm goes up. And the problem arises: what is left over if I subtract the fact that my arm goes up from the fact that I raise my arm?[43]

To find the defining mark of agency, we must surely subtract from my action of raising my arm the element, my arm rising, which it shares with my arm rising involuntarily: what is left will be the element peculiar to, and so definitive of, my action. Furthermore, the fact that my arm rises is sometimes subtracted from the fact that I raise my arm, as with the anaesthetized agent: since he is still active, what is left over will be what he has done, and will also be the essence of agency. A 'basic-action' theory, however, cannot answer Wittgenstein's question.

So what is left over? One kind of answer would specify a set of physiological events: but this is not the answer which philosophers who ask Wittgenstein's question want, or are qualified to give. What they want, and may be qualified to give, is not an empirical account of the physiological mechanisms of action, but a logical account of the defining features in virtue of which actions count as actions. It is a necessary truth that when I raise my arm, my arm goes up. An answer to Wittgenstein's question must specify a further necessary truth, that when I raise my arm, . . ., since only that would give us the defining essence of action. A physiological story, however, does not give us such a necessary truth; it is merely a contingent truth that actions involve any particular physiological events. Of course, if materialism is true, what is left over will consist ultimately in some such physiological events: but our understanding of what it is to act, and our knowledge of our own agency (which are what concern us here), do not take such events as their direct content or object.

A more plausible, indeed apparently inevitable, answer is that what is left over is some mental component of raising my arm, which causes the arm to rise. If we now ask what this mental component is, one familiar answer is that it is 'volition' or 'willing': a 'mental act' of willing the

---

[42] See Hornsby, 40.
[43] L. Wittgenstein, *Philosophical Investigations* (trans. G. E. M. Anscombe, Oxford 1963), para. 621.

movement of my arm; an act which is 'necessarily conscious and infallibly known', and which (if all goes well) causes my arm to rise.[44]

A volitionist theory seems to avoid the objections faced by a theory of bodily movements as basic actions. Even actions involving no movement involve volition; the guardsman wills to remain still. Volitions are both intentionally and causally basic to everything we do. The difference between my moving my arm, and its involuntarily moving, is that in the former case, but not the latter, its movement is caused by my willing it. And, finally, the anaesthetized agent is active in that he wills the movement of his arm; and he believes he has raised his arm because he knows he has willed its movement.

Volitionism is, of course, also familiar in legal theory. The 'act' required for any criminal liability must be 'voluntary'; and a 'voluntary act' is a 'willed bodily movement', a movement caused and controlled by the agent's will.[45]

I will not discuss the different species of volitionism here.[46] Nor will I discuss the familiar objections to volitionism:[47] that we are not conscious (as volitionism classically holds that we must be) of such peculiar mental events whenever we act; that no mental event could, logically, both have the practical character of volition, and be a cause of our voluntary bodily movements. For my concern is not with volitionism as such, but with a closely related doctrine which defines action in terms of 'trying', rather than of 'volition'.[48]

3. Action as Trying

My aim is to show how we might be led to an account of action as consisting essentially in 'trying'; why it may seem preferable to an explicitly volitionist doctrine; and why it none the less fails.[49]

[44] McGinn, 86–7 and 91: see Prichard, 'Acting, Willing, Desiring', above n. 1; Ginet, *On Action*, above n. 2, chs. 1–2; Davis, *Theory of Action*, above n. 2, ch. 1; B Aune, 'Prichard, Action and Volition', (1974) 25 *Philosophical Studies* 97; C. Ripley, 'A Theory of Volition', (1974) 11 *American Philosophical Quarterly* 141; A. I. Goldman, 'The Volitional Theory Revisited', in M. Brand and D. Walton (eds.), *Action Theory* (Dordrecht 1976) 67, at 68–9.

[45] See Moore, *Act and Crime*, above n. 12, part I; Williams, *Textbook of Criminal Law*, above n. 29, 147–8; Austin, *Lectures on Jurisprudence*, above n. 29; Smith and Hogan, *Criminal Law*, above n. 3, 40; J. Ll. Edwards, 'Automatism and Criminal Responsibility', (1958) 21 *Modern LR* 375, at 379–80; *DPP for Northern Ireland* v. *Lynch* [1975] 1 All ER 913, 933–4; *Ryan* v. *R*, above n. 15, 490–3 and 504–5; Model Penal Code, § 2.01(2) (c); LaFave and Scott, *Criminal Law*, above n. 3, 199.

[46] But see M. Brand, *Intending and Acting* (Cambridge, Mass. 1984), ch. 1; Hornsby, ch. 4.

[47] See especially H. L. A. Hart, 'Acts of Will and Responsibility', above n. 25; G. Ryle, *The Concept of Mind* (London 1949), ch. 3; A. I. Melden, *Free Action* (London 1961).

[48] Though McGinn, for instance (McGinn, ch. 5), takes 'willing' to be identical to 'trying'; see also Davis, *Theory of Action*, above n. 2, 16–17.

[49] For versions of this doctrine, see Hornsby; Ashworth, 'Sharpening', and 'Belief'; McGinn, ch. 5; D. M. Armstrong, 'Acting and Trying', [1973] *Philosophical Papers* 1; B. O'Shaughnessy,

3.1. 'To Act is to Try'

Bulstrode aims and fires at Vincy: his shot hits and kills her, as he intended. We might naturally describe his action as 'killing Vincy'. But suppose Vincy suddenly moves, and his shot misses. How should we now describe his action?

We cannot say 'he killed Vincy', since he did not. We could say 'he tried to kill Vincy': but what did this 'trying' consist in? We might say that it involved 'firing a gun, intending thereby to kill Vincy' (although in other cases 'trying to kill' involves different actions, such as administering poison, or stabbing). But it could be true that Bulstrode 'tried to kill Vincy' though he did not 'fire a gun'. Perhaps he pulled the trigger, intending thereby to fire the gun and kill Vincy, but the gun malfunctioned; or perhaps he moved his finger, intending thereby to pull the trigger, fire the gun, and kill Vincy, but the trigger was jammed. In this last case, it seems, his 'trying to kill Vincy' consisted only in moving his finger (with the intention thereby of killing Vincy).[50] We might now suggest that 'trying to kill V' consists simply in doing something (firing a gun, administering poison, pulling a trigger, moving a finger), intending thereby to kill V; and more generally that 'trying to do X' consists in doing some Y intending thereby to do X.

But Bulstrode might 'try to kill Vincy' though he does not even move a finger: he 'tries to move his finger' (as we might naturally say), intending thereby to pull the trigger, fire the gun, and kill Vincy; but he finds that his arm is suddenly paralysed. His 'trying to move his finger', which is also his 'trying to kill Vincy', does not now consist in any overt action: so what does it consist in?

Volitionists will say that it consists in making a volition, or willing the movement of his finger.[51] But perhaps this is a mistake, based on the mistaken idea that 'trying to do X' must always involve doing a distinct Y, intending thereby to do X. Why should we not just say that 'trying to move a finger' is itself the basic (not further analysable) description of what Bulstrode does here? In most cases, trying to do X does involve doing some distinct Y; and when I try to move my finger, the 'trying' is distinct from the actual movement of my finger, since the finger might not move.

The Will: A Dual Aspect Theory, ii (Cambridge 1980), hereafter O'Shaughnessy. For useful criticisms, see P. Winch, 'Trying', in his Ethics and Action (London 1972), 130; P. L. Heath, 'Trying and Attempting', (1971) 45 Proceedings of the Aristotelian Society (Supp. Vol.) 193; J. F. M. Hunter, 'Trying', (1987) 37 Philosophical Quarterly 392.

[50] His attempt to kill Vincy also involved, of course, picking up the gun and aiming it: but one could imagine a case in which the only overt conduct involved in an attempt to kill was the movement of a finger. Someone brings me a remote-control device: if I press the button, it will explode a bomb and kill V.

[51] See e.g. Ginet, On Action, above n. 2, 30.

But this 'trying' cannot be redescribed as 'doing Y', (as we might redescribe 'trying to kill V' as 'firing a gun intending to kill V'): it is, simply, 'trying'.

A Bulstrode whose shot misses 'tries to kill Vincy'. Should we not also say, however, that the Bulstrode who actually kills Vincy 'tries to kill Vincy' (though his attempt succeeds)? For they both do something, intending thereby to kill Vincy. Likewise, a Bulstrode whose gun does not malfunction 'tries to fire the gun'; a Bulstrode whose trigger is not jammed 'tries to pull the trigger'. But should we not then also say that the unparalysed Bulstrode 'tries to move his finger (successfully)'? The difference between the paralysed and the unparalysed Bulstrode is not that one 'tries to move his finger' whilst the other does not, but that one attempt succeeds whilst the other fails.

This line of thought suggests that every action, even moving a limb, involves trying; it suggests indeed that, in so far as actions typically involve moving one's body, they all involve trying to move one's body. But we might also now suggest that every action consists essentially in trying (and thus, typically, in trying to move one's body).

Consider the difference between the Bulstrode whose shot misses and the one who kills Vincy. Given this difference, the latter's but not the former's action satisfies the description 'he killed Vincy'. But it is surely not a difference in what each of them strictly did. For

the description of an action in terms of what it causes is an extrinsic description. The actions themselves, events that are finished when the agent has done his part, do not differ in any intrinsic way.[52]

'He killed Vincy' is an extrinsic description: for its truth depends on the occurrence of Vincy's death, which itself depends on external factors (the gun's working, Vincy's movements, etc.) which Bulstrode cannot (confidently) predict nor (wholly) control. He might do 'his part' (aim and fire the gun), but fail to bring about Vincy's death. Surely his 'action itself', however, must be what constitutes 'his part' in the (attempted) killing of Vincy, what it is up to him to do to bring that result about: something which has Vincy's death as an intended consequence.

If 'he killed Vincy' is an 'extrinsic description of his action in terms of what it causes', however, so too is 'he fired the gun', and 'he pulled the trigger', and 'he moved his finger'. For in each case the truth of the description depends upon the occurrence of a result which itself depends on factors outside Bulstrode's control: as the case of paralysis shows, even 'moving a finger' depends upon physical factors which are not within his control. So it seems that we 'must conclude, perhaps with a shock of surprise, that we never do more than *"try to"* move our bodies: the rest

[52] D. Lewis, 'The Punishment That Leaves Something to Chance', above n. 24, 56 n. 4.

is up to nature.'[53] However successful an agent might be, his action consists ultimately in a 'trying': that 'is all that is his'.[54]

But what is this 'trying'? It must presumably be (as 'volition' was classically taken to be) a conscious mental activity. Conscious, because the paralysed Bulstrode knows at least that he has tried to move; he is conscious of trying. Mental, because even if 'trying' is identical with some physiological process, his knowledge that he has tried does not present itself as knowledge of any such process. An activity, because 'trying' is something that he does, not something that happens to him.[55]

3.2. Trying and the Criminal Law

I have argued elsewhere that we can use the concept of 'trying' to formulate a test which will help us to deal with two problematic issues in the law of attempts.[56] A person commits a criminal attempt only if she is trying to do something that would, if she succeeds in doing it, constitute the commission of a substantive crime. By this test, one who handles what she mistakenly believes are stolen goods should be guilty of attempting to handle stolen goods only if their supposedly stolen character is part of her reason for handling them—only if the fact that they are not stolen marks the failure of her intended enterprise: if her enterprise (for example, buying a video-recorder cheaply) can succeed even though the goods are not stolen, she is not attempting to handle stolen goods.[57] By this test, a man who is reckless as to whether the woman with whom he tries to have sexual intercourse consents to it is guilty of attempted rape if she does not actually consent to it: he is then trying to do something, to have intercourse with this woman, which would (given her lack of consent and his recklessness) constitute rape if he succeeded in doing it.[58] This test, however, neither relies on nor implies the doctrine that all action consists essentially in 'trying'; we must ask what implications that doctrine does have for the criminal law.

The doctrine tells us what makes an act 'voluntary': an act is voluntary if it is something which the agent tried to do (if it is, for instance, a

---

[53] Adapting Davidson, 'Agency', above n. 2, 59; see text at n. 28 above.

[54] W. D. Ross, *Foundations of Ethics* (London 1939), 160 (Ross talks of his 'exertion'): see Ashworth, 'Sharpening', 80. I leave aside here the issue of whether 'trying' is itself an 'action', or whether I 'act' only if my trying succeeds (see McGinn, 88–90; Hornsby, 42).

[55] See McGinn, 86–7; also Armstrong, 'Acting and Trying', above n. 54, 2–3. Hornsby (Hornsby, 58–9) takes 'tryings' to be 'physical events' which need not be thought of as 'conscious occurrences': but this seems inconsistent with her description of them as 'events that the agent is particularly well placed to know about' (ibid. 44).

[56] See my 'The Circumstances of an Attempt', above n. 6; 'Attempts and the Problem of the Missing Circumstance', above n. 7.

[57] See *Anderton* v. *Ryan*, above n. 7; and text at n. 8 above.

[58] See text at nn. 5–6 above.

movement which she successfully tried to make). But this does not tell us what kind of 'act' is required as the minimal condition of criminal liability: for what the law requires is some overt act, whereas on this view 'trying' is a mental activity.[59] The doctrine might suggest, in so far as it portrays action as consisting basically or essentially in trying to move my body, that the 'act' requirement would be satisfied by any voluntary bodily movement: but this is not a plausible interpretation of that requirement.[60]

The doctrine is most clearly relevant, however, to the familiar subjectivist argument that criminal liability should depend, not on the actual outcome of the defendant's action, but on what he 'tried' to do. This is not to say that Bulstrode should be convicted only of 'trying to move his finger': we should describe his action in terms of the beliefs and intentions with which it was done, as 'trying to kill Vincy'. But it is to say that his liability should be just the same on all the scenarios sketched above. For in each case he 'tried to kill Vincy': since that 'trying' is 'all that is his', it is on that that his sentence should depend, not on the extrinsic fact of whether he actually killed her. This argument often appeals to the slogan that criminal liability should not depend on matters of luck or chance;[61] and we can call it a matter of chance, on any of those scenarios, that Bulstrode did not kill Vincy. But the argument can be strengthened by relating it to this account of action.[62] A person should presumably be punished for what he has done: if what he has done, strictly speaking, is only to try, if the trying is 'all that is his', it is for that, rather than for its extrinsic consequences, that he should be punished.

Two more radical implications might also seem to follow. First, that a Bulstrode who kills Vincy and one whose attempt fails should not only receive the same sentence: they should also be convicted of the same offence, since they have done the same thing. Second, that criminal liability should not strictly require an overt act at all. A paralysed Bulstrode is on this account no less culpable than one who kills Vincy; he too has tried, done all he can, to kill Vincy. So why should the chance fact that he failed even to move a finger save him from conviction and punishment?

I am not clear that subjectivists can consistently resist the first of these implications. Ashworth argues that such a change in the law, although

[59] Ashworth thinks that 'trying' or 'exertion' does involve some overt act: it constitutes 'a minimal actus reus ... the doing of any overt act with the necessary intention' ('Criminal Attempts and the Role of Resulting Harm', (1988) 19 *Rutgers LJ* 725, hereafter 'Attempts', 750; see also his 'Taking the Consequences' (this volume), 107). But the case of the paralysed agent shows that, according to this doctrine, the basic 'trying' is a mental activity which need have no overt behavioural effect—as Ashworth himself has elsewhere recognized ('Belief', 15–16 n. 47). [60] See s. 2.2 above.
[61] See e.g. J. C. Smith, 'The Element of Chance in Criminal Liability', [1971] *Criminal LR* 63; Ashworth, 'Attempts', 736 and 742.
[62] Ashworth, 'Belief', and 'Sharpening'; Lewis, 'The Punishment That Leaves Something to Chance', above n. 24.

'ensur[ing] that the labels of offences reflected the moral equivalence between substantive offences and "complete" attempts to commit them', would 'be alien to ordinary linguistic usage, would sometimes misrepresent the external events which took place, and would in turn blur the distinction between incomplete and complete attempts'.[63] But he has also argued that 'the limitations of language should not be allowed to override moral similarities';[64] and we could avoid linguistic problems, and the misrepresentation of 'external events', by convicting both the successful and the failed would-be killer of something like 'murderous conduct'. Furthermore, we could use the 'trying' doctrine to distinguish *more* clearly than the law now does between complete and incomplete attempts (between those where the agent has done 'his part' in the criminal endeavour, and those where he desists or is prevented before he completes 'his part'). For according to this doctrine there is something which the complete attempter, but not the incomplete attempter, tries to do: a complete attempter tries to do the last act that there is for him to do to commit the crime (he tries, for example, to move his finger on the trigger), whereas the incomplete attempter does not get to that point. The law could mark this difference by convicting the complete attempter of 'murderous conduct' (whether or not he succeeds), and the incomplete attempter of a lesser, secondary offence.

The second implication could, however, be resisted. There will anyway be few, if any, suddenly paralysed criminals whom an 'overt-act' requirement would save from conviction; and such a requirement can be justified by arguing that, even though it could, in theory, save some culpable agents from the conviction which they deserve, it protects citizens against convictions based on insecure evidence, and against intrusive policing.[65]

3.3. 'Trying' and Ordinary Usage

The doctrine that all action consists essentially in trying has one apparent advantage over explicitly volitionist theories: that we do naturally talk of people 'trying' to do things, whereas we do not ordinarily talk of people making 'volitions', or 'willing' their own movements. The doctrine can thus claim to explain action in terms of a concept which we already, pre-philosophically, apply to actions.

This apparent advantage is, however, offset by a disadvantage: that we do not ordinarily describe every action as a 'trying'; often we just say that an agent 'did X', not that she 'tried to do X'. We naturally talk of 'trying'

---

[63] 'Belief', 30–1.   [64] 'Attempts', 756.

[65] See Ashworth, 'Belief', 15 n. 47. Compare the rationale sometimes given for the 'unequivocal-act' test for the *actus reus* of attempts: see *R* v. *Barker* [1924] NZLR 865, 875; *US* v. *Oviedo* (1976) 525 F 2d 881, 885–6.

in three kinds of context, each involving the fact or the possibility of failure.

(*a*) When an action fails. If Bulstrode's shot misses, we say 'he tried to kill Vincy', rather than 'he killed Vincy'.

(*b*) When we are uncertain of an agent's success, perceiving some obstacle which creates a real chance of failure. If I doubt a student's ability to solve a logic problem, I say 'he is trying to solve it', whereas of a skilled logician solving a simple problem I would just say 'she is solving it'.

(*c*) When the agent makes a special effort to perform the action, in the face of recognized difficulties: I have to try to lift this heavy case, or to understand this complex argument, or to resist temptation. We can talk here of trying hard, or not hard enough. These cases too involve the prospect of failure: though we often succeed in doing what we thus try to do, the difficulties we must overcome bring with them a real possibility of failure.

The crucial point here is not merely that we do not in fact talk of 'trying' outside these contexts, but that it would be inappropriate to do so. It would be inappropriate to say of my skilled colleague that 'she is trying to solve' a logic problem which she predictably solves simply and effortlessly; indeed, she might well be insulted by the low estimation of her ability which that remark would imply.

One who holds that all action involves trying must thus justify her claim in the face of the fact that our ordinary use of the term suggests that only some actions involve trying, and explain why it should be inappropriate to *say* that someone tries if it is *true* that he tries. She can do this by arguing that the contexts in which we naturally talk of 'trying' reveal something, a 'trying', which must also obtain in contexts in which we would not naturally talk thus; and by arguing that the contextual factors which make talk of 'trying' appropriate or inappropriate do not bear on the meaning of 'try'.

The third context in which we talk of 'trying' gives no grounds for claiming that all action involves trying. For there is clearly a difference in how the agent goes about the action between this kind of case and that in which no special effort is required; it would, indeed, be incoherent to suggest that every action requires the kind of special effort which these actions require. The other two kinds of case, however, might ground an argument for that general claim.

Consider the first kind of case. There need be no difference in the agent's own experience of her action between doing X, and trying but failing to do X; that is how the anaesthetized agent can think, mistakenly, that he has raised his arm. '[W]hat is going on in [him] psychologically', his 'mental acts', are the same when his arm rises as when it does not rise:[66] so if he 'tries to raise his arm' in the latter case, he does so in the former too. The difference between 'I raised my arm' and 'I tried to raise my arm', is not that the latter statement describes a trying that is absent when the former is true: it is rather that the former adds to the trying the fact of success, or the latter subtracts from the former the fact that the arm rose.

Consider the second kind of case. The doubt, which leads us to say 'he is trying', 'need not impinge upon the agent himself':[67] he might be wholly confident of success. But the truth of 'A is trying to do X' surely cannot depend on factors which are thus external to A himself: if it is true that 'A is trying to do X' when such doubt is present, it must also be true when there is no such doubt.[68] 'He is trying to move the stone', I say, thinking it might well be too heavy for him. When I see that he moves it 'simply and effortlessly', I can still say 'I was right about one thing at least. I knew that [he] would try to move it.'[69]

So why should it be inappropriate to *say* 'A tried to do X' when A did X 'simply and effortlessly', if it is *true* that 'he tried'? We might explain it thus.[70] 'A tried to do X' makes a weaker claim than 'A did X': it withholds part of what 'A did X' asserts—that X was actually done. But it does not deny what it withholds: 'A tried to do X' is consistent with 'A did X'. Rather, it asserts only part of what 'A did X' asserts. But the stronger claim includes the weaker; the whole includes its parts. Whenever 'A did X' is true, 'A tried to do X' is therefore also true. It might, however, be inappropriate to say 'A tried to do X', when I know that A actually did X (simply and effortlessly), since in conversation we are normally expected to state as much as we know (of what is relevant). If I say 'Pat tried to get to London', knowing that she actually got there, I state less than I know: this is inappropriate because it may mislead my hearer, who assumes that in accordance with normal practice I am stating as much as I know, into supposing that Pat may not have got to London. My statement is true, but inappropriate because (given our normal conversational practices) misleading. Similarly, if I say 'it might be raining', when I can see that it certainly is raining, what I say is true (for if it is true that it is raining, it is also true that it might be raining): but it is misleading, and thus inappropriate, because my hearer will assume that I am stating as much as I know.

This distinction between the conditions under which it is true that 'A

---

[66] McGinn, 87; see Ashworth, 'Belief', 14–15.   [67] Hornsby, 35.
[68] Ibid.; see also McGinn, 87.   [69] Hornsby, 35.
[70] See O'Shaughnessy, chs. 9–10, especially 53–7, on the distinction between 'speech-conditions' and 'truth-conditions'; and J. R. Searle, 'Assertions and Aberrations', in B. Williams and A. Montefiore (eds.), *British Analytical Philosophy* (London 1966), 41. See also J. Hornsby, 'On What's Intentionally Done' (this volume), 55.

tried to do *X*' and the conditions under which I can properly say 'A tried to do *X*' is neither clear nor uncontroversial; it will be viewed with suspicion by anyone who sees truth in Wittgenstein's view that 'the meaning of a word is its use in the language'.[71] Nor is it yet clear why we should not say that the fact, or real chance, of failure is part of the meaning (and thus a truth-condition) of 'A tried to do *X*': that implicit in any such statement, as part of its meaning, is something like 'but he [might have] failed', so that it is false, and not merely conversationally inappropriate, when that condition does not obtain.

4. Why Action Cannot Always Involve Trying

What underpins the insistence that the fact or real possibility of failure is not a truth-condition of 'try' is a common assumption: that 'trying' must be something—some property of the agent or her action. Thus McGinn and Hornsby assume that factors independent of the agent cannot be relevant to the truth of 'she tried':[72] whether she tries must depend on some fact about her. O'Shaughnessy rejects the suggestion that 'trying' 'is not itself a real anything': it is 'a true *sui generis* element of animal psychological life'.[73] Now if that assumption is true, if 'tryings' are 'original psychological constituents of the mind',[74] we must agree that all action involves trying: for there need be no difference, as far as the agent or her 'mental acts' are concerned, between a case where we would naturally say 'she is trying to do *X*' and one where we would simply say 'she is doing *X*'. Someone who wants, as I do, to deny that all action involves trying must therefore show that assumption to be mistaken.

4.1. *What Mental Acts?*

The 'tryings' that all action supposedly involves are 'mental acts', which are 'necessarily conscious and infallibly known'.[75] But can we recognize and describe these acts?

We will not find them by looking at cases in which some special effort

---

[71] Wittgenstein, *Philosophical Investigations*, above n. 43, para. 43. See too para. 116: '[w]hen philosophers use a word . . . and try to grasp the *essence* of the thing, one must always ask oneself: is the word ever actually used in this way in the language-game which is its original home?—What *we* do is to bring words back from their metaphysical to their everyday use' [para. 116]. And see C. Travis, *The Uses of Sense* (Oxford 1989), on the idea of 'S-use sensitivity' (pp. 17–35), according to which the semantics of a statement depend crucially on the context of its utterance.
[72] See text at nn. 66–9 above.   [73] O'Shaughnessy, 45 and 55.
[74] Ibid. 44–5; see also Armstrong, 'Acting and Trying', above n. 49, 5.
[75] McGinn, 86–7 and 91.

is made to perform a difficult task. There will in such cases be phenomenological features of the agent's activity on to which talk of 'trying'
can latch. But, first, such cases reveal no distinct and unitary kind of
mental activity, since what the 'effort' consists in will depend on the particular task: the physical effort involved in trying to lift a stone is quite
different from the mental effort in trying to concentrate on a logical problem; and both differ from the 'trying' that consists in exploring different
strategies for solving a practical problem. And, second, we cannot coherently suggest that every action involves some such special effort: to talk of
'trying' in these cases is precisely to contrast them with cases in which the
agent does X effortlessly, without having to 'try'.

Nor will we find these mental acts by looking at cases in which 'trying
to do X' involves doing some Y, intending thereby to do X (as when
Bulstrode tries to kill Vincy by firing a gun). Here, 'doing Y' is constituted
as 'trying to do X' partly by the agent's intention: but intending is not the
same as trying; and it is anyway a mistake to portray intention as some
kind of mental state or activity which precedes or accompanies action.[76]
Furthermore, the kind of 'trying' which all action is taken to involve does
not consist in doing some distinct Y, intending thereby to do X: it is, rather,
'basic trying—trying to move one's body'.[77] This kind of 'trying' is revealed most obviously in cases like that of the anaesthetized agent, but is
also present when a normal agent simply raises his arm.

Suppose we ask the anaesthetized or the normal agent whether he was
aware of a mental act of 'trying' when (as he thought) he raised his arm?
He would probably be baffled by the question: but I suspect that even if
we could persuade him to answer it, his answer would be 'No': what he
(thought he) was aware of was simply raising his arm; there was no mental
act he performed in order to get it to rise.

But since the anaesthetized agent was not utterly inactive, he surely must
have done something; and since that 'something' was not 'raising his arm',
it must have been a 'trying to raise his arm', a 'trying' which also grounded
his mistaken belief that he had raised his arm. Furthermore, since there
is no subjective or psychological difference between the case in which
his arm does not rise and that in which it does, in the latter case too such
a 'trying' must occur.

These 'musts' reflect the assumption noted above, that 'trying' must be
something.[78] Someone who is both gripped by that assumption, and im-
pressed by the objection that we are not aware of such 'mental acts' of
'trying', might then suggest that 'tryings' need not always be conscious
mental acts: perhaps they are 'physical events' which need not be 'conscious

---

[76] See my *Intention, Agency and Criminal Liability* (Oxford 1990), ch. 6.
[77] McGinn, 91; see text at nn. 51–5 above.   [78] See text at nn. 72–4 above.

occurrences'.[79] Now, such a move threatens to empty the 'trying' doctrine of any interesting content. For it seems to define 'trying' as whatever it is (presumably some physiological process) that causes our voluntary bodily movements, and which also occurs when someone 'tries but fails' to move a limb: but why should we use the term 'trying' to describe such a process? Because, again, it is assumed that 'trying' must be a something. If, however, we are to retain any connection with the ordinary meaning of 'try' (and if we do not, the doctrine that all action consists in 'trying' becomes utterly uninteresting), 'trying' must at least be something that the agent does; he raises his arm by trying to raise it. But I will show that it cannot be the case that we always move our bodies by trying to move them.

4.2. *Tryings and Movements*

The 'trying' doctrine portrays every bodily action as a complex whole with two components: the trying and the movement. The relation between these components is causal and contingent: trying, normally, causes the bodily movement; but it might not do so, as when my limb is paralysed. We can most easily discern this trying, as a distinct component, in cases of action-failure: we subtract the fact that the movement occurs from the fact that the agent acted; what is left is a trying which also occurs in the normal case.[80]

There is a precisely analogous argument about perception.[81] We suppose, naïvely, that we directly perceive actual objects; I see a dagger [we suppose that we directly move our bodies; I move my arm]. But our senses can deceive us: Macbeth thought he saw a dagger, but there was no dagger [our bodies can fail us; I think I have moved my arm, but it did not move]. But even if we are perceptually mistaken, we are still perceiving; Macbeth 'saw' something [even if our bodies fail us, we are active; an anaesthetized agent 'does' something]. We might say that Macbeth saw a hallucination [the anaesthetized agent tried to move his arm]. But there is no difference for the perceiver between veridical perception and hallucination [for an anaesthetized agent between moving his arm and trying to move it]. The difference between veridical perception and hallucination thus consists not in anything intrinsic to the perceptual experience, but in its relation to the external world; from which it follows that we never directly perceive actual objects [the difference between moving my arm, and trying but failing to move it, consists not in anything intrinsic to my activity, but in

[79] Hornsby, 58–9; see n. 55 above. For similar moves by volitionists, see Davis, *Theory of Action*, above n. 2, 16–22; Aune, 'Prichard, Action and Volition', above n. 44, 109.
[80] See text at n. 43 above.
[81] See A. J. Ayer, *The Foundations of Empirical Knowledge* (London 1940), ch. 1; D. W. Hamlyn, *The Theory of Knowledge* (London 1970), ch. 6.

its relation to the bodily movement]. We cannot say that what we directly perceive are always hallucinations, since 'hallucination' implies non-veridicality: but we could say that what we directly perceive are 'sense-data'; what distinguishes veridical from non-veridical perception is that in the former case but not the latter our 'sense-data' match (and are caused by) the world [what we directly do is try; what distinguishes successful from failed action is that in the former case but not the latter the trying causes the appropriate movement]. Seeing a dagger involves two causally related components: the visual experience of a sense-datum of a dagger, and the real dagger [moving my arm has two causally related components: trying to move my arm, and the arm moving].

The 'sense-data' argument separates us, as observers, from the world: it is a contingent matter whether any of our perceptions are veridical; it is conceivable that they are all mistaken (the road to scepticism is opened). The 'trying' argument separates us as agents from our bodies: it is a contingent matter whether our tryings ever succeed; it is conceivable that they should all fail. But, as I will show, this is not conceivable; it is not a coherent possibility. The 'trying' argument must therefore be mistaken.[82]

Trying, like any mental act, requires an object: I never merely 'try'; I 'try to do *X*'. Tryings can be identified, and distinguished from each other, only by reference to their objects: trying to raise an arm is distinguished by its object from trying to move a leg. But how can we distinguish tryings from other kinds of mental act which have bodily movements as their objects: trying to raise my arm from imagining or wishing that my arm will rise?

The answer must be that trying is practical: trying to raise my arm, unlike imagining or wishing for its movement, is a way (is the normal way) of getting it to rise. But the idea that this is how to get my arm to rise is then internal to the trying; and the relation between trying to raise my arm, and the arm actually rising, is then logical, rather than contingent and causal. For if the relation were causal, we would have to discover that it obtains: we would discover (at an early age) that trying to raise an arm is usually followed by that arm rising, whereas trying to wiggle an ear is not followed by the ear moving. To be in a position to discover this, we would need to be able to try to move our limbs without yet having any idea that this might cause those limbs to move: but if intrinsic to trying is the thought that this is the way to bring such movements about, we could not do this.[83]

---

[82] I will not pursue the analogous argument against 'sense-data' here: but see Hamlyn, ibid.; A. O'Hear, *What Philosophy Is* (Harmondsworth 1985), 20–35; J. L. Austin, *Sense and Sensibilia* (Oxford 1962).

[83] This is the truth in the argument that volitions, being 'logically connected' to the movements we supposedly will, cannot be causes of those movements: see A. I. Melden,

When I try to do X by doing Y, I must know or have learned that doing Y is a possible method of doing X; and that knowledge normally depends on my knowledge of certain causal connections between events (between the trigger being pulled and the gun firing, for instance). I might discover various causal connections between mental phenomena and bodily effects: for example, that thinking about a fearful danger makes me shiver. If those mental phenomena are within my control, I can then use them as a way of bringing about those bodily effects: I cause myself to shiver by deliberately thinking of that danger. This is not, however, a possible picture of how we get to move our limbs: given the practical character of trying, we cannot imagine the young child engaging in a variety of 'tryings', and discovering that some of them do, whilst others do not, produce the effect which she tries to produce.

If trying were a mental activity which is contingently related to the occurrence of those movements we try to bring about, we could sensibly ask someone to 'try to beat his heart faster', just as we can ask him to 'try to move his arm' ('he beats his heart' is meant to stand to 'his heart beats', as 'he moves his arm' stands to 'his arm moves'). We would expect him to fail; but he could at least try. Now if asked to try to make my heart beat faster, I might know what to do: take strenuous exercise, for instance. But if asked to do as to my heart something similar to what I do as to my arm when I just move it (as distinct from, for example, moving it by lifting it with my other hand), I would be baffled. I know what it is to move my arm; I also know what it is to try to move my arm (for instance when there is an obstacle to moving it, or a chance that it will not move). But I do not know what it would be to 'beat my heart'; nor, therefore, do I know what it would be to 'try to beat my heart'.

'Trying to move my arm' (unless it is something like trying to move it with my other arm) is parasitic on 'moving my arm': I cannot try to move it unless I can normally just move it.[84] The young child does not (as the 'trying' doctrine must say) learn to move his limbs by discovering which mental acts he can perform which will cause his limbs to move—as I learn to drive a car by learning which physical actions I can do to cause the car to move as I want it to. We should rather see such minimal actions as moving a limb as exercises of the basic capacity for action (for movement) which human beings normally just have. A child does not learn how to move his limbs (which would imply discovering what he must do to get them to move): he has, and exercises, the capacity for physical movement, and learns how to do more complex actions by learning how to apply and

---

'Willing', in A. R. White (ed.), *The Philosophy of Action* (Oxford 1968), 70. See also Prichard's disarming admission that his account makes it impossible to will a movement for the first time: 'Acting, Willing, Desiring', above n. 1, 67–8.

[84] See Danto, 'Basic Actions', above n. 30, 56.

use that capacity. We learn how to do things by moving our bodies, but do not learn how to move our bodies.[85]

But what of the anaesthetized agent? He tries to raise his arm; and since his arm does not rise, his 'trying' must surely consist in doing something to get his arm to rise—something which is, as his failure shows, only contingently related to his arm actually rising. This would be true if 'trying' were a something; and it will seem to be a something if we suppose his defective action to be analogous to a non-defective action: if we suppose, that is, that because when he raises his arm something is done (an arm-raising), when he tries to raise his arm something is also done: a trying. But we should resist this reification of 'trying', just as we must resist the reification involved in supposing that when Macbeth hallucinates (seems to see) a dagger, he must see something, a sense-datum. 'He tried to raise his arm' is better translated as 'he raised his arm unsuccessfully'. The point of that translation is to emphasize that 'raising his arm' is logically prior to 'trying to raise his arm':[86] there is nothing else that he does in order to get his arm to rise; we can understand 'trying to raise his arm' only as a defective version of raising his arm.

The central mistake in the doctrine that all action consists in trying is that it puts the cart before the horse. It analyses 'A did X' as 'A tried to do X, and succeeded'. If this were right, we could first understand what it is to try, and then understand actions as trying which succeeds (this is the theoretical analogue of the idea that we learn to act by first trying, and then seeing which tryings succeed). But I have argued that acting is logically prior to trying both in practice and in understanding: rather than analyse action as trying which succeeds, we should analyse trying as action that fails (or might fail). This central mistake reflects two others. First, it reflects a misinterpretation of the meaning of 'try' in cases like that of the anaesthetized agent. It supposes that 'he tried to raise his arm' describes something which he did—something distinct from an actual arm-raising: but I have argued that there could be no such thing. Second, it supposes that this abnormal case reveals something that occurs in every case: that it reveals a 'trying' which can then be thought to occur whenever a person moves a limb. But this ignores the essential abnormality of the anaesthetized agent's case: rather than take his case to reveal more clearly what happens in all cases, we must see it as a case of action-failure which can be understood only by reference to (as a defective version of) the normal case in which he just raises his arm.[87]

[85] See D. Gustafson, *Intention and Agency* (Dordrecht 1986), ch. 2.
[86] See J. R. Silber, 'Human Action and the Language of Volitions', (1963–4) 64 *Proceedings of the Aristotelian Society* 199, at 215–20.
[87] See Wittgenstein, *Philosophical Investigations*, above n. 43, para. 606, for criticism of a similarly mistaken inference from the abnormal to the normal case.

4.3. *Understanding Trying*

Trying cannot be understood as a distinct component of 'raising my arm', as a something that I do in order to get my arm to rise: to understand it in that way leads, I have argued, to nonsense. But how, then, should we understand it?

The key is to realize that 'try' functions adverbially, rather than substantively. 'A tried to do *X*' does not describe a component of 'doing *X*': rather, it qualifies or modifies the (logically prior) action-description 'A did *X*'. In the context of such simple actions as moving an arm, 'try' serves typically to mark the fact of failure or of difficulty, or the perceived chance of failure.[88] Depending on the particular context, 'A tried to do *X*' might be roughly translated as, for example, 'A unsuccessfully did *X*', or 'A effortfully did *X*', or 'A doubtfully did *X*' [he was doing X but might have failed]: such translations make the point that 'try' does not describe something A did, but qualifies or modifies the bare statement 'A did *X*'. This is to say that the contextual features which make it appropriate to say that 'A tried' (the fact of failure, the presence of obstacles, the doubt which the agent need not share) are part of the meaning of 'A tried'; that 'A tried' is false, not just conversationally improper, when such features are absent. If we think of 'trying' as something, as an 'original psychological constituent of the mind',[89] we cannot recognize that these features are part of its meaning: but once we abandon that mistaken assumption, we can recognize that the truth of 'A tried to do *X*' can indeed depend on factors independent of A.

In the context of more complex actions, as when I say that Pat is trying to get her car to start, or that Bulstrode tried to kill Vincy, 'trying' still functions adverbially; and it still serves in part to mark the fact or chance of failure, or the presence of some obstacle or difficulty. I would not say (it would not be true) that Pat is 'trying to start her car' when she simply turns the ignition key of her reliable car, and it starts at once: I might say this if her car is notoriously unreliable, or if it fails to start when she first turns the key. In these contexts, however, 'A is trying to do *X*' also typically serves to relate A's action to some further goal. 'What is Pat doing?' you ask, as she is fiddling under the bonnet of her car; 'she is trying to get the car to start,' I reply. This does not describe an element of her activity (as 'she is cleaning the points' does). It rather relates what she is doing to a further end which she hopes to achieve by acting thus; and it expresses my uncertainty (which Pat might not share) about her success.

A proper account of the meaning of 'try' would involve looking in much

---

[88] See s. 3.3 above.   [89] O'Shaughnessy, 44–5: see text at nn. 72–4 above.

more detail at the variety of contexts in which it is used, and the variety
of tasks it performs as 'a way of setting actions in a certain context or construing them in a certain light'.[90] My aim here, however, has not been to
provide that complete account: it has rather been to show that 'try' does
not serve to pick out an element of every action.

5. The Vulnerability of Action

The doctrine that all action consists, essentially, in 'trying' alienates us,
as agents, from our bodies. If we move our bodies only by trying to move
them, our bodily movements are non-basic actions, done only by doing
something else (by trying): so our bodies become external objects, which
we must try to control. Now, certain aspects of my body are indeed
external to me as an agent: I cannot 'beat my heart' as I can 'move my
arm'. Aspects of my body which are normally within my agency can also
become external or even alien: someone who finds that a limb is paralysed
might portray it in thought and words as an external thing that refuses to
obey her. In extreme cases, the experience can be terrifying, as when a
person loses all sense of a limb as being part of him, or all sense of his own
embodiment.[91]

What is terrifying here is not just that something over which I normally
exercise control is no longer within my control, as when my computer
malfunctions: it is rather that I lose part of my self. For I am essentially
embodied: my body is not a separate object which I must try to control,
but is that through which I can try to control other objects. The 'trying'
theorist portrays the suddenly paralysed agent as someone who 'does' just
what he usually does when he raises his arm: the difference between his
case and the normal case is that his trying does not have its expected,
external effect. It would be more appropriate to say, however, that he has
lost a capacity which he normally has: the capacity (as an embodied agent)
to move, as far as the paralysed limb is concerned. The anaesthetized
agent, on the other hand, has not lost that capacity: rather, he is unaware
that his exercise of his capacity is being hindered.

But should not a proper recognition of the unpredictability of human
affairs, and the fallibility of human actions, lead us to see that our bodies
are indeed objects over which we do not have either complete or certain
control? It is always possible that the simplest of bodily actions should fail,
since they depend on factors outside our control; so perhaps the claim that

[90] Heath, 'Trying and Attempting', above n. 49, 196.
[91] See O. Sacks, 'The Disembodied Lady', 'The Man who Fell out of Bed' (both in his *The
Man who Mistook his Wife for a Hat* (London 1985), 42 and 53), and *A Leg to Stand On*
(New York 1984).

all action consists in trying marks a recognition of that fact.[92] For to say
'I am doing [will do] *X*' expresses confidence that I am actually doing or
will do *X*: since I can never be absolutely sure of doing *X* (even if *X* is just
'moving my arm'), however, all that I can strictly say is 'I am trying [will
try] to do *X*'. Analogously, the sceptic argues that we can never be absolutely certain that our beliefs are true: so we should strictly never say 'I
know that *P*', but only 'I believe that *P*'.

One response to this argument is that it misconstrues the ideas of
'control' and 'certainty' (analogously, the sceptic is accused of misconstruing
the concepts of knowledge and doubt). The fact that we can lose control
over our bodies, or lose the capacity to move, does not entail that we never
have control, or never have that capacity; nor does it entail that we can
never be certain of that control, or of that capacity. Another response is
to say that this argument does not lead us to 'trying' as a distinct component of all action: that it leads at most to the universal (and thus ultimately meaningless) qualification of every present- or future-tense action-
description. This argument might reflect, however, not a philosophical
deduction from the admitted fact that actions can fail, but a certain kind
of attitude to the world, one informed by a sense of our vulnerability to
chance or Fate. A religious believer may add 'DV' (*Deo volente*) to her
declarations of intent or purpose, expressing her recognition of the dependence of all human affairs on God's will: should we then take the claim
that all action consists in trying, that the 'trying' is 'all that is his',[93] as
expressing an analogous secular view?

This sense of our vulnerability to chance or Fate has motivated various
attempts to find something secure in human life which is not thus vulnerable.[94] The 'trying' doctrine, as now interpreted, offers us something secure
to set against the acute metaphysical insecurity which it reflects: however
doubtful the success of any endeavour, we can at least try; that at least is
within our control. The trouble with this suggestion, however, is that it
rests on

the false idea that ['trying'] is something which is 'in my power' in a metaphysically
radical sense in which other things are not: that is, that it is something the doing
of which does not itself depend on the existence of conditions.[95]

In her early work, Simone Weil looked for a conception of agency, of
'what I can do' (which is also what I am), that would be independent of

[92] See Ashworth, 'Sharpening', 80–2; 'Belief', 15; 'Attempts', 742.
[93] See n. 54 above.
[94] For a splendid exploration of some of these themes, see M. Nussbaum, *The Fragility of Goodness* (Cambridge 1986).
[95] Winch, 'Trying', above n. 49, 133. See also T. Nagel, 'Moral Luck', in his *Mortal Questions* (Cambridge 1979), 24, for the argument that our actions (our 'tryings') are as much a matter of luck as their effects.

'*hasard*', of chance and contingency.[96] Now neither my production of results in the world, nor my bodily actions, are independent of *hasard*: for 'it is a purely contingent matter that things [including my body] behave as I try to make them behave.'[97] Weil wanted to see 'thought' as a kind (the only kind) of pure activity, uncontaminated by *hasard*: similarly, a 'trying' theorist offers us 'trying' as what we can really be confident of doing. The trouble is, however, that 'thought' and trying are as vulnerable as anything else about us to chance or Fate: for I might

lose at any moment through the play of circumstance over which I have no control anything whatsoever I possess, including those things which are so intimately mine that I consider them as being myself. There is nothing that I might not lose.[98]

Just as factors outside my control can cause my carefully aimed shot to miss, or my arm to remain motionless, so they can prevent me from even 'trying': an interruption, a sudden mental breakdown (a mental paralysis) might prevent me from trying to do what I was all set to try to do. Once we deny, because of the vulnerability of human affairs to chance or Fate, that our bodily actions are truly 'ours', we must also go on to deny that even our 'tryings' are truly ours. Thus, even on this interpretation, the 'trying' doctrine must be rejected.

6. Conclusions and Implications

What emerges from this critical discussion of the doctrine that all action consists essentially in trying? What can we now say about the concept of action, and about its role in the criminal law?

The substance of this paper has been almost wholly negative. We cannot, I have argued, explain what 'action' is by analysing actions down into 'tryings': and although I have said something about how we should understand the concept of trying, I have given no alternative or positive answer to the question 'What is action?' Such an answer might seem implicit in my argument. I have denied that we can find an answer by asking, 'What is left over if I subtract the fact that my arm goes up from the fact that I raise my arm?'[99] Raising my arm is not a conceptually complex whole

[96] S. Weil, 'Science and Perception in Descartes', in her *Formative Writings 1929–41* (eds. and trans. D. T. McFarland and W. van Ness, London 1987). See P. Winch, *Simone Weil: 'The Just Balance'* (Cambridge 1989), 9–11. Similar points emerge from Wittgenstein's early struggles with the idea of the will: see P. Winch, 'Wittgenstein's Treatment of the Will', in his *Ethics and Action* (London 1972), 110.

[97] Winch, *Simone Weil: 'The Just Balance'*, 9.

[98] Weil, as quoted (with no source) by M. C. O'Drury, *The Danger of Words* (London 1973), 135.

[99] Wittgenstein, *Philosophical Investigations*, above n. 43, para. 621.

which we can analyse into its constituent elements by such a subtraction. Does this not then imply, however, that we should accept an account of bodily movements as basic actions: that what we basically or ultimately do is simply move our bodies?

There is this much truth in such a theory of basic actions: our actions typically involve bodily movements; and we do not typically move our bodies by doing anything else—by trying or 'willing'. But that theory cannot claim to lay bare the defining essence of agency. I sketched some objections to it above:[100] the considerations which lead us towards bodily movements as basic actions must also lead us beyond bodily movements to volitions or tryings. But if a search for basic actions thus leads us into error (into an untenable account of action as consisting essentially in 'willing' or trying), there must be something wrong with the search; and there is. What is wrong with such a search is that it assumes that we can come to understand what it is to act by a reductive analysis of action into its simpler, and therefore supposedly essential, constituents: but such a reductive analysis analyses out the very features which are essential to an understanding of human action.

Actions like 'raising my arm', the kinds of action on which the 'basic-action' theorist focuses, are very atypical actions. We often do things which involve raising an arm: we wave to a friend, make a bid, take a book from a shelf. But we do not typically just raise an arm. Basic-action theorists argue that we can understand these more complex kinds of action by seeing them as constructed from the basic action of raising my arm. I would rather say that we can understand 'raising my arm' as an action only by seeing the part it can play in such richer actions; and that simply 'raising an arm' can be seen as an action at all only by seeing it as an aetiolated version of such richer actions. What is missing from just 'raising an arm' is that context of meaning and intention which is central to our ordinary discourse about, to our concept of, human action: when the basic-action theorist strips away that context in order, as she hopes, to reveal the essence of action, she strips away what makes actions actions.

Her endeavour is analogous to that of one who hopes to explain the activity of painting by analysing it down into the particular brush-strokes which painters make. Painting does typically involve making brush-strokes: but rather than say that we should understand what it is to paint a picture by seeing that that complex activity consists essentially in making brush-strokes, we must recognize that we can see and understand the individual brush-strokes as aspects of painting a picture only by seeing the role which they play in that activity—an activity which can be understood only by grasping the context of meaning and purpose within which it takes place.

---

[100] See text at nn. 40–2 above.

We could call a single brush-stroke a painting, just as we can call 'raising my arm' an action: they merit such appellations, however, in virtue only of their relationship to richer, more paradigmatic instances of painting or action, not in virtue of their intrinsic character.[101]

The dimension of meaning is integral to human action;[102] and to understand actions as meaningful we must attend to intention, and to the kinds of social context in which actions can have meaning. If we are to answer the question 'What is action?' it is in this direction that we must look: but the kind of answer we can then arrive at will not consist in spelling out a basic set of necessary and sufficient conditions for action of the form 'A acts if and only if . . .'.[103] We will rather be explicating a paradigm (or, more plausibly, a set of related paradigms) of action, by reference to which other derivative or aetiolated kinds of action can be understood.

What follows from all this for criminal-law theory? It suggests that the 'element-analysis' approach, which seeks to explicate each crime by analysing it into its constituent elements,[104] is unlikely to bring us much analytical illumination, especially if it assumes that the 'conduct' element of an offence will consist in a set of bodily movements. Of course, if we assume that some such reductive analysis is necessary to a clear understanding of the law; and assume as well either that there is some objective distinction between an 'act' and its circumstances and consequences which we can hope to discover, or that for analytical purposes we must create such a distinction: then we will inevitably be driven in this direction, since the search for a general definition of an 'act' or of 'conduct' cannot but end with a definition in terms of bodily movements. But once we realize that such a definition does not provide us with a concept of action which could play any useful substantive role in explicating the conditions of criminal liability,[105] we will realize that this kind of analysis is not what we need. Likewise, if we cannot define action as bodily movement (or as willed bodily movement), we cannot say that an 'act' requirement as thus defined is a fundamental, normative condition of criminal liability.

It should be clear from what I have said that I am not going to offer an alternative definition of 'act', to serve the same role as the rejected definition of 'act' as (willed) bodily movement: my point is rather that both philosophers and legal theorists go wrong as soon as they begin looking

---

[101] Both basic-action theorists and those who analyse action as 'willing' or trying go wrong by focusing on bodily movements as the core cases of (overt) action: on this, see F. Ebersole, 'Where the Action Is', in his *Things We Know* (Eugene, Ore. 1967), 282.

[102] See Moya, *The Philosophy of Action*, above n. 40, chs. 4–5.

[103] Contrast Ginet, *On Action*, above n. 2, 1–2: the central question 'What is it for a person to act?' amounts to the question 'If "S's V-ing at t" uniquely designates a particular event, then it designates an action if and only if . . . what?'

[104] See esp. Robinson and Grall, 'Element Analysis in Defining Criminal Liability', above n. 4; and text at nn. 3–6, 29–31 above.   [105] See text at nn. 32–9 above.

for such a definition. We can say, and there is some point in saying, that criminal liability is typically for actions: but to understand the meaning or significance of such a slogan, we must begin by relating it to the paradigm of meaningful, intended action, not to a minimal notion of 'basic action'. A crime, we could say, is paradigmatically an intended or intentional action which satisfies a crime-description specified by the criminal law; and we can then go on to explain offences which (apparently) do not consist in such intended or intentional actions by explicating the ways in which they are none the less related to such paradigms.[106]

This is not the place to explain the details or implications of such an approach. It is also clear, however, that my argument here removes one of the philosophical foundations of legal subjectivism, in particular as regards the punishment of attempts. If we say that one whose attempted murder fails is just as culpable, and so should be punished just as severely, as one whose attempt succeeds, on the grounds that for each agent the 'trying' is 'all that is his',[107] we have embarked on a path which leads us inevitably to some mental act of 'trying' as 'all that is his'. If 'he killed V' is an 'extrinsic description' of his action, which includes more than is truly 'his', then so too is 'he fired a gun', and even 'he moved his hand'; what we end with, as a truly 'intrinsic' description of his action, will be something like 'he tried to move his hand'.[108] But I have argued that this is not a possible intrinsic description of his action. If, however, the proper description of the action of one who moves his hand is, simply, 'he moved his hand', then the proper description of the action of one who fires a gun is 'he fired a gun' (not 'he tried to fire a gun'), since the second description is no more 'extrinsic' than the first; and the proper description of the action of one who actually kills V is 'he killed V'.

The difference between a case in which I move my hand, and one in which I find myself paralysed, is not that in one case the trying (which is what is mine) succeeds whilst in the other it does not: it is rather that in one case there is an action (moving my hand) which is 'mine', whereas in the other case there is no such action which is mine. Similarly, if I actually kill my intended victim, there is an action, 'killing V', which is 'mine': that is what I have done, and done with intent. If I do not actually kill V, there is no action of 'killing V' which is mine, though there are other actions which are 'mine' ('firing a gun intending thereby to kill V'), which are such that I can properly be said to have tried to kill V.

---

[106] See my *Intention, Agency and Criminal Liability*, above n. 81, chs. 5.1 and 7–8.
[107] See text at n. 54 above.
[108] See text at nn. 52–5 above. Ashworth's claim that '[s]eparating the act of trying from the consequences is purely an analytical device' ('Taking the Consequences', this volume, 109), does not avoid this point: my argument has been that no such analytical separation is possible.

The implication of my argument is therefore that the actions of one who commits an offence, and of one who tries but fails to commit it, are different as actions: we cannot justify the claim that their criminal liability should be the same by arguing that in some strict or proper sense they have each done 'the same thing'. It does not, of course, follow from this that their criminal liability should not be the same; to show that one (even one central) argument for a certain position is misguided is not yet to show that the position itself is untenable. But my argument does open the way to an alternative view which, taking seriously the idea that we are convicted and punished for our actions, would explain why the difference between an actual and an attempted crime should indeed matter to the criminal law.[109]

[109] See my 'Auctions, Lotteries and the Punishment of Attempts', (1990) 9 *Law and Philosophy* 1, at 30–7. My argument there is, I admit, very far from conclusive (see Ashworth, 'Taking the Consequences', below, 118–20): I still believe, however, that once we abandon the untenable idea that criminal liability should depend on acts which are 'ours' in the 'metaphysically radical sense' noted above (see s. 5), and recognize the social meaning of ascriptions of criminal liability, we can explain why the difference between success and failure, and more generally the difference between acts which do and those which do not cause substantial harm, should matter to the criminal law.

Taking the Consequences

ANDREW ASHWORTH

1. The Problem of Luck

The consequences of one's acts do not always turn out in the way anti-cipated. What might be described as the expected result of one's conduct (e.g. a colleague whom one criticizes mildly for an error of judgment might be expected to feel bad about it) may be overtaken by unexpected contin-gencies (the colleague has just gone through deep personal difficulties but has not informed others about this) and might therefore be followed by quite unusual consequences (the colleague begins to shout, becomes over-anxious and then collapses through stress). Would it be right if one were blamed for these consequences? This is a dramatic example of the way in which a whole range of everyday acts may have unexpected outcomes. Some may turn out surprisingly well, others may have unforeseen adverse consequences. To the author of the behaviour, these myriad contingencies can be regarded as 'luck'. They are the unpredictable elements in human affairs, matters which lie outside one's knowledge and control.

But they are not the only vicissitudes of life which can be regarded as luck. They might be characterized as forms of 'outcome-luck', since they concern the results of behaviour that are afflicted with uncertainty. At least two other forms of luck may be distinguished. 'Situation-luck' might de-scribe one's good or ill fortune in being confronted with a given situation and then having to deal with it. Situations might arise out of an unex-pected turn of events (one happens upon a car accident which has just occurred; one's friend wins a large amount of money on the football pools) which then require some kind of response. Further back towards the springs of human action lies what Thomas Nagel has described as 'constitutive luck', that is, the element of chance in the temperament and inclinations with which each of us is endowed.[1]

Much could be said about the definition of these three forms of luck. One could debate whether the terms 'outcome-luck' and 'situation-luck' should be confined to occasions where the outcome or situation was un-foreseeable in some objective sense, or should be extended to cases in

---

Among those who have made suggestions for improving this essay, I record my particular thanks to Brian Bix, Antony Duff, Uma Narayan, Paul Sutherland, and Andrew von Hirsch.
[1] Thomas Nagel, 'Moral Luck', in his *Mortal Questions* (Cambridge 1979), 24 at 28. Nagel advances a fourfold taxonomy of luck, further details of which are not necessary here.

which it was unforeseen or unexpected by the agent. One could debate whether 'constitutive luck' is a convincing category, taking the argument that people can always learn to control, or to compensate for, their dispositions—a discussion which leads into issues of determinism and free will. For present purposes these debates can be left on one side, in the belief that it has at least been established that luck plays a significant role (if not various roles) in human life.

It is this proposition that led Thomas Nagel and Bernard Williams, in papers originally written in the mid-1970s, to argue that ethics simply cannot be insulated from the influence of luck.[2] Those aspects of life that, from the individual agent's point of view, seem to be matters of luck, are inescapable. Moralists would say that 'just as, in the realm of character, it is motive that counts, not style, or powers, or endowment, so in action it is not changes actually effected in the world, but intention.' Yet, as Williams urges, 'the dispositions of morality, however, far back they are placed in the direction of motive and intention, are as "conditioned" as anything else.' It is, he concluded, 'the bitter truth . . . that morality is subject, after all, to constitutive luck.'[3] From this point one could proceed in a number of ways.[4] One question would be whether it is possible to make an intelligible separation between certain 'intrinsic' elements of behaviour or dispositions which are not subject to luck, or at least not subject to outcome-luck, and other 'non-intrinsic' elements which are subject to outcome-luck. If this were possible, one might succeed in identifying some element sufficiently independent of luck to be a proper object of praise or blame. Is such a separation possible? If so, how should moral theory respond to it?

2. Exploring Outcome-Luck

We will focus here on outcome-luck, and begin by enquiring whether there is a plausible distinction between act and result which might be useful in this sphere. In an earlier essay I argued that the only element of an action which lies within the agent's control is the trying, the doing of all the acts which the agent reasonably believes necessary to achieve the desired end. Thus, if A and B each shoot at their victims from a distance of ten yards and A hits but B misses, the argument would be that intrinsically their actions are the same. Each of them tried to kill, and it is that trying alone

[2] Nagel, 'Moral Luck', previous note; Bernard Williams, 'Moral Luck', in his *Moral Luck* (Cambridge 1981), 20.
[3] Quotations taken from Williams, 'Moral Luck', 20–1.
[4] See e.g. Judith André, 'Nagel, Williams and Moral Luck', (1983) 43 *Analysis* 202.

which is sufficiently within their control, whereas what happens in the physical world thereafter may be affected by other forces and circumstances.[5]

Antony Duff has criticized this as being grounded in a dualistic account of action, in so far as it portrays the trying as a mental act distinct from the external bodily movements.[6] Since some of my explanations refer to the agent's 'exertion' as the basic unit of action which is essentially his or hers, there may be some doubt whether my account is dualistic and so open to Duff's criticisms. An exertion is not merely a 'mental act', but is the doing of something with a purpose. 'Trying' might be understood in the same sense. However, this fails to deal with the case of someone who becomes paralysed and who cannot pull the trigger despite trying: Duff argues (in this volume) that this possibility means that my account must be dualistic in that it separates the mental act of trying from the external bodily movements.[7] The counter-argument succeeds only if the paralysis cases cannot be set aside as aberrant instances that should not affect the general proposition. Elsewhere, Duff has taken the point that the argument can be reconstructed so as to avoid the difficulties of dualism:

The subjectivist argument . . . should rather be that, even if the paradigm of action consists not simply in trying, but in actually doing what I intend to do, a failed attempt does not differ from that paradigm in any way that should affect [responsibility].[8]

It therefore seems possible, for some types of case at least, to identify intrinsic elements of an action which are independent of outcome-luck.[9]

Separating the act of trying from the consequences is purely an analytical device. It is a prelude to, but does not establish, the proposition that it is wrong to blame people for unintended (or at least, unforeseeable) consequences. In the same way, the analysis advanced by Antony Duff in this volume, even if it is persuasive to the extent of establishing that consequences form part of actions and cannot be separated from them by any analytically satisfactory device, does not provide the answer to the question of whether people should be blamed for those consequences.[10] On this question of moral assessment two opposing positions have been urged, and they have been termed the subjectivist and the objectivist.[11] Let us return

[5] Andrew Ashworth, 'Belief, Intent and Criminal Liability', in J. Eekelaar and J. Bell (eds.), *Oxford Essays in Jurisprudence (Third Series)* (Oxford 1987).

[6] R. A. Duff, *Intention, Agency and Criminal Liability* (Oxford 1990), at 188 and ch. 6.

[7] R. A. Duff, 'Acting, Trying, and Criminal Liability', in this volume, 88–90.

[8] Duff, *Intention, Agency and Criminal Liability*, 188 n. See also Duff's arguments in his essay in this volume, particularly s. 2.

[9] This 'essence' would of course still be subject to constitutive luck, in that the person's dispositions and temperaments are a matter of chance, and are likely to influence behaviour. But that issue has been set aside for the moment.

[10] See the concluding paragraph of his essay.

[11] The terms 'subjectivist' and 'objectivist' are overworked in the criminal law, and care must be taken in the present context to confine them to the descriptions given.

to the example of A and B who each shoot at an intended victim, and suppose that A narrowly misses because the intended victim moves suddenly, but that B succeeds in killing his or her intended victim. On the subjectivist view, A and B are equally culpable, and the difference between them in terms of outcomes is purely a matter of chance. Their moral guilt ought to depend on the choices they make (which are sufficiently within their control),[12] not on chance outcomes (which are not). As Duff himself has expressed it:

It is through the intentions with which I act that I engage in the world as an agent, and relate myself most closely to the actual and potential effects of my actions; and the central or fundamental kind of wrongdoing is to direct my actions towards evil—to intend and to try to do what is evil.[13]

On this view, the consequences are not significant for moral blame. By way of contrast, the objectivist view treats the consequences flowing from conduct as part of the act itself, and regards any separation between act and consequences as unconvincing. For the objectivist, the consequences must be taken into account when assessing moral responsibility.

How can the conflict between subjectivist and objectivist views be resolved? The attraction of one view rather than the other may have much to do with intuition. There is certainly no foundational moral theory which can serve as an authoritative arbiter between them. What can be done is to test some of the supporting arguments, to probe their factual basis, to scrutinize their implications, and to raise questions about the account of morality which they presuppose.[14] At the very least this may demonstrate the weakness of some positions, leading to a search for better arguments, even if it fails to dislodge the underlying intuitions. It is in this spirit that we turn towards the proponents of objectivism.

3. The Objectivist Revival

Recent years have seen a revival of philosophical support for the objective view, that outcomes ought to be regarded as morally significant. Tony Honoré and Antony Duff have each advanced various reasons for taking account of consequences. Honoré's argument is developed in the context of strict liability for tort (i.e. liability to compensate without fault). Its basis is that luck is all around us in everyday life, and that inevitably 'our

[12] Note the word 'sufficiently': it could be argued that one's choices are inevitably affected by constitutive luck (see the third paragraph of this essay), but those who are not committed to a full-blooded determinism will accept that significant elements of choice remain.
[13] Duff, *Intention, Agency and Criminal Liability*, above n. 8, 113—words that are rather different in import from the views he subsequently propounds. See below.
[14] See E. Rakowski, *Equal Justice* (Oxford 1991), 6–12.

actions impinge on others, who resent it if the effects on them are harm-ful.'[15] We must accept that we live in a community where people are judged on outcomes, and we can assume by and large that good and bad luck will even themselves out over a lifetime. In effect, he argues, the only way we can come to terms with the vagaries of fortune is to see ourselves as part of a betting system in which we constantly gamble on our ability to do things successfully. We all accept this, particularly when we accept the windfall of good luck. Thus:

The person concerned, though he cannot be sure what the outcome of his action will be, has chosen to act in the knowledge that he will be credited or debited with whatever it turns out to be. Moreover we cannot opt out of the system by which we obtain credit for favourable outcomes; and so we cannot slough off the burden of discredit either. Finally, it is outcomes that in the long run make us what we are.[16]

Three aspects of this argument justify brief comment at this stage. First, it is founded largely on propositions about most people's reactions to the doings of others. There is empirical support for the proposition that in some situations people do tend to judge others on consequences which occur even if they were unintended or unforeseen,[17] but there are other situations where we tend to focus on the intention with which an act was done. Moreover, it remains open to question whether moral theory should be subservient to popular feelings or, at least, to what extent it should take them into account. Second, the step from empirical proposition to moral justification, from 'is' to 'ought', is fraught with difficulty. It is unclear that good and bad luck do tend to even themselves out over a lifetime: no evidence for this is given, and there seem to be some very unlucky people in the world. Even if the empirical proposition be granted, there seems no reason why the effect of the luck should be compounded by endowing it with legal significance, especially in the criminal law. Furthermore, the normative force of the argument rests to a large extent on a version of benefit-burden reasoning. Whether such reasoning is a sound basis for moral or political obligation, and of course whether the balance supplies that basis in a given situation, is open to question.[18]

The third point is more specific and is of particular relevance to the theme of this essay. Honoré asserts that 'it is outcomes that in the long run make us what we are.' His view is that

[15] Tony Honoré, 'Responsibility and Luck', (1988) 104 *Law Quarterly Review* 530, at 540.
[16] Ibid., at 545.
[17] See D. Indermaur, *Public Perceptions of Crime Seriousness and Sentencing* (Perth 1990).
[18] Towards the end of his essay, Honoré adverts to the issue of whether individuals who lack the general capacity to avoid mishaps (in the way that most people are able to) should be locked into the 'betting system' whereby they have to bear the consequences of the bad luck which befalls them.

Outcome-allocation is crucial to our identity as persons. . . . If actions and outcomes were not ascribed to us on the basis of our bodily movements and their mutual accompaniments, we could have no continuing history or character.[19]

To some extent this must be conceded. One does tend to associate people with the situations in which they find themselves and with the consequences which they cause, and it would be a very strange world if we were to make no reference to any aspect of a situation or to an outcome that was attributable to chance rather than to the author's design and effort. On the other hand, there is also a tendency to take account of culpability when assessing moral responsibility for outcomes, and that too can be said to be crucial to our identity as persons. It must be recalled, however, that Honoré is concerned chiefly with a person's causal responsibility for the outcome— she was the person who caused the accident, he was the person who broke the vase, etc. In the context of an essay in favour of strict liability to compensate others for harm, this is understandable. But on a broader canvas one might well wish to separate certain questions of moral responsibility: is she morally to blame for the accident? Does he have a moral duty to compensate the owner of the vase? These questions are taken up below. It is sufficient here to introduce the possibility that in terms of moral theory there may be distinct questions of at least three kinds—causal responsibility, responsibility to compensate, and moral blame—and that the arguments for one may not conclude the case for the others.

Duff's objectivist reasoning is directed, unlike Honoré's, specifically at the question of criminal responsibility for attempted harms as compared with completed harms. His first point is that if A narrowly misses the intended victim but B succeeds in causing a death, A is able to feel moral relief at not having a death on his or her conscience, whereas B can feel no such relief. This is intended as more than a psychological statement: it is to show a typical response to events which, in Duff's view, militates against any attempt to say that the acts of A and B should be treated as morally the same. In determining the proper moral assessment of conduct we must, he would argue, draw upon the kinds of sentiment which would be felt and expressed in ordinary social life. This raises the same questions as Honoré's first argument.

Duff's second point is that it is important to mark the finality of successful actions and fulfilled intentions. B can do nothing to alter the victim's death, whereas A has the opportunity to avoid bringing evil into the world. This prompts the question of the way in which this difference should be marked, and whether it is being argued that B deserves greater blame than A. That is one of the questions with which we began.

[19] Honoré, 'Responsibility and Luck', above n. 15, at 543.

The most telling of Duff's points is the third. A leading function of the criminal law and punishment is the communicative or censuring function, and a law which drew no distinction between completed and merely attempted offences would imply that the actual causing of harm is unimportant. Since this is morally the wrong message to convey, the presence or absence of harmful consequences should be marked.[20] This argument crosses the boundary from moral theory to legal theory, and raises questions about the differences (if any) between moral and legal responsibility. It is to these that we must now turn.

4. Moral and Legal Responsibility

Without attempting a general survey of the differences between responsibility in a moral sense and responsibility under the law, a few relevant distinctions can be identified. One is that, even though it may not be entirely true that legal responsibility is concerned only with the more serious wrongs, it is certainly the case that legal responsibility can give rise to the application of the coercive powers of the State. Moral sanctions may take the form of verbal criticism, or social ostracism, or even expulsion from a family home or a club, whereas legal sanctions may impose compulsory payments, exclusion from premises or from occupying a certain position, compulsory supervision, and even incarceration. A second distinction is that legal responsibility is declared by a court in public, as a result of the machinations of a formal system. This lends an authoritative and, where the proceedings are criminal, an official censuring element to the judgment which is unlikely to form part of most moral judgments. Largely because of the declaratory or stigmatizing effect of legal processes and the powerful impact of legal sanctions, fairness is generally thought to require that there be reasonably precise rules which are announced in advance: these are elements of the concept of the 'rule of law'.[21]

Before proceeding further, however, it is important to return to the proposition that legal responsibility (and, for that matter, moral responsibility) bears different meanings in different contexts. It was argued earlier that Honoré seemed to be focusing on causal responsibility or attribution. In law, causal responsibility must normally be established as a necessary step towards a finding of responsibility to compensate, and often for criminal liability, but it does not lead automatically to such a finding unless the legal regime is one of strict liability. Honoré's article amounts to an argument in favour of strict liability to compensate others for many harms, an

---

[20] Duff, *Intention, Agency and Criminal Liability*, above n. 8, 184–92, drawing also on his *Trials and Punishments* (Cambridge 1986).
[21] Joseph Raz, *The Authority of Law* (Oxford 1979), ch. 11.

argument which he advances on a moral as well as a legal plane. There is little evidence that he would apply the argument in the context of criminal liability and, if so, to what extent. Here the 'rule-of-law' values of certainty and predictability in the boundaries of liability seem particularly powerful, since conviction has a censuring function and may also be followed by a sentence which significantly restricts, or deprives the offender of, liberty.

It is not merely that citizens should be able to discover in advance whether their conduct amounts to an offence. It is also that the degree of censure should be proportioned to the degree of wrongdoing, because that both respects the offender as a choosing individual and serves to structure the official response of the courts rather than leaving it as a matter of discretion. It would be manifestly inadequate for a legal system to have a single offence stating that anyone who behaves in a way that is contrary to the good of society may be liable to conviction and punishment of up to life imprisonment. Its communicative function would be intolerably vestigial, its censuring function would be hopelessly vague, and the discretion left at the sentencing stage would confer enormous power on the courts on what would then be the key issue. This suggests that a principle of fair labelling should form part of a system of criminal law, so as to ensure that each offence is defined and labelled in a way which conveys the relative seriousness of the offence, and which confines the court's sentencing powers appropriately.[22] Of course this principle does not dictate particular formulae, and there is room for argument whether a system of criminal law which has a single, compendious offence of damage to property might also have a single, compendious offence of harm to individuals, or ought fairly to distinguish between minor assaults and serious woundings, for example. But this may illustrate a further difference between moral and criminal responsibility: in criminal law the behaviour has to be fitted into a pre-existing category which will specify certain elements and not others, whereas in moral discourse the blame may be expressed in a narrative and more individuated form.

5. Compensation and Punishment

Before returning to the question of how the law should deal with outcome-luck, one more issue needs to be discussed—the difference between compensation and punishment, or between civil and criminal liability. Some authors have set out to locate a distinction between civil and criminal liability.[23] It is clear that this cannot be done on the basis that a tort may

---

[22] See further Andrew Ashworth, *Principles of Criminal Law* (Oxford 1991), 71–3.
[23] See Jeffrie Murphy, 'Crime and Punishment', in Jeffrie Murphy and Jules Coleman (eds.), *The Philosophy of Law* (revised edition, Boulder, Colo. 1984); John Kleinig, 'Criminally

be committed by negligence whereas a crime requires intention or recklessness, because there are intentional torts and crimes of negligence and strict
liability. The paradigms differ, but the realities are overlapping. John Kleinig
has argued that a major difference is that the purpose of the criminal law
is to censure, whereas the purpose of the civil law is to rectify and to
distribute burdens.[24] One counter-argument is that civil judgments sometimes stigmatize or censure (e.g. a libel judgment, a finding of negligence
against a doctor), and that to some extent tort law is designed to deter
harmful and annoying behaviour, usually when the author was at fault.
Here, too, it might be argued that the paradigms differ although the realities are overlapping. The civil law is not chiefly an instrument of censure,
even though its judgments may occasionally have that effect. The civil law
is not primarily a means of prohibition or prevention, although that function
may be present and may be quite significant in some spheres. Indeed, a
further distinction is the procedural one that prosecutions are generally
brought by or in the name of the State, whereas civil suits are brought by
affected individuals. To suggest that the right of private prosecution is a
true counter-argument to this would be chimerical.

Some of the philosophical discussion on the civil-criminal distinction
proceeds as if the two forms of liability concern different behaviour. In
practice, considerable fields of conduct are the subject of both civil and
criminal liability, notably taking property, damaging property, and inflicting injury or death. One could therefore have both a criminal prosecution
and a civil action arising from the same set of facts. The civil action would
generally be brought by the victim in order to obtain compensation and/
or a remedy such as an injunction. Moreover, people may insure themselves against the risk of an award of damages (as is required by law when
owning or driving a car).[25] The criminal case would be brought 'in the
public interest' by an agency of the State, in order to censure and to
impose sentence. Individuals are expected to submit to the sentence per-
sonally, and insurance contracts against the risk being of convicted and
sentenced would probably be held contrary to public policy.[26] It may be
true, as Glanville Williams concluded almost forty years ago, that the
procedural difference (prosecution, criminal court) is the only true distinguishing mark of a crime.[27] But that means that it is the only criterion

Harming Others', (1986) 5 *Criminal Justice Ethics* 3; and Joel Feinberg, 'Harm to Others—
A Rejoinder', (1986) 5 *Criminal Justice Ethics* 20.

[24] Kleinig, 'Criminally Harming Others', previous note, at 5.

[25] This is not to suggest that it is *possible* to obtain insurance against any successful tort
action, simply that there is no legal impediment to doing so.

[26] There is nothing to prevent X from paying Y's fine for him, but it would not be
permissible for P to serve Q's prison sentence for her. On the doctrine of public policy in
insurance contracts, see G. H. Treitel, *The Law of Contract* (8th edn., London 1991), 382.

[27] Glanville Williams, 'The Definition of a Crime', [1955] *Current Legal Problems* 36.

which invariably works as a dividing line, not that it succeeds in capturing the predominant flavours of each mode of legal liability.

Just as criminal conviction may be followed by punishment, so civil liability may be followed by an award of compensation. Now the very idea of compensation is to provide the person who suffers loss, harm, or damage with 'a full and perfect equivalent', something which 'makes good' the harm.[28] It therefore follows that, once liability has been established, there must be an inquiry aimed at determining and quantifying the harm actually suffered. If a fairly small fault by the defendant led to a substantial loss or injury to the plaintiff, the award of damages could be high.[29] The defendant could complain that this is unfair, since it was a matter of bad luck that such harmful consequences ensued. One response to this is to point out the possibility of insurance, mentioned above, so that the effect on the individual is minimized.[30] Another response is that the misfortune has occurred, and its consequences must be borne either by the defendant (whose fault was small) or by the plaintiff (whose fault, let us assume, was nil). It is a question of distribution of the loss, and the less innocent of the two ought to bear it.[31] Indeed, since such cases always raise an issue of loss-distribution, the supposed moral superiority of fault-based systems of tort liability can be doubted, inasmuch as they allow the loss to rest with the (faultless) victim.[32]

The criminal law and punishment are differently directed. They are much more concerned with culpability, since their function is to censure, and that should be restricted to those who deserve it, to the extent that they deserve it.[33] Most of the serious offences require proof of intention or recklessness, whereas the normal minimum for compensation through civil law is proof of negligence. More especially, the criminal law would regard attempted murder as a very serious crime, even though the conduct might not have given rise to any claim for compensation at all. Thus, if we return to the example of A who shoots and misses and B who kills, B might be convicted of murder and A convicted of attempted murder. But, in terms of civil liability, B would be liable to compensate the victim's family for

[28] Robert Goodin, 'Theories of Compensation', (1989) 9 *Oxford Journal of Legal Studies* 56, at 59.   [29] *Quinn* v. *Leathem* [1901] AC 495 at 532 per Lord Lindley.
[30] Loss of 'no claims' bonus, and slightly higher insurance premiums for everyone, including the defendant.
[31] This leads to all kinds of complex arguments about the activities in which people engage and the risks which one is expected to run in everyday life, and might add strength to the argument for no-fault compensation by the State. These matters go well beyond the scope of this essay.
[32] Jules Coleman, *Markets, Morals and the Law* (Cambridge 1988), 180.
[33] This represents a paradigm: many modern systems of criminal law include large numbers of strict liability offences with minimal elements of culpability—see Ashworth, *Principles of Criminal Law*, above n. 22, 135–45—but in general these are the less serious types of offence.

the death whereas A might have no liability at all unless he or she had caused, perhaps, nervous shock in the intended victim. There might therefore be a sharp contrast between the high sentence and the absence of liability for compensation. The reason why attempted murder is treated as a serious offence is that the attempter *tried* to commit murder, which is the highest crime—and, in many cases, the failure arose from factors not intended by the attempter (e.g. someone else intervened, the aim was slightly inaccurate, the victim moved). The problem of attempts is hardly peripheral to criminal liability: it is crucial to an understanding of the difference between that and civil liability. It demonstrates the central significance of culpability in the criminal law, where the purpose is to censure and the punishment may restrict or deprive of liberty. It also indicates a difference between the concepts of harm used in criminal law and in the civil law: whereas there is no civil liability unless there is proof of harm, the criminal law is composed only partly of 'result-crimes', and many other crimes impose liability on the basis of conduct which is preliminary to the infliction of harm, merely because of the intention with which the person acted.[34]

The preoccupation with the mental or fault element in serious criminal offences has other manifestations. The culpable causing of a death will give rise, let us assume, to a right to compensation in the civil courts. The amount of compensation is unlikely to differ according to the degree of the harm-doer's culpability. But in the criminal courts the dispute will be over the classification of the conduct as murder, manslaughter, or some other grade of homicide. Murder will have the most stringent fault element and the highest sentence, whilst the other grade(s) of homicide will have lower fault elements and lower sentences. The criminal law is chiefly concerned with desert, that is, with whether or not the person deserves to be labelled as a criminal and, if so, what level of offence is fairly applicable.[35] Once again, culpability is a crucial issue.

6. Dealing with Unforeseen Consequences

Let us carry the argument further with a specific example which poses problems for both moral and legal systems. D has an argument with T in the street, which culminates in D punching T in the face such that T falls

[34] Both English criminal law and the Model Penal Code in the United States contain many offences defined in an inchoate mode, requiring a purposive act without the occurrence of any harm: for elaboration, see A. Ashworth, 'Criminal Attempts and the Role of Resulting Harm under the Code, and in the Common Law', (1988) 19 *Rutgers LJ* 725.

[35] Once again, this is a discussion of paradigms: legislatures use the criminal sanction increasingly as a swift and summary way of dealing with fairly minor infractions for which little or no fault will be required. See Ashworth, *Principles of Criminal law*, above n. 22 1–2.

down. He suffers a bruised cheek. This is both the crime and the tort of assault and battery. E has an argument with V in the street, which culminates in E punching V in the face in exactly the same way. V falls awkwardly, hits his head on the pavement and subsequently dies from a brain haemorrhage. Once again, E will be liable both in tort and in criminal law.

In the case of D, the result of the criminal prosecution should be a sentence proportionate to the seriousness of the assault. The criminal court might well make a compensation order requiring D to pay compensation to T, which might remove the need for a separate civil action.[36] Whether compensation comes from a civil action or through the criminal court, it should be such as to provide recompense for the nature and degree of the harm caused. In the case of E, however, matters are much more complex. Criminal liability in some systems, such as the English, might be for the serious offence of manslaughter. If E committed a battery upon V, from which a reasonable person would have foreseen the risk of some harm (albeit not serious harm), and death resulted, a manslaughter conviction would follow.[37] Subjectivists would argue that this is contrary to principle. E intended only a fairly minor battery, and it is unfair to impose the 'manslaughter' label when the unlucky result was unforeseen and unforeseeable. E does not deserve such a heavily condemnatory label when his culpability was much more minor.[38] Subjectivists would then carry the debate forward to the sentencing stage, arguing that E should be sentenced only on the basis of what he intended, not on the basis of the death which happened to result.[39] Whether or not a satisfactory analytical distinction can be drawn between what E tried to achieve (the assault) and what actually resulted (the death), it would be wrong to blame E morally or legally for the result, in view of the absence of culpability in relation to such a serious outcome.

Objectivists have rarely dealt specifically with this type of case, although much has been written on the alleged differences in responsibility between the attempter and the person who completes the crime. Duff's writings do not commit him to supporting a manslaughter conviction for E, but his arguments might be invoked here to assess the strength of an objectivist view. They suggest three reasons why the difference in consequences should

[36] Criminal courts have been required since 1988 to consider making such an order in every case of death, injury, loss, or damage. Any award would be deducted from any civil damages subsequently awarded. In practice, few victims bring a civil action.

[37] See further Ashworth, *Principles of Criminal Law*, above n. 22, 259–61.

[38] As the Criminal Law Revision Committee put it when recommending the reform of the law of manslaughter some years ago, 'the offender's fault falls too far short of the unlucky result': Criminal Law Revision Committee, 14th Report, *Offences against the Person* (1980), para. 120.

[39] The Court of Appeal's decision in *R v. Coleman* (1992) 13 Cr. App. Rep. (Sentencing) 508 seems to favour this view, although the sentence was probably raised a little to take account of the resulting death.

be recognized. First, there is a moral difference between the positions of D and E, since E will feel morally burdened with the death, whereas D has no such burden. That difference in sentiment may influence intuitions. Second, E cannot undo the results of his act, whereas D can resolve not to behave in that way again. And third, E should be censured for causing the death, since a law which convicted him merely of battery in these circumstances would be suggesting that the death did not matter. It is therefore possible to construct an objectivist case in support of the present English law of manslaughter, which holds E guilty of manslaughter even though he neither intended nor knowingly risked death or even any serious injury, on the ground that the fact that the wrongful act resulted in death must be marked. The imperative is connected with the communicative and censuring functions of the criminal law: a law which failed to mark the death might be taken to give official approval to the view that deaths do not matter, which would be morally the wrong message.

There are three interlinked reasons why the objectivist argument here should be rejected. Those reasons concern public perceptions of responsibility, the distinction between punishment and compensation, and the question of communication through laws. Public opinion seems to favour the view that sentences should take account of the consequences of an action, even if those consequences could be viewed as a matter of chance.[40] To accept this as a fact is not, however, to give a conclusive answer to the question of whether the law ought to reflect this view or not. For example, the view may be based on a misunderstanding. Some years ago in Wales there was a case in which the driver of a double-decker bus took a wrong turning and drove the bus into a low bridge, killing six schoolchildren who were passengers on the upper deck. The offence was said to have arisen from a tragic error of judgment and forgetfulness, and the court fined the driver £75 for careless driving. The mother of one victim criticized the sentence on the basis that her daughter's life had been valued at a mere £12.50. Now this is not simply an emotional reaction; it betrays a confusion. Lawyers might say that the sentence should be regarded as being based primarily on the offender's fault, and is nothing to do with the value of the victim's life—that is a question of compensation, to be decided separately. The driver was responsible for causing the deaths, yes. The driver was responsible in civil law for negligence, yes. But the driver's only liability in criminal law should be for the offence which matches his low culpability (careless driving), and not for any higher offence which includes death as part of its label.

Is there any reason why the law should deviate from this approach, simply because popular views sometimes tend to confound issues of compensation

[40] Indermaur, *Public Perceptions of Crime Seriousness and Sentencing*, above n. 17.

with issues of punishment? To put the question more strongly, should the
law deviate from this view if it were established that many or most people
did expect the sentence in this type of case to reflect the deaths caused
(even after the difference between punishment and compensation had been
explained)? The subjectivist would remain attached to the argument that
compensation should aim for equivalence, whereas punishment should be
based on the 'intrinsic' element of culpability or wrongdoing on the part
of the offender. Only if it proved impossible to convince people of this distinction, and if the criminal-justice system were losing public support because
of this, would there be a strong case for conceding ground to the objectivists.

The argument derived from the communicative function of the law would
certainly fail to convince the subjectivists. As a matter of historical fact,
English law has long included several offences defined in the inchoate
mode, which make no reference to the causing of a particular result.[41] For
example, both English law and the Model Penal Code in the United States
define the offence of impeding the arrest of an offender in terms of doing
acts 'with intent to impede the apprehension of an offender', irrespective
of whether the acts succeed in their goal or not. Have this and all similarly
worded offences been interpreted as communicating to criminals that it
does not matter whether or not they actually impede the arrest of offenders? Do laws drafted in this form really trivialize the harms involved in
such offences as procuring a miscarriage, perjury, bomb hoaxes, etc.?
Perhaps the issue takes on a different complexion when a death has been
caused. But it is open to question whether this is realistic when, as in our
hypothetical (yet by no means unusual) case, E intended nothing more
than a battery and by misfortune, in a way that was not reasonably
foreseeable, caused death. The fault and the result are simply too far apart
for a manslaughter label to communicate anything other than the misfortune
which befell both the victim and E. The criminal law is a censuring institution. It should censure people for wrongs, not misfortunes, and should
censure them fairly and proportionately.[42]

7. Dealing with Risk-Taking

Somewhat analogous but worthy of separate consideration is the proper
response to risk-taking. The law includes the fairly serious offence of

[41] See Ashworth, 'Criminal Attempts and the Role of Resulting Harm under the Code, and
in the Common Law', above n. 34, 764–6.

[42] The argument here has telescoped two issues which should, in a more detailed legal
inquiry, be kept apart. One is whether the legal labels of offences should refer to results
whose occurrence is a matter of luck. The other is whether, irrespective of the legal label,
courts should take account of unforeseeable consequences at the sentencing stage.

dangerous driving because failures to observe proper standards of driving
can have the most serious consequences for other human beings, notably
loss of life. Motor vehicles are more easily capable of causing death than
almost all other widely available articles. The proper standards are widely
publicized, form part of the driving test, and are often the subject of
reminders marked on the roads (e.g. double white lines on bends). A driver
who disregards one of the standards or 'rules of the road' often creates a
greater risk of collision with a pedestrian or other vehicle, and with it a
risk of property damage, personal injury, or even death.

Although the risk of harm is therefore central to the rationale for penalizing bad driving, it does not follow that the occurrence or non-occurrence
of harm is a sure guide to the relative seriousness of the offence. English
criminal law distinguishes between careless driving and dangerous driving,
the former consisting of minor deviations from the expected standards and
the latter aimed more at driving that falls substantially below the standards of a competent and careful driver. The essence of the distinction is
therefore in terms of the degree of fault. It is perfectly possible, of course,
that a minor deviation from the proper standard might have tragic consequences in a given situation. As we saw in the Welsh case described
above, a piece of careless driving might result in death. The subjectivist
response to this may be illustrated by reference to the decision in *R* v.
Krawec,[43] where a moment's inattention by a motor cyclist who was turning
right at a junction resulted in the death of a pedestrian. He had been
charged with causing death by reckless driving, but was convicted only of
the less serious offence of careless driving. The fine imposed at the trial
was, however, greater than it would have been for most offences of careless
driving, so as to mark the fact that death resulted. The Court of Appeal
held that this was the wrong approach:

> In our judgment the unforeseen and unexpected results of the carelessness are not
> in themselves relevant to penalty. The primary considerations are the quality of the
> driving, the extent to which the appellant on the particular occasion fell below the
> standard of the reasonably competent driver: in other words, the degree of care-
> lessness and culpability.

The Court therefore reduced the fine so as to reflect the culpability and not
the death. In effect, it was focusing on the 'intrinsic' conduct of the driver.

The reasoning behind this approach has perhaps received less attention
than it deserves. Indeed, a casual summary might suggest that the harm or
consequences are irrelevant on this view. This would be inaccurate. The
reason for having offences of bad driving is to prevent harm, and the two
offences of careless driving and dangerous driving are designed to label

---

[43] (1984) 6 Cr. App. Rep. (Sentencing) 367.

offenders according to the degree of their fault, small or large. This is not abstract fault: it is fault in creating a risk of harm of a certain kind. Thus, for the offence of dangerous driving as defined by the Road Traffic Act 1991, 'the driving must carry a potential or actual danger of physical injury or serious damage to property', a danger 'which a competent and careful driver would have appreciated', but which need not have involved actual risk in the particular case. When a subjectivist[44] refers to 'intrinsic culpability' or to the 'quality of the driving', this should not be taken to deny the relevance of harm. The important distinction is between the risk of harm and the actual occurrence of harm. What is crucial is the risk of harm which normally or foreseeably arises from the degree of deviation from the proper standards manifested by the person's driving. This is not affected by the materialization or non-materialization of the risk in the particular case. The cases already cited show that a small deviation from standards may occasionally have tragic consequences, whereas a gross deviation may give rise to no harm at all. Those results are matters of outcome-luck. Moral blame and criminal responsibility should be assessed on the degree of fault and the foreseeable risk of harm.

Discussions of the relationship between road-traffic offences and luck are not new. When the offence of causing death by dangerous driving was first introduced in 1956, it was pointed out that the dangerous driver was subject to a maximum penalty of two years' imprisonment, whereas if the same piece of driving happened to cause death, conviction was for the offence of causing death by dangerous driving, with its higher maximum of five years.[45] The Road Traffic Act 1991 continues this emphasis on consequences with its new offence of causing death by careless driving when intoxicated. In recommending this course, the North Committee argued that the public would expect a separately labelled offence where there was substantial culpability and the result was death.[46] This is an objectivist argument based on public opinion and on the communicative function of the criminal law, and is open to the same objections as those raised in the previous section of this essay. The Committee was less clear about the proper approach to sentencing in these cases. In this sphere, where fault is substantial, the Court of Appeal has tended to depart from

---

[44] At this point the use of the term 'subjectivist' will become particularly strained for lawyers, since we are discussing crimes of negligence which do not require fault in the sense of an awareness of risk on the part of the driver. In the present context the term refers to the separation of the fault from the consequences.

[45] See Sir Brian McKenna, 'Causing Death by Reckless or Dangerous Driving: a Suggestion', [1970] *Criminal LR* 67. The Home Secretary has recently proposed that the maximum sentence for this offence should be doubled to ten years.

[46] Department of Transport and Home Office, *Road Traffic Law Review*, Chairman: Dr Peter North (1988).

the subjectivist approach and to mark the death with a significant increase in the sentence.[47]

In principle, how should one assess the relative seriousness of these cases? Culpability and the distinction between punishment and compensation should again be the key elements. The primary criterion should be the risk created,[48] taking account of the magnitude of the harm risked and the probability of its occurrence. If the harm did occur, this may provide evidence which assists in assessing magnitude and probability, but resulting harm does not alter the intrinsic seriousness of the risk-taking. In the many cases where no harm occurred, magnitude and probability must be assessed by reference to the surrounding circumstances and any other relevant evidence. Sentence levels should then reflect the fact that the offence is really an inchoate crime of recklessness or negligence as to injury or death. In practical terms, this would probably mean harsher sentences for dangerous driving which did not result in death, and less severe sentences for causing death by dangerous driving. Those whose dangerous driving does not cause death or serious injury should not benefit from their good luck, any more than dangerous drivers who do cause death or injury should be penalized for their bad luck. In terms of liability to pay compensation, however, outcomes would be crucial and insurance would cover the payment in most cases.

8. Conclusions

The attraction of the subjectivist or the objectivist approach to outcome-luck rests largely on intuitions about fairness. But there are supporting arguments that can be tested, and much of this essay has been devoted to an examination of the arguments invoked by objectivists in favour of the view that wrongdoers should 'take the consequences'—or not—of their conduct. Some objectivists place considerable emphasis on the concordance of their approach with popular sentiments and public opinion. If intuitions lie at the foundation of both the rival approaches, this will be a significant consideration. But it cannot be conclusive unless it is also claimed that moral and legal responsibility should follow popular sentiments even when they can be shown to harbour elements of irrationality.

Three related difficulties with objectivism have been identified here. First, in some versions it fails to distinguish adequately between issues of

[47] Compare *R* v. *Boswell* (1984) 6 Cr. App. Rep. (Sentencing) 257, with the approach to careless driving taken in *Krawec*, above n. 43.

[48] Nothing will be said here on the controversial issue of whether the risk should have been knowingly created, or whether criminal liability for negligence is fair. Compare Ashworth, *Principles of Criminal Law*, above n. 22, 153–61, with *R* v. *Reid* [1992] 3 All ER 673.

causation, of liability to compensate, and of moral blame and criminal liability. Indeed, some expressions of popular sentiment perpetrate a gross confusion between punishment and compensation. If it can be shown that the intuitions, or at least what is inferred from feelings of unfairness, are tainted with confusion, their strength as guides to ethical principle is much diminished. Second, objectivists seem to underestimate the censuring function of the criminal law, and to neglect the pivotal importance of culpability in both liability and sentencing. Third, whilst their insistence on the communicative function of the criminal law is right, it does not follow that the criminal law should always communicate what people wish to hear, as it were. The communicative function might be regarded as educative, where it is clear that popular sentiments are tainted by confusion. Political paternalism of this kind is open to abuse, of course.

Subjectivism itself has difficulties. In particular, the focus of this essay on outcome-luck has left almost unargued the issues of constitutive luck and situation-luck, and yet at several points there has been reference to the importance of choices made by an individual, of culpability, and of desert. This takes for granted a satisfactory resolution of the debate over free will and determinism, one which makes these terms sufficiently meaningful when ascribing moral and legal responsibility. That has been accomplished by others.[49]

The legal implications of favouring subjectivism in matters of outcome-luck have been tested here in relation to three types of case: attempts and completed crimes; death resulting from a minor assault and battery; and dangerous driving. If a subjectivist were drafting a new criminal code, all these cases would be made to depend on the defendant's culpability rather than the outcome in the particular case. The effect of this on the form of the criminal law would be quite radical, since many offences are currently defined by reference to the result.[50] The same principle should be applied to sentencing. In practical terms, a decision to change the law in this way would depend on a political judgment of what the public (and the lawyers) would accept without significant loss of confidence in the system. Perhaps the change might be made gradually. The arguments of moral principle seem stronger, and this is therefore the direction in which the criminal law should move.

[49] See e.g. Anthony Kenny, *Freewill and Responsibility* (London 1978), and Michael Moore, 'Causation and the Excuses', (1985) 73 *California LR* 1091; see also the discussion of problems of capacity by Honoré, in 'Responsibility and Luck', above n. 15.

[50] See Ashworth, 'Defining Offences without Harm', in P. F. Smith (ed.), *Criminal Law: Essays in Honour of J. C. Smith* (London 1987), for a discussion of the implications, noting that several offences are already defined in these terms.

Foreseeing Harm Opaquely

MICHAEL S. MOORE

1. The Conceptual Problem with Foreseeability

Whether a harm was or was not foreseeable figures centrally in doctrines of proximate causation in both the law of torts and the law of crimes. The dominant test of proximate causation in torts makes a defendant liable when, but only when, the harm he in fact caused was, at the time he acted, foreseeable to him; and while foreseeability is not the dominant general test of proximate causation in Anglo-American criminal law, the concept figures prominently in the important notion of an intervening cause, where it is asked whether the event that is the intervening cause (of the ultimate harm) was itself foreseeable to the defendant at the time he acted.[1]

Apart from policy-based objections to the foreseeability test of proximate causation,[2] there have also been a number of conceptual objections urged against foreseeability. One of these stems from the ambiguity in

This paper is a revision of a paper given at the University of California, Berkeley, in March 1980. My thanks go to the participants at that discussion for their helpful comments, and particularly to Dan Dennett, Ken Kress, and Brian Loar, each of whom contributed detailed comments on that prior draft. The paper has more recently been defended at the Legal Studies Workshop, University of Pennsylvania Law School, and at the Legal Theory Workshop, University of Southern California Law Center, and my thanks go to the participants at those discussions as well. Special thanks go to Leo Katz at Penn and Michael Shapiro at USC for their helpful commentaries at these workshops, and to Stephen Morse for introducing me to the recent literature in cognitive psychology bearing on categorization.

[1] Much has been written either asserting or denying that the conceptions of proximate causation used in torts and criminal law are the same. Compare *State* v. *McFadden*, 320 NW 2d 608 (1982) (denying that there is any difference and holding the foreseeability of the harm to be determinative in both fields) with *People* v. *Warner-Lambert Co.*, 51 NY 2d 295, 414 NE 2d 660 (1980) (asserting that the proximate-cause test is more stringent in criminal law than in torts). The statement of the text is unproblematically true even in jurisdictions like New York, for foreseeability enters criminal law as a criterion of intervening causation (if not of proximate causation generally, as it is under the criminal law of jurisdictions such as Iowa). See Rollin M. Perkins and Ronald Boyce, *Criminal Law* (3rd edn., Mineola, NY 1982), 813, where the authors recognize the role of foreseeability in intervening-cause cases in criminal law while denying that foreseeability is the general criterion of proximate causation in criminal law.

[2] Namely, that any proper theory of corrective justice or of punishment will make moral responsibility at least a necessary condition of legal liability; that moral responsibility for a harm requires causation of that harm, as causation is ordinarily understood; and that the ordinary understanding of causation is *not* in terms of foreseeability. On this last point, the still-definitive treatment is H. L. A. Hart and A. M. Honoré, *Causation in the Law* (Oxford 1959).

what is meant by 'foreseeable'. On one understanding of this term, it is a normative notion: what is foreseeable is what the reasonable person—that is, the person of adequate ability to perceive danger and of adequate concern about that danger—would have foreseen. On an alternative understanding of the term, it is a strictly statistical notion: what is foreseeable is what the person of average capacities and concerns would have foreseen.

Another conceptual problem with the foreseeability test of proximate causation is the obvious vagueness of the term. Foreseeability is clearly a matter of degree that can vary along a smooth continuum, and the foreseeability test does not spell out *how* foreseeable a harm must be to be legally foreseeable.

Neither of these vagaries in the meaning of 'foreseeable' poses insurmountable difficulties for a test using the concept. With regard to the above-noted ambiguity, a legal decision-maker can simply stipulate either the normative or the statistical meaning. With regard to the above-noted vagueness, a variety of remedies is possible. One would be to quantify degrees of foreseeability in terms of degrees of probability, and to stipulate a certain level of probability as constituting foreseeability.[3] Alternatively, one might treat 'foreseeability' as akin to attributive adjectives, which lean on the nouns that they modify for their meaning;[4] this approach would create a sliding-scale foreseeability test, less probability being required for more serious harms, more probability for less serious harms.[5] Or yet again, one could do neither of these things and still have a serviceable concept none the less. After all, many legal concepts are vague, yet that does not prevent them from having a core of easy applications (even if they also have a penumbra of not-easy applications).[6]

More serious is a challenge to the coherence of the concept of foreseeability. I refer to what I shall call the multiple-description problem. The problem arises because of two considerations. The first is the well-known fact that there are many equally accurate ways to describe any particular thing. I, for example, am sometimes referred to by my proper name, but as often, by any number of definite descriptions: 'the other legal philosopher at Penn', 'the author of *Act and Crime*', 'the greatest lover of collie-dogs on the Penn faculty', as well as by a number of more colourful but, I hope, less accurate descriptions. Likewise, particular events are

---

[3] On the difference between ambiguity and vagueness, and on the possibility of remedying the latter by precise, numerical definitions, see Michael Moore, 'The Semantics of Judging', (1981) 54 *Southern California LR* 151, at 181–8 and 193–200.

[4] On attributive (or sometimes, 'syncategorematic') adjectives, see ibid. 182, 243 and 276.

[5] This would of course tend to collapse the foreseeability criterion of proximate causation toward the test for negligence.

[6] Glanville Williams, 'Language and the Law', (1945) 61 *Law Quarterly Review* 71; H. L. A. Hart, 'Positivism and the Separation of Law and Morals', (1958) 71 *Harvard LR* 593.

susceptible of alternative modes of reference that are equally accurate. A particular flood, for example, may have a name ('the Buffalo Creek Disaster'), and it will have many equally accurate definite descriptions: e.g. 'the largest flood of the year', 'the most talked-about event of the decade', 'the subject of a multimillion-dollar lawsuit', etc. The reason why persons, objects, events, and other particulars may be so variously described in our language should be apparent: such particulars possess many properties, and an accurate description of such a particular may be formed simply by referring to one or more of these properties and prefixing the description with the definite article, 'the'.

The second consideration giving rise to the multiple-description problem is the dependence of foreseeability on how a harm-event is described. Forty years ago, one of my predecessors at the University of Pennsylvania, Clarence Morris, observed that how the harm was described makes a great deal of difference as to whether that harm was foreseeable.[7] One can describe any harm particularly enough to say of it (under that description) that it was *unforeseeable*, or generally enough to say of it (under the second description) that it was *foreseeable*. Without some limits on permissible descriptions, the foreseeability rule of proximate causation is completely vacuous in the judicial decisions that it dictates.

Interestingly enough, Morris drew back from fully endorsing this sceptical conclusion about the foreseeability rule. He divided the proximate cause cases in torts into three classes:

Once misconduct causes damage, a specific accident has happened in a particular way and has resulted in a discrete harm. When, after the event, the question is asked, 'Was the particular accident and the resulting damages foreseeable?', the cases fall into the three classes: (1) In some cases damages resulting from misconduct are so typical that judge and jurors cannot possibly be convinced that they were unforeseeable. If Mr Builder negligently drops a brick on Mr Pedestrian who is passing an urban site of a house under construction, even though the dent in Pedestrian's skull is microscopically unique in pattern, Builder could not sensibly maintain that the injury was unforeseeable. (2) In some cases freakishness of the facts refuses to be drowned and any description that minimizes it is viewed as misdescription. For example, in a recent Louisiana case a trucker negligently left his truck on the highway at night without setting out flares. A car crashed into the truck and caught fire. A passer-by came to the rescue of the car occupants—a man and wife. After the rescuer got them out of the car he returned to the car to get a floor mat to pillow the injured wife's head. A pistol lay on the mat rescuer wanted to use. He picked it up and handed it to the husband. The accident had unbeknownst to the rescuer, temporarily deranged the husband, and he shot rescuer in the leg. Such a consequence of negligently failing to guard the truck with flares

---

[7] Clarence Morris, 'Duty, Negligence, and Causation', (1952) 101 *University of Pennsylvania LR* 189, at 194–200; Clarence Morris, *Torts* (Brooklyn 1953), 174–7.

is so unarguably unforeseeable that no judge or juror would be likely to hold otherwise. . . . (3) Between these extremes are cases in which consequences are neither typical nor wildly freakish. In these cases unusual details are arguably—but only arguably significant. If they are held significant, then the consequences are unforeseeable; if they are held unimportant then the consequences are foreseeable.[8]

Morris was certainly correct about there being varying degrees of predictability of the outcome of cases involving foreseeability. In some cases, one does know with reasonable certainty that the harm will be held by juries or judges to be foreseeable; in others, that it will be held to be unforeseeable. There are also cases where such knowledge is not possible.

The tempting though mistaken account of this phenomenon (of partial predictability) is to return to the vagueness of the word 'foreseeable'. As we have seen, 'foreseeable' is a vague word, in the same way as 'bald', 'heap', and 'red' are vague words. There are degrees of foreseeability, of baldness, of 'heapedness', and of redness, and although there are clear instances (and clear non-instances) of each, there are also borderline cases where one doesn't know what to say.

Although 'foreseeability' is a vague word, its vagueness has nothing to do with Morris's taxonomy of proximate-cause cases. One can see this by fixing more precisely on when the vagueness of 'foreseeable' does enter in. Once one has picked a description of the harm, then (and only then) does the vagueness of 'foreseeability' sometimes prevent one from knowing whether the harm was or was not foreseeable to the defendant. Whether a harm (under a description) was sufficiently likely to occur so as to say that the reasonable, average person would have foreseen it, may have no answer; or it may be in the core of 'foreseeable' or in the core of 'unforeseeable'. Like any other vague word, 'foreseeable' will have cases in all three categories. Yet one can only intelligibly ask the question, 'Was the harm foreseeable?' once one has picked a description of that harm. The taxonomy of Morris cannot thus be explained in terms of vagueness.

Unlike the vagueness problem, the multiple-description problem threatens the foreseeability test with complete vacuousness. In Morris's Pedestrian–Builder case, for example, if we describe the harm-event in enough detail, surely that event was unforeseeable. For example: 'the indentation on Pedestrian's skull of such and such a depth, and such and such a pattern', due no doubt to the precise movement of Pedestrian when he was hit and to the angle and rotation of the brick at the time of impact. These details, and the fortuity of the discrete physical forces that conjointly caused them, would be unforeseeable to all but an omniscient being. Likewise, in the Louisiana case that Morris references, we could redescribe the accident as follows:

[8] Morris, *Torts*, above n. 7, 174–7.

Plaintiff was on the highway, using it in a lawful manner, and attempted to rescue two persons injured by defendant's negligence, and plaintiff was himself injured in undertaking the rescue.[9]

Given the law's predilection to hold the intervention of rescuers to be foreseeable, I take it that the harm so described was foreseeable.

If these cases that Morris took to be 'unarguably' foreseeable and unforeseeable, respectively, can be transformed in outcome by more specific or more general descriptions of the harm, no case seems immune to this outcome-determinative redescription. Put another way, because of the multiple-description problem, the foreseeability test seems to decide no cases whatsoever.

It might seem that the foreseeability test just cannot be this vacuous in the face of the plain fact that each of us does have some capacity to predict the occurrence of future events. If each of us has some such predictive capacity, must there not be an average of such individual capacities, which average one might call the foresight of the reasonable person? Yet if we reflect on what our predictive capacities amount to, both individually and on average, we shall see how untouched is the multiple-description problem by this plain fact. When we predict that an event will occur in the future, or when we judge retroactively that an event that has now occurred was predictable in the more remote past, we are given a description of that event. 'Can you predict that a fire will occur in that house?' and 'Was the fire that occurred yesterday in that house predictable the day before yesterday?' are perfectly sensible questions to which we often know the answer. This is because the question asked feeds us a description of the event about which we are to make our predictions. We are never asked to predict an event described as, 'the event'; we are only asked to predict 'the fire', 'the automobile collision', 'the tree limb falling', or some other adequately described event. The problem with the foreseeability test is that it gives us no such descriptions of the harm. The test rather asks us to assess whether *the harm* that occurred was foreseeable. Unless we are to use the description, 'harm'—which our law makes plain we are not[10]—the test asks an

---

[9] This redescription is a paraphrase of the equally general description given by the plaintiff in *Hines* v. *Morrow*, 236 SW 183 (1922), which, as Morris noted, was apparently accepted by the appellate court in upholding the jury verdict that the harm was foreseeable. Morris perhaps drew back from the more sceptical implications of his insight because he thought foreseeability to be essential to proximate cause. As he had earlier put it, 'attempts to escape from the significance of foresight in the field of legal remoteness are attempts to escape from our culture.' Clarence Morris, 'Proximate Cause in Minnesota', (1950) 34 *Minnesota LR* 185, at 197.

[10] Such a very general description makes virtually all harms foreseeable. For if 'harm' is all that need be foreseeable, then so long as some sort of harm is foreseeable, any sort of harm is proximately caused. If, for example, it is foreseeable that a dock will suffer slight oil-slick damage from the defendant's negligently spilling virtually non-combustible oil into a

unanswerable question. It is like being asked by another to predict the occurrence of *x*, where *x* is some event that may occur in the future, but we are given no properties of *x* that would enable us to pick it out. Until *x* is given a description telling us some of its properties we have not yet been asked a complete enough question to be able to formulate an answer.

Consider by way of analogy a legal rule requiring us to judge whether two particular events are *similar*. No respects in which the events might be similar are specified, and the context of the rule does not give us any implicit criteria for isolating any property or properties with respect to which we are to judge the similarity of the events. Such a rule is completely vacuous, because it has not asked us a complete question. For every event-particular is similar in some way(s) to every other event-particular, dissimilar in other ways. Until we know the relevant respects in which we are to judge two events to be similar, we can give no answer (because we can equally well give both answers). The foreseeability rule of proximate causation asks just such an incomplete question. Such incompleteness renders the rule completely vacuous, even though when we ask ourselves complete-foreseeability questions (as we do in predictions in science and daily life), we often can give determinate and truthful answers.

2. Extensionality, Opacity, and Another Look at Morris's Problem

Such a sceptical conclusion about foreseeability may be welcome to those of a sceptical cast of mind generally, be they Legal Realists left over from a previous generation, or one or other of that more contemporary variety of what Morris Cohen aptly called the 'stray dogs of the intellectual world',[11] those gadflies whose persistent scepticism keeps the rest of us honest. Yet

---

harbour, then when the dock burns down (due to an extremely rare combination of conditions resulting in an unheard-of temperature igniting the oil), that harm was foreseeable. Harm was foreseeable and harm occurred, and if we are not given any more determinate description of the harm than 'harm', the foreseeability rule is satisfied.

Criminal law here differs somewhat from the law of torts, for in criminal law the *actus reus* prohibited by the relevant criminal statute will give (or presuppose) some description of the harm. 'Death of a human being' is a good example in homicide prohibitions. Yet the main use of foreseeability in criminal law's proximate-cause doctrine is with regard to intervening causation wherein it is asked, not whether the type of harm prohibited by statute was foreseeable, but rather, whether the intervening event that directly caused the prohibited harm was foreseeable (see n. 1 above). Criminal law no more gives authoritative descriptions of these intervening events than tort law does of the harm.

[11] Morris R. Cohen, 'The Place of Logic in the Law', (1915) 29 *Harvard LR* 622, at 625. I thus put aside the worries of some current stray dogs, that all law is sundered by what they call 'fundamental contradictions'.

in order to understand the present problem, one must forgo the headlong plunge into a broader scepticism about facts and factual descriptions that these sceptical intellectual fashions represent.

The multiple-description problem is in no way dependent upon scepticism about reality. Nor is the thesis hostage to Jerome Frank's corrosive cynicism about judges' or juries' capacity for finding (or sincerity in even looking for) the truth in particular cases.[12] On the contrary, one can assume some descriptions of the facts of a particular case are true, and others false, and that to enjoin legal fact-finders to find the truth in cases before them does not presuppose an unwarranted degree of optimism about human nature. Even so, the problem about the indeterminacy of foreseeability remains, for this problem is due to there being *too many true and accurate descriptions of reality*—not to there being no reality for any description to be accurate in representing.[13]

One way of understanding the discrete problem posed for foreseeability tests by the existence of many equally accurate descriptions of events, is to see why there is no analogous problem for most legal tests. Consider an old example I have used in other contexts, the agricultural exemption to the Interstate Commerce Act. A federal statute generally requires interstate motor carriers to obtain a certificate of convenience and necessity from the Interstate Commerce Commission. The agricultural exemption allows those interstate carriers who transport 'agricultural commodities but not manufactured products thereof' to do so without obtaining the certificate. Suppose a carrier is apprehended carrying frozen, plucked, eviscerated, New York dressed poultry interstate without a certificate. In deciding whether the exemption applies, a court might describe the items carried as 'eviscerated chickens'. Yet there is nothing that singles out the use of the predicate, 'is an eviscerated chicken', to describe the things in the back of the carrier's truck. One could equally truthfully describe them as 'chickens', 'frozen, eviscerated chickens', 'formerly feathered bipeds', 'cargo', or in a hundred and one other ways. All are accurate descriptions, and if truth is the only pedigree, each potentially could be used in a truthful statement of the facts.

---

[12] Jerome Frank, *Law and the Modern Mind* (New York 1930).

[13] Some Legal Realists perceived this point, although the use to which they put it was considerably different from that to which it is put herein. Walter Wheeler Cook, for example, in ' "Facts" and "Statements of Fact" ', (1936) 4 *University of Chicago LR* 233, used the point to urge that the old pleading requirement that one state the facts constituting a cause of action provided no real guidance to a pleader, given the many possibilities of different description. Similarly, Felix Cohen implicitly relied on the point in urging that there could be no value-free conception of precedent that enjoined a judge to discover the rule of a previous case from just the decision and the facts of the earlier case. ('The Ethical Basis of Legal Criticism', (1931) 41 *Yale LJ* 201; the point is more convincingly pressed home in Julius Stone, *Legal Systems and Lawyer's Reasonings* (Stanford, Calif. 1964), ch. 7, s. 12.)

So far this multitude of equally true factual statements is not much of an embarrassment. A legal fact-finder should simply sift through all factual descriptions used by witnesses, decide which are true descriptions of what happened and which are relevant to the authoritative language it is his office to apply, and ignore the rest. The only difficulties of there being so many descriptions are practical ones—that, given limited time and limited evidence, it is more difficult to find the relevant descriptions, and mistakes will sometimes be made. There is no problem of different legal conclusions depending on which description of the things carried is used.

To be sure, every legal standard, either by itself or in conjunction with others, must *potentially* license an inference to opposite conclusions. In the example just given, the Interstate Commerce Act not only provides that if an item is an agricultural commodity and not a manufactured product thereof it may be carried by a non-certificated carrier; the Act also provides that (with further exceptions here ignored) if an item is *not* an agricultural commodity, or *is* a manufactured product of an agricultural commodity, then it may be carried only on a certificated carrier. This means that the statute licenses an inference to either result: a certificate is not required for the interstate carriage of certain classes of items, but is required for all the rest. The same authoritative legal language potentially licenses contradictory inferences.

The assumption, of course, is that any one case will fall on either one side of the line or the other, that any particular item will be classed either as agricultural or non-agricultural, manufactured or not manufactured, in which event only one conclusion will be deducible *in any given case*. And this assumption is borne out by any plausible interpretation of the phrase, 'manufactured product'. Suppose an independently sufficient criterion of an agricultural commodity being transformed into a manufactured product is that it is killed. Slaughtered cattle, frozen tomatoes, and eviscerated chickens, would thus all be manufactured products. Does it matter how the things in the carrier's truck are described in order truthfully to predicate 'killed' of them? Rather clearly it does not. However you describe those items, that they have been killed is true of them. (Under some descriptions, e.g. 'cargo', one would get curious combinations; but one would not get a change of truth-value of the sentence completed by the predicate, 'is killed'.) Thus, as 'chickens', as 'eviscerated chickens', as 'formerly feathered bipeds', we will be equally truthful in saying, they have been killed. Hence, under the suggested criterion of 'manufactured product'—the 'killed' criterion— how the things in the truck are described doesn't matter.

There is a good reason for this. It is known as Leibniz' Law. Leibniz' Law holds that for any two things x and y, if x is identical with y, then anything truly predicable of x has to be truly predicable of y, and vice versa.[14] Put in other words, if two putatively distinct particulars are in reality one and the same thing, then they are indiscernible with respect to all of their properties at any one time. Thus, if x is an eviscerated chicken, and y is a formerly feathered biped, and x is the very same object as y, then anything that can be said of x can be said of y without change of truth-value.

Leibniz' Law is generally thought to be a basic characteristic of any language adequate for science.[15] Scientific laws require that they be true of given objects in the world, no matter how those objects are described. This is usually summarized by saying that the language of science is extensional. In so far as the law employs an extensional language—a language in which one may substitute different descriptions of the same things without change of the truth-values of the sentences in which such descriptions occur—the problem of arriving at contradictory decisions from the same legal standard will not arise.

'Foreseeability' does not seem like 'manufactured product' and other, more typical legal standards in this respect, for how the harm is described matters to the truth of expression of the form, 'that harm was (un)foreseeable'. Why this is so for words like 'foreseeability' has been the subject of considerable attention in twentieth-century philosophy. From Frege[16] through the important work of W. V. Quine,[17] to Quine's collaborators and critics,[18] a good deal of effort has been devoted to working out an account of various contexts in which Leibniz' Law does not straightforwardly appear to hold. These contexts have been notably two: modal contexts, for example, where one might say, 'necessarily, nine is greater than five', and the contexts of what Russell called the propositional attitudes, for example, where one

---

[14] In the symbols of the predicate calculus with quantification and identity that I will use throughout these footnotes:

$$(x)\ (y)\ [\ (x = y) \supset (Fx \equiv Fy)\ ]$$

I shall ignore interpretations of Leibniz' Law other than the indiscernibility of identicals that make the truth of the Law more questionable. See e.g. Mark Richard, *Propositional Attitudes* (Cambridge 1990), 199–200.

[15] The most sustained contemporary argument to this conclusion is W. V. Quine's, most notably in his *Word and Object* (Cambridge, Mass. 1960); see also his 'The Scope and Language of Science', in Quine, *The Ways of Paradox* (Cambridge, Mass. 1966).

[16] Gottlob Frege, 'On Sense and Reference', originally published in (1892) 100 *Zeitschrift für Philosophie und Philosophische Kritik* 25, translated and reprinted in P. T. Geach and M. Black, *Philosophical Writings of Gottlob Frege* (Oxford 1960).

[17] In addition to *Word and Object*, above n. 15, see particularly 'Reference and Modality', in Quine, *From a Logical Point of View* (Cambridge, Mass. 1953), and 'Quantifiers and Propositional Attitudes', in Quine, *The Ways of Paradox*, above n. 15.

[18] A series of essays on Quine's work on these topics is collected in Leonard Linsky (ed.), *Reference and Modality*, (Oxford 1971), in D. Davidson and J. Hintikka (eds.) *Words and Objections*, (Dordrecht 1969), and in P. Hahn and P. Schlipp (eds.), *The Philosophy of W. V. Quine* (La Salle, Ill. 1986).

might say, 'Ralph believes the man in the brown hat is a spy.' Since the latter construction is the one of importance to law, I shall focus my attention on it exclusively. Even so limited, what follows is but a sketchy summary of a view on propositional attitudes that would be controversial in any detail.

It is commonly said that there are two problems about the propositional attitudes: failure of substitutivity, and failure of existential generalization. Both are closely related,[19] but I shall discuss each in order. To revert to Quine's now classic example:[20] suppose someone, call him Ralph, believes that a man he has seen in a brown hat is a spy. Suppose Ralph sees a grey-haired man on the beach, whom he knows to be a distinguished citizen; Ralph, thinking of spies, says to himself that that man, the man on the beach, is no spy. As it turns out, 'the man in the brown hat' and 'the man on the beach' are different descriptions of one and the same man, whose name is Ortcutt, although Ralph did not know this. How should we describe Ralph's beliefs?

One thing that Ralph rather clearly believes is that the man in the brown hat is a spy. Let us represent this as follows:

(1) Ralph B (the man in the brown hat is a spy).

By hypothesis, it is also true that:

(2) The man in the brown hat = the man on the beach.

If Leibniz' Law held, (1) and (2) would yield:

(3) Ralph B (the man on the beach is a spy).

Yet (3) contradicts what Ralph himself would say about what he believes; Ralph would say that it is not the case that he believes that the man on the beach is a spy.[21] There is thus an apparent failure of substitutivity.

Turning to the second problem, failure of existential generalization: it is a rule of inference of modern logic that one may quantify open sentences with the existential quantifier. What this means in English is that if one predicates something about some one particular thing—for example, spyhood about the man in the brown hat—one is entitled to infer that

[19] For the argument that these two failures come to much the same thing, see Leonard Linsky, 'Reference, Essentialism, and Modality', in his *Reference and Modality*, above n. 18. For a more complicated view, urging that there are cases where there can be one kind of failure without the other, see Brian Loar, 'Reference and Propositional Attitudes', (1972) 81 *Philosophical Review* 43.

[20] In 'Quantifiers and Propositional Attitudes', above n. 17.

[21] To be distinguished from something else Ralph would say, namely, that he believes that the man on the beach is not a spy. The non-belief in the text would be represented by: it is not the case that Ralph B (the man on the beach is a spy); the belief just distinguished would be: Ralph B (it is not the case that the man on the beach is a spy).

'there is someone such that he is a spy.'[22] This move is known as existential generalization both because one has generalized—one is no longer talking of some one particular person but of 'someone'—and because one is committed to the existence of some thing by saying, 'There is . . .'.

Existential generalization fails for sentences like (1). If we were to apply this rule of inference to (1) it would yield:

(4) There is someone such that Ralph B (he is a spy).[23]

Sentence (4) does not follow from (1) for the reason that (3) did not follow from (1): it does not take into account the fact that Ralph's beliefs about someone being a spy depend on a particular description of that person. Describe him as 'the man in the brown hat', and Ralph believes him to be a spy; describe him as 'the man on the beach', and Ralph has no such belief. (4) fails to take this dependence upon description into account, for it asserts that it is about an object in the world—Ortcutt—that Ralph has his beliefs about spyhood; and this is not true of Ralph, for he believes that the man in the brown hat is a spy but he does not believe that the man on the beach is a spy, even though these are seemingly two different descriptions of Ortcutt. (4), accordingly, does not follow from (1), even though the rule of inference known as existential generalization says that it should.

These two peculiarities of constructions using '. . . believes that . . .' extend throughout the propositional attitudes. Mental-state descriptions using constructions such as '. . . intends that . . .', '. . . knows that . . .', '. . . is aware that . . .', '. . . wants that . . .', '. . . hopes that . . .', '. . . foresees that . . .', and the like, will share these failures of substitutivity and existential generalization. Many descriptions of actions will also utilize this kind of construction. If, for example, Ralph orders (selects, requests, seeks, asks for) the largest room in an inn, the true identity statement, 'the largest room in the inn = the dirtiest room in the inn', does not license one to conclude that Ralph ordered (selected, requested, sought, asked for) the dirtiest room in the inn.

Speaking very generally, there are only three strategies for dealing with this impasse between the demands of identity and our usage of contexts like that created by 'foreseeable', 'intend', and the like. The first strategy is to amend our notions of numerical identity and of modern logic to allow simply that there are exceptions to Leibniz' Law and existential generalization for these kinds of constructions. Such a strategy must distinguish expressions like:

(5) The man in the brown hat is a spy,

---

[22] From Sx (where 'S' is the predicate, 'is a spy') to $(\exists x)\, Sx$.

[23] $(\exists x)\, [\text{Ralph B}\,(Sx)]$. To be distinguished from the notional, Ralph B $[\,(\exists x)\,(Sx)\,]$. See below.

from expressions like (1). One would admit that Leibniz' Law, together with (5) and the identity statement given earlier as (2), would yield:

(6) The man at the beach is a spy.

But, on this view, the inference to (3) from (1) and (2) would be said to be barred because Leibniz' Law simply does not apply to the propositional attitudes.

This strategy is not only *ad hoc*, but it is wildly counterintuitive to our understanding of identity. If the phrase 'the man in the brown hat' as used in (1) truly refers to Ortcutt, so that (1) no less than (5) asserts something about Ortcutt (namely, in (1), a relation of believed-to-be-a-spy-by-Ralph), then that same thing should be assertable about Ortcutt no matter how he is described. Leibniz' Law, after all, only asserts the very plausible idea that qualitative identity follows numerical identity, that is, that anything has the same properties no matter how it is described. If identity doesn't mean this, it is hard to see what it does mean.[24]

Given that our notion of identity bars the postulating of some *ad hoc* exception to Leibniz' Law for constructions like '. . . is foreseeable', a second and more tempting strategy is to deny the insight of Morris with which we began. That is, it may be tempting to deny that how you describe the harm affects whether that harm is foreseeable. Then there would be no need to create exceptions to Leibniz' Law.

To see whether this is possible, let us return to our friend Ralph. On this view, we should take the phrase, 'the man in the brown hat', as used in (1), to refer to Ortcutt, but hold Leibniz' Law and existential generalization to be exceptionless. This view would then go on to say that Ralph does have the belief he is said to have in (3), despite his disclaimer that he doesn't; this view would also say that (4) logically follows from (1). Both of these last moves come to the same thing: what they presuppose is that the objects of Ralph's beliefs are not individuated by descriptions of real-world objects, but by the underlying identities of the real-world things (here, Ortcutt) themselves. What Ralph believes of Ortcutt under one description, he also believes under any other, on this view.

Such a view, rejecting the dependence of the propositional attitudes upon descriptions of their objects, was implicitly adopted by another of my predecessors at the University of Pennsylvania, Edwin Keedy.[25] In Keedy's

---

[24] See e.g. Neil Wilson, *The Concept of Language* (Toronto 1959), 39 ('If identity does not mean universal interchangeability, then I do not really understand identity at all'); D. Follesdal, 'Quantification into Causal Contexts', in Linsky (ed.), *Reference and Modality*, above n. 18, 56 ('tampering with the substitutivity of identity may easily make the notion of identity unintelligible').

[25] Edwin Keedy, 'Criminal Attempts at Common Law', (1954) 102 *University of Pennsylvania LR* 404.

work, the concept of intention was at issue, not belief or foresight, but
the view was none the less the one here considered. Keedy was seeking
to elucidate the common-law test for when a criminal attempt was 'legally
impossible' and therefore not punishable. The test centrally turns on the
intention of the accused: if he had succeeded in doing all he intended to
do and the result still would not have been criminal, then the attempt is
legally impossible. Two of Keedy's applications of this test were:

If A takes an umbrella which he believes to belong to B, but which in fact is his
own, he does not have the intent to steal, his intent being to take the umbrella he
grasps in his hand, which is his own umbrella. . . . If a man mistakes a stump for
his enemy and shoots at it, notwithstanding his desire and expectation to shoot
his enemy, his intent is to shoot the object aimed at, which is the stump.[26]

Unpacked, the first hypothetical asserts that from:

(7) A intends (take that umbrella)

and the true identity

(8) that umbrella = A's own umbrella

it follows that:

(9) A intends (take A's own umbrella).

This, surely, is to abuse the concept of intention. To deny significance
to differing descriptions of the intention's object is to alter radically our
understanding of what an intention is. Moreover, the altered concept is
not a serviceable one for making discriminations in culpability. Consider
the legal impossibility test for criminal attempts. On Keedy's understanding of intention, all instances of attempts become cases of non-punishable
legal impossibility. Take the pickpocket cases:

(10) The defendant intends (reach into this pocket).

Suppose the would-be pickpocket thought there was money in the pocket,
but, as it turned out:

(11) This pocket = the empty pocket.

Therefore:

(12) The defendant intends (reach into the empty pocket)?

Surely not. The remedy to prevent this kind of wholesale exculpation of
criminals who by happenstance are unsuccessful, is to give 'intent' its
normal meaning.

---

[26] Ibid., 466–7.

The same holds true for 'belief', 'foresight', and 'foreseeability'. Imagine a case involving a defendant who wielded a knife in such a way that he cut off the plaintiff's left arm. Suppose that the defendant was engaged in some other activity, but foresaw that the plaintiff would move in such a way that the plaintiff's left arm would be cut. Analogously to sentence (1) above discussed we can say:

(1a) The defendant foresaw (the cutting of the plaintiff's left arm).

Suppose that the cutting of the plaintiff's left arm was also the cutting *off* of the plaintiff's writing arm, the plaintiff being left-handed and the cut being rather severe. The following identity statement is true:[27]

(2a) The cutting of the plaintiff's left arm = the cutting off of the plaintiff's writing arm.

If 'foresaw' were given Keedy's kind of reading, it would follow both that:

(3a) The defendant foresaw (the cutting off of the plaintiff's writing arm),

and

(4a) There is some event of arm-cutting such that defendant foresaw that very event.

Just as before with respect to 'belief', (3a) and (4a) do not seem to square with what we mean by 'foresee'. (3a) does not follow from (1a) and (2a), for it matters how the harm is described. If the defendant doesn't know that the plaintiff is left-handed, or that the cut would amount to a cutting off, then (3a) is false. Similarly, the existentially generalized (4a) is false because it suggests that the defendant foresaw the harm under any description, which he didn't. 'Foresee', like 'intent' and 'belief', depends on how the object of foresight is described.

The construction, '. . . was foreseeable by . . .', will share this dependence upon description with 'foresee'. If we adopt the statistical notion of foreseeability, harms that are foreseeable are harms that the average, reasonable person in the defendant's situation would have foreseen. The average or reasonable person—the person of average foresight—foresees in the same way as do the rest of us: opaquely (that is, relative to some description of what is foreseen).

A more limited version of this second strategy (denying a dependence on description of the propositional attitudes) would be to regard the words

---

[27] Some 'fine-grained' modes of individuating particular events would not think this identity to be true. See e.g. Alvin Goldman, *A Theory of Human Action* (Englewood Cliffs, NJ 1970), ch. 1. For a defence of the 'coarse-grained' mode of individuating events, see Michael Moore, *Act and Crime* (Oxford 1993), ch. 11.

naming such attitudes as having two senses, one of which allows substitutivity and existential generalization. Such a sense would be what Quine once called the 'transparent' (or '*de re*') sense of 'belief' (to be opposed to the more usual 'opaque' or '*de dicto*' sense of 'belief').[28] 'Belief' is called transparent when it allows substitution of identicals, opaque when it resists it. Suppose in lieu of (1) one said:

(13) Of Ortcutt Ralph B (he is a spy).

According to Quine what is meant by (13) is that Ralph believes of Ortcutt, under any description or name, that he is a spy. If so, 'belief' in (13) would be used transparently. So used, (14) and (15) would follow from (13) because of Leibniz' Law:

(14) Of the man in the brown hat Ralph B (he is a spy).
(15) Of the man on the beach Ralph B (he is a spy).

Similarly, (4) would follow from (13) by existential generalization:

(4) There is someone such that Ralph B (he is a spy).

Notice that on such an account, 'belief' (and all the words used in the propositional attitudes) is irreducibly ambiguous. With a definite singular term such as 'the man in the brown hat', we may mean either (1) or (14) in our use of 'belief'. Quine initially thought that the same ambiguity could be detected when one uses the *in*definite singular term,[29] as when we say that *a* person (i.e. someone) is a spy. When we say that Ralph believes someone is a spy, we may mean (4) (there is some one particular person Ralph believes to be a spy); or we may mean:

(16) Ralph B (someone is a spy).

(16), unlike (4), means only that Ralph believes there are spies, while having no such belief about any particular person. Ralph's belief construed as (16) is not, as Quine mentions,[30] an occasion for calling the FBI, although construed as (4), it is. According to Quine's initial thought, (4) commits one to using 'belief' transparently, for no particular name or description is used in (4) with which to refer to the person believed to be a spy by Ralph.[31] (16), by way of contrast, does not commit one to using 'belief' transparently, because Ralph does not have a belief about any

---

[28] Quine, *Word and Object*, above n. 15, s. 30.
[29] Quine, 'Quantifiers and the Propositional Attitudes', above n. 17; see also *Word and Object*, above n. 15, s. 31. A singular term is one that refers to a particular thing (as opposed to predicating some quality to it); an indefinite singular term is a singular term preceded by the indefinite article, 'a', which can usually be translated as the existential quantifier, 'some'.
[30] Ibid.
[31] Ibid. Quine's intentionally paradoxical formulation: 'indefinite singular terms need referential position because they do not refer.'

particular person so that the question of the substitutability of different names or descriptions of that person does not arise.

The basic problem with this two-senses account of the propositional attitudes lies in the continued oddity of the supposed transparent sense. Notice, first of all, that 'belief' taken transparently commits one to ascribing an indefinitely large number of beliefs to Ralph if we ascribe any belief to him. If we say, for example, that Ralph believes that Ortcutt is a spy, then we would be committed to saying that Ralph has a similar belief of spyhood about Ortcutt under any name or description which a native speaker of the language (but not necessarily Ralph!) might use to refer to Ortcutt. Similarly with taking, for example, 'intention' transparently: if one asserts that Ralph intended to cut off George's left arm, one would be committed to an indefinitely large number of intentions on Ralph's part. For example, Ralph intended to cut off George's writing arm, if George is left-handed; Ralph intended to cut off George's dirty arm, if George's left arm is dirty, etc.[32] Transparency seems to commit us to a mental life and a mastery of our language far greater than we in fact have.

Secondly, taking 'belief' to have a transparent sense leads one either to ignore what the believer himself would say about his beliefs or to ascribe numerous pairs of contradictory beliefs to him. Take our friend Ralph again: if we take 'belief' in (1) as transparent, then we are committed to (3). Yet Ralph would say two things related to (3):

(17) It is not the case that Ralph B (the man on the beach is a spy).

And:

(18) Ralph B (it is not the case that the man on the beach is a spy).

(17) is the contradictory of (3);[33] to accept (3) is thus to ignore what Ralph himself would say about his beliefs. (18) is not the contradictory of (3); yet if we regard both (3) and (18) as true, we have ascribed beliefs to Ralph that have contradictory propositions as their contents.[34]

While recognizing some of these difficulties with postulating a transparent sense to 'belief', Quine none the less felt he was driven to such a sense in order to give an account of statements such as (4). More recent

---

[32] On a transparent reading of 'intention', see Michael Moore, 'Intentions and *Mens Rea*', in Ruth Gavison (ed.), *Issues in Contemporary Legal Philosophy* (Oxford 1987).

[33] For a qualification of this, see David Kaplan, 'Quantifying In', in Davidson and Hintikka (eds.), *Words and Objections*, above n. 18, 274.

[34] Which is, as Quine himself points out, *almost* to say of Ralph that he believes a contradiction. If (3) and (18) imply: (19) Ralph B (the man on the beach is a spy, and it is not the case that the man on the beach is a spy), then Ralph does believe a contradiction. Only by denying the implication of (19) from (3) and (18) does Quine avoid ascribing belief in a contradiction to Ralph on a transparent reading of 'belief'. See Quine, 'Quantifiers and the Propositional Attitudes', above n. 17.

analyses, however, have shown that the very real distinction between the two uses of the indefinite article in (4) and (16) can be maintained *without* a transparent sense of 'belief'. One cannot maintain both that 'belief' has two senses, opaque and transparent (as above defined), and that there is the relation between such senses that Quine envisioned,[35] without leading to a collapse of the distinction (between (4) and (16)) that Quine was attempting to maintain.[36] The upshot of this and the preceding considerations is that the idea of there being a transparent sense to 'belief' is a mistake.[37]

I conclude that we can tamper neither with the notion of identity nor with the description-dependence of the propositional attitudes in a way that alleviates the seeming conflict between the demands of each. Nor is Quine's purported half-way house a real option. One response to this dilemma would be to adopt the attitude of complete scepticism about terms like 'foreseeability': they are literally without any sense whatsoever. This was ultimately Quine's own attitude: if modal discourse and discourse about the propositional attitudes could not be regimented to fit within the extensional language of science, then they should be dispensed with in serious discussions.[38] Such an attitude, of course, is easier to state than to live with, particularly in a discipline such as the law, whose doctrines are heavily laced with distinctions based on the propositional attitudes of belief, intention, and foresight.

The only other alternative is to adopt the third strategy available here: we should reconstrue the seemingly clear reference of the words appearing

---

[35] Ibid. 106.

[36] Quine originally thought that one could derive a transparent usage of 'belief' from any opaque usage. If Ralph believes (opaquely) that Ortcutt was a spy, and Ortcutt truly exists, then one could say that Ralph believes (transparently) of Ortcutt that he is a spy. The problem for this view of the relation between the two supposed senses of 'belief' was pointed out by Kaplan: assume that Ralph believes (opaquely) that someone (but no particular person) is a spy. If Ralph is like most of us, he will believe (opaquely) that some one spy is the shortest spy. Thus, Ralph will believe (opaquely) that the shortest spy is a spy. Yet if there is someone who is the shortest spy, it follows from Quine's notion of the relation between the senses of 'belief' that: Ralph believes (transparently) of the shortest spy, that he is a spy. Since we are now using 'belief' transparently, we may apply existential generalization to yield: there is someone such that Ralph believes him to be a spy. What we would have just accomplished is to merge what we wished to keep separate, namely the two senses of saying that Ralph believes that someone is a spy; for the argument just completed would show that the one sense of the expression implies the other. Kaplan, 'Quantifying In', above n. 33, 220. Quine came to agree with the form of this objection. See Quine, 'Replies', in Davidson and Hintikka (eds.), *Words and Objections*, above n. 18, 337–8 and 341–2.

[37] Although Kaplan would not perhaps so state his conclusion, his analysis of the transparent sense in terms of the opaque sense has the effect of eliminating the former as a distinct sense. Kaplan's limitations on the 'exportation' of an opaque usage of 'belief' into a transparent usage become in effect limitations on the names or descriptions one can substitute (or existentially generalize over) in opaque contexts. In addition to the end of Kaplan's essay, above n. 33, see Quine, 'Replies', above n. 36, 342.

[38] Quine, *Word and Object*, above n. 15, 221.

in the objects of the propositional attitudes. Perhaps 'the man in the brown hat' in (1) or 'the man on the beach' in (3) do not refer to Ortcutt, a particular; similarly, perhaps 'the harm done' does not refer to a particular event in the foreseeability test (making one liable if *the harm done* was foreseeable). If such phrases do not refer to a particular, then there would be no necessity to say that they refer to the same particular. If the phrases 'the man in the brown hat' in (1) and 'the man on the beach' in (3) do not refer to one and the same man, Ortcutt, Leibniz' Law need not be violated by denying an equivalence between (1) and (3). Put another way: there need be no substitutivity of descriptions, because they are not descriptions of the same thing. Similarly, there is no reason to believe that one could generalize over people, as in (4), because no individual person is referred to by the phrase 'the man in the brown hat' in (1).

At this point one might appropriately ask, but if 'the man in the brown hat' in (1) does not refer to Ortcutt, the man, to what does the phrase refer? The difference between Quine and Frege lay in their answer to this question. A sceptical Quinean will say that the phrase is simply unclear in its reference—it is 'referentially opaque' in the manner of indirect discourse.[39] For Frege, by way of contrast, the phrase 'the man in the brown hat' refers to the *concept* (or sense or intension) of the man in the brown hat, but refers only 'indirectly' to the man in the brown hat himself.[40]

There are severe difficulties in working out either of these suggestions for statements like (1), where Ralph's belief seems plainly to be about a determinate particular, namely, a person he knows called Ortcutt. In some sense of aboutness, the phrase Ralph uses—'the man in the brown hat'— must be about Ortcutt, a particular. Any attempt to shift the referent of 'the man in the brown hat' from Ortcutt must accommodate this stubborn fact.

Things are more congenial for this reference-shifting strategy with regard to foreseeability. Foreseeability, like intentions and predictive beliefs but unlike present beliefs, by its nature deals with *future* events, events that have not occurred at the time the agent forms his predictive beliefs or intentions. Unlike objects or events such as Ortcutt, which exist when the subject forms his mental state, it is thus less plausible to suppose that the mental states formed about future events take those particular events as their objects. Thus, the shift-in-reference strategy holds more promise for mental states involving future events, in that we may not have to accommodate the stubborn fact we face for present beliefs and other similar

---

[39] Indirect discourse is where we paraphrase what another said, as in: 'John said that logic is fun.' Unlike direct quotation (such as 'John said, "Logic is fun" ', where the reference of 'Logic is fun' is to the exact utterance of John), the reference of 'logic is fun' is unclear in the paraphrased, indirect discourse.

[40] Gottlob Frege, 'Thought', in P. F. Strawson (ed.), *Philosophical Logic* (Oxford 1967).

mental states. I shall thus explore next what 'the harm' might refer to in the foreseeability test, if it does not refer to the particular harm-event that in fact occurred.

3. The Ontology of Foreseeability

We can see what sort of thing we might be referring to when we say that *the harm* is or is not foreseeable, if we repair to another context in which the multiple-description problem has loomed large. This is the context of causal statements proper, where we say things like, 'The spark caused the fire'. This shift of contexts is not only useful for illustration of the onto-logical possibilities for foreseeability statements; ultimately, in order to make sense of foreseeability we need to make sense of causal statements too, for we need to make sense of the idea that an agent is liable for just those foreseeable harms that he has in fact caused. We need, in other words, to link *what* it is that must be foreseeable to *what* it is that must be caused, since our liability rules in torts and criminal law assume some such linkage.

The answer that is most immediately suggested is that the *what* in both instances is the same, and that it is a particular event. The agent who sends a spark into an inflammable environment in fact causes *the fire* that ensues, and *the fire* he caused was a foreseeable consequence of his spark-emitting activity—where 'the fire' refers to a particular event that occurred at a certain place during a certain interval of time. As we have seen, this most intuitive answer gives rise to insurmountable difficulties with regard to 'foreseeability'. Many have thought that this answer gives rise to equally trenchant problems for causal statements too.[41]

Whether the latter turns out to be true depends on how one analyses the causal relation. The dominant analysis in both law and philosophy has been a counterfactual analysis: either the familiar, necessary-condition analysis of the law's *sine qua non* test, or John Stuart Mill's sufficient-condition test, or Richard Wright's necessary-element-of-a-sufficient-set test,[42] or John Mackie's insufficient-but-necessary-element-of-an-unnecessary-but-

---

[41] Some of the literature on the extensionality of causal statements includes G. E. M. Anscombe, 'Causality and Extensionality', (1969) 66 *Journal of Philosophy* 152; Adam Morton, 'Extensional and Non-Truth-Functional Contexts', (1969) 66 *Journal of Philosophy* 159; Follesdal, 'Quantification into Causal Contexts', above n. 24; J. L. Mackie, *The Cement of the Universe* (Oxford 1974), ch. 10; see also the differing views in P. Achinstein, 'The Causal Relation', A. Rosenberg and R. M. Martin, 'The Extensionality of Causal Contexts', and L. B. Lombard, 'The Extensionality of Causal Contexts: Comments on Rosenberg and Martin', all in (1979) 4 *Midwest Studies in Philosophy*.

[42] Richard Wright, 'Causation in Tort Law', (1985) 73 *California LR* 1735; Wright, 'Causation, Responsibility, Risk, Probability, Naked Statistics, and Proof: Pruning the Bramble Bush by Clarifying the Concepts', (1988) 73 *Iowa LR* 1001.

sufficient-condition test,[43] or some other variation of David Hume's general theme that causation is to be analysed in terms of necessary and/or sufficient conditions. On any of these counterfactual analyses of causation, the multiple-description problem will loom large so long as *what* is caused is taken to be a particular event. As Donald Davidson has noted, on these tests, 'the fuller we make the description of the effect, the better our chances of demonstrating that the cause (as described) was necessary, and the worse our chances of demonstrating that it was sufficient.'[44]

Davidson's point is illustrated by the attempt of some legal theorists to show that the necessary-condition analysis of causation can handle the overdetermination cases (where there appear to be two or more events, each of which was sufficient to produce the harm).[45] Where two fires converge to burn down the plaintiff's house, each fire having been capable of burning down the house by itself, it appears that because each fire was sufficient for the burning, neither was necessary, forcing the necessary-condition analysis of causation to the unpalatable conclusion that neither fire caused the burning. Not so, say the defenders of the necessary-condition analysis, such as Herbert Wechsler and the other drafters of the American Law Institute's Model Penal Code;[46] for a more detailed description of the burning —for instance, the burning of such-and-such an intensity, and of such-and-such a duration—will reveal that this (more fully described) burning would not have occurred without both fires converging as they did.

Far from rescuing the counterfactual analysis of causation, this defence reveals the incompatibility of that analysis with the idea that it is particular events that stand in causal relations. For no reason is given for why we should prefer a more detailed description of a harm-token to a less detailed one. And without some criterion for selecting the appropriate level of description, the causal relation (as analysed counterfactually) is completely indeterminate in all cases.

This dependence of all counterfactual analyses of causation upon how the harm is described leads theorists in one of two directions: either they reject the counterfactual analyses of causation in favour of a relational analysis;[47] or they reject the idea that the things eligible to be the effects of causes are particular events. It will serve our dual purposes here to explore briefly each option.

[43] J. L. Mackie, 'Causes and Conditions', (1965) 2 *American Philosophical Quarterly* 245.

[44] Donald Davidson, 'Causal Relations', (1967) 64 *Journal of Philosophy* 691, reprinted in his *Essays on Actions and Events* (Oxford 1980), 157.

[45] These theorists are critically discussed in Wright, 'Causation in Tort Law', above n. 42, 1777–80.

[46] American Law Institute, Model Penal Code and Commentaries (Philadelphia 1985), Comment to § 2.03.

[47] For a summary of relational versus counterfactual analyses of causation, see Jonathan Bennett, *Events and their Names* (Indianapolis 1988), chs. 3, 4, and 9.

Donald Davidson's choice was to reject the counterfactual analyses of causation in favour of a relational analysis. Davidson urged that 'we must distinguish firmly between causes [and their effects] and the features we hit on for describing them'.[48] Our descriptions of events like burnings properly make a great deal of difference when we are giving causal explanations, for such explanations relate facts (or propositions) about events, not events themselves, and facts, unlike events, are individuated by such descriptions. But such differing descriptions make no difference to the truth of causal statements like, 'The starting of the fire caused the burning of the plaintiff's house.' However we describe the two events, the first either caused the second, or it did not.

For reasons that I have urged elsewhere,[49] Davidson is right: we should reject counterfactual analyses of the causal relation. That allows us to maintain the most intuitive ontology for the causal relation, namely, that the relation is between particular events. Since we cannot maintain this ontology for foreseeability, that raises the question of what relation might hold between the particular events that are caused, and the whatevers that are foreseeable. Before we can settle that question, we need to settle what it is that is sensibly said to be either foreseeable or unforeseeable.

What the *what* might be that can be foreseeable can be glimpsed if we turn to those causal theorists who hang on to the counterfactual analyses of causation despite their recognition of the multiple-description problem. They have only two moves available to them. The first is to move to what might be called feature, property, aspect, or type causation.[50] The idea is this. Every particular event has many aspects, features, or properties; such particular, accordingly, is an instance of various types of event, each type being constituted by one or more of these properties. We should thus distinguish particular events (henceforth, event-tokens), like the fire that burned down the plaintiff's house yesterday, from the type of event that this fire is (among others, a fire-type of event). Causation, the argument goes, is a relation between event-types, not event-tokens. This allows one then to say that of course causal statements will seem to discriminate between different descriptions of the harm—such different descriptions in reality refer to different *types* of events, and the truth about whether there is a causal relation depends on what type(s) of events one is discussing. There might, for example, be a causal relation between the type, yellow-fire and the type, presence of sodium, even if there is no causal relation between the presence of sodium and the more general type of event, fire. This would allow one to say what it seems very intuitive to say—that the

---

[48] Davidson, 'Causal Relations', above n. 44, 155. See generally Simon Eunine, *Donald Davidson* (Stanford, Calif. 1991), ch. 2.   [49] Moore, *Act and Crime*, above n. 27, ch. 10.
[50] For a lucid exposition along these lines, see Richard Wright, 'Causation in Tort Law', above n. 42.

presence of sodium did not cause the fire as such but it did cause the yellowness of the fire—without violating Leibniz' Law.

The alternative move made by counterfactual analysts of causation is quite similar. Like the first move, it posits that the causal relation exists between universals, not particulars; but the universals are proposition-like entities, not types or properties. Since one of the idiomatic usages of the word 'fact' is to refer to these proposition-like entities, such theories are usually called fact-causation theories.[51] The fact that the fire occurred is distinct from the occurrence of the fire; the second is an event-token, the first is a fact about that event-token.[52]

The move here considered urges that only facts are causally related to one another. The fact that there was a fire was because of the fact that a spark touched highly combustible materials, for example. This move too allows for one to account for the multiple-description problem. For example, the fact that the fire burned yellow is distinct from the fact that the fire occurred at all (even though it was a yellow fire), so a fact-causation theorist could easily admit that the second but not the first fact was caused by the fact that sodium was present at the point of combustion. These are not different descriptions of the same thing, but different facts, so different causal relations can hold between them without violating the requirements of Leibniz' Law.

Similar as they are, these two moves do not amount to the same thing. Facts are not types of events. Facts are linguistic entities that can be about either event-types or event-tokens. Although the motivation for adopting these views is the same—to preserve extensionality for counterfactual analyses of causation in the face of the multiple-description problem—the ontology presupposed by each view is different.[53]

[51] e.g. see Mackie, *The Cement of the Universe*, above n. 41; J. Bennett, *Events and their Names*, above n. 47.

[52] For a book-length treatment of this distinction, see Bennett, *Events and their Names*, above n. 47.

[53] In reality, the move to types only lessens but does not eliminate the failures of extensionality for 'foreseeability' usages. Except for predicate-nominalists—those who believe that properties and types have no existence save that given them by predicates in a language—the *same* property or type can be picked out by more than one description. (On why none of us should be predicate-nominalists, see D. M. Armstrong, *A Theory of Universals* (Cambridge 1978), part IV.) This means that one can still have different descriptions of the same universal which seem to yield differing truth-values when plugged into the foreseeability formula. Suppose, for example, some instance of fire damage occurs and that it was foreseeable that some instance of fire damage would occur. Suppose further that, unbeknownst to anyone, a hermit named Jones lost his cabin to fire the day before; then another description of the same type would be, 'the type of harm that befell Jones's cabin yesterday'. Yet it was not foreseeable that there would today be an instance of the type of harm that befell Jones's cabin yesterday. This lack of any complete elimination of the failures of substitutivity for 'foreseeable' makes the fact ontology preferable to the type ontology for constructions using 'foreseeability'. Still, in the text I shall continue to discuss both variants, since the type ontology has been the most favoured amongst legal and probability theorists.

Both of these moves are for me unmotivated with respect to causation, because I reject the counterfactual analyses of causation anyway. Both such moves should be of interest in this context, however, for they are the two moves open to foreseeability theorists in order to preserve the coherence of that notion. The first would be to say that harm-tokens as such are neither foreseeable nor unforeseeable; only *types* of harms can be foreseen and thus only types of harms are or are not foreseeable. The proper legal test, on this view, would then ask: was the harm (token) in fact caused by the defendant's action an instance of any type of harm, the occurrence of some instance of which was foreseeable to the defendant at the time that he acted? The second move would likewise deny that harm-tokens are either foreseeable or unforeseeable; but it would substitute facts for types, asking only whether the fact that the harm-token (that did occur) would occur was foreseeable to the defendant at the time that he acted.

Either of these moves rescues foreseeability from failures of extensionality by allowing one to deny that different descriptions like 'damage by fire' or 'damage by shock' refer to the same thing; for fire damage is a distinct *type* of damage from shock damage—as the fact that the fire damage occurred is a distinct fact from the fact that the shock damage occurred—even if some particular damage is an instance of both fire and shock types of damage. Yet neither of these reconstruals of the ontology of foreseeability by itself lessens the complete indeterminacy of the concept, for in neither case do we yet have a criterion for picking out what type of harm—or what fact about the harm that occurred—we should use as we ask, 'Was *that* foreseeable?' And without such a criterion, both moves leave the foreseeability criterion completely indeterminate.

Herbert Hart and Tony Honoré early on noticed this about the foreseeability test for proximate causation:

> It is usually agreed that 'it is not necessary to show that this particular accident and this particular damage were probable; it is sufficient if the accident is of a class that might well be anticipated as one of the reasonable and probable results of the wrongful act.' This view, although undoubtedly law, does not in itself provide any means of determining the class of harm or accident which must be foreseeable . . .[54]

An example makes this clearer: imagine a case in which it was foreseeable to the defendant that his act would damage property of the plaintiff. For example, the defendant's winding of the plaintiff's rare clock too tight would foreseeably damage the clock. Suppose, however, that the defendant's winding of the clock too tight does not, miraculously, damage it, but does cause a neighbour (who is driving down the street) to watch the

---

[54] Hart and Honoré, above n. 2, 233, quoting from Greer LJ's judgment in *Haynes* v. *Harwood* [1935] 1 KB 146. Hart and Honoré then go on to provide their own answers to this indeterminacy, answers which we shall examine below.

defendant's excessive clock-winding so that the neighbour runs into and damages the plaintiff's car. If the type (or fact about) damage is fixed as generally as 'property damage,' then the defendant proximately caused the harm; for it was foreseeable to the defendant that some property damage would occur, and some property damage did occur.[55] By contrast, if the types (or facts about) damage are focused more narrowly, say, as 'clock-spring breaking' and 'auto-fender bending,' then there is no proximate causation under the foreseeability test; for it was not foreseeable (by hypothesis again) that an instance of auto-fender bending would occur, and while it was foreseeable that an instance of clock-spring breaking would occur, no such instance did occur. Very general types or facts make the harm almost always foreseeable (e.g. the most general type, 'harm') and there will always be specific enough types or facts so as to make any harm unforeseeable.

The upshot is that although a shift to an ontology of types or facts gets the foreseeability theorist out of the literal incoherence of violating our Leibnizian ideas about identity, such a shift does not render the foreseeability test a jot more determinate in its applications to particular cases. In order to give the foreseeability test even the limited bite that Morris thought it had, we need some way of selecting certain types of harm, or facts about harm, as authoritative. A natural thought would be that the law itself provides for such an authoritative typing of harms. Yet if one looks to the Anglo-American criminal or tort law for such details, one is bound to be disappointed. What one finds are suggestions like that of Justice Cardozo, who distinguished property-type harms from personal-injury type harms in *dicta* in his famous *Palsgraf* opinion:

There is room for argument that a distinction is to be drawn according to the diversity of interests invaded by the act, as where conduct negligent in that it threatens an insignificant invasion of an interest in property results in an unforeseeable invasion of an interest of another order, as, e.g. one of bodily security.[56]

Similarly, Viscount Simonds seems to regard *his* narrower typology of harms in *The Wagon Mound No. 1* ('fire damage,' 'shock damage') as established in law in the sense that the conventional heads of tort liability *generate* a legally natural typology.[57] The textbook maxim in torts—that

---

[55] Remember, once we eschew talking about the foreseeability of harm-tokens, we cannot refuse liability here on the ground that the harm that occurred was not the same as the harm that was foreseeable. Rather, the only question allowed us is whether the harm-token that occurred was an instance of the harm-type that was foreseeable, and with the broad type mentioned in the text, this is satisfied.

[56] *Palsgraf v. Long Island RR*, 248 NY 339, 346–7, 162 NE 99, 101 (1928).

[57] [1961] AC 388. However, since damage by fire is *not* a recognized head of tort liability, what Viscount Simonds actually appears to have believed is that the harm for which one is liable determines the type of harm that must be foreseeable. Thus, 'the test for *liability for*

'only the type of harm need be foreseeable, not the extent of the harm nor the precise means of its occurrence'[58]—also suggests that there is some such legally natural typology (although it gives but the slightest hints about what it might be).

The law has not developed these vague suggestions of Cardozo, Simonds, or Pollock. There is no distinctly legal typology of harms. If one were to summarize 'the law' on the topic, the summary by Harper and James is still about as much as one can get:

The inquiry . . . into the nature of the risks or hazards, the foreseeability of which makes conduct negligent, must be neither too refined nor too coarse. It is a matter of judgment in drawing the line . . . and this will vary from situation to situation.[59]

Juries are thus entirely on their own as they frame the types or facts about which they ask, 'Was *that* foreseeable?' Is there any reason to believe that juries exercise any but a purely arbitrary judgment when they select, as they must, some types of harm about which to ask, 'Was it foreseeable?' It has been suggested that every society 'amalgamates accidents into a relatively small number of categories',[60] and that these form the types or facts relevant to foreseeability determinations.

· There are three ways to take this suggestion. One is to think that in our normal descriptive, explanatory, and predictive activities in daily life we develop a typology of event-type that allows us to apply the foreseeability test.[61] Yet this is plainly an illusion. It is true of course that the causal laws

---

shock is foreseeability of *injury by shock*.' The assumption seems to be that the extent of a defendant's liability can be used to set the type of harm about which we can ask, was an instance of this type foreseeable? (I am indebted to Ken Kress for this interpretation of *The Wagon Mound No. 1*.) The problem with the suggestion is that defendants are liable for particular harms; these harm-tokens have many properties; there is nothing in our practices in assigning liability in either torts or criminal law that picks out one of these properties for use in framing foreseeability questions. In *The Wagon: Mound No. 1*, for example, the defendant's liability was for the destruction of the plaintiff's dock; although that particular destruction was an instance of the type, fire damage, it was also an instance of innumerable other types, such as dock destruction, property damage, twenty-five minute, yellow-fire destruction of a dock, etc.

[58] See e.g. Pollock, 'Liability for Consequences', (1922) 38 *Law Quarterly Review* 165, at 167 ('when it is found that a man ought to have foreseen in a general way consequences of a certain kind, it will not avail him to say that he could not foresee the precise course or the full extent of the consequences, being of that kind, which in fact happened.')

[59] Fowler V. Harper and Fleming James, Jr., *The Law of Torts* (Boston, 1956), ii, s. 20.5(6).

[60] Steven Shavell, 'An Analysis of Causation and the Scope of Liability in the Law of Torts', (1980) 9 *Journal of Legal Studies* 463, at 491.

[61] See e.g. H. L. A. Hart and Tony Honoré, *Causation in the Law*, above n. 2, 234 (experience has taught us to anticipate 'rainstorm' type events from dark-cloud type events, not to anticipate 'storm', 'bad weather', or 'rainstorm that lasts two hours' types of events). For a recent summary of the varying hypotheses of cognitive psychologists about what are the optimal categories for prediction and information storage, see James E. Corter and Mark E. Gluck, 'Explaining Basic Categories: Feature Predictability and Information', (1992) 111 *Psychological Bulletin* 291.

by which we both explain and predict events are themselves formed over certain types or facts (called 'natural kinds') to the exclusion of all others.[62] To this extent, those who know such causal laws do have a shared set of types of (or facts about) events. Yet this typology is far too rich to do the discriminating work demanded by the suggestion, for such a typology include the types or facts used by all known causal laws. There will be many such laws applicable to any particular event-token and, thus, there are many types that such an event-token instantiates which satisfy this criterion. A particular fire, for example, will instantiate the causally relevant types: fire, yellow fire, fire of a temperature over 1,000 degrees Fahrenheit, ash-producing fire, smokeless fire, oxidizing process, etc., etc. And if one seeks to make the typology more discriminating by allowing only those causal laws of the greatest precision, this will probably result in all harms being rendered unforeseeable.[63] For example, the most precise causal laws governing the motion of the workman's brick in Morris's earlier example are no doubt framed over very precise types of events—event-types such as cuts of certain depths and configurations connected to event-types such as rotations and velocities of a certain sort; and types of this precision are rarely if ever foreseeably instantiated on any given occasion.

The second way to take the suggestion is as a bit of the sociology of custom: without regard to the causal laws that make predictions possible, people just do clump individual events into certain types.[64] It is these familiar, ready-to-tongue types that are then used by juries as they ask and answer foreseeability questions. Yet there are two problems with this way of taking the suggestion. One is to question whether there is anything remotely approaching a typology of events with the necessary discriminating power to be found in customary categories. Take the case where the

[62] On natural kinds, see Moore, 'The Semantics of Judging', above n. 3, 204–42. See also W. V. Quine, 'Natural Kinds', in his *Ontological Relativity and Other Essays* (New York 1969); and Hilary Putnam, 'The Meaning of "Meaning" ', in his *Mind, Language, and Reality* (Cambridge 1975). Nelson Goodman's 'projectible predicates' are what I and many others would call the names of natural kinds. Nelson Goodman, *Fact, Fiction, and Forecast* (4th edn., Indianapolis 1984).

[63] See D. L. Medin, 'Structural Principles of Categorization', in B. Shepp and T. Tighe (eds.), *Interaction: Perception, Development and Cognition* (Hillsdale, NJ 1983), 203–30. See also Corter and Gluck, above n. 61, 292, where it is argued that those categories maximizing the probability that any instance of the category will have some feature F (such as being the cause or the effect of a certain type of event) will be 'the most specific categories because they tend to have the least variability in features. For example, the probability that something can fly given that it is a robin is higher than the probability that something can fly given that it is a bird.'

[64] For suggestions about such conventional clumping of types for purposes of constructing the holding of a precedent, see Frederick Schauer, 'Precedent', (1987) 39 *Stanford LR* 571. For a critique of the use of such conventional kinds in that context, see Michael Moore, 'Precedent, Induction, and Ethical Generalization', in Laurence Goldstein (ed.), *Precedent in Law* (Oxford 1987).

plaintiff's arm is cut off by the defendant's negligent action. Suppose it was foreseeable that the plaintiff's arm might be cut, but unforeseeable that it would be severed (by such a light blow with such a blunt instrument). Surely arm-cuttings and arm-severings are equally entrenched types of events in our customary way of thinking, yet that an instance of one type would occur was foreseeable, while the fact that the other would occur was not.

The second problem with this idea of using conventionally entrenched categories is a normative one. To the extent that there are such conventionally favoured ways of categorizing events, and to the extent that this is not simply in response to the natural categorization given by true causal laws, such conventional favouring is due to factors like the length of the word used in English to refer to the type, the frequency of the word's use, the average response-time taken by native speakers to recognize a particular as being an instance of this category rather than another, and the developmental sequence in which this category-name was learned *vis-à-vis* its competitors.[65] These factors seem irrelevant to the normative justifications given for the foreseeability criterion of proximate causation (either that it is *unfair* to hold a person liable for harms that he could not foresee, or that it is *inefficient* to do so, because future agents cannot take such unforeseeable types of harms into account in planning their behaviour and so liability cannot achieve its deterrent function). Word-length, developmental sequence, etc., are irrelevant to whether a category of events is a harm-type category or not, yet the normative justifications for using foreseeability demand that the relevant category under which the events must be foreseeable must be a category of *harm*.

This last objection brings out a third way to take the suggestion, which is as an observation about morality and our moral beliefs. On this line, it is only because of a shared moral theory about the significant rights and interests possessed by persons that we are able to type harms sufficiently to enquire after their foreseeability. People might have some shared typologies of harms by virtue of the interest in bodily integrity, say, being distinct from the interests in reputation or in property, or the interest in the security of one's home being distinct from the interest in other sorts of property. One would frame foreseeability questions, on this view, over those types of harms that correspond to such interests.[66]

The main problem with this view is that it yields outcomes quite at odds with those the foreseeability test is thought to give. Take the Louisiana

[65] See the extensive literature summarized in Corter and Gluck, above n. 61, 291.

[66] For suggestions on how harms might be related to rights and interests, see Joel Feinberg, *Harm to Others* (New York 1984), 31–125; Michael Davis, 'Harm and Retribution', (1986) 15 *Philosophy and Public Affairs* 236, at 239–47; Andrew von Hirsch, *Past or Future Crimes* (New Brunswick, NJ 1985), 66–71; Andrew von Hirsch and Nils Jareborg, 'Gauging Criminal Harm: A Living Standard Analysis', (1991) 11 *Oxford Journal of Legal Studies* 1, at 19–21.

case (of the rescuer shot in the leg by the deranged accident victim) that Morris took to be 'unarguably unforeseeable': the relevant interest seems to be that of bodily integrity, and the relevant type, the violation of that integrity, i.e. an injury to the body. An instance of that type was surely foreseeable to the defendant who negligently failed to guard his stalled truck with flares, since personal injuries in collisions are common; and an instance of that type in fact was caused to occur, namely the plaintiff was shot in the leg; therefore, contrary to Morris's observation, the harm *was* foreseeable.

There is, I think, a moral judgment guiding observations like Morris's here, but it has little to do with the rights and interests of persons, or, indeed, with foreseeability at all. When Morris held of such cases that 'the freakishness of the facts refuses to be drowned' and that any description that leaves out details about the use of the pistol by the deranged husband 'is viewed as misdescription', he was accurately describing the reactions of judges and juries to such cases. What explains such reactions, however, is not some implicit criterion of description that has thus far eluded us. Rather, Morris and the judges and juries he was describing are abandoning foreseeability entirely in favour of other conceptions of proximate causation. The power of the competing direct-cause and remoteness conceptions of proximate causation lies precisely in the attention these conceptions pay to these details of intervening causation. To the extent that the foreseeability theorist allows these sorts of moral insight to guide the typology of harms under which he asks, 'Was this foreseeable?' he is abandoning his theory, not saving it.

I thus conclude that the criminal- and tort-law conceptions of proximate causation in terms of foreseeability are completely indeterminate in all cases. There is no legally established typology of harm that judges and juries are to use when they ask, 'Was the occurrence of an instance of that type of harm foreseeable?' Nor do judges and juries have recourse to some unstated but shared (causal, conventional, or moral) typing of events that can fill in where law is silent.

To salvage the foreseeability criterion of proximate causation, one thus must urge that the law has to change. The reform that most readily comes to mind, of course, is to supply an authoritative typology of harms. But how is such a typology to be framed? The most promising suggestions would be along the three lines we have already explored (with reference to the alleged implicit knowledge of judges and juries), and none of these, as we have seen, will fit the bill.

Alternatively, one might think that legal reform could adopt a 'harm-within-the-risk' analysis of proximate causation. Under this approach, we should ask about the foreseeability of only those types of harms that are both: (1) types of which the harm-token that occurred was an instance, and (2) types of harms intended by the actor or foreseen by him, or types of harm the risk of which made his action negligent to perform.[67]

This would be a peculiar reform. Usually, devotees of the harm-within-the-risk analysis do not seek to salvage foreseeability but to eliminate it entirely. Under the harm-within-the-risk approach, defendants are liable to criminal and tort sanctions whenever they in fact cause an instance of any type of harm that they intend, contemplate, or unreasonably risk. There is no room or need for an additional foreseeability question under this approach.

One could, of course, also reform the harm-within-the-risk approach so that it does not supplant entirely the foreseeability question. This is easier said than done, however. Suppose we were simply to *add* the foreseeability question (restricted to the types of harms foreseen, risked, or intended) to the harm-within-the-risk question. Will it not be the case that to answer the second question will also be to answer the first? Surely any type of harm that is actually foreseen, intended, or unreasonably risked by an action was also foreseeable to that agent, rendering the foreseeability question superfluous.

A more plausible reform of the harm-within-the-risk formula would be to *substitute* the foreseeability question for the harm-within-the-risk question, using the harm-within-the-risk analysis only to frame the types of harm about which the foreseeability question is asked.[68] If the defendant intended (foresaw, unreasonably risked) *a fire*, then one asks whether it was foreseeable that an instance of the type, fire, would occur.

One problem for this suggested reform is its seeming lack of motivation: what rationale for proximate causation would make normative sense of this ungainly marriage of foreseeability to harm-within-the-risk? A second problem lies in the fact that the harm-within-the-risk analysis does not isolate a type of harm (that could give determinacy to foreseeability) when that analysis is based on negligence. There is never one type of harm, the risk of which makes an agent negligent (except for the type, harm). Rather, negligence consists in acting in the face of all types of harm that the act

---

[67] In criminal law the most authoritative adoption of the harm-within-the-risk analysis is in the Model Penal Code, § 2.03. (I use 'harm-within-the-risk' as the generic label for 'harm-within-the intent, belief, or risk'.) The Code's drafters ultimately could not stomach the seeming implications of harm-within-the-risk analysis, for they recognize liability even when 'the actual result is not within the purpose or contemplation of the actor' if 'the actual result involves the same kind of injury or harm as that designed or contemplated and is not too remote or accidental in its occurrence to have a just bearing on the actor's liability or on the quantity of his offense'. Notice that this provision frees the Model Penal Code's notion of proximate causation from the unduly restrictive grip of the harm-within-the-risk analysis only to return courts and juries to individuate types with no guidance whatsoever.

[68] This seems to be Hart and Honoré's preferred solution to the description problem. See *Causation in the Law*, above n. 2, 233 ('that class can be determined by reference to the generalizations which one would have recourse to in describing conduct as negligent').

may produce, discounted by the improbability of an instance of each type being caused to exist. Placing unlabelled rat-poison near the stove in the kitchen is negligent in part because of some probability of a poisoning, but also because of some probability of an explosion, a falling, etc. Moreover, even if we leave aside all risks but the risk that the unlabelled rat-poison would be eaten and the eater poisoned, that risk no more has a canonical description than does the corresponding harm. It might be a risk of ingesting 2.75 ounces of rat-poison, causing excessive vomiting, loss of memory, etc.; or it might be a risk of poisoning; or it might be a risk of bodily injury; etc. Which of these was *the* risk that made the agent negligent in placing unlabelled rat-poison near the stove?

Even when the harm-within-the-risk analysis produces unique types eligible to be plugged into the foreseeability formula—as it does for intended or foreseen harms, if not for negligently risked harms—the formula yields results unwanted even by friends of foreseeability. This is because the typing of harms (under which we are to ask, was *it* foreseeable) is now wholly dependent on the level of typing done by the actor as he framed his intentions or his beliefs. Return to the clock-winding example, where the plaintiff's car was run into and damaged because of a third party's undue fascination with the defendant's excessive winding of the plaintiff's clock. If the defendant's belief was that 'he might very well break the plaintiff's clock', then we type the harm that must be foreseeable as 'clock breakage', and the defendant is not liable, because although it was foreseeable that an instance of that type would occur, it did not occur. If on the other hand the defendant's belief was that 'he might very well damage property of the plaintiff', then we type the harm that must be foreseeable as 'property damage', and the defendant is liable (because an instance of that type of harm did occur and because it was foreseeable that it would). These results are not only counterintuitive, but their dependence upon the breadth of the object of the defendant's belief or intent makes them seem arbitrary.

4. Conclusion

Corrective-justice theorists of tort and retributive-justice theorists of the criminal law have good reason to reject the foreseeability criterion of proximate causation on normative grounds. For these theories demand that legal liability track moral responsibility, and moral responsibility for causing a harm requires causation of that harm in some ordinary sense, not in the artificial sense created by the foreseeability theory of proximate causation.

To this normative objection to foreseeability we should now add a conceptual objection: the multiple-description problem shows the foreseeability conception of proximate causation to be incoherent. If we take *what* is (un)foreseeable to be particular events, then (so long as we refuse a transparent reading of what 'foreseeability' means) the multiple-description problem reveals the concept to be nonsense in light of our firmly entrenched, Leibnizian ideas of identity. If, more plausibly, we take *what* is (un)foreseeable to be either types of events, or facts about events, no violation of the laws of identity need take place, but the concept is still completely indeterminate in its implications for particular cases. That indeterminacy could be reduced by legal, conventional, or moral typologies of harms, but such typologies either do not exist or, if they do, do not decide proximate-cause issues in a way that is at all intuitive, even to friends of foreseeability.

None of this makes the notion of foreseeability incoherent or indeterminate, as that concept is used as part of what is meant by negligence, and in closing it is worth saying why this is so. The negligence standard obviously requires probability judgments by both agents and the juries who judge them. Yet the negligence standard does not require that some typology of harm be adopted that precludes contradictory judgments. Quite the contrary: the Learned Hand formula for negligence, properly construed, requires the agent to assess the likelihoods of his actions producing instances of *all* types of harm (balanced against the likelihoods of those same actions producing instances of all types of benefit). The non-negligent agent *sums* the discounted value of all such types of harms, sums the discounted value of all such types of benefits, and acts only if the number is positive. In that summing process he is not imposing a binary choice (foreseeable/unforeseeable), but only seeking a probability; moreover, he does not have to choose *one* such type, because he is adding *all* such probabilities, even the smallest ones. His only problems in such summing are (1) making sure that he does not double-count (for types of harms that overlap in their extensions); and (2) the amount of information required to make this enormously complicated calculation.[69] These are serious enough practical problems in the application of the negligence standard, but they pale before the conceptual bankruptcy of the foreseeability conception of proximate causation.

---

[69] Mark Grady has undertaken to show how an adversary system can lessen the practical problem of information overload so as to ease the strain on fact-finders in making negligence determinations. Grady, 'Untaken Precautions', (1989) 18 *Journal of Legal Studies* 139.

Culpability and Mistake of Law

DOUGLAS HUSAK AND ANDREW VON HIRSCH

1. Ignorance of Law and Fact

Anglo-American criminal law treats ignorance of fact and ignorance of law differently.[1] The law is charitable to defendants whose ignorance is factual, but, generally, is uncharitable to those whose ignorance is legal.

These generalizations are subject to qualification. Ignorance of fact does not always provide a defence to liability, for its exculpatory significance depends on the distinction between reasonable and unreasonable ignorance. Reasonable ignorance of fact exculpates, except in cases of strict liability (which are comparatively rare outside the area of regulatory offences); unreasonable factual ignorance still results in liability, if the State provides that the crime can be committed negligently.[2] A few modifications have been proposed—by the Model Penal Code, for example—to the strict rule that ignorance of law is no defence.[3] Still, defendants stand a much better chance of escaping liability if they can succeed in categorizing their ignorance as factual rather than as legal. This more favourable treatment afforded to factual ignorance has generated difficulty over deciding how the contrast between mistake of fact and mistake of law is to be drawn.[4]

If pressed for an explanation of the existing disparity in the legal treatment of ignorance of law and ignorance of fact, most commentators would begin by citing the fundamental principle that criminal liability requires *mens rea*. Due to the influence of the Model Penal Code, American theorists have come to conceptualize *mens rea* in terms of four 'mental' states: purpose, knowledge, recklessness, and negligence. A defendant who is

The authors are indebted to a number of colleagues for comments on this paper: Andrew Ashworth, Tatjana Hoernle, Nils Jareborg, John Kleinig, Martin Wasik, and the editors of this volume.

[1] We will not distinguish between mistake and ignorance, although some theorists have contrasted them as follows: a defendant who is mistaken about *p* believes not-*p*, but a defendant who is ignorant of *p* need not believe not-*p*; he may have no belief about whether *p* or not-*p* is true.

[2] Our comments about existing law will refer chiefly to American doctrines, as we are more familiar with them. In the common law in America, both reasonable and unreasonable mistake of fact precluded liability for specific-intent crimes, but only reasonable ignorance of fact precluded liability for general-intent crimes.

[3] See Model Penal Code, § 2.04 (3), discussed below.

[4] Jerome Hall is probably correct to say that there is no single distinction between fact and law, but that 'what is "fact" and what is "law" differ in various contexts'. See his *General Principles of Criminal Law* (2nd edn., Indianapolis 1960), 376.

ignorant of a material fact typically lacks the *mens rea* required for liability. Suppose, for example, that murder is defined (in relevant part) as purposely or knowingly killing another human being. A hunter who kills a person believing he has shot a deer performs the *actus reus* but lacks the *mens rea* of murder. Since the offence requires both an *actus reus* and *mens rea*, the hunter simply has not committed the offence; he has not purposely or knowingly killed anyone.[5] He can avoid liability because of what Paul Robinson has described as a 'failure of proof' defence.[6] Imposing liability on the factually mistaken defendant would punish him in the absence of *mens rea*.

No parallel argument, however, suggests that a defendant who is ignorant of law typically lacks *mens rea*. The hunter who knowingly kills another human being but is ignorant that such conduct is illegal satisfies both the *actus reus* and the *mens rea* requirements for murder. This defendant possesses *mens rea* as long as he knows *that* he is killing, and knows that *what* he is killing is another human being. He need not also know that what he is doing is against the law. In case this result is doubtful, the Model Penal Code explicitly states that

Neither knowledge nor recklessness nor negligence as to whether conduct constitutes an offense or as to the existence, meaning or application of the law determining the elements of an offense is an element of the offense, unless the definition of the offense or the Code so provides.[7]

This treatment of *mens rea* in the Model Penal Code is consistent with established common-law doctrines. Justice Brennan took himself to be stating the obvious when he observed that *mens rea* 'does not require knowledge that an act is illegal, wrong or blameworthy'.[8] In contrast with the defendant who is ignorant of fact, the hunter who is ignorant of law typically possesses *mens rea*.

The Model Penal Code provision quoted above provides one significant exception, through its final clause 'unless the definition of offense or the Code so provides'. This clause refers to cases where knowledge of the law is expressly required for liability. The inclusion of such terms as 'knowing it to be illegal' in statutes converts a defendant's ignorance of law into a failure-of-proof defence;[9] a defendant who does not know his conduct to be illegal simply does not commit the offence. Most criminal statutes,

    [5] The adverb 'knowingly' modifies all material elements of the statute, according to Model Penal Code, § 2.02 (4).
    [6] See Paul Robinson, *Criminal Law Defenses* (St Paul, Minn. 1984), s. 21.
    [7] Model Penal Code, § 2.02 (9).   [8] *United States* v. *Freed*, 401 US 601, 612 (1971).
    [9] For some of the difficulties in construing terms that appear to convert knowledge of the law into an element of criminal liability, contrast *Liparota* v. *United States*, 471 US 419 (1985) with *United States* v. *Yermian*, 468 US 63 (1984).

however, do not contain such terms. Thus, defendants who are mistaken about whether their conduct is criminal usually are deemed to possess *mens rea*.

Although we have no quarrel with the accuracy of this explanation as a matter of positive law, we find it to be conclusory from a philosophical perspective. It disposes of the problem as a matter of statutory interpretation, but only by 'pushing the entire theoretical conundrum under the legislative carpet'.[10] It also assumes that the treatment of *mens rea* as contained in the common law and the Model Penal Code is an adequate normative account of culpability. What is the basis for such confidence? Why *should* a criminal code typically regard a defendant as culpable for his conduct if he is ignorant of law, but not if he is ignorant of fact?

In so far as Anglo-American writers address these questions at all, their answers tend to be couched in terms of crime prevention. It is said that the law should not encourage ignorance,[11] or that it would be unduly difficult to prove that defendants actually knew the law.[12] Such answers are inadequate because they do not address the critical issue of whether or to what extent legal ignorance affects the blameworthiness of conduct.

To provide a more satisfactory resolution of these issues, we need to recall the reasons for imposing a culpability requirement in the first place. We think that such a requirement is needed to ensure that criminal liability is imposed only on persons who are at fault for their conduct. Punishment conveys blame, and therefore should be imposed only on those whose harmful conduct involves culpable choice.[13] Punishing—and thereby holding to blame—those who are not at fault violates a fundamental requirement of justice.[14]

If this brief response is correct, it is important to ask whether the same considerations that support the culpability requirement in Anglo-American criminal law and justify a defence of ignorance of fact apply with equal force to justify the creation of a defence of ignorance of law. Is the defendant who is ignorant of law any more blameworthy than the defendant who is ignorant of fact? Are either or both of these defendants sufficiently culpable that it is just to force them to suffer the stigma and deprivation of criminal penalties? These are the kinds of questions we will address here. Because our approach emphasizes the importance of fairness and desert, we shall not confront the issues that have tended to consume most theorists who have written about ignorance of law: to what extent the

[10] See George Fletcher, 'Mistake in the Model Penal Code: A False False Problem', (1988) 19 *Rutgers LJ* 649, at 653.
[11] Oliver W. Holmes, *The Common Law* (Boston 1881), 48.
[12] John Austin, *Lectures on Jurisprudence* (3rd edn., London 1869), 498–500.
[13] See Andrew von Hirsch, *Past or Future Crimes* (Manchester 1986), 54–7.
[14] See Douglas Husak, *Philosophy of Criminal Law* (Totowa, NJ 1987), 30–4.

recognition of such a defence serves or impedes the utilitarian objectives of deterrence and crime control.[15]

We will begin by examining whether *any* difference should exist between the treatment of factual and legal ignorance. To deal with this issue, we consider a hypothetical scheme which German commentators call the 'equal-treatment doctrine',[16] according to which mistakes of law would be treated exactly like mistakes of fact. We will reject this doctrine on the ground that the culpability of the legally ignorant defendant can differ in important respects from that of the factually ignorant defendant. Next we consider wherein their culpability may differ, examining successively the case of the person who could not reasonably have ascertained the legal rule, and the person who could have but failed to do so. To resolve these issues, we would have preferred to rely on a comprehensive and general theory of culpability. We possess no such theory, however, and thus have little choice but to rely on our intuitions about when defendants who differ in some respect are or are not equally culpable.

2. The Supposed Obligation to Know the Law: An Unsatisfactory Answer

Why might a legally ignorant defendant be culpable in a way that a factually ignorant defendant is not? In so far as this question has been addressed, the most frequent explanation has been couched in terms of an obligation to know the law: the legally mistaken defendant is culpable because he has breached his obligation as a citizen to inform himself of his legal duties. The German Supreme Court, in its leading decision on the subject in 1952, cited this as its main reason for rejecting the equal-treatment doctrine.[17] Ronald Cass[18] and, more recently, Andrew Ashworth[19] have argued in similar fashion.

---

[15] For one of the few discussions of the impact of ignorance of law on culpability, see Laurence Houlgate, '*Ignorantia Juris*: A Plea for Justice', (1967) 78 *Ethics* 32. Houlgate attempts to show that the defendant who acts in ignorance of law should not be punished, because he has not voluntarily gained an unfair advantage over his fellow citizens. However, we do not subscribe to such 'unfair advantage' theories of deserved punishment, for reasons set forth in Andrew von Hirsch, *Censure and Sanctions* (Oxford 1993), ch. 2.

[16] See Gunther Arzt, 'The Problem of Mistake of Law', [1986] *Brigham Young University LR* 711.

[17] Resolution of 18 March 1952, Bundesgerichtshof, Gr. Sen. St., W. Ger., 2 BGHSt. 194. For a description and analysis of this decision, see George Fletcher, *Rethinking Criminal Law* (Boston 1978), 747–50.

[18] Ronald Cass, 'Ignorance of Law: A Maxim Re-examined', (1976) 17 *William and Mary LR* 671. Although Cass does not explicitly endorse this rationale for not allowing ignorance of law as a defence, he labels it at p. 693 as the 'most plausible' of the rationales he surveys.

[19] Andrew Ashworth, *Principles of Criminal Law* (Oxford 1991), 209.

Such an explanation is puzzling, however. Is there not (at least arguably) a parallel duty to take care to learn of factual circumstances that might lead to injury of others? Yet negligent injuries are punishable only if the law expressly so provides, and even then are treated as less serious than intentional injuries. Why, then, are not legal mistakes treated comparably?

The problem may be formulated more generally as follows. The knowing violator's breach of the law renders him blameworthy to a specified extent. Call the extent of his blameworthiness ϕ. Suppose the legally ignorant defendant is deemed to blame for his failure to know that his conduct is illegal. Call the extent of his blameworthiness μ. What is missing from Ashworth's and Cass's argument is a reason to believe that $\phi = \mu$. But unless the two quanta of blame can be shown to be the same, it is unfair to punish the two violators equally.

3. When Might the Legally Ignorant Defendant be More Culpable than the Factually Ignorant Defendant?

To account for any difference in the treatment of legally ignorant defendants, we need to decide whether there are situations in which legal ignorance seems not to reduce culpability, or to reduce it less than factual ignorance would. That, in turn, calls for a preliminary look at the underlying rationale for the defence of ignorance of fact.

Consider the paradigm case of a property-owner who shoots and kills a trespasser, believing him to be an intruding animal. Why is this defendant less culpable than a killer who knew his victim to be a human being? It is no answer to respond that he lacks *mens rea* as traditionally construed; what is needed is a reason for construing *mens rea* in such a way that factually mistaken defendants have a lesser degree of culpability than defendants who are not mistaken.

Let us propose a simple account. The reason for reducing culpability, we think, is that the factually ignorant defendant does not mean to injure his victim.[20] The property-owner who is factually ignorant has no wish to hurt a person, but only to shoot an animal. 'I meant no injury' is surely one of the most familiar pleas in extenuation in legal as well as in non-legal contexts. This plea is no artifice of the criminal law, but is basic to everyday assessments of blame. Were one to ask not about this person's criminal

[20] The Model Penal Code recognizes that the defendant may mean to inflict injury in some cases of factual ignorance. Suppose the defendant intends to inflict some injury other than the injury he actually inflicts. § 2.04(2) provides that the defence of ignorance of fact 'is not available if the defendant would be guilty of another offense had the situation been as he supposed. In such case, however, the ignorance or mistake of the defendant shall reduce the grade and degree of the offense of which he may be convicted to those of the offense of which he would be guilty had the situation been as he supposed.'

liability, but about his moral blameworthiness, the answer would be the same: he is less to blame because he meant no injury.[21] A guest may be somewhat to blame for knocking down your vase by accident, but less so than if his action had been intentional. It is worth noting that the notion of 'injury' in this plea is not just a legal one: the guest not only has no wish to violate your legal rights, he also has none to deprive you of your interests.[22]

Of course, the defendant who is reckless—who consciously disregards a substantial and unjustifiable risk of injury—is culpable as well. Although he does not actually mean the injury, he is aware that it may well occur as a result of his conduct. The culpability of the negligent defendant—who disregards a substantial and unjustifiable risk of which he should have been aware—is more problematic, and has been a matter of much controversy among Anglo-American theorists.[23] The negligent defendant does not mean to do or even to risk injury, which is why he should be blamed less than someone who acts intentionally. If he is to be blamed at all, it is because he has disregarded a risk of which he should have been aware.

Let us consider how these simple observations about the exculpatory significance of ignorance of fact pertain to the defendant who is ignorant of law. It will be necessary to distinguish several different kinds of cases in order to trace the implications.

We begin with a case in which the defendant is merely ignorant of the legal rule. He understands everything about the nature and consequence of his conduct, except that it is prohibited by law. Suppose that our property-owner intends to kill a trespasser , but mistakenly believes that he is legally entitled to kill those who commit trespass on his property. This defendant *does* mean to do injury—that is, he intends to kill his human victim. The injury of which we are speaking here is a set-back to the victim's interests: in this case, his interest in survival. Thus, our suggested basis for reducing blame—namely, that the injurer meant no injury—simply does not hold.[24]

---

[21] Strangely, not much theory is available in the way of a deeper explanation of this plea. It has been suggested that an actor manifests more disrespect for a victim by transgressing his rights intentionally rather than accidentally. It is uncertain, however, whether such an account succeeds in explaining this plea, or simply redescribes it in other terms. In any event, we will not commit ourselves to any such account. As will become apparent below, our simple description is all that our analysis will require. See Nils Jareborg, 'Uppsat och klander', (1988) 73 *Svensk Juristtidning* 722. For another account, see the 'defiance' theory proposed by Jean Hampton, 'Mens Rea', in Ellen Paul, Fred Miller, and Jeffrey Paul (eds.), *Crime, Culpability, and Remedy* (Oxford 1990), 1.

[22] This account does not extend to all factual mistakes. For example, the basis for exoneration in a case of mistaken self-defence seems different—a person is not to blame for preferring to safeguard what he believes to be his vital interests, such as survival. See Andrew von Hirsch, 'Lifeboat Law', (1985) 4 *Criminal Justice Ethics* 88.

[23] See Michael Bayles, *Principles of Law* (Boston 1987), 295–300.

[24] Our conclusion is not altered by supposing the defendant's mistake about the legal rule was reasonable, for he still intended to injure his victim. Nor does our conclusion turn on

The case just cited is one where the defendant acted purposely, but the conclusion would be the same if he acted knowingly. Suppose the defendant's aim is to terrorize future trespassers into staying away. Seeing a person on his property, he lets slip his vicious Dobermann dogs, knowing the victim is almost certain to be badly injured. Suppose he is charged with aggravated assault, under a statute that defines that offence as knowingly causing grievous bodily harm. Here, the injuriousness of the conduct is still quite clear, and the defendant can be said to have meant the injury. It would be a strange reply to say he 'meant' no injury because the wounding was not his specific aim but the known side-effect of an ulterior aim of terrorizing potential trespassers.

Why might someone be tempted to believe that the defendant is less culpable in cases in which he is merely ignorant of the legal rule? Any such temptation would seem to come from conceptualizing common crimes as a challenge to the legal order, instead of as an injury to those directly affected. Clearly, a defendant who is ignorant of the law does not mean to challenge the legal order. We are not, however, drawn to such an authoritarian conception of criminal injury.[25]

The foregoing cases involve 'simple' ignorance: the defendant understands everything about the nature and consequence of his conduct, except for its illegality. But suppose we introduce the additional element that the defendant does not know that his conduct is wrong or injurious. Take, again, our property-owner who shoots or wounds a trespasser in full awareness that his victim is a human being. However, he believes his conduct is not only lawful, but also not wrong. Is his belief exculpatory? Perhaps the answer depends on *why* he believes his conduct to be morally permissible. We can think of at least two kinds of cases in which such a belief would *not* diminish his culpability.

(i) Suppose that the defendant does not believe his act to be wrong because he has a radically defective conception of the rights of others. Any number of conceptions might qualify as sufficiently defective. He might be a moral egoist, who believes that anything that is in his self-interest is permissible. Or he might be a nihilist, who believes that nothing is wrong. Perhaps his judgment that his act is permissible depends on obnoxious

whether the mistake is about the existence of a legal offence, or about the existence of a legal justification for committing it. Our hypothetical property-owner may know of a general legal rule against homicide, but think he is legally permitted to shoot trespassers. None the less, he knows he is injuring his victim, and claims no moral justification for doing so. Thus his ignorance of law lacks exculpatory significance. But see Fletcher, *Rethinking Criminal Law*, above n. 17, 683–91.

[25] For our reasons for rejecting this authoritarian conception, see von Hirsch, *Past or Future Crimes*, above n. 13, 78–80. For a conception of criminal injury that focuses on set-backs to the person's living-standard, see Andrew von Hirsch and Nils Jareborg, 'Gauging Criminal Harm: A Living-Standard Analysis', (1991) 11 *Oxford Journal of Legal Studies* 1.

distinctions: his particular victim may belong to a minority group to which he recognizes no duties. Or he might believe that he has duties only to persons who treat him in a certain way, but that all such duties cease to exist when he is maltreated to any extent. Let us make this last assumption in the case of our property-owner: He feels he may shoot or wound the trespasser simply because he has been maltreated, however slightly, by the violation of his property rights.

The first point to notice about such a case is that reduced culpability cannot be claimed on grounds parallel to those that pertain to factually mistaken defendants. The property-owner who mistakenly believes his victim is an intruding animal has no wish to hurt a human being. In the present example, the defendant has every intention to injure. His only basis for claiming extenuation is his belief that the interests of his victim are no longer his concern.

The assertion that such a belief extenuates presupposes a relevant difference between the blame deserved by the defendant who knowingly hurts his victim, flouting his admitted duty not to do so, and that deserved by the defendant who has the same intent to do injury, but does not think he has a duty to desist. In a case such as this, it is far from obvious that such a moral difference exists. The killer who knows his action to be wrong at least concedes (in principle if not in conduct) the humanity and worth of his victim. The killer who acknowledges no such duty does not even accord his victim that worth in principle.

(ii) Suppose that the defendant does not believe his act is wrong, because he is unaware that it is truly injurious. Imagine that the defendant is aware that he is shooting a human being, but believes that his act is commendable because it speeds his victim's ascent into heaven. Here it could be argued that the defendant is less culpable because—as in the case of ignorance of fact—he does not mean to cause injury to his victim. One might reply that the defendant still intends the injury that is prohibited by law: after all, the defendant knows his victim is dead, and death is the prohibited injury. This reply seems somewhat unpersuasive, however, because the person does not believe the legal injury is a genuine set-back to the victim's interests.

The person holds this belief, however, because he fails to comprehend even in a general way what people's interests are. This comes close to not having the relevant moral norm at all, because a certain basic understanding of human interests is needed for moral standards to serve their function. Such standards are designed as practical guides to conduct, but can do so only if the person not only wishes not to injure others but also possesses a minimal understanding of what constitutes injury. Our factually mistaken defendant satisfies these conditions: he not only wishes to avoid causing injury, but also possesses some general understanding of the vital interests of other persons. He simply lacks the detailed factual knowledge in the particular case to be aware that a human being is at risk. Such a person may be seen as generally respecting other people's interests, but as having failed to be aware in this particular case that these interests are at stake. The person with the defective conception of injury is different, for he fails to comprehend even in a general way what people's interests are. Were one asked to compare the blameworthiness of the person who appreciates that killing is injurious but who kills anyway, with that of the person who kills because for some strange reason he cannot grasp that killing is injurious, the answer would be far from obvious. At the very least, any distinction in blameworthiness is far less apparent than that between someone who acts intentionally and someone who is factually mistaken.

The force of this argument diminishes, of course, as the defendant's belief that the legally proscribed result is not genuinely injurious becomes increasingly plausible. For example, suppose a defendant commits euthanasia on a suffering and incurable patient who wishes to die. A defendant who acts in ignorance of law in such a case might be entitled to exoneration or at least mitigation, as our subsequent analysis will suggest.

The euthanasia example brings to mind another kind of case, that of the morally committed violator. What if the defendant performs euthanasia knowing it to be illegal? Here, we move to a new issue, beyond the scope of this essay: that of the obligation to obey known laws. If a defendant is aware that his conduct is criminal but disagrees with the legislature about its moral status, he may generally be expected to defer to the law despite his opposition to it. The basis of this expectation, however, needs to be articulated—that is, normative reasons must be given for why the duty exists.[26] Nevertheless, this expectation has no bearing upon the defendant who is ignorant of law. No comparable demand for deference in the face of disagreement can be made to the defendant who is unaware of the applicable law and believes his conduct is morally permissible.

What is the upshot of this discussion of the 'equal-treatment doctrine'? We conclude that ignorance of law, whether or not it is supplemented by ignorance of wrongfulness, does not *invariably* reduce culpability in the same way as ignorance of fact does. Our reasoning, however, still leaves open the possibility that ignorance of law is exculpating in circumstances other than those we have described. Let us now examine what these circumstances might be.

---

[26] According to George Fletcher: 'No theory of criminal law can tolerate the wholesale acquittal of revolutionary criminals' (*Rethinking Criminal Law*, above n. 17, 748–49). Such instrumentalist accounts are deficient, however, in the absence of a moral argument that shows why citizens have (except in extraordinary circumstances) a general duty to comply with known laws.

4. Reasonable Mistakes of Law

A 'reasonable' mistake of law is one which the defendant was not careless in making. The rationale for exonerating persons who make such errors, and the criteria for exoneration, bear closer scrutiny. We believe that two types of cases need to be distinguished. In one, exoneration is based on the legality principle, and the standard of reasonableness should be an objective one. In the other, exoneration rests on the defendant's culpability, and the standard should be more subjective. We will discuss each kind of case in turn.

4.1. *'Objective' Reasonableness and the Legality Principle*

On some occasions, the particular defendant is ignorant of the legal rule simply because that rule has not been made reasonably accessible to ordinary citizens. The Model Penal Code provides examples: when the relevant enactment has not yet been published, or the person relies on a judicial opinion, administrative order, or other official interpretation of law that subsequently proves to be erroneous.[27]

Here, we believe the rationale for exoneration should be based on the principle of legality rather than on the defendant's lack of culpability. Thus the defendant should be exonerated even if he is quite aware that his conduct is injurious. The principle of legality is distinct from notions of culpability, and it should have as much application to ill-disposed persons as to well-meaning ones. The governing idea is that persons should receive fair notice of what conduct is punished. Any citizen—even one having few ethical qualms about hurting others—should have a reasonable warning of potential criminal liability, so that he can avoid the burden of criminal sanctions by taking care to keep his conduct within the law. A person is not given fair notice of his potential criminal liability unless he can inform himself of the law by a reasonably diligent inquiry. The rationale for a defence in such cases is analogous to that which prohibits retroactive or vague legislation. If the law prohibits given conduct, but the prohibition can be ascertained only with great difficulty, then the person has not been given fair notice of his potential for liability at the time of his conduct.[28]

---

[27] Model Penal Code, § 2.04 (3). The Commentaries emphasize that this subsection 'is designed to permit a limited defense based on a reasonable belief on the part of the defendant that the law is such that his conduct does not constitute an offense'. The Commentaries explain that the defence should be limited to 'situations where the act charged is consistent with the entire law-abidingness of the actor, where the possibility of collusion is minimal, and where a judicial determination of the reasonableness of the belief in legality should not present substantial difficulty'. These limitations, however, emphasize crime-prevention concerns. See Model Penal Code Commentaries, i. 274–5.

[28] The significance of the principle of legality to the problem of ignorance of law has generally been overlooked by commentators. Perhaps this oversight is due to the fact that

Although German law (as we will see) is more charitable in other respects to the legally ignorant defendant, it does not accept this rationale. The German defence of 'unavoidable' mistake of law[29] has been interpreted to apply only when the defendant is reasonably unaware of the wrongfulness as well as of the illegality of his conduct.[30] Since this defence rests on grounds of culpability, it is not always available to defendants in the situation just described.

What remains to be debated is the scope of this defence. The Model Penal Code, as just noted, construes it narrowly. But what of cases not covered by the Code in which it is plausible to conclude that the prohibition is not reasonably ascertainable? For example, should a defendant be liable if official sources are silent but the leading commentaries agree that the conduct is permissible? The answer depends on how broadly or narrowly the legality principle should be construed, a matter we leave to further discussion.

4.2. 'Subjective' Reasonableness and Culpability

In some cases, the prohibition is ascertainable, but the defendant, in his situation, could not reasonably have been expected to be aware of it. Such cases involve what might be called 'subjective' reasonableness. Suppose that a resident of country X travels on holiday to country Y, accompanied by his adult stepdaughter who is also his lover. He is charged with incest under the laws of country Y. Suppose their relationship is neither illegal nor considered reprehensible in country X. Here, the application of an objective standard of reasonableness would lead to a conviction: perusal of the laws of country Y would have indicated that the conduct is illegal. Under a subjective standard, however, the conclusion might well be otherwise: *this* individual, in his circumstances, is ill-suited to be on notice of the illegality of his conduct.[31]

Why, however, require that the legal mistake be reasonable (even if only 'subjectively' reasonable) in order to acquit? There is no comparable requirement for mistake of fact: if the person is charged with a crime requiring purpose or knowledge, even an unreasonable mistake warrants acquittal. The defendant who makes an unreasonable mistake of fact, we

the legality principle serves many diverse purposes, including the prevention of arbitrary or discriminatory law enforcement. Jerome Hall argued that the principle of legality actually provides a reason *not* to acquit the legally ignorant defendant. See Hall, *General Principles of Criminal Law*, above n. 4, 382–7. For a response, see Houlgate, *'Ignorantia Juris*: A Plea for Justice', above n. 15, 38–40.

[29] See German Penal Code, § 17.

[30] See Fletcher, *Rethinking Criminal Law*, above n. 17, 749–50.

[31] Comparable examples are provided by Fletcher, *Rethinking Criminal Law*, above n. 17, 740.

would answer, *is* somewhat culpable, albeit less so than someone who acts with purpose or knowledge. Reasons of policy, not those of culpability, point to restricting the scope of liability for negligence to offences involving gross carelessness that cause serious injuries, and to certain kinds of regulatory offences. The negligent commission of lesser injuries may be blameworthy as well, but such conduct is not sufficiently serious to merit the attention of the criminal law. With legal mistakes, the policy reasons are otherwise. Where a negligent failure to ascertain the legal rule supports an imputation of at least some culpability, there is no reason for the law to desist from punishing. For the State has good reason to encourage citizens to comply with the laws generally.

A defendant must clear two hurdles in order to sustain a defence of subjectively reasonable ignorance of law. The first, discussed in section 3, concerns knowledge of the injuriousness of the conduct. The second deals with the reasonableness of his ignorance of the legal rule. These two issues are analytically distinct. Suppose that state X adopts a new rule requiring biannual automobile inspections. The defendant, accustomed to the old rule of annual inspections, is charged with the offence of driving with an expired inspection sticker. Here, the defendant would have no reason to know that his conduct is injurious. Although he should be aware that his automobile ought to be properly maintained, annual inspections might well suffice for that purpose. The question remains, however, whether his ignorance of the legal rule is itself reasonable. It might be argued that drivers should be aware that driving is a specially regulated activity, subject to detailed—and sometimes changing—regulations. If this is the case, the defendant's ignorance of the legal rule is unreasonable, and he should not be acquitted.

Let us, then, examine these two requirements more closely.

(*a*) Was the defendant aware he was doing or risking injury? If not, did his lack of awareness show a defective moral understanding?

In offences involving individual human victims, the conduct's injuriousness is usually apparent. Our property-owner knows he is doing something terrible to the trespasser. The same holds in most ordinary offences of violence, theft, or fraud.

There may, however, be exceptions. Recall our euthanasia case. The defendant is aware he is killing the suffering patient, but the injuriousness of his conduct—seen not as the legally proscribed result, but as a set-back to the victim's vital interests—is less clear. If the suffering patient wishes to die but cannot do so without assistance, is he worse off if someone complies with his wishes and kills him? However this question might ultimately be answered, no obviously deranged moral understanding is exhibited by a defendant who believes he is acting properly in killing the patient.

What about crimes not involving identifiable individual victims? For some such crimes, the injury to unidentified individuals may be quite manifest. Reckless driving and illegal discharges of poisonous effluent are not traditional crimes, but the risk that such conduct creates to unspecified persons should be obvious. Other crimes, however, may be different. Sometimes, the evil to be prevented is clear enough, but it is a matter of judgment whether the prohibited conduct contributes significantly to that ill (as in our example of biannual vehicle inspections). In still others, the ill may not be readily noticeable at all, absent knowledge of the legal prohibition.

(*b*) Was the defendant's ignorance of the legal rule reasonable in the circumstances?

This question raises the issue of the appropriate standard of reasonableness. If that standard is drawn too stringently—as the German courts have done, in the opinion of some observers[32]—few defendants will actually be acquitted. What, then, is a proper standard?

We think that 'reasonableness' should not entail a generalized demand that the defendant make full inquiry into the legality of his every action. The circumstances must provide some 'clue'—some reason for believing— that his conduct may be proscribed.[33]

One such clue is provided when the conduct is widely understood to be illegal or to raise questions of legality. Failure to pay income taxes provides an example. Non-payment of income taxes is not obviously injurious in the sense that a person having no awareness of the law should feel morally bound to volunteer payments to the State. But paying income taxes is something citizens are routinely informed about, and hence it is a duty of which the defendant should have been aware. Thus the legal mistake would be unreasonable, unless there is something special in the defendant's situation that would deny him access to information commonly available about the obligation to pay taxes.

A second kind of clue is provided when the conduct is of a specialized kind that appears to be a candidate for State regulation. Consider the Maine summer vacationer who catches lobsters without a licence, not knowing one is required. His conduct clears the first of the two hurdles we have mentioned: catching a few lobsters is not obviously injurious to anyone (other than the beasts themselves). The question concerns the second hurdle: the reasonableness of his legal mistake. Innocent as his legal error

---

[32] See Arzt, 'The Problem of Mistake of Law', above n. 16, 725.
[33] Compare Claus Roxin, *Strafrecht: Allgemeiner Teil* (Munich 1992), 601–2.

may be, it should be plainly apparent to any visitor that lobster fishing is a special skill, conducted by many residents for a livelihood, involving a resource not likely to be inexhaustible. These facts warrant a reasonable inference—provide the clue—that the activity is one that might be regulated. Hence the defendant's mistake should not be deemed reasonable. More reflection might suggest further kinds of clues.

When such clues exist and the defendant is thus on notice, how extensive should his duty of inquiry be? Since the applicable standard is the reasonableness of his mistake, he should not be required to exhaust every conceivable avenue of legal inquiry. A duly diligent inquiry should suffice. That answer, in turn, raises the question of how much diligence is due. Would the advice of a lawyer that his conduct is legally unproblematic suffice?[34] We leave this issue to future discussion.

Because the two hurdles that the defendant must overcome for acquittal are distinct, each of them suffices to preclude acquittal, even if the other is cleared. Consider this pair of illustrations. First, a defendant rapes his wife on a boat within British territorial waters. The offence occurred the day after the House of Lords decided that spouses were no longer exempt from the rape prohibition. He believed at the time of the assault that the old rule still applied, and hence that his act was legal. Here, his legal mistake is reasonable. The former marital exemption was well known, and the defendant had no access to the new decision. Thus the second hurdle is cleared. The first, however, is not. The defendant knew his act was injurious and humiliating to his wife; thus he meant to cause injury. Or, if he did not know, his understanding of injury is too deviant to warrant exoneration. Second, consider our euthanasia case yet again. The defendant clears the first hurdle, for the reasons discussed already. But, ordinarily, he does not surmount the second. Homicide is widely understood to be regulated by the criminal law. Thus, to commit the act, without inquiring further into its legality, is not a reasonable legal mistake. Only if the defendant is, say, a recent arrival from a place where such conduct is permissible might the conclusion be otherwise.

The combined effect of these two hurdles will keep the scope of exculpation fairly narrow. This conclusion does not disturb us: a defence of ignorance of law *should* be narrow. But there will be cases in which the defence will hold: where the injuriousness of the conduct is not apparent, and no clue of the illegality of the conduct presents itself.

5. 'Unreasonable' Mistakes of Law

So far, we have discussed mistakes of law that are reasonable, either for the ordinary person ('objectively' reasonable), or for the defendant in his

---

[34] For a discussion of this issue in the German context, see ibid. 604–6.

circumstances ('subjectively' reasonable). But what of *un*reasonable legal mistakes, that is, cases in which the defendant should have known the legal rule? Here, Anglo-American law has been unwilling to allow a defence. Whatever extenuation has been granted has been dispensed at sentencing, where broad discretion has been the norm. England's new Criminal Justice Act, however, calls for sentences proportionate to the gravity of the crime and expressly authorizes sentence reductions for mitigating circumstances.[35] Thus the courts will be faced with the issue of whether and under what circumstances unreasonable mistakes of law are mitigating.

German law, meanwhile, explicitly recognizes that unreasonable mistakes of law may reduce the blameworthiness of defendants. It provides that a mistake of law, even if it does not qualify as reasonable, *may* constitute grounds of mitigation.[36] When such mitigation is found, a sentence below the normal statutory minimum may be imposed.[37] Hans-Heinrich Jescheck, a leading commentator, suggests that the word 'may' in the statute should be liberally construed, so that mitigation will often be found. He contends that only in cases of wilful blindness, indifference, manifest thoughtlessness, or actual hostility to law should mitigation be denied.[38] To what extent is this position defensible?

A defendant who makes an unreasonable mistake of law fails to clear the second hurdle we have discussed. He believes in good faith that his conduct is legal, but the circumstances have put him on notice that the law might be otherwise. When should his punishment be mitigated?

No mitigation should be allowed if the defendant fails to clear the first hurdle as well. The person who means to hurt another is not less culpable simply because he thinks that the injury is legally 'free'. However, if the defendant does overcome the first hurdle, then his culpability is reduced. The defendant meant neither to do injury nor to break the law. His fault, then, rests merely on his not having informed himself of the legal requirements under circumstances that should have put him on notice. Since that failure is merely careless, he deserves to have his punishment mitigated.

On this view, the scope of mitigation of defendants who are ignorant of law is likely to be much broader than for exculpation. Defendants who were unaware (but should have been aware) that their conduct was illegal would often be entitled to mitigation. Of course, no mitigation would be extended when the injuriousness of the conduct was plainly apparent. Thus our conclusion is consistent with the German view that permits a rather broad scope for reduced punishment.

---

[35] Criminal Justice Act 1991, s. 3(3)(a). For discussion, see Andrew Ashworth, *Sentencing and Criminal Justice* (London 1992), ch. 5.
[36] German Penal Code, § 17.   [37] German Penal Code, § 49.
[38] Hans-Heinrich Jescheck, *Lehrbuch des Strafrechts* (4th edn., Berlin 1988), 415.

6. A Reservation about our Analysis

We have claimed that a defendant who makes a subjectively reasonable mistake of law must, in order to be exculpated, not only believe in good faith that his conduct is not injurious, but also have some plausible basis for that belief. We also suggested a similar standard for unreasonable legal mistakes. Our reason for imposing this standard was sketched in section 3. We pointed out that mere legal ignorance, even if coupled with a bona fide belief in the moral rightfulness of conduct, is not necessarily extenuating, if that belief stems from a sufficiently bizarre or deviant conception of morality or of what constitutes injury.

How, though, can a standard be implemented that permits courts to assess the legitimacy of the defendant's beliefs in the morality of his conduct? Some might argue that it is never appropriate for judges to make explicit moral judgments such as these. The difference between 'normal' moral standards on the one hand, and bizarre or deviant standards on the other, is too elusive, and judges should not be required to assume the role of moral philosophers. Either the present Anglo-American rule should be followed, according to which legal ignorance seldom if ever exonerates, or else reasonable mistakes of law (coupled with a good-faith belief in the moral legitimacy of the conduct) should suffice. The intermediate position, according to which a good-faith belief in the conduct's morality should extenuate only if the defendant has a plausible basis for it, is simply unworkable.

We are troubled by this conclusion, however, because it leads to results that strike us as unjust. Simple notions of fairness—focused on culpability—point to a less restrictive treatment of legal ignorance than the existing Anglo-American rule. But permitting reasonable legal ignorance to exonerate merely when it is accompanied by a belief in the moral legitimacy of the conduct seems to produce inequitable results as well. Consider our earlier example of the yachtsman who rapes his wife. The injuriousness of such conduct, we pointed out, is plainly apparent. Suppose he nevertheless judges his conduct legitimate, because (say) he believes that women appreciate such treatment. Is his belief really an indication of reduced culpability in the same way as factual ignorance? We cannot bring ourselves to accept this conclusion.

We are aware that our proposal is not easy to implement. Our modest claim is that it represents an improvement over the current state of Anglo-American law. We do not concede that there would be insurmountable obstacles in allowing the judiciary to make the moral determinations this essay would entrust to them, and the practical experience of the German courts in applying a comparable standard seems to confirm our view.[39]

---

[39] See Fletcher, *Rethinking Criminal Law*, above n. 17, 749–55.

There remains the question of how to formulate the exclusion for such cases in a manner that is not too vague and does not leave undue discretion to individual courts. A possible formulation would be that (where the requisite legal ignorance is present) a good-faith belief that the conduct is not injurious ordinarily suffices for the defence. The exception would be created for cases in which the injuriousness of the conduct is manifest in the circumstances. We have sketched some examples in which this exception would apply, and further discussion would elicit additional kinds of cases. Rather than leaving the decision to the discretion of individual judges, a case-law jurisprudence should develop in this area, providing some principles and illustrations about the scope of the exception.

7. Concluding Thoughts

Let us review our conclusions. We began by asking why ignorance of law should be treated more restrictively than ignorance of fact. We rejected the argument that such greater restrictiveness is defensible because citizens have a moral obligation to know the law. Instead, we examined when legal ignorance might, or might not, eliminate or reduce the defendant's culpability. Our conclusion was that a defendant who is ignorant of the applicable legal rule, and has a bona fide belief that his conduct is not injurious or wrong, should ordinarily (1) be excused if his legal mistake was a reasonable one in the circumstances; or (2) have his punishment mitigated if he did not know but should have known of the conduct's illegality. We say 'ordinarily', because some more deviant kinds of beliefs in the moral propriety of the conduct would not qualify.

Our analysis provides an additional ground of exoneration, where the defendant's legal mistake is 'objectively' reasonable. Our rationale for a defence in such cases invokes the legality principle rather than considerations of culpability. Even ill-willed defendants should receive fair notice of the legal rules they are expected to observe.

What does our view suggest about the supposed obligation to know the law? It presupposes that such an obligation exists. Punishability, however, should depend on the defendant's degree of fault in infringing this obligation. If the defendant is ignorant of the legal rule without fault—that is, he makes a reasonable mistake—he is not to blame at all for his failure to know the law. Hence he can be punished only if the culpability is supplied on the alternate ground of his meaning to do injury. If his legal mistake is unreasonable, then he is somewhat culpable for his failure to learn and abide by the rule, which is why a mitigated punishment is indicated. Our analysis thus differs from Ashworth's and Cass's,[40] not in that we deny

---

[40] See text accompanying nn. 18 and 19.

there is an obligation to obey the law, but in our conclusions regarding the consequences of infringing that obligation.

Although our conclusions regarding legal ignorance resemble present German doctrine (at least in its broad outlines),[41] we did not reach them by examining that doctrine's advantages and drawbacks. Instead, we relied largely on notions of culpability. Our focus on culpability indicates that Anglo-American law, including reformist schemes such as the Model Penal Code, have been far too restrictive in their treatment of mistake of law. Notions of fairness point toward a less restrictive treatment.

[41] The details of the German doctrine contain some obscurities, including those involved in so-called 'subsumption' errors. See Arzt, 'The Problem of Mistake of Law', above n. 16, 719.

The Nature of Justification

GEORGE P. FLETCHER

Since the unification of the two Germanies in October 1990, the West has begun to apply its principles of criminal justice to crimes allegedly committed by Eastern officials during forty-five years of Communist rule. That these proceedings are undertaken raises innumerable jurisprudential conundrums, among them the problem of justifying conduct under East German statutes that the West regards as unjust. This problem came to the fore in the prosecution of, among others, two border guards, Uwe Hapke and Udo Walther, for attempting the murder of fleeing citizens of the German Democratic Republic. A 1982 statute authorized border guards to shoot all persons trying feloniously to leave the country. The guards rather sensibly appealed to this statute—informally called the *Schiessbefehl* (order to shoot)—but the court would have none of it. The statute supposedly violated the generally recognized international right to leave one's country. And if the statute was unjust, the court reasoned, it could not provide a justification for shooting someone with the intent to kill. The court declared the guards guilty of attempted murder.

Many observers equate these proceedings to the Nuremberg trials, proceedings in which an international tribunal convicted German leaders for violating the newly coined crimes against humanity and conspiring to wage aggressive war. The Nuremberg process appears to have violated the principle *nulla poena sine lege*; the prosecution of genocide as a crime against humanity was not grounded in a pre-existing statutory definition. The same charge is made today against the German courts for disregarding a statutory justification valid in the GDR. The courts, in effect, created a new crime that was not punishable at the time of its commission. Though the prosecution is understandable as a passionate effort to punish injustice, the procedures and the rationale are the same as those of the Nuremberg trials. This negative assessment of the recent German conviction of the border guards seems to be the virtually unanimous opinion of Italian scholars, indicating the radically divergent styles of legal development in post-Fascist Italy and Germany.[1]

The jurisprudential problems raised by the case of the border guards are manifold. The first question is whether a statutory declaration should be

[1] This generalization about Italian opinions is based on extensive discussions with Italian scholars in Turin, Milan, Bologna, Florence, and Trento in April 1992.

conclusive on the issue of whether homicide or attempted homicide should be treated as justified. The second is whether the judicial disregard of a statutory declaration is tantamount to the judicial recognition of a new offence. Both of these questions raise a basic problem of whether there is a fundamental distinction between those issues that we would identify as the elements of the offence, and those that are raised by way of justification. If there is no basic difference, if a justification is merely a negative element of the offence (i.e. intentional homicide requires the *absence* of self-defence as well as an act intentionally causing death), then the critics of the German decision have a strong case. If the legislature has authority to define the 'elements of the offence', then it should have the same authority over the negative elements we call claims of justification.

The claim that justificatory elements are like positive elements of the offence—except that the former require the absence rather than the presence of a factual element—has an enduring attraction. It comes in two basic forms—a conceptual and a 'positivist' variation. My aim is to argue against both of these variations in favour of what I might call an ideal theory of justification. I will back into my argument for the ideal theory by trying to clarify its opponents.

The conceptual variation holds simply that whether courts or legislatures develop the criminal law, there is no important difference between affirmative and negative elements of offences; between, say, an act causing death and the absence of self-defence. This view is expressed in the doctrine that in homicide cases, for example, an unreasonable mistake about the factual presuppositions of self-defence should be treated just like an unreasonable mistake about whether an object being shot at is a human being or an animal. As the latter form of unreasonable mistake provides an adequate foundation for a charge of negligent homicide, so, the argument goes, should the former.[2]

The positivist variation of the theory holds that there is no conceptual structure in the criminal law at all, that all there is to the definition of crimes and defences derives from the authority of those charged with the matter. This view is positivist in the sense that it assumes that the entire criminal law is enacted law: there are no principles binding by virtue of their intrinsic merit. But if there is a structural distinction between elements of the offence and claims of justification, or between claims of justification and of excuse, these distinctions would acquire their appeal not from the will of the legislature, but from their intrinsic plausibility. Whether these distinctions obtain or not depends not on legislative authority, but on whether they provide a convincing account of the immanent structure of

[2] For more on this point, see my discussion in *A Crime of Self-Defense: Bernhard Goetz and the Law on Trial* (New York 1988), 54–5.

the criminal law. So far as positivism requires all legal rules and categories to derive from legislative authority, positivists cannot concede the existence of distinctions immanent in the law. Therefore, positivists are led to the conclusion that unless the legislature has spoken otherwise, there is no relevant distinction between elements of the offence and claims of justification. For the sake of brevity, I will refer to both the conceptual and positivist theses as the 'unity' thesis.

The ideal theory of justification, by contrast, holds that despite the nominal realization of the elements of the offence, the conduct is not really wrong, not a violation of the *jus* or the Law in the ideal sense of *Recht*, *droit*, *diritto*, *derecho*, and the analogous forms in other languages.[3] A justified act conforms to the Right or the Law in a sense deeper than that captured in a legislative definition of an offence. A statutory definition should be understood as an approximation, by rule, of a principled understanding of wrongful conduct. It states the normal case of wrongdoing, but fails to account accurately for wrongdoing in the extraordinary cases that arise under conflict and under the pressure of circumstances. To deal with these extraordinary situations, we must appeal to claims of justification, such as self-defence and necessity. Under ordinary circumstances, taking the property of another without consent should be treated as theft. Under circumstances of necessity, this conventional definition breaks down; it must yield to an understanding, based on principle, that in an emergency, taking property as the lesser evil is not wrongful behaviour.

Similarly, killing is not wrong if committed in self-defence. Burning a dwelling-house is not wrong, if committed as an act of necessity to save more valuable property. Breaking and entering an abandoned cottage is not wrong if necessary to escape a life-threatening storm. To use Judith Thomson's distinction, the nominal *infringement* of the law in these situations does not amount to a *violation* of the law.[4] Satisfying the elements of the offence constitutes an infringement. An intervening justification prevents the infringement from being wrongful violation. It does not constitute full-blooded murder, arson, larceny, or burglary.

Of course they do not, the proponents of the unity thesis may respond. Killing in self-defence falls short of murder in precisely the same way that shooting and hitting a scarecrow with the intent to kill falls short of the crime. In this case, and in the other cases mentioned, one of the necessary elements of the offences—a negative element—remains unsatisfied. The ideal theory implies a structural difference between the two types of argument for non-liability. Denying an element of the offence is an assertion

[3] The reader will forgive me if I do not repeat here my oft-made comments about the difference between the two terms for law in other languages and their absence in English. For a summary, see my paper 'Two Modes of Legal Thought', (1981) 90 *Yale LJ* 970.

[4] J. Thomson, *Rights, Restitution, and Risk*, (Cambridge, Mass. 1986), 40–2.

that there is not even an infringement that needs to be justified. Asserting a justification is, to use the term from common-law pleading, an argument in confession and avoidance. A claim of self-defence confesses the infringement of a significant human interest, and seeks to avoid the implication that the conduct is wrong.

To put the difference between the two theories simply: the unity thesis maintains that in the case of justified conduct, there is no harm relevant to the criminal law. An aggressor killed in self-defence, or a home destroyed as a matter of necessity, is not a relevant invasion of protected legal interest.[5] The ideal theory insists that in these cases there is some harm that should be registered in the criminal law, but that causing this harm is justified as a matter of principle.

It bears mentioning that we are not considering the theory of excuses. Claims of insanity, duress, mistake of law, and personal necessity take as their starting-point the assumption that the conduct is wrongful. The thief who asserts starvation as an excuse does not deny that he has committed larceny. The insane killer does not deny that homicide is murder. These claims do not bear on the propriety of the act, but merely on the responsibility of the agent for authoring a wrongful act.

The two approaches to justification—the unity and the ideal theories—bear on a number of issues; their differing implications are worth rehearsing. *First*, as already mentioned, a mistaken claim about the factual preconditions of self-defence or necessity will be treated, on the unity theory, like a mistake about the elements of the offence. A mistake about whether someone is an aggressor is equivalent to a mistake about whether the person being shot at is alive. At one level, this can be understood as a point about the scope of the required intent. If the absence of self-defence is an element of homicide, then no one can be guilty of intentional homicide who mistakenly thinks that he or she is being attacked. If non-consent is an element of rape, then the required intent is the intent to have intercourse without consent. Further, if the mistake is unreasonable, then it will be treated as negligence as to an element of the offence. If the offence can be committed negligently, the negligent mistake renders the perpetrator liable. Thus, if Bernhard Goetz negligently thought he was about to be attacked, he could have been guilty of negligent homicide (had he killed one of the four putative aggressors). If the offence is not subject to negligent commission—as attempted murder is not—then the unreasonable mistake is insufficient to generate liability.

Second, the theory that claims of justification are merely negative elements of the offence leads to the view—the converse of the first implication

<hr/>

[5] This is the line taken by Paul Robinson in one of the significant early articles in this area. See Robinson, 'A Theory of Justification: Societal Harm as a Prerequisite of Criminal Liability', (1975) 23 *UCLA LR* 266.

stated above—that objective elements are sufficient to prevent commission of the offence. Think of the case in which the agent wants and intends to kill an innocent person, but in fact is subject at that very moment to a secret attack from his intended victim. The act of intended killing turns out to be an action in objective self-defence. If self-defence were just like an element of the offence, one would be inclined to think that the objective presence of aggression would be sufficient to prevent realization of the offence. If the objective fact that the intended victim is in fact a scarecrow precludes liability for homicide, then, by extension, the objective fact that the intended victim is an aggressor should have the same effect. Let us refer to this as the problem of objective justification, i.e. justification regardless of the perpetrator's ignorance of the justifying circumstances.

Though the matter continues to be debated in theory, virtually all legal systems—Italy excepted—adhere to the view that claims of justification represent good reasons for transgressing against the statute and the interest it protects. It follows that only those who have acted with knowledge of the justifying circumstances—of self-defence, necessity, or for that matter consent—should be able to claim a good reason for infringing a protected interest and rely upon a claim of justification. Admittedly, there might be stronger arguments for a position that seems so deeply entrenched in the world's legal culture. Generating a convincing rationale for requiring intent in cases of justification reminds one of other practices of the criminal law that are widely shared and intuitively accepted—for example, punishing completed crimes more severely than attempts, and retributive punishment generally—but for which theoreticians have yet to generate a compelling justification.

Third, if we may assume that the prohibitory norms of the criminal law protect specific interests, and if the norms must be stated to include the absence of justifying circumstances, then it follows that the interest protected must be stated so as to include the absence of justification. We normally say that the law of homicide protects human life, but if objective self-defence precludes finding even a nominal infringement of the law, it follows that the purpose of the law of homicide is to protect the lives of innocent, non-aggressing, human beings. Under this view, killing an aggressor is no more an infringement of the law of homicide than filling a scarecrow full of lead. In neither case does the intent to kill an innocent (non-aggressing) human being provide a sufficient basis for conviction.

Fourth, the doctrine of legislative supremacy, if applied to criteria of justification as well as to the elements of the offence, precludes the judicial recognition of new justificatory defences. In fact, in most legal systems, the courts have taken the lead in this century in developing the defence of lesser evils. Abortion cases frequently emerged as a testing-ground. The German Reichsgericht's recognition of lesser evils as an extra-statutory defence is perhaps the most dramatic example.[6] The German court's reasoning in this landmark 1927 case rests squarely on the ideal theory of justification.[7] Criminal conduct, the judges argue, depends on wrongdoing and wrongful behaviour. Conduct is wrongful only if it violates *Recht* in an ideal sense. The legislature is supreme in defining offences, but not in specifying the range of possible defences that can negate the inference of wrongdoing from the commission of an offence. Aborting a foetus to save the mother from suicide, though not justified under the abortion statute, represents the lesser evil under the situation, and therefore the act was justified in principle. As a justified act, it was not wrongful. There was no criminal liability. This kind of judicial refinement of the law would not be possible under a coupling of the unity thesis with legislative supremacy.

Fifth, legislation has a function in the field of justification (as well as in the field of excuses) which is different from its role in rendering as precise as possible the elements of the offence. Code provisions defining self-defence and necessity have the function primarily of guiding judges in deciding cases. They function, it seems, as decision rules rather than conduct rules.[8] Accordingly, these provisions governing justifying criteria may admit of a degree of vagueness that would be intolerable under the due-process principle of 'fair warning', requiring that criminal offences be defined with sufficient specificity to advise common people of their rights and obligations.[9]

The standard of necessity, for example, is defined generally to exact a comparison of the costs and benefits of following the nominal prohibition of the law. Imagine the vagueness of a crime defined to incorporate this cost/benefit judgment. It would read something like: Don't take things belonging to another unless, on balance, it is better for society to do so. When a California statute was interpreted as a prohibition against 'unnecessary' abortions, the state supreme court declared the statute void as excessively vague under the due-process clause of the Fourteenth

---

[6] Judgment of the Reichsgericht, 11 March 1927, 61 RGSt 242.

[7] One is tempted to call this a 'precedent'. According to the conventional wisdom, however, German courts do not recognize precedents. This decision had its impact, in fact, not directly, but indirectly, as a stimulus to the leading commentators to pick up the theory of 'extra-statutory' justification and to incorporate it into the law as they presented it in their textbooks.

[8] This thesis is by no means obvious. Excusing conditions function more clearly as decision rules rather than conduct rules. Claims of justification do enter into debates between individuals about whether their conduct is right or wrong. The question is whether it is the legislative language as such, or rather the general principles of justification, that enter into these debates. On the distinction between decision rules and conduct rules, see Meir Dan-Cohen, 'Decision Rules and Conduct Rules: On Acoustic Separation in Criminal Law', (1984) 97 *Harvard LR* 625.

[9] e.g. *Papachristou* v. *City of Jacksonville*, 405 US 156 (1972) (vagrancy ordinance unconstitutionally vague); *International Harvester Co* v. *Kentucky*, 234 US 216 (1914) (price and trade regulation unconstitutional).

Amendment.[10] Cost/benefit standards and standards of necessity are suitable for claims of justification but, as a general matter, they infect the definition of elements of crimes with undue imprecision.

If the unity thesis were correct, then the absence of necessity would be an element of larceny, arson, burglary, and a host of other crimes that lend themselves to justification on grounds of necessity or lesser evils. It would indeed be correct to define the injunction of common-law larceny as:

Do not take an object from the possession of the owner, with the intent to deprive the owner permanently of his property, unless necessary to avoid an imminent risk that represents a greater cost than the damage represented by taking the object.

A crime so defined would fail the due-process requirement of fair warning: the principle *nulla poena sine lege* would be frustrated. The only way to save the common-law crimes from the vice of vagueness is to filter off the defence of necessity and to treat it as a different type of issue, to which relatively lax criteria of precision may be applied.

Sixth, if the legislature is not supreme in the field of justifying criteria, the courts are free to make statutory language conform to their ideal theory of justification. A good example in the German experience is the pruning back, in recent years, of the broad sweep of the German Code provision on self-defence. That provision, Article 32 of the 1975 Code, seems to recognize the traditional German doctrine that anyone may use any amount of force to uphold any right, however trivial. So understood, the provision implies that a property-owner may use deadly force, if no less drastic means is available, to prevent a thief from escaping with a minor bounty. No principle of proportionality restrains the use of necessary force. The guiding principle of the tradition is that the 'Right need never yield to the Wrong.'

In the last decades, German scholars and courts have begun to apply a principle of proportionality to restrain the scope of Article 32. The doctrinal label is *Rechtsmissbrauch* or *abus de droit*—a doctrine, peculiar to Continental legal thinking, which resembles, more or less, the common-law principle of reasonableness.[11] The difficulty posed by this development is precisely the charge that curtailing a justification implicitly recognizes a new area of criminal liability, namely the set of cases that would be justified if the statute were strictly applied.

Seventh, there remains to be considered only the case of the German border guards posed at the outset of this article. This case differs from the problem considered in the fourth point above, for here the court was

---

[10] *People* v. *Belous*, 71 Cal. 2d 954, 458 P 2d 194, 80 Cal. Rptr. 354 (1969), cert. denied 397 US 915 (1970).

[11] On the details of 'more or less' resemblance, see my paper 'The Right and the Reasonable', (1985) 98 *Harvard LR* 949.

willing to disregard a statutory justification to the detriment of the defendant rather than add a justification for the benefit of the defence. It differs
from the sixth point, largely as a matter of degree, for in this instance the
courts went further than adjusting a defence at the fringes. Disregarding
an entire statutory defence poses the most difficult test for the ideal theory
of justification.

Let us summarize the seven items and attempt to assay the balance of
advantage between the unity thesis and the ideal theories of justification.

		Unity thesis
First	mistake about justifying fact	like mistake about element of offence
Second	objective justification	implied
Third	interest protected	includes absence of justifying factor
Fourth	recognizing new defences	not allowed
Fifth	problem of vagueness	not solved
Sixth	adjusting justification	not allowed
Seventh	disregarding statutory justification	not allowed

The ideal theory takes the opposing stand on all these counts. If justifications are asserted in a dimension of principle, while the elements are
laid down by statute, there would be no reason to treat mistakes about
justifying facts as one treats mistakes about the elements. Also, if a claim
of justification represents a good reason for violating the statute, it makes
no sense to entertain the possibility of justification by objective facts alone.
The interests protected under the criminal law are defined simply as life,
property, etc., without considering the conditions that, if present, would
justify a nominal infringement of these interests. The problem of vagueness
is solved, and further, courts have the authority to elaborate the ideal
theory of justification by recognizing new claims of justification, curtailing
other claims, and disregarding legislative pronouncements at odds with the
ideal theory.

It is hard to find a legal system that consistently adopts the implications of either the unity or the ideal theory. Because of the extraordinarily
strong positivist bent of post-war Italian jurisprudence, the Italians seem
to concur with the unity thesis on all seven points. The Model Penal Code
takes the positivist line on most of these seven points, except that it explicitly rejects objective justification; German law follows the ideal theory on
most points, except that the dominant view in German law concurs with
the Model Penal Code in treating mistakes about justificatory facts as
though they were mistakes about elements of the offence. Generally, the
unity or ideal theories do no more than incline legal systems in one direction

or another. Other arguments and theories intercede to yield different results on particular points.

As a matter of theory, the unity thesis appears to be harder to defend. Its major defects are the third and fifth points. It fails to provide an intuitively plausible account of the interests protected under the criminal law. As German theorists are fond of saying, it reduces killing in self-defence to the same format as killing a fly.[12] It also fails to solve the problem of vagueness introduced by claims such as necessity, which turn ultimately on broader questions of social costs and benefits. Of course, the advocate of the unity thesis could insist that these are mysteries of the criminal law. No one but the legislature knows what interests it seeks to protect. And if some of the defences are vague, so be it. These points hardly matter, the argument might go, as compared with the advantages gained by eliminating judicial power to curtail and disregard statutory defences.

It must be clear that, on balance, I favour the ideal theory of justification. More important than a decision for one theory or the other, however, is the way of thinking about criminal theory implicitly advocated in this essay. A case like that of the German border guards poses a problem in the foundations of criminal liability that goes beyond the immediate problem of whether a court may disregard a statutory defence. My suggestion is that the nature of justification should be assayed globally, as differing approaches to justification are manifested in the seven points, ranging from the analysis of mistakes to the problem of curtailing an overly broad statutory justification. When looked at in the light of its impact on these various points, the ideal theory cuts a more convincing figure.

The response might be: fine, we should apply the ideal where we have to, and rely upon the thesis of conceptual unity or the positivist variation whenever it serves the interests of the defendant to do so. Therefore, we will allow the courts to recognize new defences, but not to disregard a defence that protects the defendant. Although it seems to disregard the injustice of acquitting those who should be convicted, this position enjoys an undeniable appeal.

The best case for a defence-oriented version of the ideal theory would go something like this. When the legislature commits itself, in a statute, to a certain set of criteria defining criminal offences, the entire apparatus of the State, including the courts, is estopped from denying the defendant recourse to these criteria in his or her defence. Every citizen, every person subject to the jurisdiction of the State, has a right to rely on the statutory law as written. A statute is something like a promise to the citizen; the State cannot go back on its word. If the East German state promised a

[12] See Schönke-Schröder, *Strafgesetzbuch Kommentar* (23rd edn., Munich 1988), s. 23 at 177 (citing aphorism and commenting on the debate).

justification to its border guards in the form of the 1982 statute, the successor state of unified Germany cannot disregard the promise.

The problem with the theory of statute-as-promise is its overkill. It encompasses all statutes bearing on procedural matters that the State should be allowed to change retroactively, without falling foul of the principle *nulla poena sine lege*. Consider, for example, the statute of limitations. The German twenty-year statute of limitations on homicide was held to begin running first in 1945 at the end of the war, and then in 1949 when the Federal Republic took responsibility for crimes on German soil. When it was about to run out in 1965, it was extended for ten years, and before it ran out in 1975, it was abolished altogether. Is the statute of limitations a promise to the citizenry that estops the State from changing its laws retroactively? How should one decide whether it is?

The conventional starting-point for considering when legislatures may apply new legislation to crimes already committed is to distinguish between procedural and substantive rules. The legislature is free to change the former but not the latter. Thus the question raised is whether the statue of limitations should be classified as procedural or substantive. But adding this problem of classification hardly advances the inquiry, for how should we decide whether it is one rather than the other? Some courts hold that the statute of limitations is procedural, some that it is substantive. For this distinction to be of assistance, we would need a theory of substance and of procedure, and an explanation of why the question of substance *versus* procedure should matter in resolving the problem of retroactivity.

A better approach is to shift the focus from legal categories to the question: what should the actor be entitled to rely upon at the time she commits the crime? We can agree that a criminal perpetrator should be able to rely on the definition of the crime at the time of acting. If a physician removes the organs of a moribund patient with a flat EEG reading—legally dead at the time of the operation—it would be unfair to change the definition of death retroactively and thus convert to homicide that which was not homicide at the time of commission. But should she be encouraged to think to herself: 'If I commit this crime now, I am subject to prosecution, at most, for the next twenty years. This is a risk worth running'? I should think not. The purpose of the statute of limitation is not to shape the incentive-structure of those considering crimes.

A case decided not long ago in California illustrates how the labels 'substance' and 'procedure' can be misleading.[13] The defendant Snipe allegedly beat his child, and the child died twenty-one months afterwards. At the time of the acts alleged, California Penal Code, § 194, expressed the common-law rule that the defendant could be guilty of homicide only if

[13] *People v. Snipe*, 25 Cal. App. 3d 742, 102 Cal. Rptr. 6 (1972).

Should the Criminal Law Abandon the Actus Reus–Mens Rea *Distinction?*

PAUL H. ROBINSON

Many criminal lawyers, judges, and professors see the distinction between *actus reus* and *mens rea* as one of the more basic of criminal law. Along with the offence–defence distinction, it helps us organize the way we conceptualize and analyse liability. It is said to be 'the corner-stone of discussion on the nature of criminal liability'.[1] And, the concepts of *actus reus* and *mens rea* have 'justified themselves by their usefulness'.[2] I will argue that this most basic organizing distinction is not coherent. Rather than being useful to criminal-law theory, it is harmful because it creates ambiguity in discourse and hides important doctrinal differences of which criminal law should take account. I suggest that we abandon the distinction in favour of other conceptualizations.

No doubt the *actus reus–mens rea* distinction is a logical and natural extension of the obvious empirical difference between a person's conduct, which we can directly observe, and his intention, which we cannot. In the simple case—a defendant shoots someone, with the intention of injuring him—both the defendant's conduct and intention are prerequisites to liability. The concepts of *actus reus* and *mens rea* adequately capture these two facts and note the empirical difference. It is natural to extend the *mens rea* required for liability beyond an intention to injure, to include knowledge, recklessness, or negligence as to injuring another (as when one target-shoots in the woods without paying adequate attention to the possibility of campers in the overshot zone). It also is natural to extend the *actus reus* required for liability beyond an affirmative act of shooting another, to include cases of injuring another by failing to perform a legal duty (as in failing to feed one's child) and to include possession of contraband.

While such an evolution is understandable, even logical, it does not follow that the resulting distinction is one around which current doctrine should be conceptualized. We may be able to explain how we came to rely upon the distinction, but that in itself may not be adequate reason to keep it. If we are to rely upon it, we should be able to identify something that is gained by conceiving of the *actus reus* doctrines as being part of a single

---

[1] A. C. E. Lynch, 'The Mental Element in the *Actus Reus*', (1982) 98 *Law Quarterly Review* 109, at 111.　　　　[2] *Lynch* v. *DPP for Northern Ireland* [1975] AC 653, 690.

concept and by conceiving of the *mens rea* doctrines as a single concept. We should be able to articulate a common denominator among each group that makes it more convenient or more enlightening to speak of them as a group. What is the unifying characteristic of *actus reus* doctrines and of *mens rea* doctrines?

While there is some disagreement as to the meaning of '*actus reus*', which I discuss below, *actus reus* commonly is described as including, first, the requirement that liability be based on conduct that includes a voluntary act. Also part of the *actus reus* is the conduct required to constitute the offence, as well as any circumstances or results that are required to make the conduct criminal. Where a result is one of these offence elements, proof of the *actus reus* requires proof that the defendant's conduct and the result stand in a certain relation, as defined by the doctrine of causation. In the absence of an act, the *actus reus* of an offence may be found in the omission to perform a legal duty of which the defendant is physically capable, or in a defendant's knowing possession of contraband for a period of time sufficient to terminate the possession. To summarize, *actus reus* is said to include the conduct, circumstance, and result elements of an offence, as well as the supporting doctrines of causation, voluntary act, omission, and possession.

The '*mens rea*' of an offence typically is said to be the defendant's required mental state at the time of the conduct constituting the offence. Under the Model Penal Code, this generally requires proof that the defendant had intention (purpose) or knowledge, or was reckless or negligent, as to each conduct, circumstance, and result element, as the offence definition may require.[3] The required *mens rea* also may include proof of additional culpable mental states beyond that required as to each objective element. The offence may require, for example, that the defendant have a purpose to do something more than the conduct required for the offence or that he engage in the offence conduct for a particular reason.[4]

What is the unifying characteristic of the *actus reus* requirements? Are they all 'objective' in nature, as the related concept of 'objective elements' might suggest? A circumstance element of an offence may be entirely abstract, such as 'being married' in bigamy or 'without licence' in trespass. Indeed, an 'objective' element may include a purely *subjective* state of mind, such as the requirement of causing 'fear' in robbery or the requirement in rape that the victim does not 'consent'.[5] The 'subjective' nature of *mens*

---

[3] Model Penal Code, § 2.02(1).

[4] See e.g. ibid., §§ 221.1(1) (defining burglary as entering a building with 'purpose to commit a crime therein'), 213.5 (defining indecent exposure as exposing genitals with 'purpose of arousing or gratifying [his] sexual desire').

[5] See, e.g. Texas Penal Code, § 29.02(a)(2) (1974) (defining robbery as placing another in 'fear' of bodily injury or death during the course of a theft); Del. Code Ann. tit. 11, §§ 767,

rea requirements and their common character as 'mental states' are also chequered. Negligence is neither subjective nor a state of mind, of course, but rather a failure to meet an objective standard.

Perhaps the common denominator among *actus reus* requirements and among *mens rea* requirements is not to be found in the descriptive characteristics of the requirements (e.g. 'objective' or 'subjective'), but in their function. It is common to conceive of the *actus reus–mens rea* distinction in a general way as the distinction between the functions of defining the prohibited conduct and defining the conditions under which a defendant is to be held blameworthy and therefore liable for engaging in such prohibited conduct. This is the approach taken by the Model Penal Code drafters. The requirements of intention (purpose), knowledge, recklessness, and negligence may have different characteristics—subjective, objective, state of mind, legal abstraction, etc.—but they serve a single function, in the drafters' view: to assess whether the defendant is sufficiently culpable for his prohibited conduct to be held criminally liable for it.[6] Indeed, the Code refers to these requirements—intentionally (purposely), knowingly, recklessly, and negligently—as 'culpability' levels, emphasizing this common function. The objective elements of conduct, circumstance, and result, in contrast, describe the prohibited (or required) conduct, the definition of which may be modified or refined by the supporting *actus reus* doctrines. I will argue, however, that this apparent functional similarity among *actus reus* requirements and among *mens rea* requirements also is an illusion. In fact, both *actus reus* and *mens rea* requirements serve several different functions.

As the following sections in this paper try to show, what we refer to as *actus reus* requirements or as *mens rea* requirements are in fact a collection of entirely distinct doctrines. Four doctrines typically described as the *actus reus* requirements include what I shall refer to as the act requirement, the rules governing omission liability, the voluntariness requirement, and the objective elements of offence definitions. Four doctrines typically described as the *mens rea* requirement include what I shall refer to as present-conduct intention, present-circumstance culpability, future-result culpability, and future-conduct intention. While these doctrines are grouped together as *actus reus* or as *mens rea*, the doctrines within each group have no common characteristic and no common function.

Grouping the doctrines as *actus reus* or as *mens rea* is problematic because it obscures the fact that there are different doctrines at work and it

770(1), 771(1) and (3), 773(1), 774(1) and (2) (all defining sex offences to include absence of 'consent' as an element); 18 Pa. Cons. Stat. Ann., § 3922(a)(1) (1983) (defining theft by deception to require creation or reinforcement of a 'false impression').

[6] Model Penal Code, § 2.02, explanatory note and comment 1 (Official Draft and Revised Comments 1985).

misleadingly suggests that the doctrines share a common characteristic or function. This, in turn, inevitably creates confusion and invites analytic error. Criminal law would be better off if we abandoned the distinction and referred instead only to the individual underlying doctrines. If a grouping of related doctrines is useful, the doctrines might better be grouped around the three primary functions of criminal-law doctrine developed in the last section of this essay.

1. Four Doctrines of *Actus Reus*

Let me begin by demonstrating that what is referred to as the *actus reus* requirement includes at least four distinct doctrines, each of which has different requirements and a different set of rationales justifying its existence.

1.1. *The Act Requirement*

The act requirement and the voluntariness requirement, frequently treated as a single *actus reus* requirement, are related but distinct doctrines. Several writers assure that the two are treated as one by defining an 'act' as a 'willed movement'.[7] Modern codes typically keep the two separate; they define an act to be 'a bodily movement whether voluntary or involuntary'.[8] The act requirement also is distinct from the objective elements of an offence. The act requirement may be satisfied by proof of the conduct element of an offence, but it also may be satisfied by proof of a different act. Complicity, causing crime by an innocent, vicarious liability, and inchoate liability are the most obvious examples. In each instance, a defendant may be held criminally liable although he does not satisfy the conduct element of any substantive offence. The act requirement demands none the less that the defendant's liability be based upon some act. The point is that the act requirement sets a minimum condition for liability that is independent of the substantive-offence definitions. The Model Penal Code, for example, in addition to its offence definitions, requires that liability be 'based on conduct which includes [an] act'.[9] Where a code does not explicitly require an act, courts none the less tend to enforce such a requirement.[10] The act requirement does not have universal application. Liability may be imposed in the absence of an act, if the defendant fails to perform a legal duty or has possession of contraband. More on this in a moment.

Why have an independent requirement of an act? Several rationales are

---

[7] See e.g. Glanville Williams, *Criminal Law: The General Part* (2nd edn., London 1961), s. 8, hereafter *General Part*; Oliver W. Holmes, *The Common Law* (Boston 1881), 54.
[8] See Model Penal Code, § 1.13(2).   [9] Ibid., § 2.01(1).
[10] See e.g. *Scales* v. *United States* and *Robinson* v. *California*, discussed below, nn. 18–19.

apparent. By requiring an act, the law excludes from liability those persons who only fantasize about committing an offence and those persons who may indeed form an intention to commit an offence but whose intention is not sufficiently firm that it will mature into action. One might argue that such people are dangerous, at least more dangerous than persons without such fantasies or intentions, and perhaps the criminal law ought to take jurisdiction.[11] But many people may fantasize or form irresolute intentions yet never act; thus use of criminal sanctions in these cases would be inefficient. More important, so long as the criminal law continues to claim a moral foundation, liability is inappropriate, because fantasizing and irresolute intentions generally are not viewed as adequate to deserve condemnation and punishment.[12] Condemnation sufficient for criminal conviction typically follows only after an intention matures into action.

Beyond its value in barring punishment for unexternalized thoughts, the act requirement provides some minimal objective confirmation that the defendant's intention does exist. Upon observing an action consistent with the intention, we feel more sure of the defendant's intention and her willingness to act upon it. But the act requirement by itself performs this role poorly. Admittedly, some conduct may unambiguously manifest a mind bent on crime. There seems little ambiguity in the act of strangling another by the neck. But it also is the case that conduct, especially that short of a substantive offence, frequently does little by itself to indicate a culpable state of mind. The farmer lighting his pipe near his neighbour's haystack may have no intention of committing arson.

The act requirement is useful in providing a time and place of occurrence of an offence. While one's intention may range over a long period of time and many places, the conduct constituting the offence can be identified with a particular time and place. This assists enforcement of the concurrence requirement, i.e. that the required *mens rea* exist at the time of the conduct constituting the offence. An identifiable time and place also make it easier to apply various procedural rules, such as those governing jurisdiction, venue, and periods of time of limitation. Even here, however, the act requirement cannot be relied upon for too much. Frequently, an offence will contain many acts, and some offences punish so-called 'continuing acts' (such as concealment, criminal agreement, possession, or obstruction). The greater the number of acts or the longer 'a continuing act', the messier the application of the procedural rules.[13] The reason for

---

[11] Barbara Wooton, 'Diminished Responsibility: A Layman's View', (1960) 76 *Law Quarterly Review* 224, at 233.

[12] Among other things, there is some question as to whether one has sufficient control over one's thoughts to be held responsible for having them. One generally does have control of one's conduct, however, in the absence of a dysfunction that would justify an excuse.

[13] Special rules frequently are constructed to deal with this weakness of the act requirement. In the context of conspiracy, for example, see Model Penal Code, § 5.03(7).

the procedural rules sometimes may be undercut, as where jurisdiction and
venue are appropriate everywhere, and where the statute of limitation
never begins to run.

Some states, such as California, also try to use the act requirement to
resolve the thorny issue of liability and punishment for multiple, related
offences. The California Penal Code purports to allow punishment for
only one offence for a single act.[14] But the California courts have rejected
strict application of this provision where one act causes two results, such
as two deaths, or constitutes two violations of the same offence provision,
such as two instances of attempted murder.[15] The courts continue to give
deference to the provision where one act violates different provisions, such
as arson and attempted murder,[16] but even this narrow application seems
problematic. Where a defendant sets a house on fire with two people in it,
intending to burn the house and the people, why should the State have to
elect to punish for arson or for attempted murder? Why is not punishment
for both appropriate? To exclude punishment for either is to trivialize
the other offence. One also may wonder about the logic in allowing
multiple liability for the two instances of attempted murder arising from
a single act, yet denying liability for the arson and attempted murder from
the same act. What is the theory under which the State must choose
between different kinds of harms from a single act, but need not choose
between distinct but related harms from a single act? One may conclude
from the California experience that the act requirement is of little value in
solving the difficult problem of multiple offences. At best, it serves as a
starting-point for a more complex analysis.[17]

What has been discussed so far is what might be called 'the act requirement' in assessing liability. Criminal liability must be based on conduct
that includes an act. A second aspect of the act requirement concerns the
definition of offences. Nothing in the act requirement as expressed in
Model Penal Code, § 2.01 (1) requires that an offence definition contain
any act as an element of the offence. Rather, the prosecution need only
show that in the case at hand the defendant's 'liability is based on conduct
which *includes* [an] act'. On the other hand, one would not expect a
criminal code to contain provisions directed to code drafters; thus, § 2.01
(1) may not embody the full demands of the act requirement. It is natural

[14] Cal. Penal Code, § 654 provides: 'An act or omission which is made punishable in
different ways by different provisions of this code may be punishable under either of such
provisions, but in no case can it be punished under more than one.'
[15] See e.g. *Neal* v. *State*, 9 Cal. Rptr. 607, 357 P 2d 839 (1960) (defendant convicted on
two counts of attempted murder and one count of arson; because arson and attempted
murder resulted from one act, defendant's conviction for arson was dismissed, but the two
convictions for attempted murder were upheld).   [16] Ibid.
[17] For a discussion of more useful provisions determining when liability is appropriate for
multiple offences, see Model Penal Code, §§ 1.07(1) and (4), 5.05(3).

to assume that the same concerns underlying the Code's direction to judges in adjudicating cases would have application to legislatures in defining offences. That modern offences typically require an act as an element of the offence shows that legislatures are sensitive to the virtues of requiring an act.

Where legislatures are tempted to forego an act requirement, several Supreme Court cases may be read as constitutionalizing a requirement that an offence definition must on its face contain a requirement of an act. The effect and the rationale of this aspect of the requirement is the limitation of governmental power in the definition of offences. In *Scales* v. *United States*, for example, the Court barred the government from criminalizing pure membership in the Communist Party. It did, however, allow liability for 'active' members of the Party.[18] In *Robinson v. California*, the Court similarly invalidated a state statute that made it an offence to 'be addicted to the use of narcotics'.[19] Yet, these cases limit governmental criminalization authority in a very modest way. It would not be unconstitutional to criminalize *joining* the Communist Party or *taking* drugs. Thus, this aspect of the act requirement may serve only to make the government's case more difficult to prove, providing only a modest limitation on governmental criminalization authority.

To summarize, the act requirement serves to bar punishment for unexternalized thoughts, attempts to give some minimal objective confirmation that a defendant's intention does exist, provides a time and place of occurrence of an offence, offers a starting-point for resolving the thorny issue of liability and punishment for multiple related offences, and limits in a modest way governmental power to define offences. As we shall see, these rationales of the act requirement are similar in some respects to the rationales for the omission and possession rules, for those doctrines attempt to justify an exception to the act requirement. The rationales are different from the rationales for the voluntariness requirement and the objective elements of offence definitions, for those doctrines are concerned with different and generally unrelated matters. (Note that, with the constitutionalized act requirement requiring legislatures to define offences to include an act, the act requirement contained in the criminal code has little opportunity for application. It may continue to exist primarily as a vehicle for the voluntariness requirement, discussed below, and, by negative implication, as the means for defining the situations where the special requirements of omission liability must be met.)

---

[18] 367 US 203, at 222 (1961).
[19] 370 US 660, at 667 (1962). Note that neither *Scales* nor *Robinson* are in violation of the act requirement as defined in the Model Penal Code. See text at n. 9 above. In each prosecution the State no doubt could show that the defendant engaged in *some* bodily movement toward the offence.

1.2. *Substitutes for an Act: Omission to Perform a Legal Duty and Possession of Contraband*

As noted, the act requirement by itself does not have universal application: liability frequently is imposed for an omission to perform an act that one has a legal duty to perform (and for possession of contraband). But together, the requirements of an act or an omission to perform a legal duty are universal. The requirements are complementary; liability always requires proof of one or the other.[20] Not surprisingly, their rationales are parallel. That is, a defendant's failure to perform a legal duty is permitted to substitute for an act because such an omission is thought to satisfy roughly the rationales of the act requirement, or at least to satisfy them in the admittedly modest way that the act requirement itself does.

Specifically, requiring an omission to perform a legal duty helps to exclude from liability cases of fantasizing and of intentions too irresolute to be externalized. Of course, requiring only an omission does nothing to screen out mere fantasies. It is the failure to perform *a legal duty* that suggests a willingness to go beyond mere fantasizing, to have the harm or evil of the offence occur. Even then, however, the screening effect seems weak; 'letting something happen' may not carry the same implication of resolute intention that is shown in causing something to happen by affirmative action. A defendant's failure to perform a duty also provides some evidential support for the existence of an intention to have the harm or evil occur. For example, where a mother fails to protect her child from regular abuse by her boyfriend, her omission to perform her legal duty of which she is capable (perhaps by advising the authorities), may provide some confirmation of an independently proven intention or recklessness as to endangering the child that would not be present if the defendant had no such duty or capacity. Again, however, the implication is less than strong. In particular, one could argue that inaction carries no implication of intention unless it is shown that the defendant knows of his legal duty to act, a requirement that has been resisted by the law of omission. An omission also does poorly in limiting governmental criminalization authority. The government need only create a legal duty in order to criminalize an omission. Nor is an omission or its special liability requirements helpful in providing an identifiable time and place of occurrence. An omission necessarily is a continuing state.

To summarize, while an omission itself serves none of the rationales of the act requirement, when joined with the special requirement of a legal duty to act, which we presume the defendant to know, the omission does do something towards satisfying those rationales but even less than the

[20] Model Penal Code, § 2.01(1).

admittedly poor performance of the act requirement itself. It should be no surprise, then, that omission liability traditionally is limited. Legal duties to act are few in number and narrow in scope.

Another almost universally recognized exception to the act requirement is possession of contraband. Technically, possession under certain circumstances is said to be an 'act'. Under the Model Penal Code, for example,

Possession is an act . . . if the possessor knowingly procured or received the thing possessed or was aware of his control thereof for a sufficient period to have been able to terminate his possession.[21]

With the addition of the special requirement of '*knowing* receipt or control', the intent-based rationales of the act requirement are sought to be satisfied. That is, where the defendant has knowledge of receipt or control but fails to terminate possession, he appears to have made a conscious choice to keep possession. The conceptual similarity between the possession and omission doctrines is confirmed by the fact that one may view possession of contraband as a form of criminal omission. That is, the defendant's liability flows from his *failure* to dispossess himself of contraband, as he has a legal duty to do.

1.3. *The Voluntariness Requirement*

Unlike the act requirement, the voluntariness requirement *is* universal in application. Criminal liability must be based on either a voluntary act, a voluntary omission, or voluntary possession. To be voluntary, an *act* must be 'a product of the effort or determination of the actor'.[22] A defendant who injures another through convulsion or reflex muscle action, for example, is excused under this provision. Involuntary acts include, for example, 'a reflex or convulsion; a bodily movement during unconsciousness or sleep; conduct during hypnosis or resulting from hypnotic suggestion'.[23] To be voluntary, an *omission* must be an omission 'to perform an act of which [the defendant] is physically capable'.[24] To assure that *possession* is voluntary, modern codes typically require that the defendant know he has control 'for a sufficient period to have been able to terminate his possession'.[25]

The voluntariness requirement and the act-or-omission requirement obviously are related in one sense. In discussing the act-or-omission requirement, one tends to assume, often without noting, that it is a voluntary act or voluntary omission to which one refers. An *in*voluntary act or omission does not satisfy the primary rationales of the act requirement.

[21] Ibid., § 2.01(4).   [22] Ibid., §§ 1.13(3), 2.01(2)(d).
[23] Ibid., § 2.01(2)(a)–(c).   [24] Ibid., § 2.01(1).   [25] See text, above n. 21.

Permitting liability to be based upon an involuntary act or omission would do little or nothing to protect fantasizing and irresolute intentions from punishment and would provide little or no evidentiary support for the existence of a culpable state of mind. (An involuntary act may be adequate, however, to provide an identifiable time and place of the offence.)

This connection with the act-or-omission requirement helps explain why the voluntariness requirement traditionally is treated as an aspect of *actus reus*. But it is, in truth, an independent doctrine with different requirements and rationales. It applies to the act-or-omission requirement in the same sense that it applies to all other conduct, such as the conduct elements of offence definitions. Rather than protecting fantasizing and irresolute intentions from liability, or providing an anchor for application of procedural rules, or limiting governmental criminalization authority, the voluntariness requirement is designed to protect from liability defendants who admittedly have brought about a prohibited harm or evil but who cannot properly be held blameworthy for the violation, because they are unable to control their conduct. The assault that results from convulsion, hypnotic suggestion, or somnambulism is harmful and remains prohibited in the future, but the defendant at hand is not to be punished for it, because he is not morally responsible for the conduct.

The distinction between the act requirement and the voluntariness requirement also appears in Supreme Court cases. In *Robinson* v. *California*, the Supreme Court found a violation of the Fourteenth Amendment's 'cruel and unusual punishment' prohibition in a state's making it a crime for a person to 'be addicted to the use of narcotics'.[26] A mere status or condition could not be punished, the Court concluded. Some commentators took this to mean that the constitution required that criminal liability be based upon a *voluntary* act. Conviction of the addict in *Robinson* could not be permitted, they argued, because the addict could not control his status as an addict. But in *Powell* v. *Texas*[27] the Court's opinions distinguished the act requirement from the voluntariness requirement. Four of the Justices in the majority in *Powell* expressly rejected the commentators' reading of *Robinson*; they saw no constitutional requirement of a *voluntary* act:[28]

The entire thrust of *Robinson*'s interpretation of the Cruel and Unusual Punishment Clause is that criminal penalties may be inflicted only if the accused has committed some act, had engaged in some behavior, which society has an interest in preventing . . .[29]

---

[26] 370 US 660 (1962). It is not the extent of punishment that offends the constitution, but rather its use. 'Even one day in prison would be a cruel and unusual punishment for the "crime" of having a common cold.' Ibid., 667.
[27] 392 US 514 (1968).   [28] Ibid., 532.   [29] Ibid., 533.

The four dissenters in *Powell* would have constitutionalized the voluntariness requirement, and the remaining member, Justice White, indicated some agreement with this position.[30] Nothing further has been done to constitutionalize the voluntariness requirement. That the act requirement has clear constitutional status and the voluntariness requirement does not is simply another example of the distinct and independent nature of the two requirements.

Rather than being similar to the other doctrines of *actus reus*, the voluntariness requirement is analogous to, indeed it is part of, the criminal law's system of excuses. Both the voluntariness requirement and the excuse defences, such as insanity, involuntary intoxication, and duress, hold a defendant blameless despite criminal conduct, because that conduct is judged to be too much the product of forces other than the defendant's exercise of will. These exculpatory doctrines work upon a continuum of volition, with the voluntariness requirement exculpating the most extreme cases. There is considerable overlap, however, between the range of cases dealt with under the involuntariness requirement and the range of cases dealt with under the excuse defences. The fact is, many excuse defences reflect overwhelming compulsions, while many instances classed as involuntary acts, such as conduct under hypnosis or in a somnambulistic state, reflect only a mild form of coercion.

While it may have been different in an earlier era, a defence under the voluntariness requirement currently does not require absolute involuntariness. Reflex action and convulsion are certainly instances of involuntary conduct, but other less absolute dysfunctions are also recognized. There is in reality a continuum of control dysfunction even within the range of cases treated as involuntary acts. In *R* v. *Charlson*,[31] for example, the defendant hit his son over the head with a mallet and threw him out of a window, for no apparent reason. His actions were subsequently attributed to the effect of a brain tumour. While these acts may seem more willed and directed than a convulsion, their physiological explanation persuasively suggests that the defendant is not accountable for them. Further along the involuntariness continuum is conduct during sleep. In *King* v. *Cogdon*,[32] for example, the defendant stabbed her daughter to death while dreaming that the Korean War was going on in her house and one of the soldiers was attacking her daughter. The psychiatric testimony suggested that her attack manifested a subconscious hostility toward her daughter.

[30] Ibid., 548.

[31] [1955] 1 WLR 317 (jury found defendant was acting as an automaton without any knowledge of or control over his actions).

[32] This unreported case, heard in the Supreme Court of Victoria in 1950, is reported in Norval Morris, 'Somnambulistic Homicide: Ghosts, Spiders, and North Koreans', (1951) 5 *Res Judicata* 29 (defendant acquitted because the act of killing was not, in law, her act at all).

Such actions may well be the product of a defendant's effort or determination in a narrow sense. But one's subconscious desires and motivations generally are not recognized as an adequate basis for condemnation through criminal sanction. We do not generally treat people as if they can control their subconsciousness. Still further along the continuum is conduct under hypnosis. While Model Penal Code, § 2.01 (2) (c) conclusively presumes 'conduct during hypnosis or resulting from hypnotic suggestion' to be involuntary, the weight of modern evidence suggests that the effect of hypnosis on most people is not nearly so dramatic, and that its effect is only to create a discernible but not compelling compulsion.[33] The point here is simply that the voluntariness requirement concerns issues and serves purposes distinct from the act and omission requirements. The issues of voluntariness are conceptually more similar to the general excuse defences than to the other aspects of *actus reus*.

The Supreme Court's reluctance to extend constitutionalization to the voluntariness requirement may have come from an appreciation of the doctrine's conceptual identity with the excuse defences. The Court might well have seen that, no matter what the wisdom of having such a requirement, to constitutionalize it would logically have drawn the Court into constitutionalizing, or trying to distinguish, the host of other criminal-law doctrines that are based upon some degree of impairment of volition. This includes not only the general disability excuses, such as insanity, duress, involuntary intoxication, but also doctrines of mitigation, such as provocation, and extreme emotional disturbance. Criminal-law theory has struggled with and changed the accepted wisdom on these and other issues central to criminal responsibility many times during the past century. The Court might have thought it unwise to impede this continuing development by constitutionalizing and thereby solidifying matters that ought to remain fluid until we are more certain of their proper formulation.

1.4. *Objective Elements of Offence Definitions: Conduct, Circumstance, and Result*

The objective elements of offence definitions typically are included in the '*actus reus*' requirements. In modern codes, these requirements are stated independently of the act-or-omission requirement and the voluntariness requirement. The objective elements are contained in the offence definitions in the code's Special Part; the act, omission, and voluntariness requirements are contained in provisions in the code's General Part. Liability requires proof of all.

---

[33] For a more detailed discussion, see Paul H. Robinson, *Criminal Law Defenses* (St Paul 1984), ii, s. 191(c).

The objective elements of offences typically are defined to include (*i*) conduct, (*ii*) attendant circumstances, and (*iii*) a result of conduct.[34] The existence of a conduct element, if proven, will satisfy the requirement of an act, but any number of doctrines allow liability without proof of the substantive offence's conduct element, either by imputing another's conduct or by imposing inchoate liability. A minority of offences contain a result element. Homicide offences, personal-injury offences, and property-destruction offences typically require a resulting physical harm. Such offences as endangerment, indecent exposure, and falsification, typically require the defendant to cause a *risk* of a physical or intangible harm, such as danger, alarm, or a false impression.[35] Most offence definitions also include one or more circumstance elements. These frequently define the precise nature of the prohibited conduct—e.g. having intercourse with a person *under 14 years old*—or the precise nature of a prohibited result—e.g. causing the death of *another human being*.

When an offence definition includes a result element, as homicide requires a death, implicit in that result element is a causation requirement. That is, it must be shown that the defendant's offence conduct caused the prohibited result. This required relation between the defendant's conduct and the result derives from our notions of criminal accountability. A result ought to affect a defendant's liability only if it is a result for which the defendant is causally accountable. Specifically, the law appears arbitrary and unfair if it increases a defendant's liability because of a result for which the defendant is not causally accountable. The rules of the causation doctrine are the means by which the law attempts to define the conditions under which such causal accountability exists. Current doctrine typically contains two independent requirements to establish a causal connection between a defendant's conduct and a result. First, the conduct must be a 'but for' cause of the result. That is, in the language of Model Penal Code, § 2.03 (1) (a), the conduct must be 'an antecedent but for which the result in question would not have occurred'. This is sometimes called the 'factual cause' requirement. Second, the strength and nature of the causal connection between the conduct and the result must be sufficient. 'Legal cause' or 'proximate cause', as this is sometimes called, requires that the harm 'is not too remote or accidental in its occurrence to have a [just] bearing on the defendant's liability or on the gravity of his offence'. This language, from Model Penal Code, § 2.03 (2) (b) and (3) (b), is sometimes supplemented with an additional requirement that the harm is 'not too . . . dependent on another's volitional act'.[36]

---

[34] Model Penal Code, § 1.13(9) (defining 'elements of an offence').
[35] Model Penal Code, §§ 211.2, 213.5, 241.3(1)(b).
[36] e.g. NJ Stat. Ann., § 2C: 2–3.

This brief summary of the nature of objective elements of offence definitions should help illustrate that both the requirements and the issues they concern are distinct from the requirements and issues of the act-or-omission and voluntariness requirements. The definition of objective elements of offences requires a legislature to identify the wide range of harm and evil to be proscribed, and to define them in a sufficiently narrow and precise way so as to avoid prohibiting conduct that is desirable or is too trivial to warrant criminal conviction. These are not the issues of the act-or-omission and voluntariness requirements.

2. Terminological Confusion among the Doctrines of *Actus Reus*

Terminological confusion regarding *actus reus* results from two sources: from using the label to refer to different aspects of the doctrine without identifying which aspect, and from disagreement as to what is included within that label. To illustrate the first, consider the entries from several good scholars in a recent debate on 'The *Actus Reus* Requirement'. One writer, defending 'the traditional conception of the *actus reus* requirement',[37] seems to take the issue to be whether the *act requirement* is defensible: 'what objections are there to the contention that criminal liability is never imposed in the absence of such an act?'[38] It turns out that he means to refer to the voluntariness requirement as well, for he defines an 'act' as 'a bodily movement [caused] by the actor's will'.[39] Later in the same discussion, however, the phrase *actus reus* is used to mean the *conduct prohibited by an offence*: 'there exists, *for the vast majority of crimes*, a clear and separate *actus reus* requirement.'[40]

Another writer in the same debate similarly takes 'the *actus reus* principle' to mean the act requirement. He notes agreement 'for abandoning the *actus reus* principle . . . because there are many cases—status crimes, possessory offences, omissions—in which liability is sometimes imposed despite the absence of an act'.[41] But later in the same discussion, this writer too uses the phrase *actus reus* to mean the prohibited conduct of an offence: '*Actus reus* refers to the outer, physical, behavioral, objective ingredient of crime; *mens rea* refers to the inner, mental, subjective ingredient of crime.'[42] Part of the debate among these scholars concerns whether the

---

[37] Michael Gorr, 'The *Actus Reus* Requirement: A Qualified Defence', (1991) 10 *Criminal Justice Ethics* 11, hereafter '*Actus Reus* Requirement'.
[38] Ibid.   [39] Ibid.   [40] Ibid., 13 (emphasis in original).
[41] Douglas N. Husak, 'The Orthodox Model of the Criminal Defence', (1991) 10 *Criminal Justice Ethics* 20, hereafter 'Orthodox Model'.   [42] Ibid.

'*actus reus* requirement' is a universal principle.[43] The answer is dependent, of course, on what one means by the '*actus reus* requirement'. An act is not a universal requirement; voluntariness is. Another part of the debate concerns whether a 'control principle' is preferable to the 'actus reus requirement': 'I believe that the control principle performs most of the functions usually assigned to *actus reus*.'[44] Again, whether this is true or not depends upon what one is referring to with the phrase *actus reus* Certainly, a 'control principle' is an appropriate substitute for the voluntariness requirement. Some would say that the voluntariness requirement, along with the general excuses, *is* a 'control principle'. A 'control principle' would not do well, of course, as a substitute for the act requirement, the special rules governing liability for an omission and for possession, or the objective requirements of offence definitions.

My point here is not to criticize the substantive points of the debaters, many of which I agree with. I am concerned rather that use of the phrase *actus reus* makes it more difficult to engage in useful debate about the doctrines referred to by that label. In reading the debate, one wonders how many of the disagreements are substantive and how many are terminological. It seems that we have not made much progress since Jerome Hall's 1947 lament for the confusion inherent in use of the term *actus reus*.[45]

The potential for confusion is exacerbated by disagreement among writers as to which issues are included under the label. All agree that the act requirement is included.[46] The voluntariness requirement is included by most.[47] While this requirement may seem to be frequently omitted, it often is subsumed in the act requirement, as noted above, by defining an 'act' as a 'willed bodily movement'. The Model Penal Code, recall, defines an act as 'a bodily movement, whether voluntary or involuntary', then explicitly adds a separate voluntariness requirement when it requires a '*voluntary* act'.

Most writers also use *actus reus* to refer to some elements of an offence definition, but in this usage too there is disagreement as to exactly which elements are included. Some writers mean to refer to the conduct element, the behaviour required for the offence, and perhaps its attendant

---

[43] Douglas N. Husak, *Philosophy of Criminal Law* (Totowa, NJ 1987), 78; Gorr, '*Actus Reus* Requirement', 12 n. 3; Jeffrie G. Murphy, 'The *Actus* Requirement: Gorr on *Actus Reus*', (1991) 10 *Criminal Justice Ethics* 18, at 19; Husak, 'Orthodox Model', 22.

[44] Ibid., 21.

[45] See Jerome Hall, *General Principles of Criminal Law* (2nd end., Indianapolis 1960), 222–40.

[46] The '*actus reus* principle' means that '[n]o crime can be committed simply by one's thoughts or mental states.' Husak, 'Orthodox Model'; see Gorr, '*Actus Reus* Requirement', 12; Williams, *General Part*, ss. 1–3.

[47] 'The *actus reus* principle' is invoked 'to disallow liability for involuntary conduct'. See Husak, 'Orthodox Model'; see also Gorr, '*Actus Reus* Requirement', 12; Joshua Dressler, *Understanding Criminal Law* (New York 1987), 63; Williams, *General Part*, s. 8.

circumstances, but not its results.[48] Others mean to include the results of
the conduct as well, in other words, to include all of the objective elements
of the offence definition: '(*a*) A willed movement (or omission). (*b*) Certain
surrounding circumstances (including past facts). (*c*) Certain consequences.'[49] Finally, some writers go further to include the collateral doctrines sometimes required to establish liability for an offence. '[L]iability
may rest on (and the *actus reus* may accordingly consist of) an *omission*,
a *status*, or a *possession*.'[50]

With this much disagreement as to what is included within the concept,
it should be no surprise to find ambiguity, confusion, and disagreement
in discussing *actus reus*. The *actus reus* requirement, in the narrow, act-
requirement sense, is not a universal requirement. Omission liability is
the obvious exception. In the somewhat broader, act-or-omission sense,
the requirement is universal. In its most broad objective-offence elements
sense it is universal in application, but every application, every offence, is
different. In its narrow act-requirement or even voluntary-act-requirement
forms, the *actus reus* is a minor part of the requirements of liability. It is
the unusual case in which it raises issues that are in dispute. In its broader
forms—'the *actus reus* designates all the elements of the criminal offence
except the *mens rea*'[51]—it raises a disputed issue in many if not most cases.
The potential for clarity and understanding for lawyers, judges, and theorists alike would be improved if the phrase *actus reus* were never used again.

3. Four Doctrines of *Mens Rea*

The concept of *mens rea* is rather less problematic than the concept of
actus reus in some respects, but more problematic in others. There is not
significant disagreement as to what the phrase *mens rea* refers. It may be
a misleading phrase when used to include reference to negligence, but the
modern phrase 'culpability requirements' seems to avoid that problem.
The difficulties with the concept of *mens rea* arise instead from the fact
that it groups together doctrines with important differences in their
requirements and rationales.

[48] Husak seems to suggest that some writers take this view, but does not cite them.
'[D]eath is *not* part of the *actus reus*. The *actus reus* of homicide *causes* death, so that death
is a consequence of the proscribed act rather than a component of it. According to this view,
an element of liability is part of neither the *actus reus* nor the *mens rea*.' Husak, *Philosophy
of Criminal Law*, above n. 43, 124–5 (emphasis added).
[49] Williams, *General Part*, s. 11. See also J. C. Smith and B. Hogan, *Criminal Law* (3rd
edn., London 1973), 40–1; Gorr, '*Actus Reus* Requirement', 13, 15 and 25; Dressler, *Understanding Criminal Law*, above n. 47, 63. Dressler also includes causation in *actus reus*. Ibid.,
63 n. 2.
[50] Meir Dan-Cohen, '*Actus Reus*', in Sanford Kadish (ed.), *Encyclopedia of Crime and Justice*
(New York 1983), 15. See also Dressler, *Understanding Criminal Law*, above n. 47, 63 n. 3.
[51] Dan-Cohen, '*Actus Reus*', above n. 50.

Modern codes typically follow the Model Penal Code in a presumption against strict liability and for culpability.[52] The Code defines four levels of culpability: intentionally (purposely), knowingly, recklessly, and negligently. Each of the four culpability levels is specifically defined with respect to the different kinds of objective elements of an offence—conduct, circumstance, and result elements.[53] In addition, the Code specifically provides that each objective element must have a corresponding culpability element. '[A] person is not guilty of an offence unless he acted purposely, knowingly, recklessly, or negligently, as the law may require, *with respect to each material element of the offence.*'[54] If the objective elements of an offence require that a defendant take property of another without his consent, the culpability elements might require, for example, that the defendant know that he is taking property and that he be at least reckless as to it being someone else's property and at least reckless as to the owner's lack of consent.[55]

But note that the four levels of culpability do not apply in a symmetrical way to the three kinds of objective elements. When we talk of culpability as to the existence of a circumstance element, we mean the defendant's culpability as to the then *present* circumstances. Any of the four culpability levels can apply. As to the circumstance that a defendant's sexual partner is 14 years old, for example, the defendant may desire the partner to be 14, he may be practically certain (know) that the partner is 14, he may be aware of a substantial risk that the partner is 14, or he may not be aware but should be aware of a substantial risk that the partner is 14. (Apparently, the Model Penal Code drafters saw no practical significance in the difference between a defendant desiring that a circumstance exists and knowing so; the Code defines 'purposely' as to a circumstance to mean that the defendant '*believes or* hopes' that it exists.)[56] These culpability requirements are what might be called instances of 'present-circumstance culpability'.

When we talk of culpability as to a result, in contrast, we necessarily are talking of a defendant's culpability as to a then *future* event. Culpability that a defendant's conduct will cause a result, which the concurrence requirement demands exist at the time of the conduct, necessarily must be culpability as to causing a result that does not at that moment exist. Again, any level of culpability can apply. As to a defendant's culpability for causing another's death, for example, the defendant may desire to cause the death, he may be practically certain (know) that his conduct will cause the death, he

[52] See Model Penal Code, § 2.02(3) (requiring that reckless be read in as the culpability required when an offence is silent on the issue).
[53] See e.g. ibid., § 2.02(2).   [54] Ibid., § 2.02(1).
[55] For a discussion of the sometimes complex and confusing process of determining the culpability requirements of an offence, see Paul H. Robinson and Jane Grall, 'Element Analysis in Defining Criminal Liability: The Model Penal Code and Beyond', (1983) 35 *Stanford LR* 681.   [56] Model Penal Code, § 2.02(2)(a)(ii).

may be aware of a substantial risk that his conduct will cause the death, or he may not be aware but should be aware of a substantial risk that his conduct will cause the death. These kinds of culpability are what might be called instances of 'future-result culpability'.

When we talk of culpability as to a conduct element, the full range of culpability levels does not apply. Only 'purposely' (intentionally) has meaning for conduct elements. In the absence of a serious disability, a person engages in conduct only if he desires to do so, if such is his 'conscious object'. A person either wishes to engage in certain conduct or he does not. Except for those with control dysfunctions, it makes little sense to speak of a person who knows or is aware of a risk that he is engaging in certain conduct but does not desire it. The Code recognizes this in part when it fails to define 'recklessly' and 'negligently' with respect to a conduct element.[57] But the Code does define 'knowingly' as to conduct, as when the defendant 'is aware that his conduct is of that nature'.[58] What does the Code mean by being aware of the 'nature' of one's conduct? Presumably it means being aware of the circumstances and the potential results of the conduct. But that would seem to create a troublesome overlap between culpability as to conduct and culpability as to a circumstance and a result, which the Code defines separately and differently. To remind us that only 'purpose' (intention) is meaningful with regard to conduct, we may wish to call this kind of culpability 'conduct intention'.

Another important difference that characterizes culpability as to a conduct element is that it can concern either present or future conduct. For most offences, a 'present-conduct intention' is required. This requires little more than a showing that the defendant does in fact intend to perform the bodily movements that he performs. A defendant does not satisfy this culpability requirement if he does not intend to push the victim but rather does so accidentally as he catches his balance from his own fall. 'Present-conduct intention' is essentially redundant with the voluntariness requirement discussed above.

'Future-conduct intention', on the other hand, has a critical, independent role to play. It serves to show that the defendant is planning to do or have others do more than what has already been done. In defining general inchoate offences, for example, the Code typically requires that the defendant have 'the purpose of promoting or facilitating commission [of the offence]'.[59] Such 'future-conduct intention' is also present in substantive offences that are or that contain codified inchoate offences. Burglary, for example, requires that the defendant enter a building 'with purpose to commit a crime therein'.[60] Note that 'present-conduct intention' applies

---

[57] Ibid., § 2.02(2)(c) and (d).   [58] Ibid., § 2.02(2)(b)(ii).
[59] Ibid., §§ 5.02(1), 5.03(1)(a) and (b); see also § 5.01(1)(a).
[60] Ibid., § 221.1(1); see also §§ 212.1 (kidnapping) and 224.1(1) (forgery).

to an objective element of offence definition, as do the requirements of a 'present-circumstance culpability' and a 'future-result culpability'. A 'future-conduct intention' in the inchoate context, in contrast, does not apply to an objective element of the offence definition but rather exists on its own, with no corresponding objective element. Only when a 'future-conduct intention' appears in the substantive context, as in complicity, does it apply to a corresponding objective element, the principal's then-future conduct.

In some instances, the law requires that the defendant have culpability as to *another person's* conduct. For example, the general inchoate offences of conspiracy and solicitation, as well as complicity liability, require that the defendant agree with or solicit or aid another with some level of culpability as to the other person engaging in conduct constituting an offence.[61] While one normally can be only 'purposeful' as to one's own conduct, one can have any level of culpability as to causing or assisting another's conduct. One may hope and desire that another will engage in certain offence conduct; one may not desire it but may know (be 'aware that it is practically certain'[62]) that the other will engage in the conduct; one may be aware only of a substantial risk that the other will engage in the conduct; or one may not be aware but should be aware of a substantial risk that the person will engage in the conduct. Such culpability as to another's conduct can be culpability as to either the present or future conduct of another. When it concerns another's present conduct, it is simply an example of a present circumstance. When it concerns another's future conduct, which is more often the case, as in solicitation, conspiracy, and complicity, it is a form of a future result. This form of culpability requires showing that, when the defendant solicited, conspired with, or aided another, the defendant had a given level of culpability as to causing or assisting the resulting offence conduct by the other person. Culpability as to another's conduct thus does not appear to present a culpability requirement different from 'present-circumstance culpability' and 'future-result culpability'.

These four kinds of culpability requirements—'present-circumstance culpability', 'future-result culpability', 'present-conduct intention', and 'future-conduct intention'—are each included within the concept of *mens rea* (and 'culpability') and each of the four is commonly referred to using that label.[63] But, as the next section documents, these four kinds of culpability requirements perform very different functions for criminal-law doctrine.

---

[61] See e.g. Model Penal Code, §§ 2.06(3)(a), 5.02(1), 5.03(1).

[62] Model Penal Code, § 2.02(2)(b).

[63] The common law used the phrase 'specific intent' to refer to 'future-conduct intention', among other things. For kinds of culpability included in the label, see George Fletcher, *Rethinking Criminal Law* (Boston 1978), 452–4.

4. Distinct Functions

The previous sections have sought to demonstrate that the concepts of *actus reus* and *mens rea* group together what are in reality distinct doctrines with different requirements. I argue here that these doctrines also serve different functions, important differences that are masked by use of the *actus reus* and *mens rea* concepts. Criminal-law doctrine is obliged to perform at least three distinct functions: defining beforehand the conduct prohibited (or required) by the criminal law, setting the minimum conditions for liability, and setting the general grade of the offence. These most basic functions of criminal-law doctrine might be called the rule-articulation, liability assignment, and grading functions. The first, the *rule-articulation function* of the doctrine, which I have described elsewhere as defining the 'rules of conduct', provides *ex ante* direction to the members of the community as to the conduct that must be avoided (or that must be performed) upon pain of criminal sanction. The second, the *liability function*, and the third, the *grading function*, are aspects of what I have called the 'principles of adjudication'—assessing *ex post* whether a defendant who violates a rule of conduct is culpable for the violation and therefore ought to be held criminally liable for it and, if so, to what degree of liability.[64]

Unfortunately, the traditional *actus reus–mens rea* distinction (and the objective–culpability requirements distinction), despite surface appearance, do not reflect these differences in function. The doctrines traditionally included within *actus reus* do not as a group define the conduct prohibited (or required) by the criminal law. The doctrines traditionally included within *mens rea* do not as a group define the minimum conditions for liability or for aggravated liability for violating the prohibition. Instead, aspects of *actus reus* serve each of these three functions, as do aspects of *mens rea*.

The conduct and circumstance elements of offence definitions do contribute to the definition of the prohibited conduct, the rule-articulation function, but result elements do not. Unlike conduct and circumstance elements, result elements are not necessary to define the prohibited conduct. It is conduct, and not its results, that the criminal law prohibits; it is only our conduct that the law can influence. The law may claim to prohibit a particular result, but what it means by that is to direct people not to engage in conduct that would bring about (or risk bringing about) that result. An actual resulting harm may make the violation more serious,

---

[64] See generally Paul H. Robinson, 'Rules of Conduct and Principles of Adjudication', (1990) 57 *University of Chicago LR* 729. I use the term 'function' here to refer to the functions of *criminal-law doctrine generally*. Earlier in the paper I use the term 'rationale' to refer to the reasons for adopting *a particular doctrinal requirement*. The two terms are meant to refer to similar concepts.

some would argue, but the fortuity of whether the result actually occurs does not alter the nature of the conduct that constitutes the violation. The conduct remains objectionable notwithstanding the chance that the result does not occur.[65] Result elements, then, are like many *mens rea* elements in this regard. They serve to aggravate a defendant's blameworthiness and thus his liability, the grading function.

The role of the causation requirement—defining the relation between a defendant's conduct and a result that will give rise to the defendant's accountability for the result—similarly makes it a doctrine serving the grading function, not the rule-articulation function. Like the requirement of a result, the causation rules determine when a defendant's liability is to be aggravated because he is accountable for a harmful result and therefore more blameworthy. Because result elements and causation requirements are not necessary to define the conduct prohibited by the criminal law, it is not surprising that liability rarely depends upon them. If a prohibited result does not occur or if a required causal connection is not established, the defendant is typically liable for a lesser offence, such as an attempt.[66]

The rules that allow liability for an omission to perform a legal duty or for possession of contraband, rather than an affirmative act, contribute to the criminal law's definition of what is prohibited and required. The law does not provide a complete description of the rules of conduct without the requirement that persons must act in certain situations, as defined by the laws setting legal duties to act, or without the prohibition of the possession of certain things, as defined by the laws defining contraband.

On the other hand, the voluntariness aspect of the act requirement, the physical capacity to perform requirement of the omission doctrine, and the requirement in the possession liability rules that the defendant know of his possession for a period sufficient to terminate the possession, do not serve the rule-articulation function. Instead, they define the minimum conditions under which a defendant will be held condemnable for a violation by commission, omission, or possession respectively. The rules of conduct continue to prohibit possession of certain drugs, even though the person who had possession of such a drug is not to be held liable if he did not know of such possession for a period sufficient to terminate it. Filing an income-tax return remains a duty, even though the person who fails to file is not to be punished if it was physically impossible for her to file. In other

[65] In some instances, however, as when less serious harms only are risked, the societal harm of the conduct may be too small to justify criminal condemnation. Conduct creating a low risk of a minor harm may fall below the limits of minimum seriousness required for adequate blameworthiness, unless the harm actually occurs.
[66] This is always true for intentional offences in jurisdictions that have general-attempt statutes, as nearly two-thirds of the states in the USA have. See the general-attempt statutes cited at Paul H. Robinson, *Criminal Law Defenses*, above n. 33, i, s. 81(b), nn. 16, 17 and s. 83(f), n. 60.

words, the *actus reus* requirements of voluntariness, capacity, and knowledge of possession serve a liability function similar to many aspects of the *mens rea* requirements. Taking property without permission remains a violation of the rules of conduct, even though a particular defendant is not to be held liable for a taking if he was unaware of a risk that the property belonged to another person.

Neither do the *mens rea* requirements serve a single function that would justify their treatment as a single conceptual group. The requirement of culpability is said to distinguish the criminal law from other bodies of law. Without *mens rea*, there is little justification for condemning or punishing anyone. A person's conduct may be harmful; the victim may have a claim in tort; and fairness and utility both may suggest that the tortfeasor rather than the victim should bear the loss from the injury. Yet without culpability in the tortfeasor, the injury may be seen as 'accidental', perhaps unavoidable, but in any case insufficient to suggest that the tortfeasor deserves condemnation and reprobation. Thus, culpability requirements serve 'to safeguard conduct that is without fault from condemnation as criminal', to use the Model Penal Code phrase.[67]

Yet the requirements of culpability are considerably more diverse than the simple requirement that the defendant have some minimum degree of culpability with respect to each objective element, thereby assuring that the defendant's violation is not innocent and more than merely tortious. Some culpability requirements serve this liability function, of establishing the minimum culpability required for liability for the rule violation, which we might call 'base-culpability' requirements. But only 'present-conduct intention' and 'present-circumstance culpability' serve in this role. Further, as discussed above, the requirement of 'present-conduct intention' has little practical effect. It is rarely in dispute and, where it is, it is redundant with the voluntariness requirement. Thus, 'present-circumstance culpability' is nearly the exclusive culpability requirement for establishing liability.

Culpability requirements also serve a grading function, when used to distinguish between different grades of violations with identical objective elements. The culpability requirements for homicide—murder (purposeful or knowing killing), manslaughter (reckless killing), and negligent homicide—are not designed 'to safeguard conduct that is without fault from condemnation as criminal'. Rather, they define the conditions for distinguishing between grades of offences with identical objective elements. Assault with intent to commit rape, is another example.[68] The 'intent to commit rape' is used as a basis for increasing the grade of the offence over that of an assault without the intention. Burglary is a similar example. In other words, culpability requirements, such as the requirements of homicide,

---

[67] Model Penal Code, § 1.02(1)(c).   [68] Cal. Penal Code, § 220 (1988).

sometimes serve 'to differentiate on reasonable grounds between serious and minor offences', to use another Model Penal Code phrase.[69] These might be termed instances of 'aggravation culpability'. This function is performed by the requirements of either 'future-result culpability', as in homicide, or 'future-conduct intention', as in assault with intent to rape and burglary.

Finally, some *mens rea* requirements serve the rule-articulation function of defining the rules of conduct. That is, they are necessary to describe to persons the conduct that the criminal law prohibits. In the general-attempt offence, for example, the conduct and circumstance elements of the offence provide some statement of the criminal law's prohibition but, standing alone, these elements do not fully define the prohibited conduct. The requirement that the conduct constitute a 'substantial step toward commission of an offence', common in modern attempt definitions,[70] is inadequate in itself. As a purely objective matter, some conduct may constitute a 'substantial step toward commission of an offence' but in fact may be entirely innocent and acceptable conduct and is not meant to be prohibited. Such conduct becomes unacceptable and a societal harm only when accompanied by an intention to violate the substantive rules of conduct.

Lighting one's pipe is not a violation of the rules of conduct, unless it is a step in a plan to ignite a neighbour's haystack. Giving a young girl a ride in a car is not a violation of the rules of conduct, unless it is done with the intention of sexually assaulting her. Thus, to describe the minimum requirements of prohibited conduct, the definition of a criminal attempt must include a state-of-mind requirement—the intention to engage in conduct that would constitute a rule-violation.[71] (In contrast, the law can prohibit conduct that would injure another without having to refer to the defendant's mental state.) In this context, the culpability requirements play a role similar to the conduct and circumstance elements in substantive offences. Typically, such a rule-articulation function appears in what might be called 'secondary prohibitions',[72] and involves an intention to violate a primary prohibition, such as the requirement in attempt of an intention to engage in conduct that constitutes a substantive offence. In instances of incomplete attempt, it is the defendant's future-conduct intention that serves the rule-articulation function. In instances of completed conduct attempts— instances of factual and legal impossibility—it is future-result culpability and present-circumstance culpability, respectively, that serve this function.

Here, then, are three functions of culpability requirements.

---

[69] Model Penal Code, § 1.02(1)(e).   [70] See ibid., § 5.01(1)(c).

[71] The same analysis might be made for conspiracy and solicitation, although the conclusion is not so clear.

[72] The secondary prohibitions enlarge the primary prohibitions: just as one may not violate a primary prohibition, neither may one assist or attempt or solicit or conspire to commit such a violation.

'Base-culpability' requirements serve to assure that a defendant's conduct satisfying an offence's objective elements is not blameless. 'Present-circumstance culpability' does most of this work. 'Aggravation-culpability' requirements serve to aggravate a defendant's liability over the minimum. 'Future-result culpability' and 'future-conduct intention' perform most of this function. Finally, 'rule-articulation mental elements' are necessary to define the conduct to be prohibited by the criminal law. The use of the concept of *mens rea* (or 'culpability') is problematic because it groups, as one, these distinct culpability requirements that serve different functions.

The point here is that one or another of the *actus reus* requirements and one or another of the *mens rea* requirements serve each of the three primary functions of criminal-law doctrine—defining the conduct rules, setting the minimum requirements for liability, and setting the conditions of aggravation of liability beyond the minimum.[73] The correspondence between the categories of *actus reus* and *mens rea* and the rule-articulation, liability, and grading functions may be summarized as shown in the table.

5. Conclusion

I have argued here that the *actus reus–mens rea* distinction reflects no discernible underlying concept, that neither *actus reus* requirements nor *mens rea* requirements share a common characteristic or function. This does not mean, however, that I have doubts about the value of the requirements that make up the *actus reus* and *mens rea* of offences. Is the act requirement useful? Yes, although its contribution is very modest. Is the voluntariness requirement useful? Yes, although it might better be seen as part of the system of excuses rather than as having some special relationship to the elements of an offence definition. Is it useful to have the objective and culpability elements of offence definitions, the causation requirement, and the omission and possession liability rules? Yes, of course, for these requirements are all important for criminal law to perform its three primary functions: announcing *ex ante* the prohibitions (and demands) of the criminal law, identifying which violations of the law's prohibitions and demands should be punished, and providing a rough grading of the seriousness of each such violation.

Is the *actus reus–mens rea* distinction useful? No. That is, by grouping doctrines under these headings we gain no special insights into a characteristic or function that doctrines in each group share. Indeed, the groupings tend to hide important differences between doctrines. The groupings

[73] For a more detailed discussion of functional analysis, including its implications for other areas of criminal law, see Paul H. Robinson, 'A Functional Analysis of Criminal Law' (forthcoming in *Northwestern University LR*).

Three Functions of Criminal Law Doctrine

	Rule-articulation function	Liability function	Grading function
Mens rea	Rule-articulation mental elements	Base-culpability requirements: primarily present-circumstance culpability (but also includes present-conduct intention, which is essentially the voluntariness requirement)	Aggravation-culpability requirements: future-result culpability and future-conduct intention
Actus reus	Primary prohibitions: conduct and circumstance elements of offence definitions	Voluntariness requirement, in commission offences	Result elements Causation requirements
	Omission to perform a legal duty as substitute for an act	Physical-capacity requirement, in omission offences	
	Possession of contraband as substitute for an act	Requirement of knowledge of possession for a sufficient time to terminate the same, in possession offences	
	Secondary prohibitions: conduct toward a violation (attempt); assisting another in a violation		

also create terminological ambiguity—especially among *actus reus* doctrines—which can impede careful analysis of the doctrines. We are better off referring to each of the separate doctrines individually. While there may be value in retaining the concept of *mens rea* under its more descriptive modern label, 'culpability' requirements, even there we must remember that the label combines distinct requirements with different functions.

If a broader conceptual framework is desired, to help us think about and organize these doctrines, it might better look to the different functions of criminal-law doctrine—rule-articulation, liability assignment, and grading. These distinctions at least group doctrines with a discernible common ground, a ground important to the effective operation of criminal law.

Subjectivism and Objectivism: Towards Synthesis

RICHARD H. S. TUR

1. Introduction

When cases under section 1(1) of the new Act . . . first came before the Court of Appeal, the question as to the meaning of the expression 'reckless' . . . appears to have been treated as soluble simply by posing and answering what had by then, unfortunately, become an obsessive question among English lawyers: Is the test of recklessness 'objective' or 'subjective'?[1]

Lord Diplock went on to say that 'questions of criminal liability are seldom solved by simply asking whether the test is subjective or objective',[2] and these strictures were echoed both by himself and by Lord Hailsham in *R* v. *Lawrence*.[3] My own view is that it is indeed unfortunate that the recent intellectual history of English criminal law has been dominated by a dispute between subjectivist and objectivist approaches, with subjectivism in the ascendancy due in no small part to the great influence of the leading textbook in the subject[4] and to the robust opinions of the indefatigable Professor Glanville Williams.

However, 'either–or' reasoning is not necessarily to be trusted, and I seek to show that this opposition of subjectivist and objectivist approaches has produced unsatisfactory consequences in both the theory and practice of English criminal law, and has distorted its history. I propose that this tendentious opposition of subjectivism and objectivism be replaced by a synthesist approach which, I submit, better fits the practical and intellectual problems generated by the criminal law, which more sensitively registers the nuances of the subject-matter, and which more closely accommodates judicial concerns as gleaned from the accumulated case law.

Subjectivism is often presented as morally compelling, locking criminal liability into the favoured conceptual apparatus of consciousness, choice, and control. Objectivism is frequently condemned as random and unfair, visiting liability for harmful consequences on those who did not choose nor could control outcomes that they did not contemplate. A sensitive and

---

[1] *R* v. *Caldwell* [1982] AC 341, per Lord Diplock at 352G.
[2] Ibid. at 354E.   [3] [1982] AC 510.
[4] J. C. Smith and B. Hogan, *Criminal Law* (1st edn., London 1965; 7th edn., London 1992) (hereinafter 'S&H').

liberal present is contrasted with an allegedly harsh and repressive past, and those who have constructed this conception of criminal law and history have not failed to draw conclusions for law reform.

However, it is at least unlikely that any branch of law can be accurately presented simply as the outworking of any one a priori moral principle, no matter how attractive. Law is much more likely to be the result of balancing and accommodating mutually conflicting and inconsistent principles, and criminal law is rather likely to have much in common with law in general. Accordingly, an approach that seeks to synthesize rather than merely oppose subjectivism and objectivism is more likely to satisfy the first requirement of a legal theory: that it fit the facts.

In order to test this hypothesis I propose to retrace some steps in the recent history of the criminal law with a view to illustrating how patterns of academic thought may influence judicial conduct and how academic theory may foreclose moral deliberation by predetermining outcomes. In my view, both subjectivism and objectivism are such patterns of thought. It would not be so very difficult to devise a wholly subjectivist or a completely objectivist criminal code, because faithful application of the master principle will resolve or, rather, pre-empt any apparent moral problems. Much greater difficulties occur where the question is not how to apply one privileged principle but how, if at all, to reconcile the apparently opposing demands of conflicting moral principles.

2. Law as Defeasible Normative Conditional Propositions

First, I need to set out some basic notions which will, I hope, assist both in the analysis and exposition of the law and in developing my thesis. Legal theorists, at least from the time of Austin, have sought 'the key to the Science of Jurisprudence'. Austin thought he had found it in the notion of 'command', but later theorists have found that that key opens very few doors. I think that law may be best understood as a body of defeasible normative conditional propositions of the form, 'If *A* is, then *B* ought to be, unless . . .'. On the approach I favour, the '*A*' or antecedent clause contains legally determined facts and facts alone. The '*B*' clause stipulates the legally defined consequence that, according to law, ought to follow in the event that the facts determined in the '*A*' clause have occurred.

Although the 'unless . . .' clause will include already known and hitherto established circumstances defeating the imputation of the legal consequence to the legally determined facts, it is of the first importance to note that on the view I favour, the list of possible defeasing circumstances is not and cannot be exhaustively determined in advance. Indeed if all defeasing conditions could be known a priori, and were actually known, the canonical form of the legal proposition would require no 'unless . . .' clause,

because all the circumstances defeating the legal attribution of the consequence could be incorporated into the antecedent, definitional clause,
without remainder. Consider the following verse and contemplate the
difference removing the final line would make:

> If all be true that I do think
> There are four reasons I do drink
> Good food, good wine, or being dry,
> Or any other reason why!

Of course there are legal theorists and criminal lawyers who adopt a
closed rather than an open form of legal proposition. On such an approach, certainty prevails over justice. Indeed, Bentham saw certainty as
the 'grand utility of the law'.[5] One criminal-law expert has argued that
dishonesty in theft is a 'dispensable concept', proposing, in effect, that all
the circumstances of moral excuse that claims of honesty might raise can
be exhaustively defined by law.[6] As against which, Professor Smith presents
a compelling case for leaving open the circumstances of excuse and justification.[7] I am in agreement with Professor Smith. As Keble J put it: 'All
laws admit of cases of just excuse.'[8] The heads of excuse are never closed,
and justice is not beyond the age of childbirth even where the criminal law
is codified.

Taking 'assault' as an example, one might say, with the Lord Chief
Justice in *R* v. *Gladstone Williams*,[9] that it is 'an act by which the defendant, intentionally or recklessly, applies unlawful force to the complain-
ant'. As an exposition of the criminal law of England, there are several
problems with this definition, even if it is restricted to 'assault' in the
narrow sense of 'battery'; but for the present exercise, attention is drawn
to the inclusion of the word 'unlawful' in the definition.

But for that term, it is a relatively straightforward matter to render
this offence in the canonical form of a defeasible normative conditional,
substituting for '*A*' in the antecedent clause the following list of factual
elements:

(*a*) an act applying force to another; and
(*b*) intention or recklessness as to that act.

If the jury is satisfied that these facts occurred, it is entitled, perhaps
obliged, to convict *unless* there is some other factor in play, giving rise to
a defence. On my analysis, 'lawful excuse' would always be a secondary
matter of defence rather than a primary matter of definition, which would

---

[5] Cited in Mary P. Mack, *Jeremy Bentham: An Odyssey of Ideas, 1748–1792* (London
1962), 59.
[6] D. W. Elliott, 'Dishonesty in Theft: A Dispensable Concept' [1982] *Criminal LR* 395.
[7] J. C. Smith, *Justification and Excuse in the Criminal Law* (London 1989).
[8] *Moore* v. *Hussey* 1609 Hob. 93, 96.   [9] (1983) 78 Cr. App. Rep. 276, 279.

arise for consideration, if at all, only after the existence of the essential ingredients of the offence had been established.

3. Definitional Minimalism

I favour definitional minimalism, that is, a theoretical preference for economy in the definition of criminal offences whereby only the core elements ordinarily constituting the social wrong in question need be stipulated and proved beyond reasonable doubt by the prosecution. On this minimalist approach to the definition of offences, unusual circumstances that might exculpate or justify may be reserved for the 'unless . . .' clause as defeasing conditions, rather than incorporated into the definition of offences.

Subjectivism, however, tends towards definitional maximalism, that is, a theoretical preference for exhaustive antecedent clauses and therefore extended definitions of offences containing all inculpatory and exculpatory conditions in one watertight formulation. Consider, by way of illustration, the views of the Geoffrey Lane LJ in R v. *Stephenson*:

What then must the prosecution prove in order to bring home the charge of arson in circumstances such as the present? They must prove that (1) the defendant deliberately committed some act which caused the damage to property alleged or part of such damage; (2) the defendant had no lawful excuse for causing the damage; these two requirements will in the ordinary case not be in issue; (3) the defendant either (a) intended to cause the damage to the property, or (b) was reckless as to whether the property was damaged or not.[10]

It strikes me as unsatisfactory and inappropriate to expect the prosecution to prove as a general requirement in all cases that the accused had no lawful excuse, rather than to deal with lawful excuse as a secondary matter of defence if, but only if, it actually arises on the particular facts of a case.

Definitional maximalism is further illustrated in R v. *D. R. Smith*,[11] where the Court of Criminal Appeal suggests that the *actus reus* of criminal damage is (1) damaging or destroying property (2) of another (3) without lawful excuse; and that *mens rea* runs to each and all these elements on the basis of an alleged principle of the common law that to intend an act is to intend it under a full description of its circumstances and consequences. To extend *mens rea* to the ownership of the property, let alone to lawful excuse, involves doing considerable damage to the words of the statute and obviously increases the number of items that the prosecution must prove.

[10] [1979] 1 QB 695, 703.   [11] [1974] QB 354.

This extension was effected in the context of a claim of mistake. The defendant thought, wrongly, that the property in question was his own. Strictly speaking, this is a mistake of (civil) law but for the purposes of criminal law it is treated as a mistake of fact. 'Objectivist' and 'subjectivist' reasoning would have produced the same outcome on the facts of this case, in that the defendant's erroneous belief was wholly credible and reasonable and therefore it would have operated as the defence of honest and reasonable belief, even if knowledge of the ownership of the property had not been held to be an ingredient of the offence with which the accused was charged.

4. Definitional Maximalism and Mistake

An erroneous belief may lead to an acquittal either because it is logically inconsistent with the existence in the same mind of the requisite mental element or because of the principle stated by Brett J in *R v. Prince*

that a mistake of fact on reasonable grounds, to the extent that, if the facts were as believed, the acts of the prisoner would make him guilty of no criminal offence at all, is an excuse, and that such excuse is implied in every criminal charge and every criminal enactment in England.[12]

Thus an erroneous belief may be relevant at one of two stages in the criminal process: first, at the point when the prosecution seeks to establish the requisite mental element or, secondly, as a general defence which comes into play only if the prosecution has proved all the definitional elements of the offence. Mistakes of fact may be classified as 'negativing *mens rea*' or as 'a defence' by reference to whether the mistake relates to a circumstantial element of the *actus reus* qualified or not qualified by *mens rea*. Sometimes mistake will be relevant to proof of a definitional element contained in the antecedent clause of the canonical form of a legal proposition, and sometimes it will be relevant as a matter of excuse contained, perhaps tacitly, in the 'unless . . .' clause. Thus the two types of mistake of fact relate to the canonical form of a legal proposition in logically different ways.

Mistake negativing *mens rea*—what I call, for obvious reasons, 'Morgan-mistake'—is well put by Lord Scarman in *R v. Taaffe*:

the principle that a man must be judged on the facts as he believes them to be is an accepted principle of the criminal law *when the state of a man's mind and his knowledge are ingredients of the offence with which he is charged*.[13]

---

[12] (1875) LR 2 CCR 154, 170.   [13] [1984] 1 All ER 747, 749 (emphasis added).

218   *Richard H. S. Tur*

The accepted principle of the criminal law when the state of a defendant's mind and knowledge are *not* ingredients of the offence charged was,
as it appeared to Stephen J in *R* v. *Tolson*, 'unanswerably' established by
Brett J in *Prince*. Stephen J thought that:

it may be laid down as a general rule that an alleged offender is deemed to have
acted under that state of facts which he in good faith and on reasonable grounds
believed to exist when he did the act alleged to be an offence. I am unable to
suggest any real exception to this rule, nor has one ever been suggested to me ... [14]

Thus, mistake as a defence—Tolson-mistake—is doctrinally distinct from
Morgan-mistake. That distinction was preserved in *DPP* v. *Morgan*[15] by
the express refusal of their Lordships to overrule *R* v. *Tolson* and its progeny.
There are, then, two types of mistake, procedurally, logically, doctrinally,
and morally different; yet the subjectivist tendency has sought remorselessly
to assimilate all mistake-of-fact cases to one model.

The dichotomy is well illustrated by comparing the reasoning and results
in *D. R. Smith* with that in *R* v. *Phekoo*.[16] In *D. R. Smith* the Court of
Appeal first determined that knowledge of the ownership of the property
is an ingredient of the offence and then, in anticipation of the 'inexorable
logic' that later characterized the reasoning in *Morgan*, concluded that an
honest belief would suffice, reasonable or not, since the presence of such
belief in the mind of the defendant negatived the *mens rea*, and as a matter
of logic the prosecution could not prove the existence of all the essential
ingredients of the offence. Accordingly, the defendant was entitled to be
acquitted without further ado. James LJ took the Court to be 'applying the
ordinary principles of *mens rea*'—though what these principles are was left
unstated—and *D. R. Smith* enjoyed considerable popularity with the
subjectivist tendency until it was eclipsed by *Morgan*, which has been even
more plausibly presented by the subjectivist tendency as proceeding from
general principles of *mens rea* whereas *D. R. Smith*, at best, turned upon
the wording of section 5(3) of the Criminal Damage Act 1971 and, at
worst, was 'a special case ... [which] may have to be reconsidered'.[17]

Phekoo concerned the application of section 1(3) of the Eviction Act
1977, which makes it an offence for any person, with intent to cause the
residential occupier of any premises to give up occupation, to do acts cal-
culated to interfere with the peace or comfort of the residential occupier.
The trial judge ruled against a submission that a belief that the victims
were not residential occupiers was a defence and the appeal was based on

[14] [1886–90] All ER Rep. 26, 37.
[15] [1976] AC 182, 202 (per Lord Cross), 215 (per Lord Hailsham), and 238 (per Lord
Fraser).
[16] [1981] 3 All ER 84.   [17] [1976] AC 182, per Lord Edmund-Davies at 234.

the failure to put to the jury the issue of the defendant's belief that the victims were squatters.

Although the question was raised as to whether the Crown had to prove the absence of honest belief, the Court of Criminal Appeal proceeded on the basis that the distinction between honest and reasonable belief was 'not strictly material to the appeal', because the alleged defect in the direction was that the issue of belief was wholly withheld from the jury. The logical implication of that, though it is not spelled out in terms by the Court, is that the status of the victim is a circumstance not qualified by *mens rea*. That implication tacitly assumes a minimalist definition in direct contrast to the reasoning in *D. R. Smith*, where a maximal definition was expressly adopted. All this is confirmed by the concluding passages in the judgment that there must have been a reasonable basis for the asserted belief.[18] In *Phekoo*, therefore, mistaken belief operated as a defence, whereas in *D. R. Smith* it negatived *mens rea*.

5. Definitional Maximalism and Moral Assessment

Since *Morgan* was decided, there has been a series of attempts, not all successful, in the courts to extend the definitions of offences so as to apply the 'inexorable logic' that concludes triumphantly with honest mistake as a so-called defence. Attempted redefinition is illustrated in *Lavin* v. *Albert*,[19] where counsel wisely declined Lord Diplock's invitation to argue, in effect, that *mens rea* qualified the status of the victim in an offence under section 51(1) of the Police Act 1964. Redefinition occurred in *Morgan*, *Gladstone Williams*, and *Beckford* v *R*.[20] Such redefinition of offences not only adds to the burden on the prosecution but also impacts on the moral acceptability of the criminal law, as is well illustrated by a consideration of rape.

The starting-point in the moral assessment of any offence must be with the definition of that offence. Prior to the decision in *Morgan*, the definition of rape in English criminal law was distinctly minimalist. As Humphreys J put it in *R* v. *Turner*: 'on a charge of rape the Crown has to prove two things: intercourse and the non-consent of the woman.'[21] On this definition, the intercourse had to be intentional, which of its very nature it is most likely to be, but the defendant's perception of the victim's state of mind was relevant, if at all, only at the defence stage of proceedings. On that basis, any mistake about the woman's consent would be a mistake as to a circumstance not qualified by *mens rea*—i.e. Tolson-mistake—and therefore the mistake would have to be reasonable. The question to ask of

---

[18] [1981] 3 All ER 84, 93H.   [19] [1982] AC 546, 565E-G.   [20] [1988] AC 130.
[21] [1944] KB 463, 469.

this model of rape—minimalist definition plus external defence—is whether it produces ethically acceptable outcomes and, if so, what, if anything, is unsatisfactory about it?

Consider a hypothetical character, Adonis. He strongly believes that he is irresistible to women. Thus, believing that no woman could say 'No' to him, Adonis has sexual intercourse with a non-consenting woman, but such is the strength of his belief that he misinterprets her resistance and does not register her protests. Adonis honestly believes that the woman consented. Given the definition in *R* v. *Turner*, together with the *Tolson* requirement that mistake be reasonable, Adonis would be guilty of rape.

Morgan changed all that: 'it is no longer disputed that, in England, perception of the woman's consent is an aspect of the mental element in crimes of rape.'[22] The effect of this definitional revision is that Adonis must now be acquitted on a charge of rape because, as a matter of 'inexorable logic', an actual belief in consent is incompatible with the existence in the mind of the accused of the (newly) required mental element and the prosecution must fail because it cannot (now) prove all the definitional elements of the offence. Although an acquittal is logically inescapable given the widened definition, there was no a priori necessity to adopt that definition.

The question to ask of the extended *Morgan* definition is in what ways, if any, it is preferable to the *Turner* definition (plus *Tolson* defence). On moral grounds alone it is difficult to see the *Morgan* redefinition as other than a retrograde step: 'it can be argued with force that it is only fair to the woman and not in the least unfair to the man that he should be under a duty to take reasonable care to ascertain that she is consenting to the intercourse and be at the risk of a prosecution if he fails to take care.'[23] Powerful reasons might properly be expected from those who would depart from this moral principle.

The judgments in support of this departure are, however, very disappointing. There is little serious consideration of the social and moral merits of the alternative definitions of rape. Lord Cross founded his decision upon the alleged meaning of rape 'according to the ordinary use of the English language'; Lord Fraser relied on an unargued assertion about 'forms of immoral conduct . . . not intended to be struck at by the law against rape'; and Lord Hailsham proceeded on the basis of 'what seems . . . abundantly clear, that the prohibited act in rape is non-consensual intercourse, and that the guilty state of mind is an intention to commit it'.[24]

If it is allowed that the mental element in rape includes a perception of

[22] *Pappajohn* v. *R* (1980) 111 DLR (3d) 1, per Dickson J, at 11.
[23] *Morgan* [1976] AC 182, per Lord Cross, at 203B.
[24] [1976] AC 182 at 203D, 238E, and 214F respectively.

the woman's consent, then an honest belief in consent, no matter how unreasonable, necessitates acquittal because it entails the absence of the requisite mental element. The legal argument from that point on is impeccable, but the legal argument for that point is weak and unpersuasive. The House of Lords had a free and unconstrained choice between the two definitions and its adoption of the maximalist approach was not required by logic nor by legal precedent, and is difficult to justify on moral grounds. Ordinarily, on reaching such a conclusion, a commentator on the common law might advocate overruling the unsatisfactory precedent, but that option is foreclosed in England by section 1 of the Sexual Offences (Amendment) Act 1976 which puts the *Morgan* redefinition on a statutory footing.

In view of the reservations that can legitimately be expressed about its *ratio*, it is not surprising that *Morgan* has not been very popular and that various attempts have been made to circumvent it. The *Morgan* principle actually availed the accused nothing in that the House of Lords applied the proviso, taking the view that the alleged belief was so unreasonable as to be incredible. That move is not available to secure a conviction of Adonis, however, because *ex hypothesi* he does believe that the woman is consenting.

In *R* v. *Pigg*, an unreasonable mistake, far from negativing (*Cunningham*) recklessness was taken to constitute (*Caldwell*) recklessness.[25] That move is not readily available to secure a conviction of Adonis in light of *R* v. *Satnam & Kewal*[26] which held that any direction as to recklessness in rape should be based on *Morgan* without regard to *R* v. *Caldwell*. Other than its acceptability to the subjectivist tendency, quite why the later Court of Appeal decision should be regarded as controlling is unclear, particularly since *Pigg* is wholly consistent with Lord Roskill's *dicta* in *R* v. *Seymour*[27] to the effect that recklessness should be given its *Caldwell* meaning in relation to all offences unless Parliament has otherwise ordained.

The Canadian Supreme Court qualified the *Morgan* principle in *Pappajohn* v. *R*, holding that there was no room nor need for the *Morgan* direction unless there was extrinsic evidence supportive of the defendant's claim honestly to have believed that the woman was consenting. In *R* v. *Taylor*,[28] the English Court of Criminal Appeal adopted substantially the same reasoning and conclusion, though the Canadian case was not mentioned. The general issue was whether the *Morgan* direction on honest belief must always be put to the jury and, if not, when it may be dispensed with.

The court held that in cases of conflicting testimony, where the jury finds that there is evidence of non-consent, and there is no extrinsic evidence supportive of the defendant's claim, there is no room for any so-called

---

[25] [1982] 2 All ER 591. On *Cunningham*, see text at n. 75 below.
[26] (1983) 78 Cr. App. Rep. 149.
[27] [1983] 2 All ER 1058, 1064. But see now *R* v. *Sulman*, *The Times*, 21 May 1993.
[28] (1984) 80 Cr. App. Rep. 327.

defence of honest belief and no need to put the *Morgan* direction to the jury. Just as honest belief is inconsistent with the *mens rea* of the offence, as defined in *Morgan*, so that *mens rea* is inconsistent with honest belief. 'Inexorable logic' runs both ways. If, therefore, the jury concludes on all the evidence that any ordinary person in the position of the accused must have realized that the woman was not consenting; that the accused, as an ordinary person, must have so realized and therefore did; then there is no room in the accused's mind for the logically incompatible belief in consent. The doctrinal question is whether *Taylor* qualifies *Morgan* or contradicts it. That is a matter for the House of Lords in the fullness of time. The effect of current English criminal law up to the Court of Appeal would be to convict Adonis so long as his belief in the woman's consent rested merely on his own wishful thinking and mere *ipse dixit*.

If, on moral grounds, one believes that Adonis should be convicted, one is committed to conviction in the absence of *Morgan mens rea*. English criminal law already adopts that position in the case of intoxicated mistake as is illustrated in *R* v. *Fotheringham*.[29] If that is morally acceptable then so, too, is conviction of the sober man who makes an unreasonable mistake. That moral commitment calls for restoration of the *Turner* definition and the *Tolson* defence, and this discussion of rape illustrates that definition and redefinition of offences is not merely a matter of dry legal technique for committees of lawyers to determine, but one of pressing moral (and public) concern. With respect, moral commitments should determine legal definitions and not vice versa.

6. Subjectivist Redefinition and *Mens Rea*

Subjectivist redefinition of offences proceeds, in part, on the basis of an eccentric conception of *mens rea*. 'Basic *mens rea*' was defined for years in the leading textbook as 'Intention and recklessness with respect to *all* [my italics] those circumstances and consequences of the accused's act (or state of affairs) which constitute the *actus reus* of the crime in question'[30] and any modifications of this in the 'general definition' offered in recent editions[31] go more to instances where *mens rea* goes beyond the *actus reus* rather than to cases where *mens rea* does not extend to all the elements of the *actus reus*. This generalizing tendency has now been embodied in a still-further extended form in clause 24(1) of the Draft Criminal Code: 'a person does not commit a Code offence unless he acts intentionally, knowingly or recklessly in respect of each of its elements.'

---

[29] [1988] *Criminal LR* 846.   [30] S&H, 5th edn., 59.
[31] S&H, 6th edn., 70–1; 7th edn., 70–1.

Definitional maximalism has at least three noteworthy consequences. By increasing the number of elements which the prosecution must prove beyond reasonable doubt, it adds to the length and complexity of criminal trials. The (unnecessary) length and complexity of criminal trials has rightly exercised a number of judges, for example Lord Hailsham in *R* v. *Moloney*[32] and several of their Lordships in *Lawrence*. That this consequence can be attributed to the definitional maximalism inherent in subjectivism is only a hypothesis, not a conclusion, but the possibility should at least be considered in assessing the virtues of the prevailing theory of English criminal law.

A second consequence is the generalization of the *Morgan* doctrine to all and any crime with 'unlawful' (or 'without lawful excuse') as (allegedly) part of its *actus reus*, express or implied, as in *Gladstone Williams* and in *Beckford*. The argument is neat and inexorably logical. If the intention is not simply to use force or to kill but to use unlawful force, or to kill without lawful excuse, then, given their alleged beliefs, neither Mr Gladstone Williams nor PC Solomon Beckford had the necessary *mens rea*, and the prosecution 'withers on the bough'. This argument is developed in *R* v. *Kimber*,[33] where the Court of Appeal criticized Hodgson J in the Divisional Court in *Albert* v. *Lavin* for suggesting that the word 'unlawful' adds nothing to the definition of an offence. The debate has recently taken another turn with both the Court of Appeal and the House of Lords holding that 'unlawful' in section 1(1) of the Sexual Offences (Amendment) Act 1976 'adds nothing . . . and it should be treated as being mere surplusage'.[34] By contrast, in *Beckford*, the Privy Council proceeded on the basis that the *mens rea* for murder is not merely an intention to kill (or to do serious injury) but is an intention to kill (or to do serious injury) 'unlawfully'. That being so, a belief in circumstances that would render killing or doing serious injury lawful negatives the mental element for murder and must lead to acquittal.

However, in *Beckford* there was conflicting testimony. On the Crown's evidence that the slain man had his hands raised in surrender but was none the less gunned down, there was a callous execution by the defendant and another police-officer. On the defence side, this was a plain case of self-defence, since policemen investigating reports of a dangerous gunman were fired upon and returned fire, resulting in death. The Crown case persuaded the jury. On 28 March 1985 the defendant was convicted of murder and sentenced to death. On 10 October 1985 the Court of Appeal of Jamaica dismissed an appeal but gave leave to appeal, certifying as of exceptional public interest the question of whether the test for self-defence should be

---

[32] [1985] AC 905.   [33] [1983] 3 All ER 316.
[34] *R* v. *R* [1991] 2 All ER 257 (CA); [1991] 4 All ER 481 (HL).

based on what a person reasonably believed on reasonable grounds to be necessary to resist attack, or upon what the accused honestly believed.

Even treating *Morgan* as 'a landmark decision in the development of the common law',[35] the extrinsic evidence limitation established in *Pappajohn* and illustrated in *Taylor*, would determine the outcome unfavourably to the appellant. On that basis, even if there had been a misdirection, there was no substantial miscarriage of justice and *Beckford* was a case for the application of the proviso. However, unlike *Morgan*, the proviso was not applied:

Their Lordships have given anxious consideration to this submission for there is much force in it. If on the facts as they appear from the summing up the judge had left the matter to the jury on the basis of a choice between the two accounts then any misdirection as to the reasonableness or otherwise of the defendant's belief would have been of only academic interest.[36]

It appears to follow that there is little or no room or need for a direction on honest versus reasonable belief in a straightforward conflict-of-testimony case. That implication is wholly consistent with the *Pappajohn* qualification and is likely to limit the impact of the *ratio* of *Beckford*.

The Privy Council found additional problems with the conduct of the trial. The judgment continues:

However the judge did not leave it to the jury as a choice between the two accounts, for he clearly thought that there was a further possibility, namely that the defendant mistakenly believed that the deceased was armed and would shoot him if he did not shoot first. It is not readily apparent why the judge regarded this as a possible view of the facts, but their Lordships have no transcript of the evidence and must accept the view of the judge that the facts were open to such an interpretation.[37]

It is not readily apparent why their Lordships 'must' accept that the facts as proved left open the possibility of a belief that the deceased was armed, given that the jury had accepted the Crown evidence including evidence of the deceased's surrender. No transcript of the evidence is necessary to establish that the jury cannot find incompatible facts to have existed at the same time. Once a jury concludes that the defendant did not actually hold the belief asserted, it matters not whether that non-existent belief must be reasonable, if held, to constitute an answer to the charge.

Clearly their Lordships were not obliged as a matter of logic to accept the trial judge's view and, indeed, the logic of the situation appears to require its rejection. It is more probable that the trial judge's view was accepted in order to facilitate the appeal:

[35] *Beckford* v. R [1988] AC 130, 145.   [36] [1988] AC 130, 146.
[37] [1988] AC 130, 146.

In these circumstances their Lordships cannot feel with that utter certainty that is required in a case of capital murder that the jury would necessarily have returned the same verdict if they had been directed in terms of 'honest' as opposed to 'reasonable' belief.[38]

Beckford is only persuasive rather than binding authority and it is likely to be narrowly construed by English courts, given current approaches to duress and murder[39] and its potential to develop into a terrorists' charter.

A third consequence of definitional maximalism is the possible distortion of the data of English criminal law so that all crimes, whatever their statutory or common-law definition, are presented as if their *mens rea* is coextensive with their *actus reus*. Clause 24 (1) of the Draft Criminal Code, however, qualifies this with the preface 'Unless a contrary intention appears . . .', and the current edition of the leading textbook now acknowledges that 'Some offences are so defined that only intention with respect to one or more elements is sufficient. Others are defined so as to require only negligence, or no fault at all . . . .'[40]

It follows that whatever the definitional presumption embodied in the subjectivist's definition of 'basic *mens rea*', different crimes may, and do, have very different *mentes reae*. The best statement on this point remains that of Stephen J in *Tolson*,[41] who considers the phrase, '*non est reus, nisi mens sit rea*' to be 'too short and too antithetical to be of much practical value' and concludes that 'the principle involved appears . . . when fully considered, to amount to no more than this: the full definition of every crime contains expressly or by implication a proposition as to a state of mind.' On this analysis, crimes may differ as to the mental element(s) required.

7. *Mens Rea* and *Actus Reus*

There is no magic and some mystification in the traditional labels of the English criminal lawyer. It might be better to replace *mens rea* with 'mental element' or 'fault element', and *actus reus* with 'external elements', as some writers and reformers have indeed proposed. Certainly it is both unhelpful and misleading to translate *actus reus* either as 'act' or as 'circumstances' and my preference is to regard *actus reus* as including conduct, circumstances, and consequences. Plainly, different crimes may have very different ingredients and *mens rea* may qualify some but not all of these elements.

---

[38] [1988] AC 130, 147.   [39] *R v. Howe* [1987] 1 All ER 771.
[40] S&H, 6th edn., 70; 7th edn., 71.   [41] (1889) 23 QB 168, 185–7.

If one does use the traditional categories of analysis, namely *actus reus* and corresponding *mens rea*, five logically exhaustive and exclusive possibilities emerge, as follows (the presence of an element being indicated by a tick [√] and its absence by a cross [×]):

AR   *MR*

1. √   ×
   √ √   × ×
   √ √ √   × × ×   e.g. *R* v. *Larsonneur*[42]
(Some) *actus reus* but no corresponding *mens rea*

2. √ √   √ ×
   √ √ √   √ √ ×   e.g. *Prince, Phekoo, Turner*, s. 47 Offences Against the Person Act 1861
Actus reus and some corresponding *mens rea* (*actus reus* goes beyond *mens rea*)

3. √   √
   √ √   √ √
   √ √ √   √ √ √   e.g. *D. R. Smith, Morgan, Kimber, Gladstone Williams, Beckford*
Actus reus and coextensive *mens rea*

4. √   √ √
   √ √   √ √ √   e.g. *R* v. *Steane*[43] and s. 18 Offences Against the Person Act 1861
Actus reus and additional *mens rea* (*mens rea* goes beyond *actus reus*)

5. ×   √
   × ×   √ √   e.g. attempt, perhaps
No *actus reus* but some *mens rea*

I refer to the second type of crime, where not all the elements of the *actus reus* are qualified by *mens rea*, as crimes of 'partial *mens rea*' because *mens rea* qualifies some part but not all of the external elements. Although some subjectivists acknowledge that such crimes do exist, it is not infrequently claimed that all such crimes are defined by statute and that common-law presumptions of *mens rea* are not thereby impaired. However, there are instances of partial *mens rea* crimes defined not by statute but by common law.

Thus, in *DPP* v. *Newbury*,[44] Lord Salmon stated that 'an accused is

[42] (1933) 24 Cr. App. Rep. 74.   [43] [1947] 1 All ER 813.
[44] [1977] AC 500, 507.

guilty of manslaughter if it is proved that he intentionally did an act which
was unlawful and dangerous and that that act inadvertently caused death
and . . . it is unnecessary to prove that the accused knew that the act was
unlawful or dangerous.' Again, in *R* v. *Lemon*,[45] the majority held that on
a charge of blasphemous libel it is sufficient to prove that the publication
was intentional and that the matter was blasphemous, and an intention to
blaspheme is unnecessary. A similar view was taken by the Court of Appeal
in *R* v. *Gibson and Sylveire*[46] in respect of outraging public decency, it
being held unnecessary to prove an intention to outrage. 'Partial *mens rea*'
offences are to be found in the common law as well as in statutes.

   This second type of crime contrasts sharply with the third type, which
represents the subjectivist's paradigm. Plainly there are crimes where *mens
rea* runs to some but not all of the external elements, and sometimes it
may be morally preferable that this should be so, as my discussion of rape
illustrates. Subjectivism tends to obscure the existence of such crimes and,
when their existence is recognized, to treat them as objects of reform. By
thus merging conceptual concerns and moral matters, subjectivism severely limits the terms of discourse about criminal law. At the very least, the
conceptual apparatus of the criminal lawyer should be able to accommodate the full range of logical possibilities, particularly if criminal law is to
be studied historically and comparatively, where allegiance to any one moral
presupposition and conceptual paradigm is bound to be constraining.

   So long as some correspondence between *actus reus* and *mens rea* is
assumed, the antecedent factual clause in any defeasible normative conditional proposition of criminal law must logically take one or other of the
five forms outlined above, and even where this traditional correspondence
is denied only one further logical possibility emerges: an offence which has
both *actus reus* with no corresponding *mens rea* and *mens rea* with no
corresponding *actus reus*. Such an offence can be constructed by combining
the first and fifth types illustrated in the chart. By way of example, consider the imaginary offence of being HIV-positive and intending sexual
intercourse. Which form is actually exhibited by offences in any particular
legal system at a particular time will depend upon a range of factors,
including moral principles and social policies, and there is no a priori
reason to expect that all offences in even one legal system will, or should,
exhibit the same logical structure.

   But, whatever logical form an offence takes, the prosecution bears the
burden of proving the existence of all the essential ingredients of the
offence charged,[47] and in the case of mental elements that truly is a burden. Philosophically, the very existence of other minds may be problematic

[45] [1979] AC 617.   [46] [1990] *Criminal LR* 738.
[47] *Woolmington* v. *DPP* [1935] AC 462.

and no one has privileged access to the mind of another: 'The only person who knows what the accused's mental processes were is the accused himself—and probably not even he can recall them accurately . . .'[48] Even if the state of a man's mind is as much a question of fact as is the state of his digestion,[49] it is a curiously inaccessible sort of fact and, in the absence of an admission, the prosecution would always be defeated but for the availability of recognized presumptions, which legitimate inferences as to states of mind.

8. Proof of Mental Elements

Subjectivism concentrates rather too readily on general definitions of mental elements such as 'intention' and 'recklessness' and pays insufficient attention to the problem of how such elements are to be proved. It might be better to seek functional rather than semantic definitions of such terms. Juries require guidance as to the proof of these facts, and the function of the judge's direction is to provide that assistance in a succinct and intelligible form. For that reason, as Lord Hailsham says in *Lawrence*,[50] 'A direction to a jury should be custom built to make the jury understand their task in relation to a particular case.' This 'is not best achieved by a disquisition on jurisprudence or philosophy . . . [and] the search for universally applicable definitions is often productive of more obscurity than light.' Similar strictures are to be found in the judgment of Diplock LJ in *R v. Mowatt*.[51]

As to the proof of 'intention', like Lord Bridge in *Moloney*, 'I know of no clearer exposition . . . than that in the judgment of the Court of Criminal Appeal . . . delivered by Lord Goddard CJ in *R v. Steane*':[52]

No doubt, if the prosecution prove an act the natural consequences of which would be a certain result and no evidence or explanation is given, then a jury may, on a proper direction, find that the prisoner is guilty of doing the act with the intent alleged, but if, on the totality of the evidence, there is room for more than one view as to the intent of the prisoner, the jury should be directed that it is for the prosecution to prove the intent to the jury's satisfaction, and if, on a review of the whole evidence, they either think that the intent did not exist or they are left in doubt as to the intent, the prisoner is entitled to be acquitted.

The structure and legitimacy of this approach to the proof of 'intention' may be brought out first by presenting the reasoning involved in syllogistic form, and then by examining the premises.

[48] *R v. Caldwell* [1982] AC 341, per Lord Diplock at 352.
[49] *Edgington v. Fitzmaurice* (1885) 29 Ch. D 459, per Bowen LJ at 483.
[50] [1982] AC 510, 519.   [51] [1968] 1 QB 421, 426.
[52] [1985] AC 905, 929 citing [1947] 1 All ER 813, 816.

---

1. All else being equal, ordinary persons intend the near and natural consequences of their acts.
2. The accused is an ordinary person.
3. Therefore the accused intended those consequences.

The minor premiss, that the accused is an ordinary person, is itself a rebuttable presumption, going all the way back at least to the McNaghten Rules,[53] and the major premiss is presented here and best understood as a rebuttable presumption, based on common experience and ordinary usage. Since I am here concerned with the status and utility of the presumption, I need not join issue as to whether 'near and natural' is the best formulation to communicate the issues involved to a jury. However, reference to probability is plausibly thought by some to be essential to the intelligibility of the direction.[54]

Lord Bridge in *Moloney* described it (in my view correctly) as 'a rule of evidence which judges for more than a century found of the utmost utility in directing juries'.[55] Although the matter is by no means free from controversy, Lord Bridge believes (and I agree) that *DPP* v. *Smith*[56] treats this evidential presumption as irrebuttable, that is to say, as a fixed rule of substantive law. It follows from Lord Bridge's view (and again I agree) that the effect of section 8 of the Criminal Justice Act 1967 is to put intention back where it belongs, 'in the hands of the jury'. From this analysis Lord Bridge concludes (again, in my view, correctly) that section 8 'leaves us at liberty to go back to the decisions before . . . *Smith*'.[57] *R* v. *Steane* is such a case.

The appellant was convicted on an indictment which charged him with 'doing acts likely to assist the enemy with intent to assist the enemy'. As Lord Goddard CJ observed, 'The important thing to notice . . . is that where an intent is charged in the indictment, the burden of proving that intent remains throughout on the prosecution.'[58] Since the appellant asserted again and again that he never had any intention of assisting the enemy, the prosecution's case was in some difficulty, particularly given evidence of threats of internment in a concentration camp and of physical violence which had been made against the appellant and his family. It was, however, common ground and admitted that the defendant had entered the German Broadcasting System in January 1940 and had broadcast certain matters through that system. The prosecution's case, presented in syllogistic form, appeared to be:

---

[53] (1843) 10 Cl. & Fin. 200.
[54] *Handcock & Shankland* [1986] AC 455, per Lord Scarman at 472–3.
[55] [1985] AC 905, 928.   [56] [1961] AC 290.   [57] [1985] AC 905, 929.
[58] [1947] 1 All ER 813, 816.

1. A man is taken to intend the natural consequences of his acts.
2. The defendant did an act likely to assist the enemy.
3. Therefore the defendant intended to assist the enemy.

If, for any reason, the major premiss is not available, then the defendant is entitled to an acquittal simply because the prosecution has not discharged the burden of proving all the definitional elements of the offence. The major premiss may be regarded as always available under all circumstances (strict objectivism), never available (radical subjectivism), or usually but not always available (synthesism).

The defect in the way the trial was conducted was that the prosecution and the judge proceeded on the basis that the major premiss is a fixed rule of law and not a rebuttable presumption. Accordingly, the presumption was applied in circumstances where it had no legitimate application. It is one thing to conclude, as a properly directed jury may on all the evidence, that a particular defendant intended 'X' because 'X' is the near and natural consequence of the defendant's freely chosen act. It is quite another to apply that presumption to an act performed under duress: 'it is impossible to say that where acts were done by a person in subjection to the power of another, especially if that other be a brutal enemy, an inference that he intended the natural consequences of his acts must be drawn merely from the fact that he did them.'[59] The Court of Criminal Appeal therefore concluded (in my view correctly) that the conviction could not stand because proof of an essential element, namely an intent to assist the enemy, rested upon an assumption which it was unsafe to make in all the circumstances of the case.

To my mind, the judgment of the Court of Criminal Appeal in this case illustrates very clearly the acceptable operation of the presumption and identifies very precisely the defect in the trial judge's direction. However, *Steane* has appeared far from clear to some commentators, notably Professor Glanville Williams, who submits that the actual decision 'could have been reached more readily and more acceptably by recognising duress as a defence'.[60] That suggestion assumes that the defendant actually intended to assist the enemy, because before any question of defence arises the prosecution must satisfy the jury of the existence of all the essential ingredients, including the intention which is laid in the indictment. Now, the defendant may or may not have intended to assist the enemy, we know not which, and unless and until that intention is proved, the defendant is entitled to an acquittal. In this case, the presence of duress operated to abnormalize circumstances. That abnormality rendered use of the normal

---

[59] [1947] 1 All ER 813, per Lord Goddard CJ at 817.
[60] *The Mental Element in Crime* (Jerusalem 1965), 21.

presumption unsafe and unsound and therefore the prosecution 'withered on the bough' for want of proof of an essential ingredient.

Accordingly, the suggestion that the case is better analysed from the perspective of the defence of duress is misconceived in that it assumes precisely what was in issue: that the defendant actually intended to assist the enemy. Although duress is ordinarily a defence and comes into play, if at all, in the 'unless . . .' clause of the legal proposition as a matter of excuse, in some instances, as in *Steane*, it operates to negative an essential ingredient featured in the antecedent clause of the legal proposition.

Although *Steane* is frequently cited in discussions of the meaning of 'intention' as including 'purpose', that does seem to go somewhat beyond the reasoning of the Court of Criminal Appeal which was not concerned with meaning but with proof. Professor Glanville Williams correctly catches this point when he observes that 'its importance derives chiefly from its rejection of the proposition that a person is deemed to intend the natural consequences of his acts'.[61] It is very important, however, to appreciate that this 'rejection' is not absolute. What is rejected is the exclusivity of the proposition which would make all other evidence as to the defendant's state of mind irrelevant. What is preserved is the relevance of the proposition, along with all other evidence, in the determination of the defendant's actual state of mind. Understood as a rebuttable presumption, the proposition provides a method for ascertaining the actual state of mind of the defendant.

In *DPP* v. *Smith*, the defendant's intention was in issue. In summing up, the trial judge, Donovan J, said:

The intention with which a man did something can usually be determined by a jury only by inference from the surrounding circumstances, including the presumption of law that a man intends the natural and probable consequences of his acts . . . if you are satisfied that . . . he must as a reasonable man have contemplated that grievous bodily harm was likely to result . . . then the accused is guilty of capital murder.[62]

There are defects in this direction. Applying lessons from *Steane*, one relates to the meaning of 'presumption of law'. The jury might not have understood this term of art or that the presumption might be rebutted by other evidence. The Court of Criminal Appeal quashed the conviction on exactly that basis:

the presumption embodied in the . . . maxim is not an irrebuttable presumption of law. The law on this point as it stands today is that this presumption of intention means this: that, as a man is usually able to foresee what are the natural consequences of his acts, so it is, as a rule, reasonable to infer that he did foresee them and intend them. But, while this is an inference that may be drawn, and on the

---

[61] Ibid.   [62] [1961] AC 290, 299 and 303.

facts in certain circumstances must inevitably be drawn, yet if on all the facts of a particular case it is not the correct inference, then it should not be drawn.[63]

9. The Reasonable Man or the Ordinary Person?

A second defect in the trial judge's direction concerns his use of the term 'reasonable man'. Without additional explanation, members of the jury might have concluded that they were directed to treat the defendant according to the standards of a hypothetical, reasonable man and not concern themselves further with his actual state of mind. In the House of Lords, Viscount Kilmuir LC expressed his doubts about the use of this term which connotes the standard of care appropriate to civil cases but observed that 'in judging of intent, however, it really denotes an ordinary man capable of reasoning who is responsible and accountable for his actions, and this would be the sense in which it would be understood by a jury.'[64] Even if the trial judge actually meant what Viscount Kilmuir suggested, it is somewhat optimistic to assume that this is what the jury would have understood him to have meant from the words he used. Accordingly, despite the conclusion of the House of Lords that the judge's direction to the jury was correct, the better view must be that of the Court of Appeal,[65] the High Court of Australia,[66] and the Privy Council.[67]

However, criticisms of the outcome in *DPP* v. *Smith* have obscured points of general importance about the proof of intention which emerge from the case. These are developed by Pearson LJ in *Harvey* v. *Motor Insurers' Bureau*:[68]

First, it is important to note that the phrase 'reasonable man' is used in a special sense. Normally in legal mythology the reasonable man is an idealised average man, behaving always as the average man behaves in his good moments. The average man may have his bad moments when, for no sufficient reason, he loses his temper or suffers from panic, or when he becomes careless, or when he is stupid or biassed or hasty in his judgements. The reasonable man as normally understood, has no such bad moments . . . [however] the reasonable man referred to in *Smith*'s case may not only have bad moments, but also be of less than average intelligence, morality and judgment, so long as he is not insane or of diminished responsibility and is responsible and accountable for his actions. Any accused who is not putting forward a defence of insanity or diminished responsibility can be assumed to be a 'reasonable man' in that very limited sense.

Pearson LJ continues;

Then this is the syllogism. No reasonable man doing such an act could fail to foresee that it would in all probability injure the other person. The accused is a

---

[63] [1961] AC 290, 300.   [64] [1961] AC 290, 331.   [65] [1961] AC 290.
[66] *Parker* v. *The Queen* (1963) 111 CLR 610.
[67] *Frankland & Moore* v. *R* [1987] AC 576.   [68] [1964] 2 All ER 742, 748.

reasonable man. Therefore, he must have foreseen, when he did the act, that it would in all probability injure the other person. Therefore, he had the intent to injure the other person. That syllogism, however, uses the objective test as a means of ascertaining by inference the actual intention of the accused.

It would, of course, be so much better in directions to juries to abandon all talk of the reasonable man and to substitute talk of the ordinary person. The *mens rea* syllogism would then assume the form:

1. Any ordinary person in the position of the accused must have foreseen X.
2. The defendant is an ordinary person.
3. Therefore the defendant must have foreseen X; and if the defendant must have foreseen X, the defendant did foresee X.

In drawing such an inference, the jury should take account of all the evidence—particularly that given by the accused by way of explanation—and reach its decision on the totality of the evidence. In the absence of an admission, proof of intention can only be by way of inference. This *mens rea* inference will establish foresight, but since foresight is not intention, some reference to degrees of probability will also be necessary and the degree will have to be high—'little short of overwhelming'[69]—given that it is what *must* be obvious even to an individual only marginally more competent mentally than one of diminished responsibility or McNaghten insanity.

The *mens rea* syllogism reveals that the criminal law of England is neither wholly objectivist not subjectivist. Rather, it combines factors and approaches in a way that transcends the 'either–or' debate. Lord Diplock's opinions are typically terse and lucid: 'Intention can only be subjective. It was the actual intention of the offender himself that the objective test was designed to ascertain.'[70] Again, '*mens rea* is, by definition, a state of mind of the accused himself . . . it cannot be the mental state of some non-existent, hypothetical person.'[71]

10. Recklessness and the Ordinary Person

Given the aspiration to ascertain the state of mind of the accused person, rather than that of some hypothetical person, the criminal law of England has gone considerably off-course as to proof of recklessness. Since *Caldwell*, the reasonably prudent person has developed as a *standard*, which makes evidence about the accused's actual state of mind irrelevant.[72] The *mens*

---

[69] *R v. Moloney* [1985] AC 905, per Lord Bridge at 925H.
[70] *Hyam v. DPP* [1975] AC 55, 94.   [71] *R v. Caldwell* [1982] AC 341, 354.
[72] *Elliot v. C (a minor)* [1983] 2 All ER 1005; *R v. Bell* [1984] 3 All ER 842.

rea syllogism proceeds on the basis of what any ordinary person must foresee. Any ordinary person lighting a bonfire in a stack of straw must foresee the risk of some damage but in R v. *Stephenson* there was psychiatric evidence that the defendant was schizophrenic and might not have the same ability to foresee or appreciate the risk as a mentally ordinary person. Given that abnormality, the minor premiss is falsified and it is unsafe and unsound to rely on the syllogism.

In R v. *Mowatt*,[73] Diplock LJ stated that:

In the absence of any evidence that the accused did not realise that it was a possible consequence of his act that some physical harm might be caused to the victim, the prosecution satisfy the relevant onus by proving the commission by the accused of an act which any ordinary person would [be bound to] realise was likely to have that consequence.

But what of the presence of any evidence that the accused did not realize that it was a possible consequence? Evidence of 'rage, excitement or drunkenness' exercised Lord Diplock in *Caldwell*.[74] Such evidence could create difficulties in proving beyond reasonable doubt 'recklessness', whether defined in R v. *Cunningham*,[75] as foresight of the particular kind of harm; or defined in *Mowatt*, as foresight of some harm.

Intoxication requires special consideration,[76] but in principle anger or excitement are treated as normal incidents and, so long as these do not amount to insanity or diminished responsibility, it is a question of fact for the jury whether the angry or excited accused realized the possible consequences.[77] R v. *Parker*[78]—an angry man in a telephone booth—is illustrative. Even allowing for the defendant's understandable anger, no reasonable jury would have acquitted on a charge of simple criminal damage, and the Court of Criminal Appeal could see nothing unsafe or unsatisfactory in the result.

Doctrinal difficulties were generated by the perceived need to fit the *Cunningham* direction to the facts of *Parker*, and that raises a wider question about how comprehensive and binding 'model' directions should aspire to be, given the very broad range of circumstances in which judges must direct juries. However, once it is established that an ordinary person in the position of the accused must have realized the risk, and there is no evidence of relevant abnormality, the jury is entitled to conclude that the accused actually realized the risk, notwithstanding any denials which are, in all the circumstances, incredible.

---

[73] [1968] 1 QB 421, 427.   [74] [1982] AC 341, 352.
[75] [1957] 2 QB 396.   [76] *DPP* v. *Majewski* [1977] AC 443.
[77] *Harvey* v. *Motor Insurers' Bureau* [1964] 2 All ER 742, per Pearson LJ at 748.
[78] [1977] 1 WLR 600.

11. Recklessness and the Extraordinary Person

The question remains, however, as to the effect of evidence of abnormality such as schizophrenia, retarded mental development, stress psychosis, hysterical amnesia, or premenstrual syndrome.[79] Ordinarily such evidence is introduced, if at all, in connection with the defence of insanity (or diminished responsibility), but there may be some logical space for psychiatric evidence to throw doubt on the inference of the requisite mental element by challenging the minor premiss that the accused is an ordinary person. There may be evidence of mental abnormality to a degree sufficient to throw doubt on the operation of the *mens rea* syllogism without amounting to affirmative proof on the balance of probabilities of insanity.

In *Stephenson*, 'a very experienced consultant psychiatrist' testified to a long history of schizophrenia and that the defendant did not have the same ability as a mentally normal person. None the less, the trial judge directed in terms of risks obvious to any reasonable person and the jury convicted on a charge of arson. The defendant had pleaded guilty to a charge of burglary and was subjected to a probation order for three years with a condition of medical treatment. On appeal, it was held that since the jury had not been left to decide whether the appellant's schizophrenia might have prevented the possibility of risk entering his mind at all, the conviction was unsafe and would be quashed. However, the appeal court did not interfere with the sentence and Geoffrey Lane LJ concluded his judgment with the observation that 'the mere fact that a defendant is suffering from some mental abnormality . . . does not necessarily mean that on a particular occasion his foresight or appreciation of risk was absent.'[80] Indeed, had the matter been properly put to the jury for it to decide in the light of all (including psychiatric) evidence, it would have been open to the jury to find against the accused and convict.

In *R v. Bell* the defendant pleaded not guilty to a charge of reckless driving on the basis, *inter alia*, that he was 'possessed by God'. Medical evidence was adduced that his behaviour was symptomatic of stress psychosis, that he was now cured, and that detention in a mental hospital would be deleterious to his health. Defence counsel asked the judge to direct the jury that it was open to it to return a plain verdict of not guilty because of the absence of *mens rea*. However, the judge ruled that the issue of insanity could not be withdrawn from the jury and that only two verdicts were open to it: (*i*) guilty of reckless driving; or (*ii*) not guilty by

---

[79] *R v. Stephenson* [1979] QB 695, *Elliott v. C* [1983] 2 All ER 1005, *R v. Bell* [1984] 3 All ER 842, *R v. Isitt* [1978] *Criminal LR* 159, *R v. Sandie Smith* [1982] *Criminal LR* 531.
[80] [1979] QB 695, 704.

reason of insanity. On counsel's advice, the defendant changed his plea to guilty and appealed against the judge's ruling.

The appeal was based on the proposition that the judge was wrong in law in ruling that on a charge of reckless driving, medical evidence of mental illness, not amounting to insanity under the McNaghten Rules, could not be relevant to the state of mind of the defendant, namely that he had failed to give any thought to the possibility of there being a risk. Robert Goff LJ quoted a passage from Lord Diplock's judgment in *Lawrence*:[81]

If satisfied that an obvious and serious risk was created by the manner of the defendant's driving, the jury are entitled to infer that he was in one or other of the states of mind required to constitute the offence [sc. EITHER giving no thought to the possibility of risk OR recognizing that there was some risk and proceeding] and will probably do so; but regard must be given to any explanation he gives as to his state of mind which may displace the inference.

At first blush this might seem to be most helpful to the appellant, but Goff LJ concluded that the inference that the accused gave no thought to the risk was not displaced by evidence tending to show that because he was seriously deranged he gave no thought to the risk. The trial judge was therefore correct, according to the Court of Criminal Appeal, to rule that failure to give thought 'for whatever reason' was sufficient in conjunction with driving in such a manner as to create an obvious and serious risk.

This outcome is manifestly unjust and renders wholly nugatory Lord Diplock's strictures that regard must be given to any explanation which may displace the inference. With respect, it seems that the very notion of an inference may have been misunderstood. If criminal offences are to be constituted by one's being absent-mindedly at the scene of a serious and obvious risk, no inference whatsoever is necessary. Either one thought about the risk and took it, or one did not think about the risk at all. A priori, one must either have thought or not have thought about the risk and therefore all evidence and all inference is rendered irrelevant.

What I venture to suggest Lord Diplock may have had in mind and what certainly makes the best Diplockian criminal-law theory that can be constructed is the wholly unexceptional reasoning in *Parker*: 'it seems to this court that if he did not know, as he said he did not, . . . he was, in effect, deliberately closing his mind to the obvious.'[82] The inference here is obvious:

1. Any ordinary person must have realized that there was a risk.
2. Mr Daryl Clive Parker is an ordinary person.

3. Therefore Mr Daryl Clive Parker must have realized that there was a risk or, if he insists that he did not, he must have deliberately shut his mind to it.

No such inference can or should be taken on the facts of *Bell*, where the accused was 'glassy-eyed' when driving according to one witness and appeared 'deranged and incoherent' to the police when apprehended. There can be no inference to any deliberate closing of the mind to an obvious and serious risk in such circumstances simply because it cannot be said that the accused is an ordinary person. It follows on this interpretation of Caldwellian and Lawrencian recklessness that evidence of mental abnormality may, in rare cases, raise sufficient doubt as to whether the prosecution has proved the requisite mental element.

12. Conclusion

Caldwell and *Lawrence* were not popular decisions with the subjectivist tendency, which was rather too astute to stigmatize all that is not radical subjectivism as extreme objectivism. Whatever the merits of that reading of Lord Diplock's criminal jurisprudence, and they are not obvious, it is at least possible to argue that Robert Goff LJ in *Elliot* v. *C (a minor)* and in *Bell*, despite all protestations that he was merely applying clear law as he was bound to do, actually converted defensible synthesism into indefensible objectivism by, in effect, treating the minor premiss in the *mens rea* syllogism not as a rebuttable presumption but as a fixed rule of law. There is a clear case on the arguments of this paper to depart from these two decisions and to treat mentally abnormal offenders with the respect and compassion that their circumstances merit.

The overall conclusion is that subjectivism is unacceptable on practical, doctrinal, conceptual, and ethical grounds given its impact on the doctrine of mistake, its definitional maximalization, and its overly narrow conception of the moral mission and merit of the criminal law. Objectivism is unacceptable, too, on like grounds, given its contrived conviction of the mentally abnormal offender, and for its tendency to remove questions of fact from the jury and to impose fixed rules of law which render all and any evidence about actual states of mind of real human beings wholly irrelevant. Arguably—and this paper has canvassed some of the arguments—synthesism is an altogether clearer, more coherent, and ethically more acceptable reconstruction of criminal law.

Diminished Capacity

STEPHEN J. MORSE

Stress, intense emotion, mental disorder and defect, intoxication, trauma, and other causes of abnormal mental states can impair rationality and self-control, abilities which are thought crucial to ascriptions of moral responsibility. In addition to insanity, diminished capacity in its many incarnations is the major legal doctrine that responds to mental abnormality. After first briefly outlining preliminary assumptions about responsibility and criminal justice, this chapter defines diminished capacity's two variants: the *mens rea* and partial-responsibility variants. The chapter then addresses in depth the justifications and implementation problems for each variant, with special attention to partial responsibility and the problematic issue of 'internal coercion' or 'compulsion'. Discussion of difficult special issues concludes the chapter.

1. Some Preliminaries

Simplifying and clarifying assumptions about human action and criminal justice proper will avoid ensnarement in foundational disputes and accusations of unselfconscious question-begging.[1]

First, I assume with both Strawsons[2] and many others that the truth of determinism is irrelevant to the moral and legal responsibility of normal and abnormal agents alike. Second, causation *per se* is not an excuse for behaviour.[3] More specifically, if abnormal mental states can sometimes operate as the predicate for an excuse, it is not solely because they are part of the causal chain that produces the behaviour in question.[4] Third, with

Jennifer Spotila furnished excellent research assistance. The editors of this volume, Stephen Shute, John Gardner, and Jeremy Horder, and my colleagues and friends, Heidi Hurd, Leo Katz, John Monahan, and Michael Moore, provided helpful comments. Alan Schwartz generously permitted me to teach him about coercion, an experience that taught me much as well. Finally, I gratefully acknowledge my intellectual debt to Herbert Fingarette.

[1] Because the assumptions are so commonplace and well defended, I will make no attempt to defend them and will simply cite representative writers who do make such a defence.

[2] G. Strawson, 'Consciousness, Free Will, and the Unimportance of Determinism', (1989) 32 *Inquiry* 3; P. Strawson, 'Freedom and Resentment', in G. Watson (ed.), *Free Will* (Oxford 1982), 59.

[3] M. Moore, 'Causation and the Excuses', (1985) 73 *California LR* 1091.

[4] S. Morse, 'Psychology, Determinism, and Legal Responsibility', in G. B. Melton (ed.), *The Law as a Behavioral Instrument* (Lincoln, Nebr. 1986), 35; 'Excusing the Crazy: The Insanity Defense Reconsidered', (1985) 58 *Southern California LR* 777; but see also L. Reznek, *The Philosophical Defence of Psychiatry* (London 1991), 204–6.

rare exceptions, moral desert for one's actions is at least necessary to justify criminal punishment.[5] Finally, desert is primarily dependent on the agent's mental states.[6] In legal terms, and again with rare exceptions, desert is proportionate to the agent's *mens rea* and to the reason that the mental state was formed (and to the amount of harm caused).

Although each of these assumptions and the criminal-justice system they support are controversial within jurisprudence and philosophy,[7] each assumption is mainstream and in most cases regnant within the dominant liberal and moderately individualistic conception of criminal justice. Because I believe that this conception of criminal justice is also desirable, I hope this contribution provides further defence for the current arrangements, by buttressing their justifications.

2. Diminished Capacity Defined[8]

Despite the congeries of confusing and often inconsistent terms used for the myriad doctrines and practices of diminished capacity[9] there are only two variants, the *mens rea* variant and the partial-responsibility variant.[10]

A defendant raising the *mens rea* variant claims that his or her alleged mental abnormality was inconsistent with forming the *mens rea* required

---

[5] H. L. A. Hart, *Punishment and Responsibility: Essays in the Philosophy of Law* (Oxford 1968); N. Morris, *Madness and the Criminal Law* (Chicago 1982). Moreover, if one is a pure retributivist, desert may be sufficient to justify punishment.

[6] See generally, R. A. Duff, *Intention, Agency and Criminal Liability: Philosophy of Action and the Criminal Law* (Oxford 1990), esp. chs. 4 and 5; J. Hampton, 'Mens Rea', (1990) 7 *Social Philosophy and Policy* 1.

[7] See N. Lacey, *State Punishment: Political Principles and Community Values* (London and New York 1988), 58–78; see generally, A. W. Norrie, *Law, Ideology and Punishment: Retrieval and Critique of the Liberal Ideal of Criminal Justice* (Dordrecht 1991).

[8] In this largely descriptive section of the chapter, I shamelessly cannibalize an earlier article on the same topic: S. Morse, 'Undiminished Confusion in Diminished Capacity', (1984) 75 *Journal of Criminal Law and Criminology* 1. Confusion in recent American decisions and commentary has declined. See e.g. *US* v. *Cameron*, 907 F 2d 1051 (1990); *US* v. *Pohlot*, 827 F 2d 889 (1987), *cert. denied* 484 US 1011 (1988); *P* v. *Saille*, 820 P 2d 588 (1991). Alas, this is not always the case. See e.g. M. Mendez, 'Diminished Capacity in California: Premature Reports of its Demise', [1991] *Stanford Law & Policy Review* 216.

[9] The terminological confusion has not abated recently, although most courts now understand how others are using the various terms. They continue to develop new terminologies, none the less. See *US* v. *Cameron*, 907 F 2d 1051, 1062–3 (1990) (describing the situation as a 'war of labels' and creating a new set of labels—'affirmative defence psychiatric evidence' and 'psychiatric evidence to negate specific intent').

[10] I coined these terms in 'Undiminished Confusion', above n. 8. I still believe they are the most concise, clear, descriptive terms and will continue to use them in this contribution. For a different, influential categorization, see P. Arenella, 'The Diminished Capacity and Diminished Responsibility Defenses: Two Children of a Doomed Marriage', (1977) 77 *Columbia LR* 827.

by the definition of the crime charged. For example, a defendant might claim that rage, mental disorder, and alcohol together rendered him unaware that his actions would kill or cause serious bodily to his victim, and thus that he cannot be guilty of murder.[11] Or, another defendant may argue that his personality disorder and stress prevented him from premeditating and forming the purpose to kill.[12] For a final example, a killer might allege that command hallucinations and delusions were inconsistent with planning the killing of her victim and prevented her from forming the purpose to kill him.[13] The *mens rea* variant is not an affirmative defence: the defendant is simply using evidence of mental abnormality, like any other evidence, to cast doubt on the prosecution's prima-facie case.[14] If the defendant succeeds, he or she is simply not guilty of the crime charged, because the prosecution is not able to prove the definitional *mens rea* element of the crime. Thus, the first defendant might not be guilty of purposely or knowingly killing, and the other two might not be guilty of premeditating and purposely committing homicide.

A substantial majority of American jurisdictions have legislatively or judicially adopted the *mens rea* variant, although most have cabined the doctrine with various, largely unjustified restrictions.[15] Discussions in the courts and commentaries of the English, Canadian, and Australian approaches to the *mens rea* variant have been hampered by disputes about the admissibility of expert mental-health evidence to prove it. Although a firm, consistent conclusion is difficult to draw, it appears that in general a defendant may always try to demonstrate that the requisite *mens rea* was not formed, but may support this contention with expert evidence only if he or she was suffering from a severe mental disorder or had a subnormal intelligence.[16] In most American jurisdictions and in England, the use of

---

[11] e.g. *State* v. *Carroll*, 577 A 2d 862 (1990).

[12] e.g. *Commonwealth* v. *Zettlemoyer*, 454 A 2d 937 (1982); *Zettlemoyer* v. *Fulcomer*, 923 F 2d 284 (1991).

[13] e.g. *People* v. *Bobo*, 3 Cal. Rptr. 2d 747 (1990). We shall return below to the question of whether and to what degree any of the claims raised by the hypothetical cases in the text are credible.

[14] See American Law Institute, Model Penal Code (Philadelphia 1962), § 4.02.

[15] 'Undiminished Confusion', above n. 8. For example, courts limit the doctrine to cases involving so-called 'specific intent' or to the issue of premeditation. Detailed discussion of these limitations is beyond the scope of the present contribution and the interested reader is referred to the cited article for a full discussion.

[16] *R* v. *Turner* [1975] QB 834 (CA); *R* v. *Weightman*, [1991] *Criminal LR* 204; R. Mackay and A. Colman, 'Excluding Expert Evidence: Tale of Ordinary Folk and Common Experience', [1991] *Criminal LR* 800 (discussing critically *Turner* and the English experience generally); R. Pattenden, 'Conflicting Approaches to Psychiatric Evidence in Criminal Trials: England, Canada and Australia', [1986] *Criminal LR* 92. See also, M. Beaumont, 'Psychiatric Evidence: Over-Rationalising the Abnormal', [1988] *Criminal LR* 290. Limitations on the use of expert evidence have been much criticized. See Mackay and Colman, and R. Pattenden, above; A. Samuels, 'Psychiatric Evidence', [1981] *Criminal LR* 762.

voluntary intoxication to negate some *mentes reae* is treated as a separate doctrine,[17] but this, too, is a form of the *mens rea* variant.

The partial-responsibility variant is an affirmative defence. The defendant claims that even if he or she possessed the *mens rea* required by the definition of the crime charged, mental abnormality rendered him or her less than fully responsible. So, for example, in addition to claiming that they lacked *mens rea*, our hypothetical defendants might also allege that their various abnormalities impaired their reason and ability to control themselves. Even if they committed their crimes with the requisite *mens rea*, each might claim that mental abnormality diminished his or her responsibility for wrongdoing.

The typical outcome of this partial, affirmative defence is that the defendant is convicted of a lesser offence or receives a reduced sentence. Although no Anglo-American jurisdiction has adopted a general partial-responsibility variant applicable to all crimes, all have adopted specific doctrines that are instances of partial responsibility. In the United States and England, the following doctrines and practices are examples: the provocation doctrine, which reduces intentional killings from murder to voluntary manslaughter;[18] the English doctrine of 'diminished responsibility', which reduces a murder to manslaughter if the defendant was suffering from an abnormality of mind that substantially impairs mental responsibility;[19] the Model Penal Code's 'extreme mental or emotional disturbance' doctrine, which also reduces conduct that would otherwise constitute murder to manslaughter (whether it is fashioned as a definition of manslaughter or as a partial, affirmative defence);[20] sentencing criteria and practices that consider mental abnormality a mitigating factor;[21] creative judicial interpretation of the definitional *mens rea* elements of some crimes that permits the *mens rea* requirement to operate as a partial, affirmative defence.[22] Consulting the specific language and the justifications for these doctrines and practices demonstrates that they are all of a piece.[23] Moreover, the indirect adoptions of partial responsibility are fraught with illogical limitations.[24]

---

[17] See e.g. Model Penal Code, above n. 14, § 2.08; *DPP* v. *Majewski* [1977] AC 142.
[18] e.g. California Penal Code, § 192(a); Homicide Act 1957, s. 3.
[19] Homicide Act 1957, s. 2.
[20] Model Penal Code, above n. 14, § 210. 3 (1) (b); New York Penal Law, § 125.25.1 (a).
[21] 42 *Pa. Cons. Stat. Ann.* §§ 9711 (e) (2) and 9711 (e) (3); *United States Sentencing Guidelines*, §§ 5K2.12 and 5K2.13.
[22] e.g. *Comm.* v. *Gould*, 405 NE 2d 927 (1980). See generally, S. Morse, 'Diminished Capacity: A Moral and Legal Conundrum', (1979) 2 *International Journal of Law and Psychiatry* 272, for a description of the most famous American example of this practice, found in a series of influential California Supreme Court decisions that tortured the standard definitions of *mens rea* terms in the law of homicide.
[23] See the discussion in s. 6 below.   [24] See s. 6 below.

3. The *Mens Rea* Variant Justified

The *mens rea* variant is logically straightforward and unproblematic: the defendant is simply attempting to cast doubt on the prosecution's prima-facie case, using evidence about his or her abnormal mental state. The justice of the *mens rea* claim is similarly simple: because desert is largely proportionate to the culpability of the agent's mental state, and because criminal conviction and punishment are maximally intrusive exercises of State power, fairness requires providing defendants with a reasonable opportunity to defeat allegations of guilt. If an agent, in an emotional storm of rage and distraction, really did not intend to kill or seriously injure his victim, does he *deserve* to be punished as if he did possess these mental states?[25] Indeed, if one consults cases to discern the reasons for denying the defendant this right, one discovers consequentialist justifications irrelevant to moral desert, or a confusion of the *mens rea* claim, which is *not* an affirmative defence, with the insanity defence, which is.[26] Thus, any genuine difficulties with the *mens rea* variant must be implementation problems, to which we now turn.

4. The *Mens Rea* Variant Implemented

Amid the welter of arguments opposing the *mens rea* variant, only two have possible validity: fears for public safety and problems with expert mental-state evidence. Examining these claims requires preliminary general exploration of the meaning of *mens rea* terms and the effect of mental abnormalities on *mens rea*.

Contrary to the apparent misunderstanding of many mental-health professionals, legal *mens rea* terms have ordinary language meanings. The meaning of 'intent' is the same whether the intent is to kill (in violation of a homicide statute), to write poetry, or to play bridge: it is simply to have the purpose to engage in the particular conduct or to achieve the result. If the agent is legally conscious, no moral analysis or capability for it, or any other type of substantive reflection or ability, is required to satisfy the legal requirement of intent.[27] So, for example, whether or not one reflects on the moral heinousness of homicide before or during killing,

[25] For an interesting account of when essentially normal agents should be held accountable for lacking culpable, subjective *mens rea*, see J. Horder, 'Cognition, Emotion, and Criminal Culpability', (1990) 106 *Law Quarterly Review* 470.

[26] 'Undiminished Confusion', above n. 8, 5–20. Because the confusion, when it exists, is so patent and erroneous, I shall spend no more time on this point.

[27] Indeed, there is dispute about whether *mens rea* should encompass more than purpose and knowledge. Cf. J. Gardner and H. Jung, 'Making Sense of *Mens Rea*: Antony Duff's Account', (1991) 11 *Oxford Journal of Legal Studies* 559. These disputes are far removed from attempts to 'thicken' ordinary-language, mental-state terms. Compare the discussions of dissociative states and psychopathy in ss. 10 and 11 below.

if it is the agent's purpose to cause the death of another, the agent intends to kill. Similarly, the 'conscious awareness of risk' component of recklessness means solely that the defendant must actually be aware of the risk hazarded. It does not mean that the defendant must reflect or have the capacity to reflect on the morality of running the risk. Many might argue that *mens rea* terms *should* include such requirements, because it is unjust to hold fully responsible those who do not meet them; but this is simply not the law.[28]

A final issue concerning the meaning of *mens rea* is engendered by the term 'capacity'. The ultimate legal question is whether a defendant possessed *mens rea* in fact. Having a particular capacity is not a specific definitional element of any crime. Nevertheless, if a person lacks a capacity to do something, it is entailed that the agent could not do it. A defendant who lacked the capacity to form a specific *mens rea* on a particular occasion surely did not form it. Thus, evidence about capacity is logically relevant to the ultimate legal question, but experts rarely have sound scientific or clinical knowledge of whether a normal or abnormal defendant lacked the capacity to form a particular *mens rea* and, as we shall see, claims about capacity create confusion.

The empirical relation between mental abnormality and *mens rea*, properly understood, is quite uniform: mental abnormality, even if severe, seldom if ever reduces the general capacity to form *mens rea*, and it rarely prevents the formation of *mens rea* on a particular occasion.[29] Although a contrary conclusion may seem intuitive, and conclusions about mental states always involve folk-psychological inferences that can never be physically demonstrated, the conclusion in most cases of subjective *mens rea* is blindingly clear.[30] Stress, mental disorder, intoxication, and other mental abnormalities may give people crazy reasons for forming *mens rea* and they may weaken self-control, but they negate subjective *mens rea* exceedingly rarely. On the other hand, mental disorder may prevent a person from forming reasonable beliefs and thus may negate negligence on H. L. A. Hart's view that a person must be capable of meeting the reasonable-person standard to qualify for negligence liability.[31] For example, a person who delusionally believes that she can puncture the vital organs of others with a knife without doing them harm[32] lacks intent to kill and

---

[28] As we shall see in ss. 10 and 11 below, the justice of such claims is better addressed by affirmative defences.

[29] 'Undiminished Confusion', above n. 8; H. Fingarette and A. Hasse, *Mental Disabilities and Criminal Responsibility* (Berkeley, Calif. 1979), 66–8.

[30] Indeed, trial and appellate courts are frequently faced with absurd claims to the contrary. See *Zettlemoyer*, above n. 12, which characterized the defendant's claim that he did not premeditate as 'nothing short of preposterous'.

[31] *Punishment and Responsibility*, above n. 5, 152–4.

[32] Cf. *People v. Strong*, 37 NY 2d 568 (1975).

awareness that her behaviour risks death and, on Hart's view, may not be negligent because she is incapable of getting the facts right. Of course, if, *pace* Hart, one adopts a thoroughly objective negligence standard, then this defendant is liable. In any event, cases in which mental disorder negates (Hart) negligence are as rare as cases in which it negates subjective mental states. Of course, in many cases of severe mental abnormality, the defendant's understanding of what he or she is doing may be substantially clouded by factual mistakes or emotional agitations, and a full defence of legal insanity, for example, may be appropriate. But a claim that *mens rea* was negated is seldom true. Indeed, my research has unearthed only two examples.[33]

Even if mental abnormality rarely negates *mens rea* and even if it more rarely disables the capacity to form requisite mental states, evidence of such abnormalities may support a claim that no *mens rea* exists. Consider a defendant who claims to have killed in response to command hallucinations coupled with delusional beliefs: if we believe that she acted 'on the spur of the moment' in response to a combination of her delusional beliefs and command hallucinations, then it is simply the fact that she did not 'premeditate' in a jurisdiction that interprets the term to require actual forethought and cool reflection. This defendant may have been able to premeditate despite her command hallucination, but the presence of such hallucinations supports a claim of instantaneous rather than carefully planned action. In general, mental-abnormality evidence more often supports claims of no premeditation than other *mens rea* claims. Intense emotion, intoxication, and various forms of mental disorder may not obliterate the capacity to premeditate, but they enhance the credibility of a claim that one did not premeditate on this occasion.

Here is another example of how evidence of abnormality may strengthen a claim of no *mens rea*, even if does not prevent the agent from forming *mens rea*. Assume that on a cold winter evening a destitute person is abroad in the streets of a deserted part of a city. As a result of mental disorder, intoxication, or some other abnormality, the person becomes confused and disoriented and can't find the way home. Cold and tired, she breaks into a warehouse in order to get warm and sleep. The police arrest the wanderer in the midst of the break-in and charge her with burglary on the theory that the person intended to commit theft. In this case, the mental abnormality strongly supports the defendant's claim that there was

[33] *People* v. *Wetmore*, 583 P. 2d 1308 (1978) (defendant charged with burglary based on intent to steal lacked *mens rea* because he delusionally believed he was in his own apartment taking his own goods); *People* v. *Kosma*, 749 F Supp. 1392 (1990) (prosecution unable to demonstrate that incarcerated and delusional defendant who sent an objectively threatening letter to an ex-president *intended* the letter to be a threat as the applicable statute provided). See also the results of an anecdotal survey of California public defenders described in n. 34 below.

no intent to commit a felony in the warehouse and thus that there cannot be guilt for burglary. Note that the claim is not that the defendant lacked the capacity to steal. The defendant might very well have been able to form such an intent, but simply did not do so on this occasion, and evidence of mental abnormality makes this story more believable.

Analysis of the relation between mental abnormality and *mens rea* thus discloses that evidence of mental abnormality will seldom be relevant to assessing the existence of *mens rea*, and cases in which defendants are acquitted outright because *mens rea* is lacking will almost never occur. All limitations on the *mens rea* variant that are meant to prevent outright acquittal are both unfair and unnecessary. A system of criminal justice that presumes innocence and is committed to fairness can hardly prevent a defendant from using generally acceptable evidence to cast doubt on the prosecution's case. And even if defendants were allowed to do so in every case, acquittals would rarely occur.[34] Public safety would not be compromised if the *mens rea* variant were adopted without limitation.

A stronger case can be mounted against the use of expert evidence. Contrary to the assertions of some critics, the problem is not that evidence concerning insanity is more scientifically and clinically sound than evidence concerning *mens rea*. They are equally sound (or unsound) and mental-state evidence is admissible in a broad range of civil and criminal contexts, from testamentary capacity to competence to stand criminal trial. The difficulty is that so much expert testimony concerning *mens rea* is utterly incredible. In case after case, experts testify that the defendant lacked capacity to form *mens rea* when it is clear beyond doubt that the *mens rea* was in fact present. What explains such bewildering claims? Some experts may be honestly mistaken about the requirements of *mens rea* and others may be willing to compromise honesty to achieve a result which they believe is just,[35] often by using patently false claims about lack of capacity. In either case, courts are deluged with absurd claims and the critics are right to complain. The solution, however, is not to exclude expert testimony categorically or to restrict it to cases of severe abnormality. The better response is preliminarily to consider each claim carefully and sceptically, and to exclude evidence that has no prima-facie claim to relevance. In cases of prima-facie relevance, courts should try to limit experts to testimony about actual *mens rea* formation, excluding speculative

---

[34] I performed an admittedly unscientific, non-random poll of California public defenders to determine what happened during the one year, 1982, when an unlimited *mens rea* variant was in effect in that state. None of my respondents could identify a case in which a plausible claim of complete *mens rea* negation arose. There were a small number of cases in which claims of lack of premeditation were plausibly supported by evidence of mental abnormality. A more recent example is *Bobo*, above n. 13.

[35] R. Restak, 'Psychiatry in the Courtroom', *Psychiatric News*, 7 August 1992, 3.

testimony concerning capacity[36] and conclusions about the ultimate legal issue of whether *mens rea* was formed in fact.[37]

5. The Partial-Responsibility Variant Justified

Unlike the *mens rea* variant, which is a simple denial of the prosecution's prima-facie case, the partial-responsibility variant is a genuine excuse. The defendant is claiming that, whatever may be the case about the other elements of criminal liability, including *mens rea*, mental abnormality diminishes his or her responsibility for criminal conduct. The justification of partial responsibility thus depends on the general theory of excuse. The theory of excuse I adopt requires that on the occasion in question the agent was capable of minimal rationality and acted without coercion. Mistake, infancy, and so-called 'cognitive' tests of legal insanity are examples of irrationality excuses, and duress and so-called 'volitional' tests of legal insanity are examples of coercion.[38] This section discusses the irrationality and coercion justifications in detail, concluding with a brief discussion of whether a history of emotional deprivation should provide an independent justification for partial responsibility. The following sections address the theoretically justified scope and implementation of partial responsibility.

[36] See California Penal Code, § 28 (a), which prohibits admission of testimony concerning the *capacity* to form *mens rea*, but which permits testimony concerning whether the defendant *actually* formed *mens rea* (at least in the case of so-called 'specific intent' crimes).
[37] See California Penal Code, § 29 (experts prohibited from testifying about whether *mens rea* was formed in fact); Federal Rules of Evidence, § 704 (b) (experts prohibited from offering an ultimate opinion about legal insanity or other mental states in federal criminal trials). Prohibiting experts from testifying about the ultimate legal issue is of course controversial, and some consider the ultimate-issue rule incoherent. None the less, strong arguments to the contrary have persuaded the American Congress and many state legislatures that the prohibition should apply to mental-state questions in criminal trials.
[38] Some scholars, such as my colleague Michael Moore, wish to distinguish between cognitive and volitional excuses, such as mistake and duress on the one hand, and status excuses, such as infancy and insanity, on the other. See 'Causation and the Excuses', above n. 3. Although there is considerable merit in such categorizations, I do not believe much turns on the alternative chosen and I prefer the suggestion in the text because it seems more parsimonious. For example, an insane person may be excused in an appropriate case, because at the time of the crime he or she was incapable of minimal rationality concerning the criminal conduct charged, even if the person was capable of minimal rationality about a wide range of other matters. Very young children as a class come closest to fitting status conception, but the reason for their non-responsible status is their lack of rationality, and even children, especially as they mature, are quite capable of being held accountable in some contexts, if not in others. Finally, it may seem odd to think of the mistaken agent, who acts in non-culpable ignorance, as a candidate for an irrationality excuse. Although this person, unlike the insane agent, may be capable of getting the facts right, in a sense the mistaken agent is incapable of rational, practical reasoning *on the occasion*, because his or her reasoning includes untrue factual premises.

5.1. Irrationality and Partial Responsibility

The minimal rationality the law requires for responsibility is not an exalted or complicated notion. In the words of Susan Wolf, rationality is the ability 'to be sensitive and responsive to relevant changes in one's situation and environment—that is, to be flexible'.[39] It is the ability minimally both to get the facts right according to the applicable epistemology and to reason instrumentally, including weighing the facts appropriately and according to a minimally coherent preference-ordering. A more formally precise definition of instrumental rationality might include the following criteria: (1) employing means that an agent believes will achieve a preferred goal; (2) believing, empirically plausibly, that the means chosen will achieve a preferred goal; (3) attempting to achieve a goal the agent believes is superior to relevant others in the circumstances; (4) using the most effective means to achieve a goal, unless the agent can give an independent and superior reason for choosing the less effective means; and (5) believing, empirically plausibly, that the means chosen are the most effective.[40] Irrationality is the opposite of all the above. It is by no means clear, however, that more precise definitions are desirable for legal-responsibility assessments. All formal definitions found in the literatures of economics, philosophy, and psychology are contestable and, in any case, all are related to the vaguer definition with which we began. Furthermore, definitions should be no more precise than the context requires,[41] and the criminal law's definition of rationality must necessarily be open-textured to permit argument about what the law requires in a vast array of circumstances.[42] Thus, no absolute or partial defect in the informal or formal criteria of rationality is either necessary or sufficient to justify a legal finding or irrationality. Rather, the criteria are guides to an assessment of the agent's overall functioning.

Discussion so far has focused on instrumental rationality, but whether the rationality of ends, as opposed to facts and means, can be assessed is also a vexing question about which there is no consensus among philosophers.[43] In general, we tend to consider the agent's ends irrational if they are not plausibly intelligible within widely defined cultural conventions. So-called kleptomaniacs, who recurrently steal objects not needed for

---

[39] S. Wolf, *Freedom Within Reason* (New York 1990), 69.

[40] I previously offered a closely related definition. 'Psychology, Determinism, and Legal Responsibility', above n. 4, 60–1, based on S. Bice, 'Rationality Analysis in Constitutional Law', (1980) 65 *Minnesota LR* 1, at 9–17.

[41] See Aristotle, *Nichomachean Ethics* 1. 3.

[42] Aristotle, *Nichomachean Ethics* 2. 9.

[43] For recent views, compare D. Gauthier, *Morals By Agreement* (New York 1986), with M. Slote, *Beyond Optimizing: A Theory of Rational Choice* (Cambridge, Mass. 1989).

personal use or monetary gain in order to relieve increasing tension,[44] may represent cases of unintelligibility. Cases involving an agent who evidences clearly irrational goals coupled with otherwise unimpaired rationality rarely arise in criminal law, however.[45] Although irrational ends are possible according to some accounts, they do not present a substantial practical problem.

The primarily instrumental definition of rationality which I offer, and which the law adopts, does not imply perfection; it therefore includes both the 'normal' infirmities of perception, inference, and judgment which are well documented by cognitive psychology and related disciplines, and the influence of emotions on practical reasoning.[46] It is the commonsensical notion of bounded rationality which we use all the time. Finally, although the definition is relatively 'thin', it permits an enormous range of ways in which mental abnormality may cause cognitive misfirings: crazy beliefs and emotional storms can produce factual mistakes, poor reasoning, failures of perception, and a host of other cognitive glitches which may appropriately be termed instances of irrationality. Avoiding harm-doing is difficult if one cannot understand what one is doing or what one's legal duties are. At the extreme, of course, legal insanity provides a total excuse for rationality failures produced by mental disorder or defect.[47]

Rationality as defined, however, clearly ranges along a continuum, from fully rational by anybody's standards, to completely lacking rationality by anybody's standards. Consequently, if rationality is a criterion for responsibility, then responsibility, too, should in theory be matter of degree which ranges along a continuum. Even if someone is not fully excusable, his or her rationality may be non-culpably compromised to a substantial extent, thus mitigating the deserved blame and punishment. If a wildly delusional agent intentionally *and* premeditatedly kills her victims for deluded reasons, she surely deserves less punishment than an undeluded killer-for-hire. Similarly, if an agent kills intentionally or with awareness of the risk of death, but in a 'blind', depersonalized state of rage caused by mental disorder and consequent intoxication, he is surely less rational and responsible than if he had killed while sober and in full possession of his faculties in order to collect the proceeds of an insurance policy on the victim's life.

---

[44] American Psychiatric Association, *Diagnostic and Statistical Manual of Mental Disorders [DSM-III-R]* (Rev. 3rd edn., Washington 1987), 322–3. For purposes of discussion throughout this chapter, I shall assume the validity of the *DSM-III-R* categories, but as the manual itself admits, many of the categories have not been fully validated. *DSM-III-R*, p. xxiv.

[45] The question of the rationality of goals will be discussed in more detail in ss. 5.2–4 below.

[46] See R. Nisbett and L. Ross, *Human Inference: Strategies and Shortcomings of Social Judgment* (Englewood Cliffs, NJ 1980). On the role of emotions in getting the facts straight, see Horder, 'Cognition, Emotion, and Criminal Culpability', above n. 25.

[47] This includes the 'settled' insanity that chronic intoxication may cause.

Ordinary morality makes differential, excusing allowances on a sliding
scale of diminished rationality, and in principle the law might do so as
well.

5.2. *Internal Coercion and Partial Responsibility*

The more difficult issue is how to understand claims about coercion resulting from mental abnormality: claims that are variously fashioned as 'coercion', 'involuntariness', 'irresistible impulse', 'compulsion', 'volitional' or
'control' problems, and the like. In the remainder of this section I shall use
these phrases interchangeably, because they all address the same conceptual domain of excuse and there is no uncontroversial reason to prefer any
of them as optimal.

The almost universal acceptance of excusing claims of duress and coercion in criminal and civil law testifies to the implicit assumption that an
excuse on these grounds should sometimes obtain. That is, the law often
accepts that there are appropriate cases for excuse when the person claims,
'I could not help myself'. Nevertheless, understanding of coercion is far
less well established than understanding of defects of rationality. Although
rationality is a normative concept about which there is no consensus among
philosophers, psychologists, and others, there is a rough, common-sense
consensus about the meaning of 'everyday' rationality and its place in
practical reason. In contrast, no consensus about the meaning of 'coercion'
exists among 'experts' or laypeople. Consequently, my strategy is to begin
with a choice among competing models of *inter*personal coercion, about
which much has been written. Coercion claims based on mental abnormality are usually 'one–party' cases, however. It is therefore necessary to apply
the chosen two-party model to such cases to determine whether conceptual
and practical progress is possible.

Theories of coercion may be classified into two types, empirical and
moral. The former rely on analogies to cases of physical compulsion and
suggest criteria for when a non-physically compelled agent is deprived
psychologically of the ability to behave otherwise. Psychological pressure
or some negative, affective calculus are the variables that do the work.
(Remember that determinism is irrelevant to such criteria because if determinism were true and always produced coercion, then all action would be
coerced.) The claim is that psychological compulsion makes it literally
impossible for the person *not* to perform the allegedly compelled action.[48]

[48] See J. Gardner, 'The Activity Condition in Criminal Law', in H. Jung, H. Müller-Dietz,
and U. Neumann (eds.), *Recht und Moral* (Baden-Baden 1991), 67, 73 and 79. Gardner also
claims that the analogy to physical compulsion is virtually perfect and not metaphorical, and
that the psychologically compelled agent does not choose.

Moral theorists abandon the quest for an empirical test because they believe that it is technically impracticable and normatively undesirable. They
claim that the analogy to true physical compulsion is inapt and that we
lack the understanding and expertise to 'measure' the ability to do otherwise in the absence of physical compulsion or threats, such as a gun to
one's head, which can be commonsensically assessed. Therefore, most
empirical conclusions about coercion, especially those based on purely
internal causes such as mental abnormality, are simply that: conclusions,
unsupported by evidence. Even examples that intuitively support the empirical view, such as impulse disorders and substance abuse, derive their
force from conceptual and factual premises which are far weaker and
more controversial than their proponents assume.[49] Moreover, virtually
all general empirical work addressed to the problems is unpersuasive or
marginally relevant.

Finally, and perhaps most importantly, intuitions about psychological
coercion that depend on the analogy with mechanistic, physical causation
are often inconsistent with our considered moral evaluations, and thus the
former should not guide the latter unless the intuitions are well supported
and the considered moral evaluation is unjustified.[50] The facts upon which
the analogy rests are highly problematic, however, and, as we shall see,
coercion excuses do not depend on the presence of 'pressure', and coerced
agents do act for reasons. They are not automatons, and their movements
are actions. Further, we believe, upon moral reflection, that the ability to
resist should and does vary according to the circumstances,[51] and yielding
to the desire should excuse only in some circumstances. For example, we
do not excuse a drug-dependent person who commits armed robbery or
similar heinous crimes to obtain money to buy drugs, no matter how much
pressure to have a fix the agent alleges to have felt. The analogy to an
irresistible physical cause is simply too far-fetched properly to persuade us
that such serious wrongdoing should be excused.

I have been convinced by the arguments of the empirical sceptics and
moralizers, such as Fingarette[52] and Wertheimer,[53] that a moralized approach is conceptually and practically preferable, despite its own problems.[54] Moreover, moral models dominate discussion of the problem. Using

[49] See e.g. H. Fingarette, *Heavy Drinking: The Myth of Alcoholism as a Disease* (Berkeley,
Calif. 1988); A. Schwartz, 'Views of Addiction and the Duty to Warn', (1989) 75 *Virginia
LR* 509.   [50] See A. Wertheimer, *Coercion* (Princeton, NJ 1987).
[51] See C. Elliott, 'Moral Responsibility, Psychiatric Disorders and Duress', (1991) 8 *Journal
of Applied Philosophy* 45, at 47.
[52] *Mental Disabilities and Criminal Responsibility*, above n. 29.
[53] *Coercion*, above n. 50.
[54] More detail concerning the arguments is found throughout this section and ss. 7 and 8
below on the implementation of partial responsibility. On the problems with Wertheimer's
moral model, see e.g. J. Bickenback, 'Critical Notice', (1990) 20 *Canadian Journal of Philosophy*
577; T. Honoré, 'A Theory of Coercion', (1990) 10 *Oxford Journal of Legal Studies* 94.

a moral model, then, the working criteria for a coercion excuse are as follows:

First, the person is subjected to an unjustifiable threat: that is, unjustifiable circumstances that will make the person worse off compared to some baseline, if she doesn't perform the wrongful act.

Second, performing the wrongful act and suffering the threatened consequences for failing to perform it are both aversive choices, but doing the wrongful act is an excusable alternative because it is unfair to require the agent to refrain under the circumstances.

Third, the person is not responsible either for placing herself in or for failing to avoid the circumstances that produced the hard choice.

In other words, coercion exists when the agent is not physically forced to act, but unjustifiable circumstances produce a hard choice and the agent cannot fairly be expected to avoid choosing to do wrong. Even though the person has a choice among actions—that is, no superior force is physically moving her body—there is no 'real' or 'acceptable' alternative, and the person cannot be expected to act otherwise.

Why adopt this particular, moral test of coercion? Various writers have attempted to grapple with the criteria for coercion but, although virtually all adopt a moral model, no particular test has achieved any consensus among philosophers. Each is subject to challenging counter-examples that expose fuzziness in the concepts, such as the difference between threats and offers, or that lead to results that seem undesirable. Consequently, one must simply make a choice and the test chosen is, I believe, at least consistent with the various duress and coercion criteria in criminal and civil law.[55] Moreover, the first criterion distinguishes threats, which are usually thought to decrease choice and increase coercion, from offers, which are usually thought to increase choice and decrease coercion, even if the offer is one the offeree 'can't refuse'. Some would argue that offers and mixed cases ('throffers') can also be coercive, but this is a minority view that would tend to excuse people most observers would wish to hold responsible. The threat must be unjustified because, within a moral model, a person should yield to a morally or legally sanctioned threat. Finally, even if unjustified threats are a necessary element, setting the baseline is itself problematic. As Wertheimer demonstrated, the baseline can be statistical, psychological, or itself moralized.[56] I agree that the last is the best approach because it will yield a test for moral and legal excuse that doesn't collapse into conventionalism or unbridled subjectivity.

Turning to the second criterion, the threatened consequence and the wrongful act must both be aversive outcomes, or the person is not facing

---

[55] e.g. Model Penal Code, above n. 14, § 2.09.   [56] *Coercion*, above n. 50, 206–11.

a hard choice. If the consequence is desired, the circumstance is no threat, and if the person desires independently to perform the wrongful act, then again there is no hard choice because the threat does not furnish the motive for the wrongful act. But how hard must the choice be to warrant an excuse? This is the question that morality and the law must decide according to the circumstances of each context in which it arises. Once again, we are adopting a moral test that depends on social judgment, and, as will be discussed below, the law generally requires very substantial threats before it will excuse agents for criminal conduct. Finally, even if the agent is coerced according to the first two criteria, an excuse will not obtain if the agent was responsible either for placing himself or herself in the situation or for failing to employ possible resistant strategies. An agent who causes or fails to prevent the circumstances of his or her own excuse should not profit thereby.[57] Although the third criterion is not specific to coercion,[58] it is especially important when mental abnormality furnishes the coercive circumstances, because strategies of resistance are often a genuine possibility.

Duress furnishes a handy example of the working of the test. Suppose a gunslinger threatens to kill you unless you kill someone else. The balance of evils is neutral, so the justification of necessity is unavailable; the excuse of duress is your only hope for acquittal if you comply with the gunslinger's threat and kill. Consider the application of the three criteria: first, you have been unjustifiably threatened because the gunslinger had no right to make such a proposal to you, dying is (presumably) a worse-off state than living, and no sensible baseline would include the gunslinger's threat. Second, killing another may be excusable under the circumstances because, arguably, neither the law nor morality can fairly expect you to die, even to save an innocent. And third, let us suppose that you were not responsible for placing yourself in the circumstances. Thus, the criteria are satisfied and the excuse of duress may obtain.[59] Observe, finally, that if our miscreant gunslinger instead threatened to break your arm unless you killed, the law would not excuse you no matter how cowardly, afraid, and

[57] See generally P. Robinson, 'Causing the Conditions of One's Own Defense: A Study in the Limits of Theory in Criminal law Doctrine', (1985) 71 *Virginia LR* 1.

[58] The third criterion is not specific to a theory of coercion, because the law often fails to grant an excuse or justification when the actor is responsible for causing the conditions that necessitated the excused or justified conduct. The law is blaming an agent for conduct that would otherwise be blameless because the agent was blameworthy earlier. For example, the Model Penal Code, above n. 14, § 2.08, holds a drunken agent liable for recklessness even if intoxication deprived the agent of conscious awareness of the risk he or she was running. The justification is that the agent was reckless in becoming drunk.

[59] Many jurisdictions will not permit a duress excuse to homicide, but the Model Penal Code, above n. 14, § 2.09 and following jurisdictions do so. That there is dispute about the scope of duress suggests once again that the issue is primarily moral and not psychological. If it were the latter, there would be no reason to limit the doctrine.

subjectively pressured you felt. On the moral view, there is a real alternative: our society can fairly ask one to suffer a fracture rather than kill an innocent.[60]

Note a few things about the example. If you kill, you do so as the result of a quite intentional choice, and indeed, you might feel entirely cool and unafraid as you choose the obviously rational alternative for you under the circumstances. Thus there is no rationality problem to excuse and the claim is pure coercion, but what is the meaning of coercion here? No pathology of will exists: you *may* not feel any sense of pressure or 'irresistibility' as you choose the rational alternative. Indeed, if given time, you may deliberate about your choice in the fullest sense. The law and morality will excuse you, however, because you were unjustifiably placed through no fault of your own in a threatening circumstance that left no acceptable alternative. The basis for the excuse is that it is unjust to condemn and punish people who cannot fairly be expected to undergo awful harms, even if they must commit other terrible acts to avoid harm to themselves.

Now, can the objective, moral model of coercion be applied to one-party, *intra*personal, cases? The problem of intrapersonal involuntariness may be characterized generally as follows: you want to do something that you know you shouldn't do, but you feel as though you must do it anyhow because the pain of not doing it will be unbearable. Put another way, you experience intense and unpleasant emotion that can only be alleviated by wrongful action. Although some positive pleasure or at least the 'positive' experience of 'release' will accompany the wrongdoing, the primary motivation is the avoidance of dysphoria. Now, if you don't know what you are doing or that it is wrong, this is a standard rationality problem and casts little light on pure inner compulsion. Suppose, however, that you know rationally that you shouldn't perform the wrongful act because you correctly believe that it is wrong, but you feel that you can't help yourself because it will simply be too awful not to perform it. For example, you know that you can't afford to lose any more money gambling, but feel that you must place that next bet. Or an agent feels overwhelmed by intense rage that can only be alleviated by violent action. Or a person desires to have sexual contact with a child, despite knowing that doing so would be exploitative and harmful. Most of the classes of diagnoses that involve alleged pathologies of the will—the impulse disorders,[61] drug dependence,

---

[60] The subjectivists will immediately object, however, that this argument misses the point: if you are cowardly, they will claim, you may experience the threat as irresistible; therefore you couldn't help yourself and it is unreasonable and unfair to punish people who are unable to behave differently. But not only is this an undesirable outcome that will threaten to undermine any just blaming, it also requires an empirical assessment that cannot be made accurately, as s. 7 below shows.

[61] The American Psychiatric Association provides the following 'essential features' of 'impulse control disorders': (1) failure to resist an impulse, drive, or temptation to perform an

so-called paraphilias,[62] and compulsions[63]—fit this characterization. In many cases of these types, the sufferer feels a dysphoric building of tension, anxiety, or other unpleasant affect that seemingly can be alleviated only by doing the wrong thing.

Do the generic two-party criteria apply to the analogous one-party case? First, make the simplifying assumption that you are not responsible for your desires. Aristotle would demur,[64] but many would agree, especially if the desire were considered pathological or if the agent experiences the desire as alien to him or herself, as in cases of compulsive hand-washing. And let us assume further, that you make every effort to avoid those situations that elicit the problematic desire. Despite your efforts, however, the desire arises and you will feel much worse than you now do unless you behave wrongly by acting on it. Although the threatened dysphoria from non-fulfilment of an unwanted, 'abnormal' desire and from the continuation of unpleasant mental or emotional states cannot sensibly be described as a wrongful or morally unjustified 'threat', the despairing desirer surely does not 'deserve' to be threatened. Consequently, it is reasonable to consider the threat 'unjustified'. (In contrast, if positive pleasure were the primary motivation for wrongdoing, fulfilment would be an 'offer'.) In sum, assume that the agent faces an unjustifiable internal threat and is not responsible for having the pathological desire, for placing herself in environments likely to elicit it, or for otherwise failing to attempt reasonable resistance strategies.[65] Again, the critical question is whether performing the wrongful action to avoid the threatened or continued dysphoria is excusable.

On the moral view, if the wrong thing desired is small beans, then it may be reasonable to do it rather than to suffer substantial dysphoria. Suppose, for example, that the compulsive hand-washer's desire to wash builds to a crescendo just as his spouse is telling him something terribly important and he rudely and insensitively leaves to go to wash. The spouse

act harmful to the self or others; (2) increasing sense of tension or arousal before committing the act; (3) experiencing either pleasure, gratification, or release at the time of committing the act. *DSM-III-R*, above n. 44, 321.

[62] *DSM-III-R* generically defines these disorders as marked by recurrent sexual urges and fantasies directed at non-human objects, at the suffering or humiliation of oneself or one's partner, or at children or other non-consenting persons. The disorder exists only if the person has acted on these urges and fantasies or is distressed by them. *DSM-III-R*, above n. 44, 279.

[63] Compulsions are defined as disorders marked by (1) repetitive, purposeful, and intentional behaviours performed in response to an obsession, or according to certain rules or in a stereotyped fashion; (2) the behaviour is designed to neutralize or to prevent discomfort or some dreaded event or situation, but the behaviour in not realistically connected to what it is designed to neutralize or prevent; (3) the person recognizes that the behaviour is excessive or unreasonable. *DSM-III-R*, above n. 44, 247.

[64] Aristotle, *Nichomachean Ethics* 3. 5.

[65] See A. Mele, *Irrationality: An Essay on Akrasia, Self-Deception and Self-Control* (New York 1987), esp. chs. 2 and 4.

wouldn't like it, of course, but if she has any charity in her, she would excuse him. Or, suppose that the paedophile unlawfully possesses child pornography as a means of gratifying his unwanted sexual urges. An excuse might not be unthinkable. Or, suppose that an enraged, cruelly jilted lover spews despicable epithets at the rejecting other. We might very well forgive the cruel words. But suppose, in contrast, that the hand-washer's crescendo of desire to wash his hands peaks just as his spouse chokes on some food and will die without immediate assistance. Or, suppose that the frustrated paedophile has intercourse with a passive child. Or, suppose that a drug-dependent person can obtain the money for the next fix only by committing armed robbery or burglary. In the latter cases—the choking spouse, the molesting paedophile, and the withdrawing, drug-dependent robber—the moral test would hold that the person must bear the dysphoria rather than cause dreadful harm.[66]

5.3. *The Analysis of One-Party Coercion*

Although the moral analysis of two-party coercion cases appears profitably applicable to one-party cases of 'internal' coercion, the analysis is complicated.

First, note again that one-party coercion cases are not instances of physical compulsion, in which an external or internal physically irresistible cause, such as a much stronger person or a neuro-muscular reflex, moves a person's body although the person does not intend the movement and may even try valiantly not to perform it. In these cases, a person literally has no choice and has not 'acted'. In contrast, the coerced agent has a desire/ belief set that rationalizes her bodily movement when he or she washes to avoid dysphoria, strikes out in rage, sexually molests a child, reaches once again for the bottle, or lays down yet another bet at the roulette wheel. Because many wish to excuse at least some people who yield to strong, allegedly pathological, desires they analogize goal-directed, intentional actions driven by such desires to truly involuntary movements. By this analogy they hope to strengthen the case for excuse; but remember that the use of the words 'coercion', 'compulsion', 'involuntary', and 'irresistible' in these cases is moral and metaphorical. It does not have the literal, material definition that obtains in cases of physical compulsion. It is simply a loose characterization of those circumstances in which we excuse those who behave wrongfully in response to pathological desires. The rational victim

[66] Note that the subjective view would simply inquire whether the person was psychologically capable of acting differently. The agent would be excused if she was able to persuade that the potential dysphoria allegedly made her feel helpless in the face of the desire, no matter how dreadful the wrongdoing and even if she had an acceptable alternative. This point is discussed further in s. 5.4 below.

of the threatening gunslinger who kills to avoid her own death is surely not acting involuntarily, except in the moral sense that we might excuse her.

Second, the agent suffering from strong, arguably pathological, desires exercises choice when she intentionally acts to satisfy her desires. To hold that no choice is exercised is confusing, loose talk that begs the important questions. There is no doubt that choice can be constrained, limiting the person's alternatives in the circumstances, but the decision to act or not to act is nevertheless a choice, even under the most constraining circumstances. Thus, deciding which constraints should excuse will require a moral theory about excusing. Consider Martin Luther's claim: 'Here I stand; I can do no other.' Although there was 'pressure' and no 'real' alternative for Luther, he certainly chose. Or, consider the following case: suppose you decide to add a room with a bath to your house and entertain bids on the same plans from two contractors, A and B, who are equally skilled, equally reputable, equally likeable, and equally efficient. A bids $60,000; B bids $45,000. Remember that all things are equal. Do you exercise a choice when you choose B, as any rational person would? Of course you do, although you would rightly claim, when you turned A down, that you really had no meaningful choice. Note in this case that the absence of meaningful choice would not allow you to claim coercion and avoid paying B. This situation involves an offer rather than a threat, of course, and thus fails to meet the moralized coercion criteria, but it does demonstrate first, that choice is involved even when there is 'pressure' and no 'real' alternative, and second, that the absence of meaningful choice does not *per se* excuse. The coercion problem is not lack of any choice. It is yielding to an unjustifiable choice in the absence of acceptable alternatives.

Some contend, contrary to the analysis offered so far, that the analogy of psychological to physical compulsion is near perfect, and that the psychologically compelled agent does not choose. A standard way of attempting to support these conclusions employs hierarchical theories of motivation, such as those most famously deployed by Harry Frankfurt.[67] The central notion is that we are responsible for actions only if they are produced by desires that we identify with or ratify by evaluating them according to higher-order desires. For example, some argue that agents lack the ability to act differently and do not choose to act unless they are identified with, assent to, or ratify their desires, as the hand-washer, paedophile, and drug-dependent person presumably do not.[68] Although hierarchical accounts are

[67] See e.g. 'Freedom of the Will and the Concept of a Person', 'Identification and Externality', and 'Identification and Wholeheartedness', in H. G. Frankfurt, *The Importance of What we Care About: Philosophical Essays* (Cambridge 1988), 11, 58, and 159 respectively.   [68] e.g. Gardner, above n. 48, 74–9.

attractive, the concept of identification is itself problematic and seems to do little work in the justification of excuse.

As Gary Watson has shown,[69] higher-order volitions are just desires themselves and there is no reason to make them the touchstone of deliberation or any other criterion for responsibility. Moreover, what seems to give them authority is that they are *evaluative*, they mark what we consider worthwhile. But one can fail to identify with what one values, and behave in ways one does not value, from a more general standpoint. Watson argues that defining an evaluational system just in terms of what one does without regret abandons an explanation of self-determination that is based on identification by evaluation. Watson concludes that the notion of identification is 'elusive' and that defining it as a type of 'brute self-assertion seems totally unsatisfactory'.

The other difficulty with hierarchical theories of responsibility is that ratification or identification does not do the work for which it is designed. An intensely greedy person, who accepts greediness as part of himself or herself, may feel 'powerless' in the face of temptation, even if we consider these desires normal (albeit undesirable).[70] By contrast, a person with unwanted but weak paedophilic urges may have the ability to resist temptation, even if these urges are rightly called pathological. The identification criterion would condemn the former and excuse the latter, but this appears to be a perverse result that needs far more explanation. If we assume that the 'identified' agent has the ability to resist, but the 'unidentified' agent does not, then the ability to resist, not identification, is doing the work, and the empirical assumption about resistance-ability needs further support. It is not immediately apparent why identification is coterminous with the ability to resist. Nor is it apparent that a person faced with even a dreadfully hard choice produced by his own wanted or unwanted desires is not choosing. For example, the American Psychiatric Association's definition of compulsive behaviour is that it is purposeful and intentional: the agent is hardly an automaton. Hierarchical accounts do not convincingly disprove the claim that the analogy of psychological compulsion to physical compulsion is metaphorical. And, finally, suggestions that the agent has no choice beg the difficult empirical and moral questions concerning human abilities, and concerning what the law and morality can demand when choice is unjustifiably constrained.[71]

---

[69] G. Watson, 'Free Action and Free Will', (1987) 96 *Mind* 145, at 149–51.

[70] See the discussion of the 'moneyphile' in s. 5.4 below for further elucidation.

[71] Finally, should a person with unfortunate desires, who may have tried without avail to change and who has finally accepted her unpleasant fate because she has no alternative, become an enhanced candidate for moral appraisal because she has 'ratified' her desires? After all, there is no positive evaluation; there is simply 'brute acceptance' because life provides no alternative.

The third general consideration about one-party cases is that the agent's conduct in response to so-called irresistible impulses, including impulses produced by intense emotions like rage, is decidedly intentional and, in important ways, rational: the agent acts wrongfully 'on purpose' for the perfectly rational reason that she wishes to avoid seemingly unbearable dysphoria. In the case of some impulse disorders and compulsions, such as kleptomania, the desire itself may seem irrational, but satisfying the need to avoid pain is surely not irrational. Moreover, for many people affected by the so-called paraphilias, some impulse disorders, and drug dependence, satisfying the desire produces positive pleasure as well as the avoidance of pain, and seeking pleasure is surely a rational reason to form an intention. Observe, parenthetically, that in cases where the agent satisfies the desire by wrongful conduct both to avoid dysphoria *and* to seek pleasure, the test of reasonableness for yielding to the desire is complicated on either the moral or empirical view. If the motive for satisfying the desire is purely pleasure, then there is no threat and no compulsion, no matter how strong the desire is. Of course, if a person's ultimate goal is irrational, craving for it collapses into a rationality problem.

Fourth, even if a person has intense, irrational desires that cause great dysphoria, this does not mean that there is some defect with the will or volitional capacity. Some modern theories of action posit the will or volition as an operative variable, especially as a functional state that translates desire/belief sets into action.[72] Other theorists think of volitions as actions (of the will).[73] Some think that the concept can be dispensed with,[74] and others, most notably Ryle, believe the concept of the will is preposterous.[75] Such disputes should certainly give pause to those who facilely discuss problems of the will and volition and assume that they understand both those problems and their bearing on responsibility. But, in any case, problems of coercion are quite distinct from what might be termed 'pathologies' of the will, especially if the will is conceived as a functional state. The functional mental state that produces action successfully satisfying an intense, irrational desire is as intact as the functional mental state that produces action satisfying an equally intense, rational desire. The 'problem', if there is one, is irrationality, not volitional defect.[76]

Fifth, in one-party (and two-party) cases, if threatening circumstances prevent one from thinking rationally, then a rationality problem exists

---

[72] A. Donagan, *Choice: the Essential Element in Human Action* (London 1987); M. Moore, *Act and Crime* (Oxford 1993), ch. 6.
[73] e.g. C. Ginet, *On Action* (Cambridge 1990).
[74] e.g. A. Mele, *Springs of Action: Understanding Intentional Behavior* (New York 1992).
[75] G. Ryle, *The Concept of Mind* (London 1949).
[76] Fingarette and Hasse make this point very clearly. See *Mental Disabilities and Criminal Responsibility*, above n. 29, 55–65.

that can be dealt with according to the rationality criteria for diminished capacity or, conceivably, the insanity defence. Many of the cases we term 'volitional' or involuntary fall under this description. Indeed, some would claim that all cases are like this, even in the absence of obvious irrationality. Suppose, for example, that the person is not rendered distraught by threatening circumstances. Imagine that a person is petrified but rational: she has her wits about her but feels that she must kill because she is morbidly afraid of bodily injury. Many commentators would treat this case, too, as a rationality problem. The morbidity of the fear is itself irrational and the intensity of it makes one unable in any meaningful sense to weigh the competing alternatives.[77]

The sixth, related observation about one-party cases is that they rarely involve pure impulse problems in the absence of substantial irrationality and there is persistent confusion in the literature between rationality problems and so-called volitional defects. For example, in a recent article,[78] Dr Richard Rogers cites the case of a woman suffering from major affective disorder who, in the depths of her hopeless dysphoria, attempts suicide and the homicide of her children to 'end their suffering'. Although Rogers treats this case as one of defective volition, note that the depressed mother's assumption that the children's suffering is somehow indistinguishable from hers is a psychotic, gross misperception of reality, as is her belief that her situation is genuinely hopeless. Although there are clearly rational homicides and arguably rational suicides, this case presents neither and terming it a volitional problem, especially the slaughter of the children, achieves no gain in comprehension.

But we can recharacterize the case, of course. Focusing solely on the suicide, we could treat the threat of unbearable, unending dysphoria as meeting the first compulsion criterion, and then treat the suicide as an acceptable alternative under the circumstances. But most of us do not believe that suicide is the only real alternative. We know that even the most severe depressions are self-limiting, that most respond to various treatment modalities, and that virtually all severe depressions compromise the sufferer's ability to think rationally about her situation. Few would claim that this person is rational about herself, her disorder, and her future. If her situation really was hopeless, then the case might represent an entirely rational suicide that posed no volitional problems. Rogers also raises the case of a person with major mania, but once again the problem that ultimately causes legal trouble is the person's beliefs and perceptions about herself and the world. The manic person does not knowingly do

[77] Note that if this case is treated (wrongfully) as a coercion case, the empirical model would excuse and the moral model would not.
[78] R. Rogers, 'APA's Position on the Insanity Defense: Empiricism Versus Emotionalism' (1987) 42 *American Psychologist* 840.

wrong because elevated mood somehow impels her to do so. Rather, the mood disorder distorts her perception of reality and the consequent rationality of her practical reasoning.

Except, possibly, for the impulse disorders and related diagnoses, it is difficult to envision a case in which the defendant was suffering from a severe mental disorder with marked coercive features, but was substantially rational. Virtually all cases that would justify acquittal by reason of insanity or partial responsibility demonstrate that marked irrationality infected the practical reasoning that motivated the criminal conduct. Crazy beliefs and perceptions are the touchstone. Nevertheless, the confusion of irrationality and volitional problems persists.

Seventh, an enduring mistake in analysing one-party cases is the belief that abnormal cognitions are somehow more coercive or compelling than normal cognitions. An agent motivated by crazy beliefs is classically irrational, however, and there is no need to resort to coercion analysis. But in any case, it is a logical error to believe that mistaken perceptions and beliefs, whether normally or abnormally generated, are more compelling in practical reasoning than accurate perceptions and beliefs.[79] The delusionally mistaken belief of the persecuted paranoid that she is about to be attacked and must use self-defensive force is no more 'compelling' than the accurate belief of a police-officer that she must use deadly force in justifiable self-defence. Both have the same survival desires and there is no reason to doubt that both experience these desires with equal intensity. The unfortunate paranoid is, of course, irrational and in appropriate cases will be excused on that basis. The paranoid might not have attacked but for the delusional belief, but the problem is not lack of self-control; it is the irrational belief. If a person simply *felt*, without any apparent reason, that she had to attack an innocent victim or suffer some dreadful dysphoria, the case would be far more purely volitional, but also clinically unlikely.

Eighth and last, if there are cases of purely impulsive, thoughtless conduct, where the agent is incapable of any form of reflective awareness about her desires—cases that might be termed impetuous among the normal, or explosive disorder among the abnormal[80]—these are clearly cases of irrationality by any reasonable criteria of rationality.

In sum, although preliminary analysis of one-party cases suggests that pure cases may exist and fit the paradigm for excuse, cases of pure internal coercion, compulsion, or 'volitional' problems are extremely rare. Moreover, many would treat as rationality problems those cases of arguably 'irrational' ends that might otherwise be characterized as purely volitional, like the paedophile, the kleptomaniac, the pathological gambler, or the

---

[79] Cf. J. Wakefield, 'Disorder as Harmful Dysfunction: A Conceptual Critique of *DSM-III-R*'s Definition of Mental Disorder', (1992) 99 *Psychological Review* 232, at 237.
[80] *DSM-III-R*, above n. 44, 321–2 ('Intermittent Explosive Disorder').

cool coward who will commit any harm to avoid injury to self, no matter how slight. Nevertheless, infrequency alone is insufficient reason to deny a partial-responsibility excuse if it is justified in principle.[81] Let us therefore consider such cases in more detail.

5.4. *Pure One-Party Coercion?*

How should morality and the law respond to a case of a pure internal coercion—that is, a case of a person who uses rational but wrongful means to avoid dysphoria threatened by arguably rational desires? Can these cases be treated as based on mental abnormality and on that ground as justifying a moral or legal excuse? Can these cases ultimately be distinguished from rationality problems?

Most laypeople and many clinicians would probably treat pure coercion cases as instances of clear-headed akrasia—that is, normal weakness of the will—and would hold the agent fully responsible because he does not seem sufficiently mentally abnormal. Suppose that a generally law-abiding person is none the less exceptionally avaricious and greedy: a moneyphile, if you will. If this person is faced with a tempting situation in which the theft of a large sum of money is easily accomplished with little chance of detection, she may steal. How do we explain this case? One possibility is that she was so overcome by her desires that she failed to think straight about the moral and legal consequences of what she was doing. If so, the excuse, if any there be, is once again irrationality. If an agent 'loses control', that is, does something that she would not otherwise do, as a result of a cognitive glitch, this is a rationality problem. The alternative possibility is that the agent recognizes the reality of the situation in all its moral relevance, but is somehow *unable* to refrain from acting wrongly because she fears mounting dysphoria or the like. This is the classic case of 'irresistible impulse'.

Do we excuse the moneyphile? The usual answer is negative: moneyphilia is considered a character-trait rather than a disorder, and we believe that an agent is responsible for her character and able to maintain both cognitive rationality and self-control in the face of the strong desires her character produces, even when tempted directly. How is this case distinguishable, though, from paedophilia or gambling? Simply referring to the latter as mental disorders rather than character-traits begs the crucial question. Are our 'normal desires' up to us more than our 'abnormal/pathological desires'? We are all in large measure the product of biological endowments and environments over which we had no control and many

---

[81] Practical concerns that may also be reason not to provide a partial-responsibility excuse in coercion cases will be discussed in s. 7 below.

of our central desires are firmly established well before we reach the age of genuine, independent moral reflection on those desires. Moreover, what reason is there to believe that it is more difficult to learn to control abnormal desires than immoral desires?[82] And if we try to distinguish the cases on the ground that paedophilia and pathological gambling desires are irrational and moneyphilia is not—as is implied by the locution, 'abnormal desires'—then we have redefined the problem once again as a rationality problem.

Another approach is to suggest that the desires of the paedophile or pathological gambler are necessarily stronger than the moneyphile's desires and that non-fulfilment will produce correspondingly greater dysphoria than in the case of the moneyphile. But this won't work either. There is simply no scientific or clinical evidence that 'abnormal' desires are necessarily stronger than 'normal' desires and thus that abnormal desires are uniquely able to threaten one with unbearable dysphoria. The moneyphile faced with an unattended pile of the ready may feel as much 'pressure' as the paedophile unwittingly left alone with an attractive child. An extraordinarily strong desire for power, fame, or wealth motivates people to diverse unseemly conduct, and for some people, paedophiliac and other allegedly abnormal urges are mild and avoidable even under the most devastatingly tempting circumstances. What is the relevance of the source of the desire, except that some are 'abnormal', that is, irrational, thus collapsing the analysis into the rationality domain once more? If desires or ends conceptually cannot be irrational *per se*, providing a principled way to distinguish these cases is difficult.

A final attempt to distinguish desires that diminish responsibility from those that do not employs the hierarchical view of motivation discussed above, which requires for responsibility that the agent identify with or ratify his or her desires according to higher-order desires.[83] Although hierarchical accounts initially seem promising responses to compulsive states,[84] for the reasons given earlier—difficulties with the identification concept and with whether failure to identify is genuinely the basis for excuse—this approach is unlikely to solve the dilemma.

Perhaps the soundest approach is simply to define as abnormal any extreme desire that can threaten unbearable dysphoria, no matter how rational it might be in milder forms, and to limit one-party coercion excuses to such cases. Indeed, most of us think there is something more than

[82] Here I am assuming that one can distinguish between abnormal and immoral desires. To the extent that one believes it is impossible rationally to desire immoral ends, then the distinction collapses. See generally, R. Milo, *Immorality* (Princeton, NJ 1984). This point is discussed further in the discussion of the psychopath's responsibility in s. 11 below.

[83] See above s. 5.3.

[84] See Watson 'Free Action and Free Will', above n. 69, 148.

a little wacky about wanting anything 'too much'. Now, how much is 'too much' will of course depend on the circumstances, including social conventions. An extreme desire to end hunger in one's society is less likely to be considered irrational than an equally extreme desire to possess the finest collection of matchbook covers in one's neighbourhood. (And, how one tries to satisfy the desire will be judged as a matter of instrumental rationality.)

How should we respond to cases of wanting something 'too much'? First, are desires so excessive appropriately characterized as rational? And when people are motivated to act wrongfully as a result of such extreme desires, do we believe that they are capable of rationally weighing the situation? I don't have answers to these questions, but my hunch is that most people would conclude that neither extreme desire nor practical reasoning that includes such desire is rational. Moreover, in many cases involving such extreme desires, it is probable that the ability to reason well in the face of the relevant temptation will be compromised substantially.

Finally, on the moral view, how can threatened, undesirable, subjective states ever justify a rational agent's wrongdoing? The moral, objective test does not ask an empirical, phenomenological question that requires an answer about an unknown level of ability to refrain. The expectation of reasonableness is not a psychological variable, but a moral standard, and we assume that all can refrain from wrongful conduct, albeit some with greater difficulty than others. Thus, if it would be unfair to require a person to refrain from causing harm—as in the case of person who acts in response to the threatening gunslinger—the law will excuse her even if she is capable of refraining. Conversely, as a moral matter, we simply expect people to bear significant harms before they will be excused for harming others. Indeed, most American jurisdictions provide a duress defence only if the defendant had been threatened with death or grievous bodily harm, and most provide no duress defence to the crime of murder. The reasoning in two-party cases is that only the most seriously harmful threats can excuse, and in many jurisdictions no threat excuses taking a life. Understanding why the one-party case should be different is obscure. Consequently, to justify even partial excuse for all but the most petty crimes, an agent would have to demonstrate that extraordinary fear of dysphoria drove her to unlawful conduct. In virtually all cases, however, fear that strong, or feelings that intense, would surely result from irrational beliefs or perceptions or would compromise rationality to a substantial degree.

Observe that if we adopted a subjective, empirical model for internal coercion, we would excuse anyone who persuaded us that she acted for fear of dysphoria, even if the source of her dysphoria did not seem objectively intense and she committed a genuinely horrendous deed. Still, much as some people might terribly fear even slight physical harms, others might have similar difficulty bearing mildly unpleasant emotions. 'Pressure' is 'pressure', whether its source is objectively justifiable or not. So, the empirical model is hard put not to excuse the physical or emotional coward who really is afraid. One may object, however, that if the source of the dysphoria was weak and the need to avoid it so terrible, then the problem must be character-based lack of self-control. But this is simply another way of saying the person is a coward. In either case, the agent felt as though she could not help herself. And is the empiricist willing to hold people responsible for their characters? How, at the age of self-reflection and maturity, can a profound coward justly be expected upon threat of punishment to develop the courage to fight and conquer the cowardice? If this expectation is unreasonable, the internal coherence of the empirical model requires that this person must be excused. But excusing in such cases would be a morally perverse result based on a technology that we lack. Finally, if an agent is willing to do something horrendous to avoid objectively mild sources of dysphoria, one suspects once again that the agent's ability to weigh the alternatives rationally is impaired.

In the end, do pure coercion cases exist that require excuse? Although I am sympathetic to claims that the rationality of desires or ends is difficult to assess, I am finally convinced, by malignantly circular reasoning perhaps, that it must be irrational to want to produce unjustified harm so intensely that failure to satisfy that desire will create sufficient dysphoria to warrant an excuse. Moreover, in a very small class of cases, such as kleptomania or necrophilia, the agent's goal—described as theft *for no reason* or sexual desire *for the dead*—may simply seem unintelligible. The justification for the excuse in all these cases is then irrationality, not coercion. Even if clinicians routinely consider what they conceive to be volitional problems in their clinical practice, it does not follow that the law must adopt a conceptually misguided excuse. As Joseph Livermore and Paul Meehl argued in their justly celebrated article on the virtues of *McNaghten*, a morally justifiable insanity defence based on purely cognitive considerations is feasible.[85] Even if pure coercion cases provide theoretically independent grounds for partial responsibility (and legal insanity), the profound conceptual difficulties already considered and consequent assessment and implementation problems, to be discussed presently, suggest great caution before adopting the excuse.

5.5. Deprivation and Partial Responsibility

Should a history of emotional or other deprivation provide an independent ground for a partial-responsibility excuse? Many claim that deprivation

---

[85] J. Livermore and P. Meehl, 'The Virtues of *M'Naghten*' (1967) 51 *Minnesota LR* 789; reprinted in C. A. Anderson and K. Gunderson (eds.), *Paul E. Meehl: Selected Philosophical and Methodological Papers* (Minneapolis 1991), 338.

can cause irrationality[86] and an unfortunate history properly elicits sympathy, but should deprivation itself excuse? If deprivation produces nonculpable irrationality, then irrationality is the basis for the excuse. If, however, it simply produces character flaws or anti-social predispositions, why should a history of deprivation create more ground for excuse than any other non-culpable developmental cause of such flaws or predispositions?

The true basis, I believe, for the intuition that deprivation should excuse is sympathy for those who have suffered. Although such responses are entirely understandable, deprivation is not clearly relevant to responsibility ascriptions, and the proper legal response to the rational and uncoerced but relevantly deprived criminal is problematic. As Martha Klein has demonstrated, deprivation can be argued to be relevant only if it is the cause of the actor's *morally reprehensible* state of mind that produced the criminal act.[87] Klein also suggests that in such cases the offender deserves less punishment because he or she 'has paid in advance' by his or her previous suffering. The payment-in-advance principle has intuitive appeal, but note that it is not an argument about partial responsibility. Rather, a fully responsible miscreant is simply being punished less *after* the offence because he or she has been punished *before* the offence by the very conditions that produced his or her culpability. Viewed from the vantage point of an entire life, the offender his been fully punished, albeit in large measure by agencies other than the State. There are also practical problems with this suggestion, such as identifying causal suffering, calibrating the proper deserved punishment post-offence, and dealing with the danger to public safety that less-punished, responsible agents represent. But for our purposes the crucial point is simply that a history of deprivation itself does not furnish grounds for partial responsibility, even when it is causally relevant to the agent's offence.

6. The Scope of Partial Responsibility

If partial responsibility is justifiable, should it be limited? The myriad indirect partial-responsibility doctrines are really the same doctrine

---

[86] The explanation for the higher rates of severe mental disorder among the socially disadvantaged is elusive. The two dominant hypotheses are social causation and social selection or drift. The most recent large-scale epidemiological attempt to resolve the question discovered that social selection may better explain the higher rates of schizophrenia, but that social causation may better explain depression in women and antisocial personality and substance abuse in men. B. Dohrenwend, I. Levav, P. Shrout, S. Schwartz, G. Naveh, B. Link, A. Skodol, and A. Stueve, 'Socioeconomic Status and Psychiatric Disorders: The Causation–Selection Issue', (1992) 255 *Science* 946.

[87] M. Klein, *Determinism, Blameworthiness and Deprivation* (Oxford 1990), 84–91 and 172–6.

expressing the same moral judgment.[88] For example, there is no real difference in principle and language between English 'diminished responsibility', which applies only to murder and reduces convictions to manslaughter, American capital-sentencing mitigation criteria, such as 'lack of substantial capacity to appreciate the criminality of one's act', which serve only to avoid the death penalty, and the Federal Guidelines' diminished-capacity provision, which applies only to non-violent crimes and permits a downward departure from the normally mandated sentence. As another example, is the reason for reducing an extremely emotionally disturbed killer's crime from murder to manslaughter different from the reason for reducing the sentence of a convicted murderer because there is convincing evidence in the pre-sentence report that the murderer was similarly disturbed when the homicide occurred? More important, what principle of desert and fairness suggests that partial responsibility should apply only to some crimes and not to others? For example, if a mentally abnormal, partially responsible murderer deserves a partial excuse, does not an equally mentally abnormal, partially responsible armed robber, arsonist, rapist, or thief also deserve the excuse? The same principle guides all these cases and should apply to all crimes. Moreover, legislatures and courts have already demonstrated that the evidentiary concerns are manageable. Thus, only considerations of public safety could justify limitations, but as I argue below, this problem can be solved by a rational sentencing-response to a finding of partial responsibility.

I conclude that there is ample theoretical justification for a partial-responsibility excuse based on irrationality.[89] I am less certain about internal coercion, especially since I believe that all arguable claims are probably either clear irrationality cases or can be properly redefined as such. None the less, despite the coherence of the justification for partial responsibility, whether the law should adopt the generic excuse is entirely dependent on one's vision of how much rationality is required for full legal responsibility. I have argued in detail elsewhere that very little is required for criminal responsibility, that the law should not adopt a generic partial-responsibility excuse (most assuredly not one based on internal coercion), and that extant indirect partial-responsibility doctrines should be abandoned.[90] I still maintain that view, but for those who have more stringent requirements for responsibility, partial responsibility is clearly rational and a sensible response to it can be devised.

---

[88] See above, s. 2.

[89] This conclusion and the previous analysis that supported it is most closely like Fingarette and Hasse's illuminating proposal for an excuse based on 'disability of mind' (DOM). See *Mental Disabilities and Criminal Responsibility*, above n. 29, 199–261.

[90] Morse, 'Undiminished Confusion', above n. 8; see also, Morse, 'Excusing the Crazy', above n. 4.

7. Partial Responsibility Assessed

Because the law is concerned with whether the agent was irrational or internally coerced, the fundamental inquiry in all cases concerns the agent's psychological phenomenology: what were the agent's thoughts and feelings? Needless to say, we cannot directly 'read' each others' minds or measure the strength of feelings. Nevertheless, most people are quite expert at identifying and assessing other peoples' reasons for action. Relatively orderly and predictable human interaction is possible only because we are all able within reasonable limits to make inferences about our fellow humans' mental states from behaviour, including speech acts. Moreover, assessing the rationality of another person's reasons for action requires only that we identify those reasons and then evaluate them according to our operative, normative theory of rationality. Of course, how much irrationality is required to justify excusing is a moral and legal matter.

In contrast, judging the strength of another's desires and dysphoria or fear of it is a Herculean endeavour. Unlike rationality cases, there is no relatively clear phenomenon to match against a roughly consensual normative standard. Indeed, this is a major difficulty with the empirical model of intrapersonal coercion: it is well known that we cannot distinguish between irresistible impulses and those impulses simply not resisted. No established metric exists to determine the magnitude of impulses, desires, or feelings. That two independent observers trained in the same system of assessment would agree that a subject exhibits desires of a certain strength, or is unable to refrain from acting, does not entail that the system is valid, and I know of no such measurement system with established validity.[91] Furthermore, it is difficult to disentangle the strength of desires, the strength of temptations, and the capacity for self-control. There have been numerous studies of impulsiveness and self-control in the psychological and psychiatric literature,[92] and people do commonsensically note individual differences in these traits. Moreover, we talk about the will and self-control as if these are independent psychological entities which are well understood and reliably identifiable. But the studies often contradict each other, measures of supposedly the same variable correlate poorly, findings

---

[91] Rogers's system, above n. 78, discussed in this section below, is primarily about rationality and is unvalidated.

[92] See e.g. E. Barrat and J. Patton, 'Impulsivity: Cognitive, Behavioral and Psycho physiological Correlates', in M. Zuckerman (ed.), *Biological Bases of Sensation Seeking, Impulsivity, and Anxiety* (Hillsdale, NJ 1983), 77; S. Dickman, 'Functional and Dysfunctional Impulsivity: Personality and Cognitive Correlates', (1990) 58 *Journal of Personality and Social Psychology* 95; A. Logue, 'Research on Self-Control: An Integrating Framework', (1988) 11 *Behavioral and Brain Sciences* 665.

are often based on suspect self-reports, and, most importantly, the studies do not address (and folk psychology does not know) whether and to what degree people are *unable* to refrain from acting. Neither in psychology, nor in philosophy, nor in folk psychology is there a reasonably uncontroversial understanding of these matters. Finally, we do not know how mental disorder affects self-control in general, apart from its more clear role in affecting perception and belief, which are variables central to rationality.

The strongest contrary claims in the literature fail both conceptually and empirically. For example, in an article about legal insanity that purports to demonstrate that volitional problems can be reliably identified,[93] Rogers provides 'representative criteria for assessing volitional capacity'. But inspection of the criteria Rogers proposes disclose that they are firmly in the camp of folk psychology and most describe failures not of volition or the will, but of rationality in the face of strong desires, emotions, impulses, and the like. For instance, Rogers's criteria ask: what did the defendant perceive as his or her alternatives to the criminal behaviour? Or, did the criminal behavior include planning or preparation? One criterion begs the question by asking: 'Was the *loss of control* [emphasis added] caused by a strong emotional state (e.g. rage reaction) or intoxication, or both?' None of these criteria individually, nor all of them taken together, can demonstrate with acceptable scientific precision whether and to what degree a defendant lacked the capacity to behave lawfully under the circumstances. And virtually all are designed to uncover rationality defects rather than defects of volition. In a later article using *four* forensic psychiatrists as subjects, Rogers and colleagues claim that they empirically establish that volitional criteria are practically important and logically distinct from cognitive criteria. But the article shows only that the tiny number of subjects believe they can distinguish and use volitional criteria. No evidence demonstrates that the subjects in fact use volitional criteria that are independent of rationality, and nothing in the study, contrary to its blithe assurance, supports the conceptual validity of independent volitional problems.[94]

Proponents of an independent coercion or volitional excuse often try to justify its adoption in the face of conceptual and assessment problems by *correctly* arguing that our understanding of the causes of cognitive or rationality defects is as primitive as the understanding of the aetiology of inner coercion. Although true, this argument is irrelevant to the differential difficulty of assessing *existing* irrationality and inner coercion. The law's concern is *not* why glitches occur. Rather, to evaluate responsibility the

[93] Rogers, 'APA's Position on the Insanity Defense' above n. 78.
[94] R. Wettstein, E. Mulvey, and R. Rogers, 'A Prospective Comparison of Four Insanity Defense Standards', (1991) 148 *American Journal of Psychiatry* 21.

law needs to know only whether and to what degree glitches occur. Understanding the causal background may in some cases be probative about whether an excusing condition exists, but no particular cause is required to justify the excusing condition.[95] For example, if we are convinced that a person was in the throes of non-culpable irrationality, we excuse the agent, even if we do not know what produced the abnormality. The causes of cognitive and volitional defects are equally obscure, but for the reasons suggested above, we can empirically identify and assess each others' reasons for action far better than we can empirically identify and assess each others' strength of desire or intensity of feeling. Although there are no conclusive studies that prove this point, I believe that the opposite claim is so counterintuitive that it is fair to place the burden of persuasion on those who disagree.

Ultimately, coercion assessment may collapse into rationality assessment. Virtually all cases of so-called irresistible impulse will prove on close analysis to be instances of irrationality, especially if the law continues to specify that an abnormality is required. Even the common-sense basis for judging volitional problems is often a disguised rationality criterion. For example, the 'policeman at the elbow' test, which is usually understood as a volitional standard, is, I think, better interpreted as a rationality test. Those who offend in the face of certain capture have either rationally decided for political or other reasons that the offence is worth the punishment, as in cases of civil disobedience, or they are irrational. We generally tend to conclude that intense internal coercion was operative if conduct was so irrational that we cannot make any sense of it; otherwise, why would the person do it? Again, however, rationality is the real issue.

Still assuming, however, that cases of pure internal coercion exist, the best we can do is to ask the agent to tell us how she felt and to observe psychophysical signs, such as trembling or perspiring, that may also provide a clue. The moral test asks only for phenomenological description and then weighs it in the moral balance. By comparing the intensity of the threatened dysphoria to the conduct chosen to avoid it, we can make the moral and legal decision about whether partial responsibility is warranted. This we can try to do without kidding ourselves by treating the pseudo-scientific enterprise of assessing volitional problems as if it were an empirically valid inquiry. Even when performed rationally, however, assessments of internal coercion are at best questionable. On both theoretical and practical grounds, the law should treat internal-coercion claims with great caution.

[95] One may object that we must identify causes such as mental disorder, but the same evidence that proves the presence of mental disorder also proves the substantive part of an irrationality test. Moreover, there is no need to identify the cause of the mental disorder.

8. Sentencing Partially Responsible Agents

How should the law respond to justifiable claims for partial responsibility? Both irrationality and fear of dysphoria are continua, and therefore partial responsibility is also a theoretical continuum. But can the law sensibly and even-handedly make fine judgments about morally relevant discrete, marginal differences in rationality and fear of dysphoria? Simply to pose the question is to suggest, I believe, that the answer must be negative. Disagreement about the normative issues and deficient assessment-technology make this task impossible within the constraint of treating like cases reasonably alike.

If the law were to adopt a generic partial-responsibility excuse, the best compromise between concerns of justice and the inability accurately and finely to calibrate responsibility would be simply to offer the fact-finder the option of a new verdict, 'guilty but partially responsible' (GPR). GPR is a general analogue to 'diminished responsibility' that applies to all crimes, expressing a finding that at the time of the crime the defendant was legally responsible, but not fully so because he or she was irrational or internally coerced by mental abnormality. If proven, GPR triggers a legislatively mandated reduction in sentence.[96]

I propose that partial responsibility should be decided by the fact-finder rather than by the sentencing judge, because it represents the community's moral judgment and I have a preference in such cases for community decision-making in the high-visibility context of the trial. In contrast, I am quite neutral about the appropriate reduction in sentence that should follow. Many schemes seem sensible, including reducing the sentences for all crimes by the same percentage (for example, all partially responsible criminals receive a reduction of fifty per cent for all crimes) or differentially reducing sentences depending on the seriousness of the crime (for example, all partially responsible murderers receive a twenty per cent reduction and all partially responsible petty thieves receive an eighty per cent reduction). Such fixed schemes clearly contradict the continuous nature of partial responsibility, but for the reasons given above it is impossible to be more fine-grained without increasing arbitrariness. These proposals are probably not politically feasible,[97] but alternatives such as 'guilty but mentally ill'

---

[96] I suggested this option previously in 'Diminished Capacity', above n. 22. I still believe it is the only sensible solution if partial responsibility as a separate generic excuse should be adopted. This verdict is quite unlike the justly maligned 'guilty but mentally ill' verdict adopted by about one-quarter of the American states, which does not entail a finding of diminished responsibility, and which permits the maximum penalty for the crime charged, including death.

[97] John Monahan describes the proposal as a 'punishment sale' for partially crazy criminals. Alas, I fear that it would be characterized this way.

Stephen J. Morse

are morally bankrupt, and it is difficult to envision other, adequate responses to the legally sane, but only partially responsible criminal.

9. Implications of Partial Responsibility: New Defences

Courts and legislatures are currently inundated with arguments in support of creating new affirmative defences based on endlessly proliferating alleged discoveries of new 'syndromes', such as battered spouse, battered child, holocaust survivor, PMS, and a host of others. When proposed as justifications, these new defences are theoretically confused. If justifiable, these defences are partial-responsibility claims and should be treated generically as such. The battered-spouse syndrome has had the greatest legal effect and is the most well known, so I shall use it as my example, assuming for purposes of discussion that the syndrome itself is reliably identifiable and valid.[98]

The common scenario giving rise to the issue involves a battered spouse or significant other suffering from the syndrome, usually a woman, who is arguably unable to leave the battering relationship because the syndrome negatively affects her self-esteem and makes her dependent on the batterer. After killing the batterer when there is no obviously immediate threat of death or serious injury, she then claims that she acted in self-defence and uses evidence of the syndrome to support the claim. The issue is how the evidence relates to the plea for exculpation. The strongest argument, if empirically true, is that syndrome sufferers (and perhaps battered significant others in general) become hypervigilant and hypersensitive to cues indiscernible to others that indicate that a battering episode is imminent. If so, the defendant's deadly attack fits squarely within the standard justification of self-defence because she *is* in immediate danger of death or serious bodily harm, and the defendant requires no new doctrine for exculpation.

Suppose, however, as often occurs, that the victim of battering attacks when the batterer is not threatening immediate harm.[99] Even if the woman correctly fears that an attack will occur when he awakes or at some future time, what justification is there for killing the batterer when leaving is a genuine possibility? All justifications are restricted by the requirement that no reasonable alternative to harm-doing is available, and in the hypothetical

---

[98] Of course, there is evidence to the contrary. D. Faigman, 'The Battered Woman Syndrome and Self Defense: A Legal and Empirical Dissent', (1986) 72 *Virginia LR* 619. Nevertheless, entering that debate here is a needless distraction from the central theoretical and practical point.

[99] See e.g. *P* v. *Yaklich*, 50 *Criminal Law Reporter* 1256 (1991) (battered spouse hired two people to kill her husband; killers were paid with the proceeds of the husband's life-insurance policy; spouse not entitled to self-defence instruction).

case, there is an alternative. To modify the imminence requirement to permit the use of deadly force in these situations deprives self-defence of its status as a justification.[100] Proponents of the defence argue that the sufferer cannot leave or seek other remedies because her syndrome prevents her from doing so. This argument implicitly concedes, however, that a blameless rationality defect disables the agent from pursuing the reasonable alternative. Consequently, the sufferer's real claim is an irrationality excuse rather than the justification of self-defence.

Those who nevertheless wish to treat the syndrome-suffering defendant's conduct as self-defence respond perplexingly that the reasonable-person standard should be 'subjectivized' to endow the reasonable person with the characteristics of the accused, namely, that she suffers from the syndrome. Then, it is argued, the reasonable syndrome-sufferer does reasonably believe that she is in imminent danger. But this move empties the categories of 'reasonableness' and rationality of all sensible content. Should a person suffering from paranoia who kills in 'self-defence' be judged as a 'reasonable paranoid'? The reasonable irrational person is a mythical creature in a world in which rationality bears any relation to objectivity.[101]

If the new syndrome simply provides evidence to support properly understood extant justifications or excuses, there is no need for new doctrine. Often, however, as in most battered-spouse cases, the evidence does not fit standard defences. In such cases, the newly discovered syndromes actually best support a partial-responsibility excuse, and at the extreme perhaps, a claim of legal insanity. Whatever specific syndrome or disorder was operative, the excusing claim is always that the defendant was not fully rational when he or she acted. Irrationality, not the cause of it, is the predicate for excuse. A defendant suffering from an abnormality that does not render him or her sufficiently irrational should not be excused, despite the abnormality. Consequently, rather than individuating these defences by the variable that produces the excusing irrationality or internal coercion and treating the abnormality itself as the excuse, evidence of the abnormality should be used in appropriate cases to establish the unitary excuse of partial responsibility. In the case of battered-spouse syndrome, for example, evidence concerning the syndrome may strongly support the defendant's claim that she suffered from a rationality defect when she killed her spouse.

[100] I am assuming, probably *incorrectly*, that in most cases there is a reasonable alternative, such as resort to law enforcement or retreat to a shelter, which the woman can turn to with complete safety. If not, then the imminence requirement may be satisfied and self-defence would be justified.

[101] The often ongoing and long-term relationship of the spouses renders the actual situation in such cases more complicated than the brief description and analysis in the text suggest, but pursuing the implications of the complications does not alter the ultimate analysis. S. Morse, 'The Misbegotten Marriage of Soft Psychology and Bad Law', (1990) 14 *Law and Human Behavior 595*, at 601–8.

10. Dissociative States and Responsibility

Dissociative states pose vexing problems for understanding the relation between mental abnormality, *mens rea*, and partial responsibility. These states involve a disturbance or alteration in self-consciousness that ranges along a continuum from normal to severe.[102] Normal examples might be 'highway hypnosis', the phenomenon of driving quite competently for some distance without either concurrent self-consciousness or later memory of having done so. Pathological examples include fugue states, sleepwalking, or episodes of depersonalization, in which a person becomes detached from the usual sense of self and may feel like an automaton. Intense emotions such as rage or severe stress can trigger such states, which, again, can range along a continuum of severity. The standard criminal-law doctrine that responds to such states is automatism or unconsciousness.

Should these doctrines be understood as negations of *actus reus* or of *mens rea*, or as affirmative defences? On the one hand, the dissociated defendant has been able successfully to engage in conduct demonstrating accurate understanding of the environment and goal-directedness, suggesting that the bodily movements are intentional actions.[103] These are certainly not cases of reflex or physically compelled movement. Consider the case of Huey Newton. After becoming unconscious as a result of being shot in the abdomen in a conflict with police-officers, Newton was able to wrest a gun from one of his attackers, to shoot one, to run away, and finally to go to the emergency room of a nearby hospital.[104] On the other hand, in dissociative states consciousness is not fully integrated because the normal 'oversight' function, the ability self-consciously to observe oneself, is missing or severely diminished. This function is crucial because it enables us to perceive our conduct and to behave more adaptively by correcting ourselves. In moral terms, the oversight function operates as a censor: its absence facilitates 'unthinkingly' immoral behaviour.[105] Intoxication has the effect of 'weakening control' because it inhibits self-observation and censorship.

Now, whether dissociative states should be treated as negating *actus reus* or *mens rea* or as providing an affirmative defence is a normative question.[106]

---

[102] See D. Spiegel and E. Cardena, 'Disintegrated Experience: The Dissociative Disorders Revisited', (1991) 100 *Journal of Abnormal Psychology* 366.

[103] Dissociative states are often followed by amnesia. Amnesia for conduct does not necessarily entail a lack of awareness or full intentionality during the conduct. One may be fully aware and later amnesic, or dissociated with or without later amnesia.

[104] *People v. Newton*, 8 Cal. Rptr. 394 (1970).

[105] Psychoanalytic theory postulates that these two functions of consciousness are superego functions, but one need not adhere to Freud's theoretical structural model of the mind to recognize the existence and importance of these functions.

[106] For the argument that voluntariness can be treated as part of either the *actus reus* or *mens rea*, see G. Williams, *Criminal Law: The General Part* (2nd edn., London 1961), 11–15.

If responsibility requires action and action is predicated upon the capability for minimal self-consciousness, then action is probably absent in *severe* dissociative states such as sleepwalking. Similarly, if mental states such as purpose and knowledge, which are also foundational for responsibility, require self-observation, then mental states are negated. Can one have a purpose without being at all self-consciously aware of what one is doing? But if self-observation is not required for action or intention, and outright acquittal of unconscious defendants would threaten public safety, then an affirmative defence (and the possibility of post-acquittal commitment in appropriate cases) seems desirable.

Assuming that dissociation is severe, obliterating morally required, minimal self-consciousness, I am inclined to treat these cases as raising claims of affirmative defence. Although by doing so we run the risk of depriving *actus reus* or *mens rea* of their moral importance, practical concerns dictate that we treat these cases this way. First, the outcome in either case is excuse and outright acquittal, unless the crime charged includes a lesser, negligence crime. But negligence convictions are not appropriate because it is unreasonable to treat the severely dissociated person as capable of behaving as a reasonable person.[107] The defendant who acted in a dissociated state is more like a legally insane agent than he is like an agent who harmed as a result of a reflex movement, or like a rational defendant who made a mistake of fact that negated *mens rea*. In any case, justice will be done if dissociated defendants are acquitted by virtue of an affirmative defence. Second, claims of dissociation are difficult to establish, easy to fake,[108] and may be easy to raise in common cases of dangerous, violent agents whose conduct is triggered by rage and other strong emotions. Consequently, there are many reasons to place the burden of production and perhaps also the burden of persuasion on the defendant: justifiable acquittal will be rare, the defendant has the best access to the necessary evidence, and public safety will be unduly compromised by wrongful acquittals.

Before concluding discussion of dissociative states and *legal* unconsciousness, it is necessary to distinguish the psychodynamic use of 'unconscious', which carries no necessary implications for excuse, but which is sometimes confused with the legal doctrine.[109] Adherents of psychodynamic

---

[107] Cf. Hart, *Punishment and Responsibility*, above n. 5, 152–4, arguing that it is just to punish negligence only if the defendant was capable of behaving reasonably.

[108] Consider the dispute about whether the most exotic form of dissociative disorder, multiple personality, exists at all. H. Merskey, 'The Manufacture of Personalities: The Production of Multiple Personality Disorder', (1992) 160 *British Journal of Psychiatry* 327; but see D. Lewis and J. Bard, 'Multiple Personality and Forensic Issues', (1991) 14 *Psychiatric Clinics of North America* 741.

[109] See *Pohlot*, above n. 8, which succumbs to the confusion. The court uses my analysis of the legal doctrine of unconsciousness in 'Undiminished Confusion', above n. 8, to deal with the other type of claim because, unfortunately, I did not draw the distinction in that article. Happily, however, the court still reaches the right result.

psychological theories claim that much of human behaviour is caused by psychological motives that are dynamically unconscious, that is, prevented from reaching awareness because recognition of them would provoke dreadful anxiety and other unpleasant feelings. An example of such motivation might be the bank robber who robs to pay gambling debts, but who executes his crimes in a manner that virtually ensures that he will be caught. A psychodynamic formulation of the causes of his action might include the hypothesis that the robber unconsciously feels unworthy and guilty and desires, without being aware of it of course, to be punished. As a result, and again without being aware of it, he commits his robberies in an unnecessarily incompetent manner, guaranteeing capture, conviction, and punishment.

Assuming the validity of such hypotheses, what is their bearing on *mens rea* and excuse?[110] First, note that dynamically unconscious motivation does not negate *mens rea*. The hapless bank robber may not have been aware of the 'real' reason why he robbed the bank, but he surely robbed it with the full *mens rea* required by the definition of the crime. Moreover, he was fully conscious in the legal sense. Thus, dynamically unconscious causes have no bearing on the *mens rea* variant unless they can be used to support an otherwise unlikely claim that *mens rea* was not formed in fact. But the presence of such causes does not *per se* negate *mens rea* and, in virtually all cases, claims that particular unconscious motivation in fact negated *mens rea* will be simply incredible. No story about unconscious motivation, no matter how clinically or scientifically credible, should or could convince us that an armed person who walks into a bank and demands money from a teller at gunpoint lacks the *mens rea* for bank robbery.

Even if it does not negate *mens rea*, should dynamically unconscious motivation have excusing force? The robber was quite consciously rational: he knew the relevant facts about the world and his conscious reason for robbing the bank—to obtain needed money—was certainly rational, if not laudable. Thus, only if dynamically unconscious causes somehow 'compel' conduct can they excuse; but why are dynamically unconscious causes any more compelling than the other, myriad causes of behaviour of which we

---

[110] There is reason to have more than reasonable doubts about the validity of such assumptions. See S. Morse, 'Failed Explanations and Criminal Responsibility: Experts and the Unconscious', (1982) 68 *Virginia LR* 973. For the more sanguine view, see R. Bonnie and C. Slobogin, 'The Role of Mental Health Professionals in the Criminal Process: The Case for Informed Speculation', (1980) 66 *Virginia LR* 427. Treatment in the depth it deserves of the relation between dynamically unconscious motivation and responsibility goes far beyond the scope of this chapter, but a brief sketch of the answer is possible. For a far fuller treatment, see the articles cited above in this note. For a recent attempt to integrate dynamic and cognitive accounts of unconscious mental processes, see M. Power and C. Brewin, 'From Freud to Cognitive Science: A Contemporary Account of the Unconscious', (1991) 30 *British Journal of Clinical Psychology* 289.

are unaware? If the presence of dynamically unconscious causes or other unperceived causes negated responsibility, no one would ever be responsible, because such causes are always operative. As long as the agent is consciously rational and not constrained by a perceived, blameless hard choice, he or she is responsible.

11. Psychopathy and Responsibility

The traditionally conceived psychopath is firmly in touch with the reality of the environment, including the schedule of rewards and punishments that the law and ordinary folk will impose for various sorts of behaviour, and is able to engage in successful, formal, instrumental reasoning. Nevertheless, the psychopath lacks empathy and conscience,[111] traits whose absence surely predispose an agent strongly to selfish, antisocial, and perhaps criminal conduct. The question is whether psychopaths should be excused partially or wholly for their deeds. There is no hint of internal coercion in these cases, so if an excuse is to obtain, it must be irrationality.

I confess at the outset to great ambivalence about the proper moral and legal response to the psychopath's harm-doing. On the one hand, the psychopath knows what he is up to, what the rules are, and what will happen to him if he is caught for breaking them. From this vantage, the psychopath seems undoubtedly rational and many wish to hold him fully responsible if the only claim for excuse is psychopathy.[112] On the other hand, he lacks attributes that give people perhaps the best reasons not to

[111] Although the validity of the diagnostic category has been denied and there is much disagreement about the modal characteristics of psychopathy, I assume for purposes of discussion (and believe) that such people exist. The modern understanding of the concept begins with H. Cleckley, *The Mask of Sanity* (5th edn., Augusta, Ga. 1988), and the best recent, empirical work is by Robert Hare and associates. See e.g. R. Hare, T. Harpur, A. Hakstian, A. Forth, S. Hart and J. Newman, 'The Revised Psychopathy Checklist: Reliability and Factor Structure', (1990) 2 *Psychological Assessment* 338. The characteristics of the 'traditional' psychopath described in the text are not necessary criteria for the seemingly related disorder, 'Antisocial Personality Disorder', which is defined more behaviourally by the American Psychiatric Association in *DSM-III-R*, above n. 44, 342–6. See also R. Hare, S. Hart, and T. Harpur, 'Psychopathy and the *DSM-IV* Criteria for Antisocial Personality Disorder', (1991) 100 *Journal of Abnormal Psychology* 391. Nevertheless, a lack of conscience and empathy would surely predispose a person to the types of antisocial conduct that are criterial for Antisocial Personality Disorder.

[112] See e.g. Model Penal Code, above n. 14, § 4.01(2), which provides, for the purpose of excusing responsibility on the basis of mental disease or defect, that the terms mental disease or defect 'do not include an abnormality manifested only by repeated criminal or otherwise anti-social conduct'. This section is arguably meant to exclude psychopaths from those who can properly claim legal insanity. See American Law Institute, *MPC and Commentaries (Official Draft and Revised Comments) Part I Secs. 3.01–5.07* (Philadelphia 1985), 174–5. In contrast, some have argued that the psychopath should be entitled to raise a legal insanity claim as long as the diagnosis is not based *only* on repeated antisocial conduct. See *State v. Werlein*, 401NW 2d 848 (1987).

harm others and thus operate as powerful moral, emotional, and intellectual inhibitors of harming others. Viewed thus, the psychopath seems 'morally insane', unable to reason successfully and practically about moral issues, or to include moral concerns among his or her reasons for action.[113] Both characterizations are correct, of course, so the question is whether the law should adopt a standard of rationality that is 'thin', requiring only knowledge of the world and its rules and the ability to reason instrumentally in a formal sense, or one that is 'thick', requiring moral content in addition. If one adopts the former, no excuse is necessary; if the latter, partial responsibility or complete exculpation, depending on the agent's degree of psychopathy, is appropriate. I have not yet resolved this point satisfactorily for myself, so I must be content with simply raising the issue. Finally, accepting an excuse for the psychopath does not put society on a slippery slope which will inevitably lead to the claim that none of us is responsible for what we do because none of us is responsible for who we are. Once again, the predicate for responsibility is rationality, not causation. We are all caused, but we are not all irrational.

12. Conclusion

Although diminished-capacity claims are not difficult to understand if the distinction between the two variants and their differential justifications are clear, current law too often confuses or illogically limits both variants. The *mens rea* variant is straightforward and should be adopted without limitation. The partial-responsibility variant is easily predicated upon irrationality, but internal coercion provides a more problematic justification. Whether the law should adopt a generic partial-responsibility excuse is a difficult normative question, but if it does, a reasonable solution to sentencing concerns is possible.

[113] P. Arenella, 'Convicting the Morally Blameless: Reassessing the Relationship between Legal and Moral Accountability', (1992) 39 *UCLA LR* 1511; S. Wolf, 'Sanity and the Metaphysics of Responsibility', in F. Schoeman (ed.), *Responsibility, Character, and the Emotions: New Essays in Moral Psychology* (Cambridge 1987), 46. Wolf writes that, 'these characters are less than fully sane. Since [they] lack the ability to know right from wrong, they are unable to revise their characters on the basis of right and wrong, and so their deep selves lack the resources and the reasons that might have served as a basis for self-correction.' Ibid. 58. In other words, they are morally irrational in that they lack the ability to reason accurately and morally. Hampton, '*Mens Rea*', above n. 6, 14–15.

Value, Action, Mental Illness, and the Law

K. W. M. FULFORD

1. Introduction

The insanity defence, diminished responsibility, a plea of incompetency, civil commitment, contractual incapacity . . . the law is perhaps nowhere more problematic than at its points of contact with psychiatry.

The difficulties in the relationship between law and psychiatry operate at three levels. At the level of professional practice there is a plain communication gap.[1] Lawyers have little understanding of the phenomenology of mental illness, while psychiatrists have difficulty adapting their diagnostic concepts to legal criteria—the *Diagnostic and Statistical Manual* (or *DSM*), the official classification of the American Psychiatric Association, actually includes a disclaimer against its use in administrative and legal contexts.[2] This communication gap reflects a conceptual divide, between medical and legal modes of madness:[3] as a medical discipline, psychiatry is concerned with disease theories of insanity; the law, on the other hand, operates primarily with everyday concepts of rationality. But the conceptual divide itself reflects a deeper metaphysical split. Psychiatry, modelled as it is on scientific medicine, is inherently deterministic, in its theories of the unconscious as in its assumptions about brain-functioning, while the law normally assumes freedom of choice. And through this split is introduced a range of further issues: about causation, knowledge, intentionality, and the very relationship between mind and brain.

It is the middle level of difficulty, the conceptual level, with which we will be mainly concerned in this chapter. It will be argued that, tricky as the difficulties between law and psychiatry undoubtedly are, they have been compounded by the adoption of a faulty picture of the concept of mental illness. The standard view—in law no less than in psychiatry—is that mental illness should be understood on an essentially scientific model

I am grateful to Antony Duff, Christopher Howard, and the editors of this book, for their detailed and most helpful comments on an early draft of this article.

[1] See the editorial in (1990) 58 *Medico-Legal Journal* 61.

[2] American Psychiatric Association, *Diagnostic and Statistical Manual of Mental Disorders* (3rd edn., Washington 1980).

[3] N. Eastman, 'Psychiatric, Psychological, and Legal Models of Man', (1992) 15 *International Journal of Law and Psychiatry* 157.

of bodily disease, one capable in principle of analysis in terms of factual norms of bodily and mental functioning. This view, it will be suggested, is not so much wrong as incomplete. Facts and failure of functioning are indeed important elements in the conceptual structure of medicine. But so also are the less well-recognized elements of value and failure of action. These latter elements, moreover, although relatively problem-free in physical medicine, may be highly problematic in psychiatry, and not least at its points of contact with law. As a strategy for tackling the problems in this area, then, modelling mental illness on bodily disease amounts to focusing on the wrong half of the conceptual framework of medicine. We should be seeking rather to make explicit and to clarify the elements of value and of action-failure in the meaning of illness.

The extraordinary range of the phenomena of mental illness is often neglected in discussions on the relationship between law and psychiatry. Hence this chapter starts with an outline of these phenomena. These amount to what the philosopher Gilbert Ryle would have called a map of the 'logical geography'.[4] Standard accounts of mental illness—fact/function accounts—are shown to be inconsistent with certain important features of this map. Adding the elements of value and action-failure, on the other hand, provides a more consistent account. In the context of this more complete, or 'full-field' theory of mental illness, the significance of these two elements—value and action-failure—for our understanding of the relationship between law and psychiatry is then explored. Broadly, a full-field theory of mental illness is shown to bridge the conceptual divide between the two disciplines, this in turn providing a basis for improved communication at the level of day-to-day practice. These results are achieved, however, only at the cost of facing squarely the metaphysical difficulties that underpin practice in this area. It is argued finally, therefore, that in tackling these difficulties, philosophy and psychiatry should move towards a closer working partnership of the kind which already exists between psychiatry and science.

2. The Phenomena of Mental Illness

We begin, then, with the phenomena of mental illness. These are shown schematically in the Figure at the end of this chapter, together with a glossary of case-vignettes and brief definitions. It should be said straight away that as a map of psychiatry this is not intended to reflect a well-developed theory of the classification of mental disorders. That we lack such a theory is itself a reflection of the inadequacy of current accounts of

---

[4] Gilbert Ryle, *The Concept of Mind* (London 1949).

the concept of mental illness.[5] None the less, the map does represent a number of features of the conceptual terrain of psychiatry which any theory of the meaning of mental illness must explain. *Any* theory, note, since explaining the features of the map of psychiatry is a criterion for the success of philosophical theory, a criterion which is neutral with regard to whether mental illness turns out, ultimately, to be a valid concept. We will be looking at some of the arguments for and against mental illness in the next section. But a propsychiatry theory, endorsing the validity of mental illness, must explain why the map has the features it has; while an anti-psychiatry theory, denying the validity of the concept, must explain why the map appears to have these features.[6]

A first and perhaps most obvious feature of the psychiatric terrain, set out in this way, is the sheer diversity of mental disorders. At the centre of the map are the psychoses. Characterized by delusions, hallucinations, and certain kinds of disordered thinking, these are severe disorders which are central to psychiatry in the sense (*inter alia*) that they correspond broadly with the traditional 'insane'. The defining characteristic of psychotic disorders is what is called 'lack of insight'. In this context this means that psychotic patients, as against non-psychotic patients, characteristically lack insight into their disordered mental condition. With a phobia, say, the patient will normally complain of his irrational fear, rather as one might complain of a pain. But with delusions of persecution, for example, a typical psychotic symptom, what is wrong, from the patient's perspective, is not that he is ill but that people are persecuting him.

Psychotic disorders include depressive (with depressed mood) and manic (with elevated mood) psychoses, paranoid states (relatively fixed delusional states, not necessarily of persecution), and the schizophrenias. These disorders are sometimes called 'functional psychoses' to distinguish them from 'organic psychoses'. In the latter, psychotic symptoms are associated with what are called in psychiatry cognitive impairments—memory loss and falling IQ (as in dementia), or disturbances in the level of consciousness (as in acute states of intoxication). The organic disorders are due to gross brain pathology (tumours, metabolic disturbances, etc.), and thus connect through neurology to physical medicine (off the map to the right). The remaining disorders are all non-psychotic: counting anticlockwise, they include disorders of affect (anxiety disorders and non-psychotic depression); hysterical disorders (in which apparently physical symptoms—blindness, paralysis, amnesia—are produced by psychological causes); obsessive-compulsive disorders (e.g. compulsive hand-washing, obsessive

---

[5] K. W. M. Fulford, 'Closet Logics: Hidden Conceptual Elements in the DSM and ICD Classifications of Mental Disorders', in J. Z. Sadler, M. Schwartz, and O. Wiggins (eds.), *Philosophical Perspectives on Psychiatric Diagnostic Classification* (Baltimore, forthcoming).
[6] K. W. M. Fulford, *Moral Theory and Medical Practice* (Cambridge 1989), ch. 1.

counting—like a bad case of getting a tune stuck in your head); mental
'trauma' (acute, as in 'battle fatigue'; chronic, as in grief); behavioural
disorders (conduct disorders in children, psychopathy in adults); appetitive,
or biological-drive disorders (anorexia; sexual problems, including decreased
libido and anomalies of sexual-object choice; alcoholism and other addic-
tions); and mental subnormality and the developmental disorders of
childhood (such as delayed sphincter control, walking, and talking).

It is important to see that the diversity here is in the disorders themselves, the experiences and behaviours by which they are characterized,
rather than in their underlying causes. Psychiatry stands in this respect in
contrast to physical medicine. Disease theory in physical medicine, built up
from scientific knowledge of bodily pathology, infectious agents, social,
psychological, and other causal factors, is highly elaborate. But the actual
symptoms of physical illness, although in their particulars varied enough,
fall into no more than three principal categories: sensation (e.g. vertigo,
nausea), movement (including paralysis), and perception (e.g. blindness).
The conceptual field to be covered by a theory of physical illness is thus
relatively circumscribed. The symptoms of mental illness, on the other
hand, are considerably more varied. They may indeed include disturbances
of sensation, movement, and perception. But they extend to disorders of
such conceptually diverse phenomena as memory, affect, volition, belief,
thought, appetite, and desire.

A second feature of the psychiatric terrain represented by the map is a
marked variation in the extent to which different conditions or groups of
conditions are uncontentiously regarded as mental illnesses. This variation
is partly as between mental illness and other kinds of pathology: dementia
is an illness but is part-way to physical illness; grief is like trauma;
psychopathy, being long-term and relatively unvarying, is closer to disability than disease; mental subnormality *is* a disability. But the variation is
also as between illness and conditions which are not properly disorders (in
a medical sense) at all. The psychotic disorders are the least equivocal in
this respect. They have been widely, though (like many physical disorders)
not universally, regarded as illnesses from classical times[7] and in many
different cultures.[8] Obsessive-compulsive disorders, too, and anxiety and
depression, to the extent that they occur in the absence of stress and of loss
respectively, are readily thought of as illnesses.[9] But hysteria merges with
malingering, conduct disorders and psychopathy with delinquency, and
alcoholism with drunkenness.

This variation in the status of disorders as mental illnesses is medico-
legally significant in that it correlates closely with the variation in the

[7] Ibid., ch. 10.   [8] J. K. Wing, *Reasoning about Madness* (Oxford 1978).
[9] *Report of the Committee on Mentally Abnormal Offenders*, Chair: Lord Butler, Cmnd.
6244 (1975).

status of these conditions as excuses in law. Thus, psychotic disorders are, again, the central case. Of all mental illnesses they are the least contentious example of mental illness as a distinct species of legal excuse.[10] And it is psychotic disorders which are most likely to be treated on an involuntary basis under civil law.[11] Other severe mental disorders, less centrally placed in the map, are more likely to be introduced in mitigation than as an excuse—a phobia, say. Correspondingly, involuntary treatment, even of a life-threatening disorder such as anorexia, is highly contentious.[12] And the legal status of more peripherally placed disorders may be dubious indeed: psychopathy—'moral insanity' in the nineteenth century—is notorious in this respect;[13] but the status of hysteria[14] and sexual disorders[15] has been widely debated; and intoxication has been thought by many, from Aristotle onwards,[16] actually to increase, rather than to excuse from, responsibility.

A third feature of the map of psychiatry is its marked evaluative colouring compared with physical medicine. This is partly a difference between illness (the patient's subjective experience) and disease (scientific knowledge of specific illnesses and their causes). Illness is the dominant concept in psychiatry, disease is the dominant concept in physical medicine. But even comparing like with like, mental illness with physical *illness*, it is the former which is the more value-laden. This is evident in various ways: the uncertain status of a number of conditions at the edge of the map (described above) is in part an uncertainty between medical and moral categories (disorder as against delinquency, and so forth); the diagnostic categories employed in psychiatry are often ethically problematic (hysteria, homosexuality, and psychopathy, as just noted); some disorders are actually defined by reference to social-evaluative norms (e.g. the *DSM-III*, although a self-consciously scientific classification, defines conduct disorder, and certain sexual disorders, by reference to social-evaluative norms);[17] and much

---

[10] N. Walker, *Crime and Insanity in England* (Edinburgh 1967).

[11] T. Sensky, T. Hughes, and S. Hirsch, 'Compulsory Psychiatric Treatment in the Community, Part 1. A Controlled Study of Compulsory Community Treatment with Extended Leave under the Mental Health Act: Special Characteristics of Patients Treated and Impact of Treatment', (1991) 158 *British Journal of Psychiatry* 792.

[12] E. H. Kluge, 'The Ethics of Forced Feeding in Anorexia Nervosa: A Response to Hebert and Weingarten', (1991) 144 *Canadian Medical Association Journal* 1121.

[13] C. Elliot and G. Gillet, 'Moral Insanity and Practical Reason', (1992) 5 *Philosophical Psychology* 53.

[14] T. S. Szasz, 'Malingering: "Diagnosis" or Social Condemnation', (1956) 76 *Archives of Neurology and Psychiatry* 432.

[15] J. Bancroft, in S. Bloch and P. Chodoff (eds.), *Psychiatric Ethics* (2nd edn., Oxford 1991), ch. 11.

[16] Aristotle, *Nichomachean Ethics* 3 (ed. J. L. Ackrill, London 1973).

[17] American Psychiatric Association, *Diagnostic and Statistical Manual of Mental Disorders*, above n. 2, 280.

of the pressure to include a number of new diagnostic entities in *DSM-IV* has actually been described by the authors of this classification as reflecting pragmatic considerations.[18]

We will see in the next section that this feature of the map of psychiatry is one which has received considerable attention in the literature on the meaning of mental illness. There is a further feature, however, which, though actually more significant conceptually, has been relatively neglected, namely the remarkable oddity of some psychiatric symptoms. Again, psychotic disorders come out centrally in this respect. Without actually suffering, say, depression, phobia, or obsession, we can gain some understanding of these phenomena as extensions of ordinary experience, much indeed as we can of pain, vertigo, and other symptoms of bodily illness. But psychotic symptoms include such existentially paradoxical phenomena as thought insertion— having thoughts in your head, and which you are (in this sense) thinking, yet which you experience as the thoughts of someone else (e.g. case 2 in the glossary). This is a key symptom of schizophrenia, a major psychotic disorder. More generally, hallucinations, although taken to be real by the patient, may be bizarre—visual perceptions outside the visual field, for example. And delusions, although commonly false beliefs, may take other more remarkable logical forms. They may be true beliefs (beliefs known to be true at the time of diagnosis,[19] value judgments (depressive delusions of guilt may be factual or evaluative in form),[20] or the paradoxical delusion of mental illness.[21] There is a danger, therefore, a danger which we will find later has been realized in the case of delusions, that the strangeness of these symptoms will be glossed over, that they will be assimilated falsely to less obscure phenomena, more adaptable to the requirements of an exclusively scientific model of disease.

3. Theories of Mental Illness

As noted at the start of the last section, there has been a wide-ranging debate about the meaning, indeed the very validity, of the concept of mental illness.[22] Much of this debate can be understood directly in terms

[18] A. Frances, M. B. First, T. A. Widiger, G. M. Miele, S. M. Tilly, W. W. Davis, and H. A. Pincus, 'An A–Z Guide to DSM-IV Conundrums', (1991) 100 *Journal Of Abnormal Psychology* 407.

[19] K. Vauhkonen, *On the Pathogenesis of Morbid Jealousy, with Special Reference to the Personality Traits of and Interaction between Jealous Patients and their Spouses* (Copenhagen 1968).

[20] K. W. M. Fulford, 'Evaluative Delusions : Their Significance for Philosophy and Psychiatry', (1991) 159 *British Journal of Psychiatry* (supplement 14) 108.

[21] Fulford, *Moral Theory and Medical Practice*, above n. 6, 204–5.

[22] A. Clare, 'The Disease Concept in Psychiatry', in P. Hill, R. Murray, and A. Thorley (eds.), *Essentials of Postgraduate Psychiatry* (New York 1979).

of the features of the map of psychiatry just outlined. That there should be a debate at all is a product of the relatively uncertain status of some conditions as mental illnesses—the conditions on the edge of the map. It has been widely, if tacitly, assumed that difficulties in the *use* of the term mental illness reflect obscurity of *meaning*.[23] Then again, the wide diversity of views which have been expressed about the meaning of mental illness reflects the diversity of forms of mental illness. Indeed, many of these views can be understood as focusing on one part of the map while neglecting others. Thus mental illnesses have been thought to be nothing more than learned abnormalities of behaviour,[24] or, reflecting the stress-related disorders, a normal response to an abnormal situation.[25] Then again, a number of authors have argued that psychiatry is merely a device adopted by society for the control of its more troublesome deviants.[26] Each of these theories embodies an important truth about mental illness: learning theory has led to valuable psychological treatments; life difficulties can be important in the aetiology of all mental disorders, not just 'adjustment reactions'; and psychiatric diagnoses are notoriously at risk of being misused as a means of social control.[27] But as theories of the meaning of mental illness, all of these fail to capture the features of the conceptual map of psychiatry as a whole.

More comprehensive theories have been developed by both opponents and supporters of mental illness. Among the former is Szasz.[28] Drawing on the relatively value-laden nature of mental illness, he argues that the concept as a whole is an invalid extension of the concept of physical illness. Mental illness, he says, is defined by reference to ethical and legal norms, whereas physical disorders are defined by objective norms of bodily structure and functioning established by straightforward scientific means. In arguing against mental illness, therefore, Szasz effectively collapses mental disorders to the moral categories off to the left of the map. The corresponding arguments of the supporters of mental illness, on the other hand, effectively collapse mental disorders the other way, to physical disorders. This is because both sides in the debate, those for as well as those against mental illness, take the mark of validity to be conformity to physical illness. Hence, where Szasz regards the evaluative connotations of mental illness as essential, his opponents—Kendell,[29] for example, and Roth and

---

[23] Fulford, *Moral Theory and Medical Practice*, above n. 6, ch. 1.
[24] H. J. Eysenck, 'Classification and the Problem of Diagnosis', in his *Handbook of Abnormal Psychology* (London 1960), ch. 1.
[25] R. D. Laing, *The Politics of Experience* (London 1967).
[26] M. Foucault, *Madness and Civilization: A History of Insanity in the Age of Reason* (New York 1973).
[27] S. Bloch and P. Chodoff, *Russia's Political Hospitals* (Southampton 1977).
[28] T. S. Szasz, 'The Myth of Mental Illness', (1960) 15 *American Psychologist* 113.
[29] R. E. Kendell, 'The Concept of Disease and its Implications for Psychiatry', (1975) 127 *British Journal of Psychiatry* 305.

Kroll[30]—have sought to define them away, to show that mental illness is 'really' as scientific a concept as physical illness. Boorse[31] has developed an interesting variant of this approach by exploiting the prima-facie distinction between concepts of disease (incorporating specialized medical knowledge) and illness (reflecting the patient's actual experience). Illness, he says, whether in physical medicine or psychiatry, is indeed a value-laden notion; it is just a disease which is serious enough to be incapacitating. Disease, though, as the more fundamental notion, is defined, ultimately, by reference to reduced life and/or reproductive expectations, these being objective criteria of disturbed functioning, bodily or mental. The conclusion of all these arguments, however, to the extent that they depend on showing that mental illness is the same as physical illness, is not that mental illness is a legitimate species of illness in its own right, but that it is physical illness after all.

Even these more comprehensive theories are partial, therefore. Szasz and the anti-psychiatrists focus on the evaluative aspects of the concept of mental illness; Boorse and the pro-psychiatrists focus on its connections with physical illness. We will see later that both these positions have been influential, directly or indirectly, in discussions about the relationship between law and psychiatry. As a conceptual debate, however, this polarization nicely illustrates Wittgenstein's view of philosophical problems as delusions (we should call them rather illusions) of language; that is, problems arising from a tendency to take too narrow or one-sided a view of the concepts involved in a particular area of discourse.[32] In medicine, specifically, the importance of science has made it natural that both sides of the debate about mental illness should have assumed a scientific paradigm of physical illness, relying respectively either on the similarities (pro-psychiatry) or differences (anti-psychiatry) between it and mental illness. If we take Wittgenstein's 'cure', however, and look at the actual use which is made of the concept—as set out in the map of psychiatry—we see that what is needed is an account which does justice equally to the similarities and differences between the two kinds of illness.

It is considerations of this kind which have led to the appearance in recent years of what I have called elsewhere 'full-field', as opposed to 'science-half-field', views of the conceptual structure of medicine.[33] According to theories of this kind, the logical elements emphasized in conventional theories—fact, disease theory, and disturbance of functioning—are indeed

[30] M. Roth and J. Kroll, *The Reality of Mental Illness* (Cambridge 1986).
[31] C. Boorse, 'On the Distinction between Disease and Illness', (1975) 5 *Philosophy and Public Affairs* 49.
[32] L. Wittgenstein, *Philosophical Investigations* (2nd edn., trans. Anscombe, Oxford 1958).
[33] K. W. M. Fulford, 'The Concept of Disease', in S. Bloch and P. Chodoff (eds.), *Psychiatric Ethics* (2nd edn., Oxford 1991), ch. 6.

important, but they amount to an incomplete (or half-field) view of the conceptual structure of medicine. Full-field theories add the element of value to that of fact, the patient's experience of illness to medical disease theories, and an analysis of the experience of illness in terms of incapacity or failure of action to the analysis of disease in terms of failure of function.

We shall be looking at how theories of this kind work in more detail in the remainder of this chapter. But once the illusion of an exclusively scientific medicine is broken, they are not implausible. Etymologically, illness and disease, whatever their scientific content, are value terms: and sociologists have long emphasized the value-laden natures of these concepts.[34] Similarly, from a patient's rather than a doctor's perspective, what matters is the experience of illness.[35] And this experience consists in incapacity; this is what it is to be a patient rather than an agent. Moreover, there are close conceptual links between action and function: writing the words on this page, for example, might be thought of in the context of medical science as my hand, arm, nerves, etc. functioning; but in everyday contexts it would be more natural to think of it as an action I am performing. Given links of this kind, therefore, if disturbance of function is indeed important in the conceptual structure of medicine, as is recognized in conventional theories, then disturbance of action should be as well.

In the next two sections, then, we will consider how these full-field theories can contribute to better understanding of the phenomena of mental illness and hence of the difficulties in the relationship between psychiatry and law. We will look first at what we can learn from the element of value in these theories, and then turn to the analysis of the experience of illness as action-failure.

4. Mental Illness, Value, and the Law

There has been a considerable interplay between the debate about mental illness and discussions of the relationship between law and psychiatry. In this section we will explore this interplay with particular reference to the accounts given by conventional and full-field views of the status of mental illness as a distinct species of legal excuse. There are of course other closely related questions, such as the competence of the mentally ill in a number of contexts in civil law, of fitness to stand trial, of mitigation at the stage of sentencing, and so on. Each of these raises important issues in its own right. But the intuitive status of mental illness as an excuse has been

---

[34] P. Sedgewick, 'Illness—Mental and Otherwise', (1973) 3 *The Hastings Center Studies* 19.

[35] D. Lockyer, *Symptoms and Illness: The Cognitive Organization of Disorder* (London 1981).

subject to a number of specific legal interpretations which help to focus discussions of the relationship between law and psychiatry.

The essential practical difficulty arising from the status of mental illness as an excuse is where to draw the line. It will be recalled from our map of psychiatry that psychotic disorders, at the centre, are intuitively the paradigm case. But this shifts the line-drawing difficulty from mental illness in general to psychotic disorders in particular. The radical anti-mental-illness arguments of Szasz and others represent one response to this difficulty: to dissolve it, by abolishing the very distinction between normal and mentally abnormal offenders. Wootton, an agnostic rather than an atheist about mental illness, would also abolish the distinction, except that where Szasz would collapse disease to criminality, she would collapse criminality to disease.[36] Lord Denning's views in *Bratty* v. *Attorney-General for Northern Ireland* have something of this. He argues that the notion of 'disease of the mind' within the McNaghten Rules should include more that just the psychoses.[37] These indeed 'are clearly diseases of the mind'. But '*any* mental disorder which has manifested itself in violence and is prone to recur is a disease of the mind. At any rate it is the sort of disease for which a person *should be detained* in hospital . . .'[38]

We have already touched on some of the theoretical arguments against eliminativist positions such as these. But, as Moore has pointed out, it is their dissonance with the demands of practical reality which is perhaps the strongest argument of all.[39] If there is a theoretical argument to show that a deeply depressed mother, who kills her baby in the belief that he is a child of Satan, should be denied treatment, then so much the worse for the theoretical argument. Equally, if there is a theoretical argument to show that the dissident, even the violent dissident, let alone the merely delinquent, should be denied the right to punishment under the law, then, again, so much the worse for the theoretical argument. Scepticism challenges us with the trickiness of the concept of mental illness. This *is* important practically. It can lead, as the Mental Health Movement in Italy showed, to liberalization of the treatment of the mentally ill.[40] But as the Italian experience has also shown, the real importance of scepticism is to remind us of the vulnerability of psychiatry to the abuses represented by either sceptical extreme, extreme criminalizing of mental disorder or extreme medicalizing of crime.

[36] B. Wootton, *Social Science and Social Pathology* (London 1959).
[37] *Bratty* v. *Attorney-General for Northern Ireland* [1961] 3 All ER 523, at 527 ff.
[38] Ibid. (emphasis added).
[39] M. S. Moore, 'The Legal View of Persons', in his *Law and Psychiatry: Rethinking the Relationship* (Cambridge 1984).
[40] S. Ramon and M. G. Ginichedda (eds.), *Psychiatry in Transition: The British and Italian Experiences* (London 1988).

The conventional science-based response to scepticism, on the other hand, although no less subject to theoretical objections, of the kind outlined earlier, would seem to offer definite attractions from a practical point of view. It holds out the prospect, at least in principle, of allowing expert psychiatric evidence to be based on determinate factual information, thus putting the psychiatrist on the same footing as any other medical expert. And it holds out this prospect apparently consistently with the intuitive status of psychotic disorder as the central case of mental illness as an excuse. The Butler Committee, for example, took just this line: acknowledging the central place of psychotic disorders, it argued that psychiatrists, although indeed unable to give a satisfactory overall definition of psychosis, could none the less identify with a high degree of inter-subjective agreement (hence, objectivity) individual psychotic symptoms.[41] Philosophers, too, have adopted a similar approach. Flew, for example, concerned with the value-laden nature of much psychiatric diagnosis, identifies the falsity of psychotic delusions as providing an objective test for the presence at least of serious mental illness, and hence, in Flew's words, 'the one sure defence against the abuse of psychiatry'.[42] Again, Moore argues that although the medical concepts—including the notion of psychotic mental disorder—are indeed inherently value-laden, they embody only what he calls a 'thin theory' of the good; that is, they are defined by reference to 'goods' which are so basic that everyone must acknowledge them as necessary for whatever particular ends they may individually embrace.[43]

A full-field account shows, however, that it is specifically from a *practical* point of view that these conventional science-based accounts are most clearly misdirected; and misdirected in much the same way that the eliminativist accounts of the extreme sceptic are misdirected, namely that they turn their back on the real difficulties. To see why this is so we need to look briefly at the explanation suggested by such accounts of the relatively value-laden nature of mental illness (the third of the features represented by the map of psychiatry). In the science-half-field view, either these value connotations have to be eliminated (as pro-psychiatrists have argued), or mental illness itself has to be eliminated (as the anti-psychiatrists have argued). But in a full-field account it turns out that the evaluative connotations of mental illness and the factual connotations of physical illness are both legitimate reflections of the status of illness itself as a value term. The key point here is that people differ more widely in their evaluations of experiences such as anxiety (a typical symptom of mental illness) than of experiences such as pain (a typical symptom of physical illness): for

---

[41] See *Report of the Committee on Mentally Abnormal Offenders*, above n. 9.
[42] A. Flew, *Crime or Disease?* (New York 1973).
[43] See Moore, 'The Legal View of Persons', above n. 39.

most people anything but the mildest physical pain is at best a necessary evil; yet many people enjoy horror films, or seek out the thrill of dangerous sports, while others avoid such experiences at all costs. But as Hare,[44] Urmson,[45] and others have pointed out, differences of this kind lead to variations in the strength of the evaluative connotations even of such all-purpose value terms as good and bad: thus 'good apple' has mainly factual connotations because most people in most contexts judge sweet, clean-skinned, etc., apples to be good. Hence, for this reason alone, if illness is a value term, we should expect it to have more marked evaluative connotations used (as in psychiatry) of experiences such as anxiety, compared with its use (as in physical medicine) of experiences such as pain: 'mental illness' is like 'good picture' in this respect, 'physical illness' like 'good apple'.[46]

According to a full-field interpretation of the medical concepts, then, the relatively factual connotations of the concept of physical illness are due, not to it being a purely factual concept, but to the value judgments it expresses being relatively uncontentious. This is the feature which conventional science-half-field theories, such as those of Boorse, are able to exploit. Similarly, Moore's 'thin theory' of the good, like 'moral descriptivism' before it, is linked to those goods about which more or less everyone agrees. But this brings us back to the practical limitations of theories of this kind in relation to mental illness. For mental illness, on this view, differs from physical illness precisely in that the value judgments it expresses are relatively contentious. This *is* the difficulty (or one important difficulty) about mental illness. This is why it has relatively value-laden connotations. Hence, in relation to mental illness, a thin theory at best limits the diagnosis of mental illness to conditions which are uncontentiously illnesses. This can indeed be important practically, as a protection against the over-medicalization of crime. But the evaluative connotations of mental illness, reflecting as they do *legitimate* differences in our evaluations of phenomena such as anxiety, represent a *legitimate* variation in what counts as mental illness. Hence a 'thin' theory, just to the extent that it protects against crime becoming over-medicalized, increases the risk of disease becoming over-criminalized.

The idea that medical diagnosis involves an essential element of value, on the other hand, may seem to err the other way. This is Boorse's starting-point: in the absence of scientific criteria for the presence of disease, he claims, there is no limit to the medicalization of life's problems, including crime.[47] Much the same objection used to be raised by moral descriptivists

[44] R. M. Hare, 'Descriptivism', (1963) 49 *Proceedings of the British Academy* 115.
[45] J. O. Urmson, 'On Grading', (1950) 59 *Mind* 145.
[46] K. W. M. Fulford, 'Is Medicine a Branch of Ethics?', in G. Gillett and A. Peacocke (eds.), *Personality and Insanity* (Oxford 1988), ch. 8.
[47] Boorse, 'On the Distinction between Disease and Illness', above n. 31.

against non-descriptivism, that in insisting on the logical separation of 'is' and 'ought', it made any value judgment logically possible. However, as Hare and other non-descriptivists regularly pointed out, the logical separation of description and evaluation leaves the full range of *psychological* limits to our value judgments intact.[48] This is the case, too, with mental illness, understood as an evaluative concept. It is just not true that all judgments of mental illness, even to the extent that such judgments hinge on negative value judgments, are equally plausible: the variation in the status of conditions as mental illnesses across the map of psychiatry is a direct reflection of this. Moreover, far from leaving psychiatry vulnerable to abuse, recognizing and making explicit the evaluative logical element in the diagnosis of mental illness can be shown to be protective precisely because it makes plain the nature of the difficulty.

We can get a clearer picture of how all this works out by considering the implications of a full-field view for the role of the psychiatrist as an expert witness. At first glance, the suggestion that there is an irreducibly evaluative element in the conceptual structure of medicine, and one which is essentially open and contentious in respect of diagnoses of mental illness, may seem to have left the role of the psychiatrist as an expert witness considerably compromised. Under the rules of evidence, an expert is essentially an expert to the facts. These need not be arcane: but the expert should be 'acquainted with' some area of knowledge with which the average jury person chosen at random—the person on the Clapham Omnibus—is unlikely to be familiar. The expert indeed was originally a 'man of science': and this is how psychiatrists, at least, understand their role, as drawing on their 'special knowledge to help the court'.[49] There is thus a prima-facie conflict between the central idea of the expert as an expert to fact, and the central claim of this section that there is an important element of evaluation in diagnoses of mental illness.

We should remember, though, that a full-field view is just that: a *full*-field view. It does not exclude or diminish the importance of science in medicine. Rather, it clarifies its proper role. At a practical level, then, much will go on as before. Anything which is genuinely empirical in psychiatric evidence will be as fully represented in a full-field theory as in any science-half-field theory. And the potential of psychiatric testimony at a straightforwardly descriptive level should not be underestimated. In the first place, the psychiatrist is 'acquainted with' a variety of mental states which, if only because they are unusual, are unlikely to fall within the experience of the average member of a jury: we noted earlier that this is true especially of the psychotic symptoms, such as thought insertion, which are jurisprudentially crucial. However, even with more familiar conditions,

---

[48] R. M. Hare, *The Language of Morals* (Oxford 1952).
[49] M. G. Gelder, D. Gath, and R. Mayou, *Oxford Textbook of Psychiatry* (Oxford 1983), 740.

such as grief, it is not always intuitively obvious how different people will feel, react, and behave. The psychiatrist has expert knowledge at least of the range of possibilities. Some of these may indeed be counterintuitive: for instance, anxiety, although normally sexually inhibiting, may not be so in certain abnormal states.[50] Again, there is often a good deal of relevant detail that the expert can fill in. Depression, for example, whether or not pathological, affects people in widely different ways. A standardized method of assessment, such as the Beck Depression Inventory,[51] can help to give a clear picture of the range and severity of the symptoms in a particular case. Instruments of this kind, like all 'tests', have to be appropriately chosen and administered, and their results interpreted—all roles for the expert. Used properly, moreover, they have the further advantage of being of known 'reliability', a measure of inter-subjective agreement. Hence an expert can say how likely it is that the evidence will be consistent in a given area. An important general point in this respect is that many symptoms of psychiatric illness (and especially psychotic symptoms) are as reliably identifiable as the signs and symptoms of bodily illness:[52] psychiatry, contrary to popular opinion, is thus at no disadvantage here. Standardized instruments, moreover, may help to reveal hidden difficulties: in dementia, for example, the true extent of the intellectual loss may be masked by a relative preservation of social skills—standard tests of IQ will reveal this. Conversely, as is often the case with people with learning difficulties (or mental handicap), such tests may reveal the true extent of their abilities.

With testimony of this kind, we can think of the psychiatrist as being on a par with the forensic scientist, giving evidence on, say, the presence of a bloodstain. In so far as any description is value-free, the psychiatrist, like any other expert, can offer testimony without raising questions of value, let alone medical value. But the psychiatrist can also give evidence which is on a par with that of the forensic pathologist, that is, as to the presence of diseases. To see why this is so we need to look briefly at the account which a full-field theory gives of the relationship between illness and disease. As conventionally conceived, for example by Boorse, illness is defined by reference to 'scientific' concepts of disease. But once both illness and disease are recognized to be evaluative in nature this relationship is reversed, the meaning of disease being derived from that of illness rather than vice versa. This reversal of the relationship between illness and disease depends on the general point about the logic of value terms noted earlier in this section, namely that the strength of the factual connotations

[50] H. M. C. Warwick and P. M. Salkovskis, 'Unwanted Erections in Obsessive-Compulsive Disorder', (1990) 157 *British Journal of Psychiatry* 919.
[51] A. T. Beck, C. H. Ward, M. Mendelson, J. Mock, and J. Erbaugh, 'An Inventory for Measuring Depression', (1961) 18 *Archives of General Psychiatry* 561.
[52] A. Clare, 'The Disease Concept in Psychiatry', above n. 22.

of a value term reflects the extent to which the criteria for the value judgment it expresses are settled or agreed upon. In a full-field view, just as this explains the difference in value connotations between mental and physical illness, so it helps to explain the difference in value connotations between illness and disease. According to this approach, illness, with its more marked evaluative connotations, is used of any condition that may be negatively evaluated as an illness, while disease, with its more factual connotations, is restricted to the subclass of these conditions which are so evaluated by most people most of the time. This subclass of course includes not only symptomatically defined diseases (such as migraine) but also diseases defined by the causes of these conditions, including those defined by disturbances of bodily or mental functioning. But the logical relationship, the flow of meaning, is from the experience of illness to underlying causal condition, not, as in the science-half-field view, from underlying causal condition to illness.

There are a number of indications that, notwithstanding the hegemony of science in medicine, this is how these terms are actually used.[53] To return, then, to psychiatric evidence: while questions of value are implicit in testimony as to the presence of disease (as distinct from conditions defined in purely descriptive terms), such questions are by definition largely uncontentious, and, hence, as indeed in much of physical medicine, can be ignored. In practice, therefore, whatever the objections of the extreme anti-psychiatry movement, evidence that someone is suffering from, say, schizophrenia, is in this respect on a par with evidence that they are suffering from migraine (a symptomatically defined bodily disease).

Up to this point, a full-field view has much the same consequences—for the psychiatrist as an expert witness—as the conventional, science-based view, and indeed as 'thin' theories of the nature of illness as a value term. To the extent that psychiatric diagnoses involve genuinely empirical questions, to the extent even that such diagnoses involve questions of value which are genuinely uncontentious, the role of the psychiatrist as an expert witness is the same in a full-field theory as in either of these more familiar alternatives. And her role even up to this point may be difficult enough: the courts often ask for certainty where nothing more than tentative opinion is possible; or for a categorical (yes/no) interpretation of data which is continuously variable; or for a straight-line causal account of events which are inextricably cross-linked. But the essential advance represented by a full-field view is to see that in addition to such empirical difficulties, psychiatric diagnoses may also involve genuine difficulties of evaluation.

This is not to say that the psychiatrist has *no* role as an expert witness in relation even to difficulties of this kind. There are difficult jurisprudential

[53] Fulford, *Moral Theory and Medical Practice*, above n. 6, ch. 5.

questions here, not indeed limited to psychiatry: about the role of experts on questions of public morality—on the difference between art and pornography, for example; and about the respective roles of the expert and the jury in reflecting, or leading, the attitudes of society. An expert may be consulted on what is a 'good' picture; and would consider herself in this an expert on intrinsic merit as well as on value in the market-place. Beauty, in the well-worn phrase, may be in the eye of the beholder; and there is a sense in which the expert cannot dictate individual taste; but there is also a sense in which the eye can be trained, sensibilities refined, and judgment developed; and all in ways which are not reducible to mere consensus. Aesthetic values, then, may be a 'matter of acquaintance'; and if aesthetic, why not other values, medical, or indeed, moral? After all, in totalitarian societies, religious or ideological, there is no perceived conflict in the idea of an expert on the correctness of one's views: there are indeed experts, mostly self-styled to be sure, on 'political correctness' in many university campuses in America at the present time.

Still, granted all this, it remains an unavoidable consequence of a full-field view of medicine that we should expect questions of value to arise in the diagnosis of mental illness which, at least in a liberal society, are legitimately open in the sense that they reflect differences in individual value-systems. At this point, then, the expert may have to defer to a jury. Rather as in a flower show, the expert may be able to identify a particular species (a question of fact), or tell us whether a particular bloom is a good example of that species by reference to Horticultural Society criteria of excellence (mutually agreed criteria of value); but the expert would be beyond her brief, in a horticulturally liberal community of gardeners, in trying to dictate which species or blooms we should individually admire.

As we noted earlier in this section, the idea that there may be questions of value of this kind involved in psychiatric diagnosis is not a recipe for anarchy. Even with aesthetic values, as in the gardening case, there will be a degree of consistency within a given community. The point is rather that the determination of questions of value of this kind should not turn, uniquely, on the values of one individual or indeed class of individuals. And the acknowledgement of this, far from leading to the abuse of psychiatry through the indeterminacy of judgments of mental illness, could have a number of salutary consequences. We have already seen that it could help to clarify the kinds of question to which, as an expert on the 'facts', the psychiatrist can legitimately be expected to testify. But it could also help to improve the case-by-case consistency of the law: if questions of value are not recognized for what they are, false conflations and artificial distinctions are that much more likely to occur. So one role for the (philosophically minded) psychiatrist may be to flag the relevant questions of value when they arise. And this could in turn help actually to reduce the likelihood of the abuse of psychiatry. I have argued elsewhere that although administrative, political, and professional factors may be important in abuse becoming widespread, the underlying vulnerability of psychiatry to abuse arises in part from a failure to recognize the evaluative element in psychiatric diagnosis for what it is.[54] This has led to the appropriation to psychiatry of a spuriously scientific authority. It is as a protection against such abuses that in civil law decisions about compulsory psychiatric treatment, instead of being left to psychiatrists alone, are shared (with a social worker, relative, and so on). The effect of this can be understood in full-field terms as providing a balance of evaluative considerations in considering questions of capacity. Similarly, then, in criminal law, deferring in part to a jury is not a dilution of the authority of psychiatry but a method by which, to the extent that psychiatric diagnoses turn on open, contentious questions of value, they may indeed be weighed in a liberal ethical scale.

It may now be said: are we not short-changing the psychiatrist as an expert witness? Surely, like any other medical expert, the psychiatrist can go beyond, as it were, surface appearances to underlying causes, beyond illness and symptomatically defined diseases to the underlying bodily and mental causes of illness? Well, there is certainly scope for this. There is less scope for it in psychiatry than in physical medicine for the good practical reason that our knowledge of brain mechanisms and other relevant aetiological factors is limited. But so far as the relevant causal links are demonstrable, causally defined disease categories are in principle as available in psychiatry as in physical medicine. The difference, though, is the one noted above, that in a full-field theory the flow of meaning is from illness to disease. Hence the mere demonstration of a cause of an experience or behaviour is not, as is often assumed in conventional theories, sufficient to show that someone is ill. If a condition (psychopathy, say) is only equivocally an illness, the causes of that condition will be only equivocally diseases. This, of course, leaves open the question of what marks out illness from other negatively evaluated conditions, including delinquency. It is to this that we turn in the next section.

5. Mental Illness, Action-Failure, and the Law

In the preceding section, the status of illness and disease as value terms, being a key logical element of a full-field view of medicine, was shown to be consistent with an important feature of the map of psychiatry, namely

[54] K. W. M. Fulford, A. Y. U. Smirnoff, and E. Snow, 'Concepts of Disease and the Abuse of Psychiatry in the USSR', (1993) 162 *British Journal of Psychiatry* 801.

296 K. W. M. Fulford

the more value-laden nature of mental illness compared with physical illness. This in turn had implications for the role of the psychiatrist as an expert witness. In this section the same line of argument will be run for the second key element of a full-field view, the analysis of illness as a particular kind of action-failure. This will be shown to explain the other features of the map of psychiatry: the diversity of psychiatric disorders, the oddity of some psychotic symptoms (including the remarkable logical range of delusions), the variation across the map in the status of these disorders as mental illnesses (in particular, the central place of psychiatric disorders in this respect), and the correlation between this variation and the variation in the status of different mental conditions as legal excuses. Again, as in the preceding section, the account will have implications for the role of the psychiatrist as an expert. In this section, though, its main significance will be to underline the need for closer co-operation between philosophers and psychiatrists on future research in this area.

First then, the diversity of psychiatric disorders. Both conventional science-half-field and full-field views are broadly consistent with this feature of the psychiatric map. In the case of the former, this can be understood as reflecting a diversity in the kinds of mental functioning which may become disturbed. Lewis developed an early and detailed version of such an account;[55] and many disorders, dementia for example, are appropriately conceived in this way. Other disorders, however, are not so easily understood in functional terms. They *can* be so understood. But in a full-field view account they are more readily understood as reflecting different kinds of failure of action. As with the evaluative natures of the medical concepts, this is not an implausible idea in principle, once the illusion that medicine is an exclusively scientific discipline is broken. The 'machinery' of action, after all, as Austin used to call it,[56] is complex: it involves, indeed, all those phenomena we noted earlier as encompassing the range of possible symptoms of illness, physical as well as mental—movement, perception, sensation, appetite, volition, and so forth. Each of these phenomena, moreover, is on the face of it incorporated at different points or in different ways into the structure of action. Hence, in so far as they are involved in failures of action, we should expect these failures to be correspondingly diverse. All this *could* be put in functional terms, of course. But in point of fact, even in the standard (and self-consciously 'scientific'), medical classifications of psychiatric disorders, the language used is often that of action rather than function: In *DSM-III*, for example, the hysteric's symptoms are said to be 'not under voluntary control';[57] similarly, factitious disorder (as opposed to

---

[55] A. Lewis, 'Health as a Social Concept', (1953) 4 *British Journal of Sociology* 109.

[56] J. L. Austin, 'A Plea for Excuses', (1956–7) 57 *Proceedings of the Aristotelian Society* 1.

[57] American Psychiatric Association, *Diagnostic and Statistical Manual of Mental Disorders*, above n. 2, 244.

malingering) has a 'compulsive' quality;[58] and in ICD-9 the alcoholic's drinking (as opposed to that of the mere drunk) is not on his 'own initiative'.[59]

If an action-failure account of mental illness is at least plausible in
relation to the diversity of psychiatric disorders, however, it is essential
to an adequate account of the psychotic disorders. A science-half-field
account fails here essentially because it is obliged, in effect, to collapse the
non-organic psychotic disorders (at the centre of the map) to the organic
(half-way to the physical disorders). Thus as early as 1934, Lewis showed
that a 'cognitive' account of insight failed to distinguish between psychotic
and other ways in which insight might be lacking.[60] Yet such is the power
of the science-half-field view that this result has been taken to impugn
the psychotic/non-psychotic distinction, rather than to point the need for
a different way of understanding insight. Similarly, with specific psychotic
symptoms the conventional, science-based view has taken itself to be on
more secure ground. But the definition of delusion, the central psychotic
symptom, in most textbooks as (*inter alia*) a 'false' belief, neglects the
fact that (among their other possible logical forms) delusions may be true
beliefs. And even where this is recognized, it is assumed to be merely
epiphenomenal to some putative underlying disturbance of cognitive functioning, delusions being understood to be unfounded beliefs. Such an interpretation would indeed preserve a scientific view. The difficulty, however,
is that despite the best efforts of the cognitive psychologists, no such
disturbance of cognitive functioning has yet been demonstrated.[61] Delusions
occur in conditions, such as dementia, in which there are disturbances of
cognitive functioning. But these impair delusional-belief formation just as
they impair the formation of normal beliefs. The best-quality delusions—
elaborate, complex, highly systematized and well sustained—occur in what
are called the mono-symptomatic delusional disorders in which there is
little or no associated pathology at all (e.g. case 3 in the glossary). Of
course, it could be that there is some characteristic disturbance of cognitive functioning waiting to be discovered. Given, however, the central place
of these disorders on the psychiatric map, if impaired functioning were a
sufficient basis for the analysis of mental illness, we should expect the
relevant impairment of cognitive functioning to be more obvious than it is.
Overall then, as no less an advocate of the science-based view than Boorse

[58] Ibid., 285.
[59] World Health Organization, *Mental Disorders: Glossary and Guide to their Classification in Accordance with the Ninth Revision of the International Classification of Diseases*
(Geneva 1978), category 305.0.
[60] A. J. Lewis, 'The Psychopathology of Insight', (1934) 14 *British Journal of Medical
Psychology* 332.
[61] D. R. Hemsley and P. A. Garety, 'The Formation and Maintenance of Delusions:
A Bayesian Analysis', (1986) 149 *British Journal of Psychiatry* 51.

has noted,[62] disturbed-functioning accounts of the psychotic disorders are inconsistent with their given status as the paradigm mental illnesses.

In a full-field view, however, drawing on the resources of an action-failure account of illness, psychotic disorders come out naturally in their proper place, at the centre of the map. Without going into the details,[63] the bottom line in such an account is that in a full-field view these disorders, and the irrationality of delusions in particular, should be understood primarily in terms not of defective cognitive functioning, but rather of defective reasons for action. That is to say, instead of seeking to define delusion by reference to some specific disturbance of memory, logical reasoning, IQ, attention, and so forth—defects which are indeed important in conditions such as dementia (case 4 in the glossary)—we should look rather to a defect in practical reasoning, in the reasons we have for the things we do. The essential features of this account are, first, that it explains the specific kind of loss of insight by which psychotic disorders are characterized, directly in terms of a feature of the experience of illness, a feature common to physical as well as mental illness. This explanation, it should be said, is not merely in general terms: it generates a series of differential diagnostic tables covering each of the three main classes of psychotic symptom, thought disorder (including thought insertion described earlier), hallucination, and delusion.[64] Then, second, it is consistent with, and indeed explains, the logical range of delusions. The key point here is that just as a delusion may take the form either of a statement of fact or of a value judgment, so also may reasons for action. In my example earlier, my (immediate) reason for moving my hand across the page is, either, 'I am writing' (fact), or, 'I like, etc., writing' (implied value). This in turn leads, thirdly, to an explanation of the central place of psychotic disorders. Thus for most illnesses, physical as well as mental, there is a well-defined action but some downstream difficulty in carrying it out. These 'executive' difficulties range from motor paralysis through loss of control to a disturbance of volition. Actions, however, are in a sense actually *defined* by the reasons for which they are done—the movement of my hand across this page is the action of writing (rather than, say, brushing away a fly) only because writing is my (immediate) reason for moving my hand. Hence, if the reasons themselves are defective, there is a constitutive rather than merely executive failure of action. There is, in this sense, no *action* at all.

[62] C. Boorse, 'What a Theory of Mental Health Should Be', (1976) 6 *Journal of Theory of Social Behaviour* 61.

[63] Fulford, *Moral Theory and Medical Practice*, above n. 6, ch. 10.

[64] K. W. M. Fulford, 'Thought Insertion and Insight: Disease and Illness Paradigms of Psychotic Disorder', in M. Spitzer F. Uehlein, M. A. Schwartz, and C. Mundt (eds.) *Phenomenology, Language and Schizophrenia* (Heidelberg 1993).

As in the preceding section, then, where a science-half-field account fits the features of the map of psychiatry at best only uncomfortably, a full-field account fits them like a glove. Even set out fully, this account still amounts to a framework for research rather than a thoroughly worked out theory.[65] However, the prima-facie correspondence with the given features of psychotic disorders, including their central place in the map of psychiatry, makes this a promising framework. At the risk of repetition, it should be said again that a full-field account is not exclusive of the elements of the science-half-field account. It is effective because, or to the extent that, it makes explicit the elements of value, illness, and action-failure alongside the science-half-field elements of fact, disease, and failure of functioning.

The importance of this is evident if we apply the above picture to our understanding of the last of the features of the map of psychiatry, the variation in the status of different kinds of mental disorder as legal excuses. Thus, many of the established legal 'tests' in this area can be understood as drawing on one or other element of the conventional science-half-field view. Insane automatism, arising from 'disease of the mind', is, by the *Quick* test at least, indeed a *disease*—it is a 'malfunctioning of [the] mind . . . caused by a bodily disorder in the nature of a disease'.[66] Similarly, non-insane automatism is not due to disease of the mind because (like trauma, perhaps) it is clearly the result of some external factor—it is 'caused by the application to the body of some external factor such as violence, drugs, including anaesthetics, alcohol and hypnotic influences . . .'.[67] And perhaps the best-known test of all, *McNaghten* insanity—a failure (from disease of the mind) to 'know the nature and quality of the act' committed or to 'know that it is wrong'—is cast in explicitly cognitive form.[68]

Tests of this kind, like the value-free definition of mental illness considered in the last section, have the merit of avoiding the over-medicalization of crime. They have been widely criticized, however, as being *over*-exclusive. And these criticisms can now be understood as corresponding with a number of the arguments, derived from a full-field account of mental illness, also outlined in the last section. The *Bratty* and the *Quick* tests draw on the causal element in disease theory; but this is at one remove from the relevant mental state of the accused. Again, the 'disease' approach is legitimate to the extent that a condition is widely construed *as* an illness. But without this caveat it fails to recognize that the flow of meaning, described in the last section, is from illness to disease, not vice versa. And as to *McNaghten* insanity, it was the transparent injustices arising from an exclusively cognitive account of insanity which led to the introduction of a plea of 'diminished

[65] K. W. M. Fulford, 'Mental Illness and the Mind–Brain Problem: Delusion, Belief and Searle's Theory of Intentionality', *Theoretical Medicine* (forthcoming).
[66] *R v. Quick* [1973] 3 All ER 347.   [67] Ibid.
[68] *McNaghten's Case* (1843) 10 Cl. & Fin. 200.

responsibility' as a defence to a murder charge.[69] This defence, as we should expect, has been criticized as being too broad. But *McNaghten* insanity, though appropriate to some cases, is certainly too narrow. A full-field view, moreover, suggests precisely the sense in which it is too narrow, namely that it excludes impairments of practical reasoning. And that this is a crucial exclusion follows directly from the account of psychotic disorder just outlined. With such disorders, we noted, there is 'no action'. But 'no action' means 'no intent'. To the extent, then, that intent is material to responsibility,[70] psychotic disorders, in a full-field account of mental illness, automatically emerge in their intuitively correct position, as the central case of mental illness as an excuse.

The cashing out of this account in practical terms raises issues about the role of the psychiatrist as an expert which, in part, are similar to those described in the last section, about the relationship between fact and value in psychiatric diagnosis. It is worth adding here, though, specifically in relation to attributions of responsibility, that exclusively 'factual' conceptions of mental illness, although advocated from the perspectives of a number of disciplines, have consistently failed to meet the needs of practice. The Butler Committee, for example, sought to define psychotic mental illness by reference to a list of specific psychotic symptoms: psychiatrists, they argued, should restrict their evidence as experts to whether or not, as a matter of fact, these symptoms were present, broader questions of 'responsibility' being left to the jury.[71] But this proposal was not incorporated in the Mental Health Act 1983, which in other respects drew extensively on the Butler recommendations. In the bioethics literature, similarly, responsibility has been analysed in terms of a series of 'competences', each of which is capable in principle of objective assessment. But if these are compared with the patients actually treated as incompetent, on grounds of mental illness, they fit only those cases (like dementia) which are properly understood in cognitive terms.[72] Again, among philosophers, as we saw earlier, delusion has sometimes been identified as providing an 'objective' test of mental illness. Yet this entirely fails to recognize that in addition to false factual beliefs, delusions may take the form of value judgments and even of true factual beliefs. And even where philosophers of law, on rather different grounds from those advanced here, have come to see insanity as a species of defective practical reasoning, they have tended, consistently with the science-half-field view, to conclude that this places judgments of insanity

[69] H. L. A. Hart, *Punishment and Responsibility: Essays in the Philosophy of Law* (Oxford 1968).
[70] R. A. Duff, *Intention, Agency and Criminal Liability* (Oxford 1990).
[71] See *Report of the Committee on Mentally Abnormal Offenders*, above n. 9.
[72] K. W. M. Fulford and T. Hope, 'Psychiatric Ethics: A Bioethical Ugly Duckling?', in R. Gillon (ed.), *Principles of Health Care Ethics* (London, forthcoming).

outside the scope of medical expertise. Moore[73] and Duff[74] have both argued along these lines.

A full-field view offers a radically different approach here. Acknowledging that practical reasoning is the province as much of morals as of science, it none the less claims that a specifically *medical* kind of failure of practical reasoning is involved in psychotic disorder. Medicine and morals are thus part and parcel in this construction. Just how the parcel should be unpacked for the courts is a matter for further medico-legal research. But in a full-field view, as we saw earlier, such research, if it is to illuminate the relevant medical sense of irrationality, must be concerned as much with philosophical questions about the nature of action as with scientific questions about brain functioning. It is to the relationship between philosophy and psychiatry that we turn next.

6. The Philosopher as an Expert

After a long period of relative estrangement, philosophy and psychiatry have recently started to move back towards the kind of close working relationship which they enjoyed at the turn of the century. The relative neglect of psychiatry by philosophy, and of philosophy by psychiatry, has been a product, *inter alia*, of the science-half-field view: so long as psychiatry was thought to be no more than a scientific poor relation of physical medicine, the two disciplines—with the partial exception of (the scientifically equivocal) psychoanalysis—appeared to have few interests in common.

In a full-field view on the other hand, it is clear that the relationship between philosophy and psychiatry should be as close as that which already exists between psychiatry and science. The importance at least of philosophy for psychiatry has been evident at each stage of the argument outlined in this chapter. The difficulties from which we started, in the relationship between law and psychiatry, although difficulties in day-to-day practice, are primarily conceptual rather than empirical in nature. Then again, the picture of these difficulties to which we came, as arising from a too-restricted (or half-field) view, and hence the need for an initial map of psychiatry, was a direct application of Wittgenstein's account of the nature of philosophical problems. Moreover, an important overall feature of this map, the relative strength of the evaluative connotations of mental illness, has been found to follow directly from the logical properties of

---

[73] Moore, 'The Legal View of Persons', above n. 39.
[74] R. A. Duff, 'Mental Disorder and Criminal Responsibility', in R. A. Duff and N. E. Simmonds (eds.), *Philosophy and the Criminal Law* (Wiesbaden 1984).

value terms discussed in detail in the meta-ethical literature. (The whole debate about mental illness can be understood as a *forme fruste* of the is–ought debate.)[75] And the internal topography of psychiatry, in particular the central place of psychotic disorders as (*inter alia*) a species of legal excuse, has been found to be more readily explicable in terms drawn from the philosophy of action rather than from cognitive science.

All this is, of course, far from exhaustive of the philosophical possibilities. Recent work in moral philosophy on the contingent nature of value judgments, raising anew the possibility of objective 'moral facts',[76] is directly relevant to our understanding of the nature of psychiatric diagnosis and hence of the role of the psychiatrist as an expert witness. So also, though in a reverse direction, is work in the philosophy of science on the social embeddedness of scientific theories.[77] In respect of the social context, indeed, the view presented here is in its own terms partial. As noted earlier, a full-field view broadens our perspective. It is the parts of bodies and minds which, as constituents of disease theories of disturbed functioning, are the focus of the science-half-field view. But the focus of a full-field view is, rather, the experiences and actions of persons. However, persons, in turn, must be understood in a social context. And this is important, moreover, especially in relation to law and psychiatry. For the very concept of psychotic loss of insight, as the defining characteristic of all psychotic symptoms, is itself a socially-relative concept. The psychotically ill patient was described earlier as failing to identify him or herself as mentally ill. It is in this sense, specifically, that the psychotic patient lacks insight. But this is to say, in the terms of our map, that those who are located by everyone else most confidently at the centre, are just those who, *contra* everyone else, locate themselves off the map altogether. This is the central enigma presented by these disorders.

The relationship between philosophy and psychiatry should not be all one way, however. Just as science has benefited from medicine (diabetes leading to the discovery of insulin, for example), so philosophy, besides contributing to psychiatry, has much to gain from it. This is not a new idea. As early as 1956, Austin pointed philosophers to the importance of abnormal psychological phenomena;[78] and Wilkes,[79] Glover,[80] and others, have recently followed Austin's lead. The importance of psychiatry for philosophy can be appreciated in part from the features of our map. The plain oddity of many symptoms of mental illness has been the attraction

---

[75] Fulford, *Moral Theory and Medical Practice*, above n. 6.
[76] J. Dancy, *Moral Reasons* (Oxford 1993).
[77] M. Hesse, *Revolutions and Reconstructions in the Philosophy of Science* (Brighton 1980).
[78] J. L. Austin, 'A Plea for Excuses', above n. 56.
[79] K. V. Wilkes, *Real People: Personal Identity without Thought Experiments* (Oxford 1988).
[80] J. Glover, *I: The Philosophy and Psychology of Personal Identity* (London 1988).

for most recent authors: multiple-personality disorder, for example, in which a number of different people appear to be severally present in one body, has figured prominently.[81] But it was as much the diversity of these phenomena that Austin had in mind, a diversity which both tests and extends philosophical theory. It is not enough, for example, to point in a general way to the central enigma of psychotic disorders as an indication of the social embeddedness of reality. Once the remarkable variety of these phenomena is recognized, any serious epistemological theory must seek to explain the full logical range of delusional beliefs, the links between these and other psychotic symptoms (e.g. hallucinations), the differences between delusional and other pathological forms of belief (beliefs may be obsessional, for example), and the location of all these in conceptual 'space' as pathological rather than normal, false and, indeed, true beliefs.

Psychiatry has a further and less well-recognized significance for philosophy, however, in that it provides a pressure of practical necessity which is wholly lacking from much theoretical speculation.[82] This is partly a matter of plain humanity. The problems with which we have been concerned in this chapter are conceptual. But on their determination in the courts people's lives may literally hang. The practical nature of these problems has also a more directly theoretical relevance, however. For the fact that they *are* practical problems means that any philosophical account of them which fails to make some difference to practice, albeit just a difference of understanding, is suspect. The standard tests of success of a philosophical theory—internal consistency, comprehensiveness, economy, elegance—are simply not sufficient where the need for theory arises in a context of practical necessity. The demand that the philosopher as an expert should have a contribution to make to resolving the difficulties in the relationship between law and psychiatry is thus not a matter merely of justifying the philosophical payroll. It is a direct constraint on theory.

7. Conclusions

In this essay, recent work on the concepts of illness and disease has been described, in which the logical elements of evaluation and of action-failure have been given equal prominence alongside the better recognized elements of fact and failure of functioning. A full-field view of medicine, as it has

---

[81] G. R. Gillett, 'Multiple Personality and the Concept of a Person', (1986) 4 *New Ideas in Psychology* 173; S. E. Braude, *First Person Plural: Multiple Personality and the Philosophy of Mind* (London 1991).

[82] Fulford, 'The Potential of Medicine as a Resource for Philosophy', (1991) 12 *Theoretical Medicine* 81; Fulford, 'Philosophy and Medicine: The Oxford Connection', (1991) 157 *British Journal of Psychiatry* 111.

been called, in contrast to the more conventional science-half-field view, has given us the conceptual resources necessary to explain the main features of the logical geography of psychiatry: its more value-laden nature compared with physical illness (this being a direct consequence of the more open nature of our evaluations of mental phenomena); and the central place of psychotic disorders (these being characterized by a constitutive rather than by any of a range of executive kinds of action-failure).

Although not developed for this purpose, a full-field picture of medicine helps to bridge the gap between law and psychiatry at least at the conceptual of the three levels of difficulty outlined at the start of this chapter. At this level the gap between the two disciplines is indeed no less than a gap between the scientific models of madness (as disturbances of functioning) to which most medical thinking is limited, and the everyday model of rationality (as practical reasoning) which is the basis of law. A full-field view shows, however, that the actual use which is made of the concept of mental illness in psychiatry, right down to the fine-grained detail of the descriptive psychopathology of delusions, reflects and is directly dependent on a model of madness itself as a disturbance of practical reasoning. This model has been implicit rather than explicit, in law no less than in psychiatry, essentially because of the importance and prominence of scientific disease theories in medicine. This has led a majority of authors to contrast medicine (as science) with morals (the realm of practical reasoning). A full-field picture shows on the contrary that medicine is as much a part of morals as of science.

If a full-field view helps at the conceptual level, however, it is certainly no sinecure at the level of day-to-day practice. The gap between law and psychiatry at this level was identified originally as a communication gap. As such, the contribution of a full-field view is one of clarification, a contribution we explored briefly in relation to the role of the psychiatrist as an expert witness. But the outcome of this was to show that our difficulties at this level are in a sense more profound even than we had appreciated; the variable status of many conditions as mental illnesses was found to be (in part) a reflection of our diversity as human beings; and psychiatric diagnosis thus turned out to be inherently rather than merely contingently problematic.

Still, just recognizing this could help to improve the relationship between the courts and psychiatry. So long as we continue to work with a model of psychiatry as no different from physical medicine, we encourage unrealistic expectations: that evidence for the presence of mental disorder will one day be as decisive as that for physical disorders; that with advances in the brain-sciences the discrepancies between psychiatric testimony will soon disappear. This is a recipe for increasing frustration. A recognition on the other hand, as in a full-field theory, of the limits of science in medicine, could increase understanding and help build mutual confidence and respect. The courts would continue to insist on the highest standards of professional competence in the collection and presentation of the facts in a given case, including the extent to which the condition of the accused conforms to the criteria for an established disease concept. But there would be a clearer recognition of the dividing line between the expert's proper role as illuminating the facts, and the value judgments which form part of the ultimate questions appropriately reserved to the jury. There is already a degree of recognition of this in relation to questions of responsibility. A full-field theory provides a framework for the further definition of the proper role of the psychiatrist as an expert on questions of this kind.

At the practical level, then, a full-field view, although not resolving our difficulties as such, is a basis for transforming our attitudes towards them. In the science-half-field view these difficulties are thought of, pejoratively, as reflecting the underdeveloped state of psychiatric science. In a full-field view they are seen rather to be a reflection of the inherently more problematic nature of psychiatric medicine. In physical medicine questions of value, although arising in principle, can be ignored in practice because they are generally uncontentious: but in psychiatry such questions have to be squarely faced (and this in addition to all the empirical problems involved in investigating the brain). Where, therefore, in the science-half-field view, psychiatry is thought of as no more than a simple-minded relative of physical medicine, in a full-field view, on the contrary, physical medicine is seen to be a less complicated relative of psychiatry.

Much the same transformation of view is implied by a full-field view at the third of our three initial levels of difficulty, the philosophical. It is perhaps a further reflection of the hegemony of medical science that notwithstanding the prima-facie links between intention and the status of mental illness as an excuse, the difficulties in the relationship between law and psychiatry have been relatively neglected by philosophers of law. These difficulties are perceived as being at the periphery of their concerns, the product of a few wild-strain notions, readily enough corralled once we have an adequate understanding of the core legal concepts of intention and responsibility. But in a full-field view, the difficulties in the relationship between law and psychiatry move from the periphery to centre-stage. For in fully assimilating medical concepts of insanity to the framework of practical reasoning within which the law operates, a full-field view shows these difficulties to be symptomatic of problems in the conceptual framework of law as a whole. On this view, then, it is because we do not have an adequate understanding of intention that we have difficulty with the boundaries of mental illness as an excuse. It is because our ordinary notions of responsibility are ill-formed that the sense in which the deluded person is not responsible is elusive. No theory of intention, then, if not a theory of mental illness; no theory of responsibility, if not a theory of insanity.

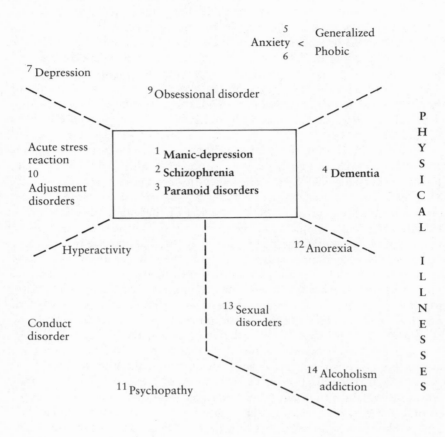

A conceptual map of psychiatry. The variety of mental disorders can be set out schematically, as in this diagram. Although not representing a well-established classification of these disorders, the map illustrates a number of the features of the conceptual terrain of psychiatry which any theory of the meaning of mental illness must explain. Brief descriptions and a number of illustrative case-vignettes are given in the accompanying glossary. For more detailed descriptions, see M. G. Gelder, D. Gath, and R. Mayou, *Oxford Textbook of Psychiatry* (Oxford 1983); J. Leff and A. D. Isaacs, *Psychiatric Examination in Clinical Practice* (Oxford 1978); and C. S. Mellor, 'First Rank Symptoms of Schizophrenia', (1970) 117 *British Journal of Psychiatry* 15.

GLOSSARY—EXAMPLES OF PSYCHOLOGICAL DISORDERS

(All cases based on real patients but with biographical details disguised)

1a. Manic-Depressive Illness: Depressed Type
Psychotic disorder with depressed mood. The psychoses are severe disorders with loss of insight shown characteristically by delusions, hallucinations, and certain forms of thought disorder (e.g. thought insertion—*see case* 2).

> *Mr S. D. Age 48—Bank Manager. Presented in casualty (with his wife) with a three-week history of 'biological' symptoms of depression [early waking, weight loss, fixed diurnal variation of mood] and delusions of guilt [believed he caused the war in former Yugoslavia]. History of attempted suicide during previous similar episode. Denied that he was depressed but said he needed something to help him sleep.*

1b. Manic-Depressive Illness: Manic Type
Psychotic disorder with elevated mood.

> *Miss H. M. Age 25—Novice Nun. Brought by superiors for urgent out-patient appointment as they were unable to contain her bizarre and sexually disinhibited behaviour [running away from convent and soliciting 'for the Lord']. Showed pressure of speech [continuous talking], grandiose delusions [that her minor charities are saintly acts of 'great and enduring moral worth'], and auditory hallucinations [female voices telling her she is Mary Magdalene].*

2. Schizophrenia
Psychotic disorder with specific delusions, hallucinations, and disorders of thought ('first-rank' symptoms), together with a large number of other disturbances, especially of affect and volition.

> *Mr. S. Age 18—Student. Emergency psychiatric admission from his college. Behaving oddly [found wandering, in bemused and agitated state]. Complained that people were talking about him. Showed thought insertion [John Major 'using my brain for his thoughts'] but no cognitive impairment (see case 4).*

3. Paranoid Disorders: e.g. Othello Syndrome
Psychotic disorders with well-developed delusional symptoms (not necessarily of persecution) and little other pathology. In the Othello syndrome the paranoid system is built round delusions of infidelity.

> *Mr A. Age 47—Publican. Seen by general practitioner initially because his wife was depressed. However, Mr A. complained of anxiety and impotence. GP suspected alcohol abuse. After some discussion, Mr A. suddenly announced that 'the problem' was that his wife was 'a tart'. Once started, he went on at length about her infidelity, drawing on a wide range of evidence, some of it bizarre [that she washed their towels on a different day; pattern of cars parked in street had changed].*

4. Dementia

Psychotic disorder with progressive impairment of 'cognitive' functions—viz. memory, attention, orientation (time, place, person), and general IQ. Due to gross brain pathology, hence sometimes called 'organic psychosis'. Acute (and usually reversible) disturbances of cognitive functions occur in confusional states (e.g. after blow to head, or with intoxication). Visual hallucinations are common.

> *Mrs G. M. Age 65—Shopkeeper. Referred by general practitioner when her customers complained that she had started to forget their orders. Family confirmed she had become forgetful and at times seemed confused. She had been complaining of seeing rats in her storeroom but there was no evidence of these. Initially denied problem but on cognitive function testing unable, e.g. to recall a simple name and address after a gap of five minutes.*

5. Anxiety Disorder—Generalized

Sustained periods of anxiety with associated bodily symptoms in absence of appropriate cause.

> *Mrs B. Age 35—Teacher. Presented to general practitioner complaining of a constant sense of anxiety for which she could give no reason, developing over about 3 months. Had always been a worrier but coped well with a stressful job. Had difficulty getting to sleep and bodily symptoms [palpitation and difficulty swallowing].*

6. Anxiety Disorder—Phobic

Pathological anxiety related to a specific object or situation and leading to avoidance.

> *Mrs R. D. Age 23—Housewife. Visited by district nurse at home as she had failed to attend for post-natal follow-up. She explained that she had become afraid to go out because of a fear of thunder. This had been a lifelong fear but had become worse since she gave up work to have her baby. Even approaching the front door produced feelings of panic with bodily symptoms [palpitation, hyperventilation, tingling in her fingers].*

7. Depression—Non-Psychotic

Pathological depression of mood without psychotic features.

> *Mr R. J. Age 32—Bricklayer. Presented to general practitioner complaining of feeling miserable and difficulty getting to sleep. For some months he had lost his enjoyment of life and tended to lie awake at night worrying about the future, even though he had no particular problems at present. Physical examination was normal and he had not lost weight.*

8. Hysterical Disorders

Physical symptoms [e.g. paralysis, blindness, memory loss] with psychological causes.

> *Miss H. P. Age 30—Secretary. Admitted to neurology ward and transferred to psychiatry under protest. Unable to move right hand. No evidence of physical lesion. History of depression and self-injury.*

9. Obsessive-Compulsive Disorder
Recurrent mental content (obsession) or behaviour (compulsion) typically recognized by patient to be irrational and resisted but unsuccessfully (like a bad case of getting a tune 'stuck in your head').

> *Mr O. C. Age 27—Bank Clerk. Three-year history of progressive slowness. Referred with recent depression and anxiety following suspension from work. Showed severe and progressive compulsive checking which he saw as 'ridiculous' but was unable to stop.*

10. Acute Reaction to Stress
Marked psychological reaction to sudden stressful stimulus. Adjustment disorders are corresponding reactions to more chronic situations, e.g. a grief reaction which becomes excessively extended. These disorders are in many respects the psychological counterpart of physical trauma or wounds.

> *Mr J. B. Age 55—Doctor. Involved in serious car accident while returning from an emergency call-out late at night. No head injury. Was unable to recall the accident. Felt anxious, distressed, and unable to cope with his work for several days. Then developed a brief, self-limiting manic reaction.*

11. Psychopathic Personality Disorder
Personality disorders differ from illnesses in being more or less fixed features of the way a person feels, thinks, or behaves. With psychopathy the disorder is manifested mainly in repeated delinquency. The conduct disorders of childhood have similar manifestations but are self-limiting. Hyperkinetic syndrome of childhood is pathological overactivity.

> *Mr P. P. Age 23—Unemployed. Seen in casualty by duty psychiatrist. Brought in by girlfriend because he was threatening to kill a rival. Had been drinking. History of repeated criminal assaults. Promiscuous.*

12. Anorexia Nervosa
Pathological disorder of eating in which patient refuses to eat, exercises excessively, and abuses laxatives. Self-induced vomiting is common. Typically perceive themselves as fat despite extreme emaciation together with physiological and other changes of starvation.

> *Miss A. N. Age 21—Student. Four-year history of intermittent anorexia. Currently seriously underweight, exercising and using laxatives; amenorrhoeic. Refusing admission on the grounds that she is 'too fat'.*

13. Sexual Disorders
These may involve (*a*) pathological changes in sexual drive and/or function, or (*b*) disorders of sexual-object choice (e.g. sadism, paedophilia).

> *Mr R. P. Age 22—Post-Graduate Student. Attended student counselling service complaining of difficulty maintaining an erection. Had a steady girlfriend and normal sexual interest and drive. Struggling to finish his doctoral thesis.*

14. Alcoholism and Drug Addiction
Abuse of alcohol or drugs which is out of the patient's control. There is often denial of the problem.

Mr A. R. Age 38—Shopkeeper. Self-referral to general practitioner from Relate (marriage guidance counselling). Over several years had increased his alcohol consumption and was now drinking a bottle of spirits and several pints of beer every day. Without a drink in the morning his hands shook. His wife was threatening to divorce him and he had lost many of his customers. However, he was ambivalent about the referral, arguing that he had the problem 'under control'.

15. Mental Subnormality and Developmental Disorders of Childhood

With mental subnormality there is pathologically low IQ together with varying degrees of emotional and behavioural abnormality persisting from birth. The developmental disorders of childhood include delays in reaching normal milestones, e.g. persistent urinary incontinence ('bed wetting'), delayed walking, talking, or reading.

Index of Subjects

action:
  basic vs. non-basic 80–5, 103
  as condition of criminal liability 34, 48,
    190–202, 295–301
  descriptions of 6–7, 77, 216
  failure of 95, 98, 296–301
  and intention 6, 18, 55–7, 109–10, 300
  vs. omission 77, 194–5
  and responsibility 5–6, 18, 70, 77–80,
    275, 295–301
  and what is done 7, 56, 61–3
  and trying 6–8, 58–60, 85–102, 108–9
  see also agency
actus reus, see mens rea
agency 4–5, 27–39, 56–7
  vs. welfare 24–7, 49–53
  see also action; welfare; values
attempts, criminal 34–5, 38, 48, 58, 82–3,
    88–90, 118, 136–7, 209, 226
  see also trying
automatism 16, 48–9, 62, 299

blame, see culpability

causation 143–54, 199, 207, 266, 278
  and responsibility 18–20, 239, 269–70,
    278, 296–301
choice 22–4, 29, 37, 110, 159, 257–8
  see also freedom
civil liability 30–1, 34–5, 114–17, 125,
    143–54, 208
coercion 37, 250–65
  see also duress; excuse
compensation, see punishment
consequences 8–10, 38–9, 53, 79, 86–90,
    105–6, 117–23, 199, 206–7
  see also luck; trying
control 5–6, 18–19, 70–1, 77–8, 100–1,
    195, 197–8, 201, 213, 239, 257
culpability 33–4, 72–4, 116–17, 157–74

defences, see offences vs. defences
descriptions:
  actions under, see action
  events under 9–10, 126–43
determinism, see free will
duress 24, 39, 230–1, 253–4, 264
  see also coercion; excuse

excuse 16–17, 35–6, 197–8, 215–17,
    247–50, 288

vs. justification 2, 39, 178, 180, 272–3
  see also justification
expert evidence 241–2, 304–7
ex ante rules vs. *ex post* rules 12–17,
    176–81, 183–6, 206–10, 214–17

foreseeability 9–10, 117–20, 125–30,
    143–54
freedom 19–20, 23–31
  see also values
free will 18–19, 24–5, 28–9, 80, 107–8,
    239, 279

harm (or injury) 11–12, 161–5, 173, 178
  principle 5, 21–5, 52
  see also wrongs

insanity, see mental illness
intention 33–5, 63–9, 77–8, 136–7, 178,
    228–33, 243–4

judges vs. legislators 12, 15, 179–80,
    183–4, 192–3, 198
justification 12–13, 175–86, 215
  vs. excuse, see excuse

labelling, 'representative' or 'fair' 8–9,
    89–90, 133–4, 206–10
legislators, see judges vs. legislators
luck 8–9, 89, 108–10
  see also consequences; trying

mala in se vs. *mala prohibita* 4, 11–12,
    24–5, 42–4, 46, 51–3, 169–70
mens rea 42–3, 47, 202–6, 217–25, 243–7
  vs. actus reus 13–17, 24, 33–4, 61–3,
    75–9, 81–3, 157–9, 187–90, 200–2,
    206–10, 225–8
  proof of 48, 191, 194, 227–37, 268
mental illness 35–6, 234–7, 248–62,
    268–70, 281–95
  vs. mental disease 16–19, 284–7, 296–9
mistake:
  of fact 24, 31, 35, 52–3, 176, 178,
    217–25
  fact vs. law 157–66
  of law 10–13, 36, 44, 157–60, 166–71,
    217

nullum crimen sine lege (or *nulla poena
  sine lege*) principle 12, 15, 166–7,
    175, 180–1, 184

objectivism, *see* subjectivism
obligation to obey the law 12, 160–1, 165
offences vs. defences 13–17, 176–81,
　　214–22, 240–2, 274–7

philosophy, uses of 1–2, 73–4, 172,
　　305–7
punishment 2–3, 32–3, 38, 42–3, 52–3,
　　113–17, 119–23, 266
　　and compensation 32, 35, 114–17

reasonableness 31, 35–6, 126, 166–72,
　　181, 218, 232–7, 273
Recht 12–13, 177, 184–6
recklessness and negligence 47, 69, 233–7,
　　244–5, 213
　　see also risk-taking
responsibility 5–6, 8–9, 18, 34–5, 69–73,
　　77–80, 154, 190–3, 249, 257–8, 278,
　　305
　　partial or diminished 232–3, 247–74,
　　303–4
　　see also action
risk-taking 31–4, 120–3

scepticism 26, 49, 130–1, 288–9
strict liability 42–4, 46–9, 51–3, 69,
　　110–12, 157
subjectivism 42–4, 47, 51–3, 89–90,
　　105–6, 109–13, 216, 222, 227–8
　　vs. objectivism 26–7, 31–2, 39, 42–3,
　　51–2, 114–17, 123–4, 188–9, 213–37

trying 6–9, 48–9, 58–60, 85–102, 108–10
　　see also action; attempts; consequences

values 27–31, 32–7
　　vs. facts 286–95, 305–7
　　intrinsic vs. instrumental 3, 4–5, 14,
　　46–9
　　liberal 19–20, 40–2
　　see also agency; freedom; welfare
voluntariness 7, 39, 48, 77, 84–5, 88,
　　195–8, 201

welfare 4–5, 23, 40–9
　　see also agency; values
wrongs 10–14, 21–2, 31–7, 177, 180,
　　185–6, 216
　　vs. harms (or injuries) 11, 21–2, 24

Index of Names

Aristotle 20
Ashworth, A. J. 89–90, 160–1, 173
Austin, J. 214
Austin, J. L. 296, 302

Beck, A. T. 292
Bentham, J. 215
Boorse, C. 292, 297–8
Brennan J 158
Brett J 218
Bridge, Lord 228, 229

Cardozo J 148–9
Cass, R. 160–1, 173
Cohen, M. 10, 130
Cross, Lord 220

Davidson, D. 144–5
Denning, Lord 288
Dickson CJ 53
Diplock, Lord 213, 219, 228, 233, 234, 236, 237
Donovan J 231
Duff, R. A. 55, 58, 63–4, 66–74, 109–10, 112–13, 118–19, 300–1

Enker, A. 82

Feinberg, J. 21–5, 52
Fingarette, H. 251
Flew, A. 289
Frank, J. 131
Frankfurt, H. G. 257
Fraser, Lord 220
Frege, G. 133, 142

Glover, J. 302
Goddard, Lord 228, 229
Goff LJ 236, 237
Grall, J. A. 82

Hailsham, Lord 213, 220, 223, 228
Hall, J. 201
Hare, R. M. 290, 291
Harper, F. V. 149
Hart, H. L. A. 147, 244–5
Hodgson J 223
Holmes, O. W. 36
Honoré, A. M. 110–12, 113–14, 147
Hornsby, J. 93
Hume, D. 144

James LJ 218
James, F., Jr. 149
Jescheck, H.-H. 171

Kant, I. 28
Keble J 215
Keedy, E. 136–8
Kendell, R. E. 285
Kilmuir, Viscount 232
Klein, M. 266
Kleinig, J. 115
Kroll, J. 286

Lane LJ 216, 235
Leibniz, G. W. von 132–6, 139, 142, 146, 148, 155
Lewis, A. J. 296
Livermore, J. 265
Luther, M. 257

McGinn, C. 93
Mackie, J. L. 143–4
Meehl, P. 265
Mill, J. S. 143
Moore, M. S. 288–9
Morris, C. 127–9, 136, 148, 150, 152

Nagel, T. 107–8

O'Shaughnessy, B. 93

Pearson LJ 232–3
Pollock, F. 149

Quine, W. V. 133–4, 139, 141–2

Rawls, J. 41
Robinson, P. H. 82, 158
Rogers, R. 260, 269
Roskill, Lord 221
Roth, M. 286
Ryle, G. 259, 280

Salmon, Lord 226–7
Salmond J 49
Scarman, Lord 217
Simonds, Viscount 148–9
Smith, J. C. 215
Stephen J 218, 225
Strawson, G. 239

Strawson, P. 239
Szasz, T. S. 283, 285

Thomson, J. 177

Urmson, J. O. 290

Watson, G. 258
Wechsler, H. 144

Weil, S. 102–3
Wertheimer, A. 251
Wilkes, K. V. 302
Williams, B. 108
Williams, G. 115, 213, 230–1
Wittgenstein, L. 84, 93, 286, 301
Wolf, S. 248
Wright, R. 143